ALBUM

European Perspectives

European Perspectives

A Series in Social Thought and Cultural Criticism

Lawrence D. Kritzman, Editor

European Perspectives presents outstanding books by leading European thinkers. With both classic and contemporary works, the series aims to shape the major intellectual controversies of our day and to facilitate the tasks of historical understanding.

For a complete list of books in the series, see pages 359–360.

ALBUM

Unpublished Correspondence and Texts

ROLAND BARTHES

Established and presented by Éric Marty
With the assistance of Claude Coste for
"On Seven Sentences in *Bouvard et Pécuchet*"

Translated by Jody Gladding

COLUMBIA UNIVERSITY PRESS   NEW YORK

Columbia University Press
Publishers Since 1893
New York   Chichester, West Sussex
cup.columbia.edu
Album: Inédits, correspondances et varia copyright © 2015 Éditions du Seuil
English translation copyright © 2018 Columbia University Press
All rights reserved

Library of Congress Cataloging-in-Publication Data
Names: Barthes, Roland. | Marty, Éric, 1955– editor. | Gladding, Jody, 1955–
    translator. | Coste, Claude author.
Title: Album: unpublished correspondence and texts / Roland Barthes; established
    and presented by Éric Marty; with the assistance of Claude Coste for On Seven
    Sentences in Bouvard et Pâecuchet; translated by Jody Gladding.
Description: New York: Columbia University Press, 2018. | Series: European
    perspectives | Includes bibliographical references and index.
Identifiers: LCCN 2017039160 | ISBN 9780231179867 (cloth: alk. paper)
Subjects: LCSH: Barthes, Roland—Correspondence. | Critics—France—
    Correspondence.
Classification: LCC P85.B33 A4 2018 | DDC 801/.95092—dc23
LC record available at https://lccn.loc.gov/2017039160

Cover design: Evan Gaffney

Cover images: photo of Roland Barthes by Arthur Woods Wang, Photographs of
Authors and Ranchers, Yale Collection of American Literature, Beinecke Rare
Book and Manuscript Library; draft of letter from Roland Barthes to Jean-Paul
Sartre: Roland Barthes Collection, Bibliothèque Nationale de France (BNF);
Divertissement in F Major, dedicated to Philippe Rebeyrol: Philippe Rebeyrol
Archives, l'Institut Mémoires de l'Édition Contemporaine (IMEC); note to Roland
Barthes from Jean Cocteau: "Thanks to the Comité, Jean Cocteau"; letter to
Roland Barthes from Georges Perec: Roland Barthes Collection, BNF.

CONTENTS

FOREWORD

Éric Marty

Reading in R. B. what he does not say but suggests, I imagine that for Werther passionate love is only a detour to death. After reading *Werther*, there were no more lovers, but more suicides. And Goethe passed off to Werther the temptation of death, but not his passion, writing not to keep himself from dying but through the movement of a death that no longer belonged to him. "That can only end badly."

—Maurice Blanchot

Posthumous time is as complex and subtle as life time. It is woven of events, surprises, waiting, mourning (survivors die as well), encounters (new readers), betrayals, neglect, alliances, sorrows, disappointments, and of course joys. In that posthumous time, there is also a place for what Proust called *temps retrouvé*, that time when forgotten feelings, scents, words, truths, and faces are revived thanks to the effects of recollection. In putting together this album celebrating Roland Barthes's centenary, I continually had that feeling of accessing a *temps retrouvé*, immediately prompting a concern for helping readers gain access to it as well. From the letters from the sanatorium, where Barthes is very often immersed in the darkness of disease and its surrounding silence, to the last letters that revive Barthes's exchange with another writer now deceased, Hervé Guibert, strange and often scintillating bits of the past emerge. It is a past that may well have constituted for Barthes himself, in his lifetime, an invisible part of his life, a virtual part. We remember so little of the letters we have written and even when we do remember them, what can be gathered from them—what is gathered here from so many exchanges with so many correspondents—constitutes an expected tableau, a tapestry woven of so many threads that even its author could not have imagined it.

This album comprises five large sections—preceded by a prelude devoted to the death of Barthes's father—in which the letters exchanged, written, and received by Barthes constitute the main part of the text, with inclusions of unpublished material (from Barthes's text from 1947 on the sanatorium to his notes on "Vita Nova"). Chronology—since it is an entire life we find here—was our guide, as well as our desire to let that life unfold through what correspondence expresses best: friendship. Thus we have in some way inflected the chronology through a form of cartography whereby chapter titles are also something like stages in a writing career, in a writer's life. It is worth noting, moreover, that Barthes may be among the last of our authors for whom producing a posthumous collection of letters is possible, given the evolution of the act of writing itself, since his death, and the gradual disappearance of letters that makes the epistolary act revolutionary. That fact as well confers upon this collection a flavor or scent of a time regained. It is also the time regained of a certain idea of what writing means.

Nevertheless we know that a "correspondence" is an artifact, and it is an illusion to think we might rediscover Barthes's actual life there. Thus this collection is not in any way an exact reflection of things or a life, except as an erotic of the everyday, even if we may think that some of the letters in this body of complex and moving materials may have something seemingly decisive about them. Just as others are seemingly insignificant, simply a brief note or polite response. Nevertheless we have included them because, for those who love letters, in the very brevity of a polite phrase there lies an entire message full of meaning. Sometimes it is simply the writer's name itself that matters because it allows us to complete the cartography of friendship that we are attempting to draw.

Letters are lost, burned, and torn up, and this collection does not pretend to be exhaustive. Thus the reader will not find here Roland Barthes's letters to some of those closest to him: François Wahl, his friend and editor; Severo Sarduy, Wahl's companion; Jean-Louis Bouttes, whom Barthes refers to as "the Friend" in his final work, *Vita Nova*. They did not keep his letters. Not long ago I myself, for example, destroyed the letters that Roland Barthes had sent to me. The decision to include only unpublished letters led us to omit those Barthes wrote to Frédéric Berthet,[1] Leyla Perrone-Moisés,[2] and Michel Archambaud,[3] among others. There are so many gaps, perhaps sometimes linked to oversights or negligence on our part, but most often due to the physical contingency of those fragile things that letters are. We deeply regret not having found a single letter from or to François Braunschweig, who was so close to Barthes and to whom Barthes dedicated his *Essais critiques* in 1964. We were also refused rights in a few cases, we ran into all sorts of complications that denied us access to certain correspondences, and we were met with silence on the part of some of Barthes's friends whom we solicited. Phillipe Sollers wanted to publish a certain number of Barthes's letters separately.[4] Michel Foucault, who was Barthes's closest friend in the 1960s, with whom he went out almost every evening, often to wrestling halls or, for example, to see a B movie like *Maciste* in a movie theater in Belleville, as on a January evening in 1963, is only represented by a very small sampling. There is only one letter from Barthes to Pierre Klossowski and none from Klossowski to Barthes, although they were very good friends. Other names are missing or poorly represented. There are no letters from or to Marguerite Duras, whom Barthes visited often in the 1960s, or from Henri Lefebvre, for example, with whom Barthes was very close. These absences are compensated for by presences that are unexpected (Maurice Blanchot), moving (Jean Genet), or surprising and therefore all the more delightful (Georges Perros).

A very popular author of historical accounts of World War I, Paul Chack (1876–1945), devoted an entire chapter in one of his books, which appeared in 1927, to the naval action in which Louis Barthes, the father of Roland Barthes, died on the night of October 26–27, 1916.[1]

Roland Barthes must have known of this hagiography, as he must have known of the letters his mother received following his father's death from the military, letters he kept with the account of the naval battle. We are reproducing them here as a kind of prelude to the album, as part of the archives of the fatherless writer who nevertheless had letters establishing his father's legend in death. Like Claude Simon and Albert Camus, Barthes belongs to that generation of intellectuals and writers orphaned by the Great War. More precisely, all his work erases the father, neutralizes patriotic and even familial and patriarchal mythology. In *Roland Barthes par Roland Barthes*, published in 1975, this is his comment on two photos of his father in uniform: "The father, dead very early (in the war), was lodged in no memorial or sacrificial discourse. By maternal intermediary, his memory—never an oppressive one—merely touched the surface of childhood with an almost silent bounty." In the same book, mentioning one of his teachers who began the school year by listing on the blackboard the names of students' relatives who had "fallen on the field of honor," Barthes notes both how he was the exception in being the only one "who could claim a father" and how, at the moment when the blackboard was erased, "nothing was left of this proclaimed mourning." A father without a tomb since his body went down with the wreck of the ship that he commanded, *Le Montaigne*.

This play of mark and erasure is characteristic of the modern palimpsest thanks to which Barthes constructs a new art of autobiography. It seemed to us that as a prelude to this book we could offer exactly what it was that, in order to write, Barthes never stopped erasing and thereby inscribing, since basically that is the very principle of this album.

*   *   *

Madame [Louis Barthes],

It is with the keenest regret that I am confirming the news of the horrible misfortune that has so suddenly stricken you and your deepest affections.

The name of your dear husband will remain in my memory as one of a brave, loyal, and courageous officer, prepared to make any sacrifice to fulfill his duty to the very end. That task, so often thankless and riddled with dangers, he accomplished with the highest, most elevated feeling, setting an example for all through his energy and his zeal. Of him, Madame, I have only words of praise to offer you; I considered him to be by far the best officer under my command, and all those who witnessed him at work in all circumstances are unanimous in deploring his loss.

Death struck him down at his battle post.

Although wounded in the head, he continued to give orders as precisely as ever; but a second shell hit him directly in the chest. Unfortunately his body could not be recovered and disappeared with the vessel when it sank. The ship was then located four kilometers north of Cape Gris-Nez.

I know from experience the dreadful pain that you must feel and that grips your heart as a beloved and cherished wife; but nevertheless, Madame, overcome your grief, think of your dear little son who brought you both joy, and tell yourself that your dear husband died in fulfilling his duty toward and for France.

He bears with him the sincere regrets of those who knew him and he will remain an example for those who have survived him.

Please accept, Madame, the assurance of my respectful and most sincere condolences.

Signed: Le Bihan
Commander of the Second Patrol Squadron
Calais

*   *   *

Chief of the Flotilla Division of the North Sea

Dunkirk, November 7, 1916

Madame,

So that you receive testimony that is—insofar as human things can be—worthy of your husband's valor and your sacrifice, I have asked that he be given the Military Cross and Citation by an authority higher than my own. But I can wait no longer to express to you my respectful compassion and the deep regrets that M. Barthes leaves behind. I saw little of him because my flotillas are widely dispersed, but I knew him well enough for him to inspire in me a lively sympathy and absolute confidence in his value and character.

The last time I saw him, as I was telling him how I regretted that certain regulations did not yet permit me to compensate him as he deserved and as I would like, he answered me in such a way—with such dignity and simplicity and so loyal and fine a look—that his noble heart was clearly revealed to me and my eyes brimmed with tears of emotion; these visions matter in life and are not forgotten.

Thus I know, Madame, whom you have lost and the grief before which I bow.

Commander Le Bihan has written to you. You know what took place that night of October 26–27: your husband sensing something serious in Pas-de-Calais and placing himself and his two small ships resolutely between the trade routes that he was supposed to guard and the enemy's likely position. Then the sudden arrival of five warships. He could have extinguished his lights and hidden in the darkness. No! Duty called him to recognize those ships and demand if they were enemies or allies. Such knowledge was essential at any cost in order to sound the alarm if necessary and to inform our forces. Barthes ordered the reconnaissance signal to be given. Terrible fire, at point-blank range, hit *Le Montaigne*. Seriously injured, the Commander fell, but he commanded still; clearly, carefully he gave the order that had to be given. A second volley of enemy torpedoes carried his soul to where those souls go who put duty before life, before all else. Duty, whatever it is, is a form of the Divine Order—we know this—and swift is the infinite reward for those who sacrifice themselves to that order.

Le Montaigne sank a short time later. With difficulty, places were found in the small crafts for the able-bodied and the wounded. Impossible to bring the dead. But before leaving the ship, Second-in-Command Courant and Quartermaster Clermont assured themselves again that their Commander was no longer alive. I interrogated them on their observations; there is no possible doubt.

Hence the tomb of the Commander of the *Montaigne* is the bridge of his ship; it is the battle post that he did not desert. I well understand, alas, that you would wish for a different one where you could pray or where later you could bring your dear child to pray. But your gaze and your prayers ascend higher than the tomb.

Be so good as to accept, Madame, my humble respects and my affliction, shared by all those who knew, esteemed, and loved the one for whom you grieve.

Captain Exelmans[2]

ENCOUNTER IN THE ENGLISH CHANNEL ON THE NIGHT OF OCTOBER 26–27, 1916, BETWEEN GERMAN DESTROYERS AND THE TRAWLER *LE MONTAIGNE*

Account rendered by the survivors of *Le Montaigne* to Lieutenant Guénée, Commander of the trawler *L'Élisabeth*.

About ten o'clock, the second-in-command of the *Montaigne*, who was on watch, noted in the northeast the existence of rapidly appearing lights that seemed to be flashes of artillery fire. He informed Commander Barthes, who was not concerned at first and made no changes in his orders. About eleven o'clock, the lights were accompanied by the muffled noise of artillery fire. The commander mounted the bridge, where he remained after confirming the accuracy of the information. It seems clear that from that moment Commander Barthes grasped the imminence of the danger, but was too self-disciplined to let anything show; he continued his patrol duty, increasing the precautionary measures already taken, but without disclosing his opinion.

At ten past midnight, black shapes were perceived at a short distance. The commander gave the order to put posts on alert and send reconnaissance signals. Immediately, searchlights from the destroyers were unmasked. One of them was so close that, afraid of interfering with English torpedo boats, Commander Barthes retreated so as not to approach it. Almost immediately the Germans opened fire.

The first cannon fire struck the 57mm artillery that was in front. The men who had reached their weapons were thrown into the sea. The second shots struck the bridge; a piece of shrapnel hit Commander Barthes in the head. The wound seemed serious but not life threatening. Very calmly, the commander gave the order to the second-in-command to steer to Griz-Nez (*Le Montaigne* was about six nautical miles north-northeast of the cape) and to ground the boat if that became necessary.

He had hardly finished giving those instructions when a third volley struck the wireless telegraph booth and exploded, killing the commander instantly. All this happened in a matter of seconds. The fourth shots did serious damage to the helm. From that moment on, shots followed one after another so rapidly that the men could not keep track of where they hit. A fire that broke out in front must have convinced the Germans that the boat was going to blow up because they stopped firing.

As *Le Montaigne* sank, the second-in-command had the two dinghies lowered into the water. In the first, they put the wounded, and the able-bodied men who remained tried their best to collect the dead but access to the bridge was impossible; a shell that had exploded below had destroyed the ladder. Also the boiler was threatening to blow up, the rear of the ship was rising above the water, and the front had sunk many meters. The second-in-command believed it necessary to abandon the dead and leave *Le Montaigne* in haste as it was about to engulf the second dinghy in its nose dive toward the bottom.

The first dinghy was rescued by *La Madeleine* about one thirty, the second about three o'clock by *L'Élisabeth*, commanded by M. Guenée. Everyone paid respectful and heartfelt tribute to their late lamented commander whom they deeply loved.

ACKNOWLEDGMENTS

I would first like to thank the institutions that retain the letters we are publishing, and to say how friendly, helpful, and welcoming their staffs have been to us.

We are thinking in particular of the Bibliothèque Nationale de France and its manuscript department, the Institut Mémoires de l'Édition Contemporaine, the Bibliothèque Littéraire Jacques-Doucet, and the Bibliothèque Nationale Suisse. Among individuals, we would like to mention Marie-Odile Germain, Olivier Corpet, André Derval, Stéphanie Cudré-Mauroux, and the list goes on. Among Barthes's correspondents, those holding rights, or those who alerted us to groups of letters, I would like to name Dominque Bourgois, Renaud Camus, Françoise Canetti, Marie-Claude Char, Antoine Châtelet, Antoine Compagnon, Marco Consolini, Raoul Delemazure, Marguerite Derrida, Bernard Faucon, Emmanuel Gabellieri, Christine Guibert, Pierre Guyotat, Éric Hoppenot, Julia Kristeva, Monique Lévi-Strauss, Patrick Longuet, Laura Marin, Alexandru Matei, Gilles Nadeau, Michel Pateau, Sylvie Patron, Frédéric Poulot, Christian Prigent, Antoine Rebeyrol, Jean-Loup Rivière, Jean Starobinski, Jude Stéfan, Catherine Veil, Michel Vinaver, and the list goes on.

But our thanks go above all to Michel Salzedo, the brother of Roland Barthes, without whose faith and friendship this album would not have been possible.

My gratitude goes as well to the Institut Universitaire de France, of which I am a member and thanks to which I was able to produce this work.

NOTE

When we place the date of a letter in brackets, that indicates a conjecture on our part. Most of the time we have completed abbreviations except when they are significant as such. We have made spelling consistent in certain cases and corrected a few mistakes made by Barthes or his correspondents regarding proper nouns. We have nonetheless respected Barthes's capitalization style.

Barthes's own notes are indicated with asterisks, while editorial notes are numbered. [Editorial notes for Barthes's own notes are in square brackets.]

Any time a letter is held by one of the institutions previously cited, we indicate that. No reference indicates the letter belongs to a private collector. These are institutions where the letters from or to Roland Barthes are held: Bibliothèque de l'Arsenal (BA); Bibliothèque Littéraire Jacques-Doucet (BLJD); Bibliothèque Nationale de France (BNF); Bibliothèque Nationale Suisse in Berne (BNS); Institut Mémoires de l'Édition Contemporaine (IMEC).

1915: Birth of Roland Barthes in Cherbourg, November 12, son of Lieutenant Louis Barthes and Henriette Binger.

1916: Death of Louis Barthes, October 27, in naval action in the North Sea on the patrol boat, *Le Montaigne*.

1916–24: Roland Barthes lives with his mother in Bayonne, in the town of his paternal grandparents. Studies piano with his Aunt Alice.

1924: Moves to Paris with his mother. She works in a bookbindery in Courbevoie. In November enters primary school at the Lycée Montaigne.

1926–27: Schooling interrupted by a stay in Capbreton for the birth of his brother Michel, April 11, 1927, child of his mother and André Salzedo, with whom she has an affair.

1927–30: Returns to Paris and resumes studies at the Lycée Montaigne, sixth grade. Regular summer vacations in Bayonne at the home of Barthes's paternal grandmother and aunt, the Allées Paulmy.

1930–34: Studies at the Lycée Louis-le-Grand through the baccalaureate.

1934: First onset of tuberculosis, May 10. A stay in Bayonne until the end of August, and then beginning in September 1934, a "free cure" in Bedous with his mother and his brother Michel through summer 1935.

1935–36: Return to Paris, October 1935. Lives on Rue Servandoni in the Sixth Arrondissement. Classical literature studies at the Sorbonne. Founds the Groupe de Théâtre Antique de la Sorbonne with Jacques Veil in 1936. Performance of *Perseus* by Aeschylus on May 3, 1936, directed by Maurice Jacquemont, costumes by Jean Bazaine, music by Jacques Chailley, masks by Jean Daste.[1] Barthes plays the role of Darius.

1937: Summer stay in Debrecan, Hungary, where he is teaching assistant at the university.

1938: Summer trip to Greece with the Groupe de Théâtre Antique.

1939–1940: Teaches at the high school in Biarritz, where he lives with his mother and his brother.

1940–41: Temporary teacher at the Lycée Voltaire and the Lycée Carnot in Paris. Takes singing lessons with his friend Michel Delacroix under the direction of Charles Panzéra. Defends his advanced degree thesis, "Evocations et incantations dans la tragédie grecque," in October 1941 under the direction of Paul Mazon at the Sorbonne.

1941: Relapse of pulmonary tuberculosis in October. First treatments in Paris.

1942: In January, enters the Sanatorium des Étudiants de France in Saint-Hilaire-du-Touvet in Isère. First publication in the spring: "Culture et tragédie" in the first issue of *Cahiers de l'étudiant* (edited by Robert Mallet, Paris).[2]

1943: Postcure stay from January to July at the Paris clinic of Doctor Daniel Douady, Rue de Quatrefages, Fifth Arrondissement. Relapse in July. Second stay at Saint-Hilaire-du-Touvet from July to February 1945. Meets Robert David and Georges Canetti.

1944: Jacques Veil assassinated by the Gestapo in Marseille in January. Plans to study medicine. Enrolls to study for the preparatory degree for medicine, then withdraws.

1945: Beginning in February, one-year treatment in the Leysin Sanatorium in Switzerland (with a brief interruption in the month of September for a new postcure).[3] In spring, he begins a systematic reading of the complete works of Michelet, which he indexes. Enters the Miremont Clinic in Leysin on October 10 for a right extrapleural pneumothorax.

1946: Returns to Paris, February 28. The effects of Barthes's tuberculosis will follow him throughout his life (regular medical visits, examinations, hospitalization, for example, in 1968). In spring, the first sketch from *Le Degré zéro de l'écriture*, "L'Avenir de la rhétorique." Postcure in Neufmoutiers-en-Brie during the summer. In September Barthes writes a piece on the exhibition of Dominique Marty's set designs (Nina Dausset Gallery, 19 Rue du Dragon, Fifth Arrondissement, Paris). Begins doctoral thesis on Michelet at the Sorbonne under the direction of René Pintard (1903–2002).

1947: Meets Maurice Nadeau through the intermediary Georges Fournié, a militant Trotskyite whom Barthes met in Leysin. Course in social services in June. Publishes his first article, "Le Degré zéro de l'écriture," in *Combat*, August 1. In November Barthes takes a position as librarian and then teacher at the Institut Français in Bucharest, whose director is his friend Philippe

Reybeyrol. In Bucharest Barthes meets Jean Sirinelli and Charles Singevin. Makes friends with the Romanian filmmaker Petre Sirin (1926–2003).

1948–49: The Institut Français is closed at the order of the Communist regime in November 1948. Having become a cultural attaché, Barthes remains in the Romanian capital until September 1949. In July 1949, Barthes writes a report for the Ministry of Foreign Affairs on the intellectual and academic situation in Romania ("Politisation de la science en Roumanie").

1949–50: Teaching assistant at the University of Alexandria in Egypt, where he arrives in November 1949. Meets Algirdas Julien Greimas, with whom he becomes friends. New series of five articles in *Combat*, from November 9 to December 16, 1950, sketches from *Le Degré zéro de l'écriture*.

1950–52: Works at the Department of Cultural Relations for the Ministry of Foreign Affairs. First articles in *Esprit*. Meets Albert Béguin. First approaches the publishers Gallimard and Seuil with the idea of publishing *Le Degré zéro de l'écriture*. Meets Jean Cayrol.

1952: Student researcher at the CNRS in lexicology. Meets the linguist Georges Matoré. Begins a new thesis with Charles Bruneau on "the vocabulary of relations between the state, employers, and workers from 1827 to 1834, according to legislative, administrative, and academic texts." His secondary study is the critical edition of *De l'éducation militaire* by Charles Fourier, under the direction of Matoré. Publication of the "first" of the *Mythologies* ("Le Monde où l'on catche") in *Esprit* in October. First articles in *L'Observateur*, where Nadeau works.

1953: Publication of *Le Degré zéro de l'écriture* by Éditions du Seuil in March.[4] First articles on the theater in *Les Lettres nouvelles*, edited by Maurice Nadeau. Founds *Théâtre populaire* with Robert Voisin in spring. Teaches courses in French civilization to foreign students at the Sorbonne. Meets Jean Genet at the home of Marguerite Duras and Dionys Mascolo, Rue Saint-Benoît, Sixth Arrondissement, Paris.

1954: Publication of *Michelet par lui-même*. Loses his grant from the CNRS in lexicology following a harsh report by Georges Matoré. In June he attends the production of *Mother Courage* by the Berlin Ensemble directed by Bertolt Brecht. First pieces on Alain Robbe-Grillet in *Critique*. He becomes friends with Jean Piel. First contact with Jean Starobinski regarding Michelet.

1954–55: Literary advisor to Éditions de l'Arche, directed by Robert Voisin. Is introduced to Michel Foucault through Robert Mauzi. Meets Michel Vinaver. Makes friends with Georges Perros, Michel Butor, and Pierre and Denise Klossowski, who form a circle of friends.

1955–56: New grant from CNRS (sociology) as research assistant to the laboratory of Georges Friedmann. The research topic is "social signs and symbols in human relations" and the focus is "contemporary civilian clothing." Georges Friedmann and Ignace Meyerson are the directors of this work. Meets Maurice Merleau-Ponty with regard to the question of clothing.

1956: Indicates a desire early in the year to take up singing lessons again with Charles Panzéra, but abandons this plan a few months later. During the summer Barthes writes "Le Mythe aujourd'hui," which will be the postscript for *Mythologies*. Participates in the founding of *Arguments* with Edgar Morin, Jean Duvignaud, and Colette Audry, a review created in December following the Soviet intervention in Hungary. Also sees Henri Lefebvre frequently. Meets Gérard Genette. Meets François Wahl, who will be one of his closest friends and his editor at Seuil—a bit later, in 1961–62, meets Wahl's companion, the Cuban writer Severo Sarduy.

1957: Appearance of *Mythologies*.

1958: Barthes does not take part in the extreme left's denunciation of de Gaulle's rise to power as "fascist." First stay in the United States in summer, teaches at Middlebury College, meets Richard Howard, the future translator of his work. Stays in New York.

1959: CNRS grant as research assistant ends. First publications of texts on a semiology of fashion.

1960: Named chairman of the Sixth Section at the École Pratique des Hautes Études, directed by Fernand Braudel, who supports his candidacy. Refuses to sign the *Manifeste des 121* launched by Maurice Blanchot on the "right to insubordination," but signs an "Appel à l'opinion" in *Combat* on October 6, with Claude Lefort, Edgar Morin, Maurice Merleau-Ponty, and Paul Ricoeur, advocating for peace in Algeria. Meets Claude Lévi-Strauss and Marthe Robert. Becomes friends with Lucien Goldmann.

1961: Puts Etchetoa, the family house in Hendaye, on the market in order to buy a house in Urt, where he will often stay for long periods of time. Attends Michel Foucault's thesis defense on May 20. Summer travels to Canada and the United States for lectures. Meets Pierre Boulez. First contact with the *Tel Quel* group through the intermediary of Jean-Edern Hallier.

1962: Given tenure at the École Pratique des Hautes Études as Director of Studies ("Sociology of Signs, Symbols, and Representations"). Beginning of Barthes's "seminar," which is attended by Jean Claude Milner, Jean Baudrillard, Jacques-Alain Miller, and Luc Boltanski, among others. Participates in the start of the *Revue internationale* with Maurice Blanchot. First encounter with Louis Althusser in October.

1963: Appearance of *Sur Racine*. At the end of August, Barthes completes a new version of *Système de la mode*, the final draft of which will not be completed until April 1964, and will not be published until 1967, delayed by the appearance of *Essais critiques* (1964) and *Critique et vérité* (1966). Meets François Braunschweig in November. Makes friends with Claude Simon. Joins the editorial board of *Critique*. First contact with Philippe Sollers—first dinner May 21—beginning Barthes's association with the *Tel Quel* group. Meets Jean Beaufret through the intermediary of Michel Foucault.

1964: Georges Perec and the Moroccan poet and intellectual Abdelkébir Khatibi attend Barthes's seminar. Makes the acquaintance of Jacques Derrida in March thanks to Phillipe Sollers. On April 21 attends Jean-Paul Sartre's lecture on Kierkegaard at UNESCO. On September 19, Pierre Klossowski reads him his *Baphomet*. Meets Charlotte Delbo through the intermediary of Henri Lefebvre (lunch on December 7 in the company of Jean Baudrillard). First contact with Jean-Luc Godard in December. Makes friends with Jacques Nolot, whom he meets at the Cannes Film Festival, according to Nolot. In 1989 Jacques Nolot will write the screenplay for the film *J'embrasse pas* (1991), made by André Téchiné, to whom Barthes had introduced him.

1965: Encounters with Francis Ponge in March, especially at Paule Thévinin's home. Appearance in autumn of *Nouvelle critique ou nouvelle imposture*, a violent tract against Barthes's *Sur Racine* written by Raymond Picard, Éditions Pauvert. Accepts and then declines to appear in *Alphaville* by Jean-Luc Godard.

1966: Publishes *Critique et verité* in response to Picard. On March 19, Barthes participates in the defense panel for Jean Baudrillard's thesis, with Henri Lefebvre and Pierre Bourdieu. In March–April, meets Italo Calvino, Pier Paolo Pasolini, and Alberto Moravia in Italy. First visit to Japan from May 2 to June 2 at the invitation of his friend Maurice Pinguet. First encounters with Julia Kristeva. Participates in the large colloquium held in Baltimore from October 18 to October 21 at the invitation of René Girard, with Jacques Lacan, Jacques Derrida, Paul de Man, Tzvetan Todorov, Lucien

Goldmann, and others. Founds *La Quinzaine littéraire* with Maurice Nadeau and François Erval.

1967–68: Second stay in Japan, from March 4 to April 5, 1967. Teaches at Johns Hopkins University in Baltimore from September to December. Appearance of *Système de la mode*. First publication of "La Mort de l'auteur" in *Aspen Magazine*, an American journal of contemporary and underground art, under the title "The Death of the Author," published in French the following year. Begins his seminar on Balzac's *Sarrasine*. Third stay in Japan from December 17, 1967, to January 11, 1968. Follows the events of May–June 1968 sympathetically but with some remove. With regard to May 1968, writes "L'Écriture de l'événement." Publishes his first piece on Japan, "Leçon d'écriture," in *Tel Quel* (Summer 1968).

1969: Begins the "Incidents" file that will go through many titles—"Roman," "Journal-Texte," "Stromates"—until taking its definitive title in the mid-1970s, "Vita Nova." Meets Pierre Guyotat.

1970–71: Teaches at the University of Rabat in Morocco. Becomes friends with Joël Lévy-Corcos. Appearance in 1970 of *S/Z* and *L'Empire des signes*.

1971: Publication of *Sade, Fourier, Loyola*. Appearance of a special issue of *Tel Quel* devoted to Barthes. Begins a regular practice of painting and of what he calls "Graphies." Barthes's great texts on painting (André Masson, Bernard Réquichot, Leo Steinberg, Cy Twombly, and others) are directly linked to them. Meets Pierre Soulages in May. Becomes friends with André Téchiné. Guest professor in Geneva at the invitation of Jean Starobinski and Jean Rousset, parallel to his teaching at the École Pratique des Hautes Études.

1972: Appearance of *Nouveaux Essais critiques*, preceded by the reissue of *Le Degré zéro de l'écriture*. Meets Tony Duvert in February and Jean-Louis Bouttes in April. Shooting of the short film *Roland Barthes par Roland Barthes* (six minutes, thirty seconds) by Jacques Scandelari and André Téchiné, produced by Pathé. Writes *Le Plaisir du texte* in the summer, which will appear in the *Tel Quel* collection in 1973.

1973: Supports Tony Duvert's book *Paysage de fantaisie* for the Médicis Prize, for which he has just served as judge. Teaches classes in Paris broadcast from New York University. Meets and becomes friends with Patrick Mauriès. Makes friends with Christian Prigent. Also meets Frédéric Berthet during a conference in Lyon in January.

1974: Plays the role of the narrator in a work by André Boucou-rechliev, *Thrène*, recorded January 19. In March becomes friends with Renaud Camus. Travels in China with Philippe Sollers, Julia Kristeva, François Wahl, and Marcelin Pleynet from April 11 to May 4. Publishes "Alors, la Chine?" in *Le Monde* on May 24, a piece that will be severely criticized. Begins his seminar on the "lover's discourse" which he will continue the following year.

1975: Seminar on *Bouvard et Pécuchet* at the Paris 7 University in spring. Meets Cy Twombly on May 25 through the intermediary of Yvon Lambert. Writes on this artist in September–October of the same year. Becomes friends with Antoine Compagnon. Publication of *Roland Barthes par Roland Barthes*. Begins analysis with Jacques Lacan on June 29, which he breaks off after three sessions. Begins piano lessons with his friend André Boucourechliev.

1976: Elected professor at the College de France, March 14, as proposed by Michel Foucault, for the chair of "Literary Semiology."

1977: Barthes gives his inaugural lecture at the College de France on January 7. Meets Hervé Guibert in early February, and then Yann Lemée, the future Yann Andréa, in May. Cerisy Colloquium titled "Prétexte Roland Barthes" led by Antoine Compagnon, June 22–29. Publication of *Fragments d'un discours amoureux* in the month of March. Returns to the question of photography already broached in the 1960s with texts on Richard Avedon, Daniel Boudinet, Bernard Faucon, Wilhelm von Gloeden, Robert Mapplethorpe, and others. Death of Barthes's mother on October 25. Begins his "Journal de deuil."

1978: In February, Barthes participates in musical analysis seminar ("Le Temps musical") with Gilles Deleuze and Michel Foucault at the Institut de Recherche et Coordination Acoustique/Musique, directed by Pierre Boulez. In April, plan for a literary conversion, plan for a novel. In autumn Barthes begins his course "La Préparation du roman," which he will continue in the year 1979–80. In summer Barthes plays the role of William Thackeray in the film by André Téchiné *Les Soeurs Brontë*, released in 1979. Begins the "Chronique" in December, which he will publish each week in *Le Nouvel Observateur*; abandons it in March 1979.

1979: Second encounter with Cy Twombly in the month of April. Appearance of *Sollers écrivain*. From late August until December Barthes makes a series of sketches of plans for the future work "Vita Nova." Writes a preface for *Tricks* by Renaud Camus. Meets Gilles Châtelet in October.

1980: Appearance of *La Chambre claire*. On January 27 goes to Bologna to give a short speech at an award ceremony for his friend Michelangelo Antonioni. Plans to stay in Venice for the Pop Art exhibition scheduled to open March 22. On February 25, Barthes is hit by a van while crossing the street in front of the Collège de France. Dies on March 26 in La Pitié-Salpêtrière hospital.

ALBUM

1

From Adolescence to the Romance of the Sanatorium
1932–46

1. Roland Barthes to Philippe Rebeyrol (IMEC)

The relationship between Philippe Rebeyrol (1917–2013) and Roland Barthes is quite exceptional in Barthes's history since, as the selection of letters offered here shows, their correspondence extends from adolescence, from the 1931–32 school year when they were both in the second level at the Louis-le-Grand Lycée, to the time of Barthes's death when Rebeyrol was the French ambassador in Athens.

We are only publishing a small number of the letters from Barthes to Rebeyrol, which are housed at the IMEC (Rebeyrol's letters have not been found). The first one dates from August 1932, the last one from March 25, 1979 (in which Roland Barthes cancels his plans to visit Tunis as the invited guest of Rebeyrol, who was the French ambassador there, because he wants to write the book that has not yet been titled *La Chambre claire*). Admitted to the École Normale Supérieure in 1936, graduating with a history degree in 1941, Philippe Rebeyrol became a diplomat after the war. He was of great help to Roland Barthes during his return from the Leysin sanatorium. In addition to his significant diplomatic career, Philippe Rebeyrol maintained his intellectual life as well, as is clear from the many texts that he wrote on Baudelaire, Manet, and Spinoza, some of which still remain unpublished.

*   *   *

[Bayonne,] August 13, 1932

My dear friend,

I was waiting to be completely settled here in Bayonne before writing to you. That happened quite some time ago now, since I left Paris very soon after you did, that memorable July 13 (Speeches, E*** Prize, letter from the Prince of Conti to Molière, Goodbyes, etc.)[1] If I haven't written to you sooner, it's because, first of all, I lead a very busy life, and then because I'm afraid I'll bore you and remind you of your bad comrade from a bad past. I have decided to, nevertheless, because I hope that you will answer me and tell me what has become of you, what you're doing and thinking about (I don't want to pry). As for me, I'm in the process of becoming an ascetic; I read very erudite things, I educate myself, I meditate. Which, in short, makes me a decidedly boring fellow. As for what I'm doing, I do many things: I read (not so bad). I play music and—I am very proud of this—I'm learning Harmony (which is even more difficult than Math). I also play a little bridge but I am really very bad at it. For me, the ideal hands are the ones where I'm the dummy. Finally, I walk a bit along the coast, and I'm hoping to spend a few days in Spain, if the good weather holds. As for what I'm thinking about, it's simple, I am always thinking about the same things. Often it's politics, but I have no one to talk to. Nevertheless I'm trying to convert my grandmother, who reads *Le Figaro*, to Socialism. She has already confessed that she would prefer revolution to war. Of course she does not know that I'm immersed in Jaurès (I hope that doesn't compromise him).

I have not abandoned my literary loves, which are—as you know—some Mallarmé and much Valéry. You absolutely must listen to the *Prelude à l'après-midi d'un faune* by Debussy while reading Mallarmé's eclogue at the same time: it's perfect. I will not go on too long about it, because I don't know if you have the same admiring and enthusiastic feelings toward Valéry. Maybe you have found another star that outshines *Narcissus*.[2]

In which case, let me know, we can debate it on the sidewalk of the Rue de Rennes. However, I think the real truth is that you are hardly thinking of all this during vacation, and you're right. But I'm a fussy old man who, when he has a new craze, wants to tell everyone about it and you would be surprised if I *could* (I employ a language against purism, you remember) write a letter without mentioning Jean Jaurès and Valéry. With regard to poetry, and at the risk of inviting your wrath, I hope that you're writing it again and that you would like to share it with me. You know, I do not say this with any irony; I am speaking very seriously. Besides, we have agreed once and for all, I believe, that being in accord on this subject, we can speak of it quite freely and frankly.

Excuse my three pages, my running on, my egoism. But you must read between the lines that I think of you often and I hope for your news very shortly. And if you need inspiration in order to write to me, may it arrive soon. Anatole France says that the beginning of the school year reunites students who have much to tell one another.*[3] Will that be the case for all of us? I hope so, and also hope that we might arrange to get to know each other a little better than just during breaks and on the Rue de Vaugirard. Don't you agree?

My dear friend, I'll close now. My regards to your parents, please, and to you, my very affectionate thoughts.

Barthes
I received two letter, each as kind as the other, from Oaulid and Huerre. Two good friends (along with others) whom I am happy to know.[4]
Allées Paulmy
Bayonne

*   *   *

[Bayonne,] August 30, 1932

My dear friend,

Let me congratulate you on having defended the passion of the great poet. I doubt that you convinced your interlocutors because interlocutors are never convinced. But if that's how it is, it doesn't matter; it's enough if only the initiated are never disappointed. And if I had needed some kind of initiative to fathom Valéry, I believe your argument would have provided it for me. I understand you very well: Valéry's great charm is how, in the work of inquiry, he unites the reader's thought to his own, in such a way that the thought actually comes alive only if the reader contributes his share. If he does not form this bond, this communion of ideas and feeling, Valéry remains dead to him, incomprehensible, snobbish (when someone doesn't please you, he is a snob or poseur). I don't want to say that we are inspired by the gods in understanding (since our rich French language has only this word to express the idea), in understanding, I say, Valéry, but he awakens in us something very poetic, very new, and very beautiful; can we accuse him of obscurantism? Sensible understanding is no longer, I think, the supreme sensation of happiness felt by man. I have the intuition that there is something beyond. I have just today read an article—maybe you've read it as well—on Valéry and his origins; on his mother's side, he comes from an old

---

*This quote is a consequence of my erudition. You see, I choose my authors.

Genoese family. One of his ancestors played an important role in the history of Genoa. His father was Corsican. I knew that Valéry had lived in and loved Genoa, but truly it seems to me that his poems are a thousand miles from the Italian spirit.

You ask me what I'm reading and what I think of Jean Jaurès. I might have a hard time not getting carried away. Until today, I was a socialist—very pretentious for a boy of sixteen—partly as a way to contradict the whole reactionary, nationalist clan. Having read Jaurès, it is impossible to maintain a lukewarm position, the middle course so dear to the French. Jaurès makes socialism an expression of such magnitude, such power and truth, almost of such sanctity, that one cannot resist it (as for me, I had no intention of resisting it). Reading the works of Jaurès, we see that he answers—having anticipated them—all the objections—the poor objections that, eighteen years after his death, and because of his death, miserable, vicious journalists are going to raise against the sincerity, integrity, and nobility of socialism as he defined it. Blum's socialism is, for that matter, fairly far removed from Jaurès's; that is what I presented when, in our school's government, I established a distinction between SFIO and Socialiste Français.[5] But probing more deeply, we see that in Jaurès's work, it is much less a matter of politics than of humanity, which is why it's so admirable; everything he says is wise, noble, humane, and, above all, good.* So his "Discourse à la Jeunesse" on peace is a masterwork of eloquence and emotion. Also wonderful are the pages he wrote in four days of war (and his death); they clarify remarkably the attitude of the socialists in that period, so discredited by a hateful spirit that exploits the misfortunes of a people and the goodness of a man. Nevertheless I will admit to you that, if one were to be frank and not daunted by a few small moral difficulties, Jaurès-the-conciliator is very difficult—impossible—to reconcile on one particular subject. If one has the courage it takes, this creates one of those small spiritual crises whose absence we deplore in some among us. But let's save that for our future conversations (because I hope there will be some). So I'm reading a fairly thick collection of Jaurès's selected writings.[6] You know that Jaurès

---

*Despite Lesserre, I cannot write without adjectives. [Pierre Lasserre, an intellectual close to Action Française, author especially of a very critical essay on French Romanticism, makes the adjective one of the signs of Romantic decadence. For example, with regard to George Sand's *Lélia*, he speaks of a "deluge of nouns and epithets." In *Le Romantisme français: Essai sur la révolution dans les sentiments et dans les idées au XIXᵉ siècle* (Amsterdam: Nabu, 2010), 202. (Originally published in Paris by Mercure de France in 1907.)—ED.]

wrote hardly any books (aside from a *Histoire de la révolution*, I believe).[7] *L'Armée nouvelle*, which makes up very sizable volumes, is simply collected articles from *L'Humanité*.[8] But the book I'm reading is quite well done and I do not need to tell you it's at your disposal. Because you will like Jaurès (I think—all political considerations aside—because even at his best, Herriot is very far from Jaurès).[9] He fills me with enthusiasm and now I feel that I admire him, him and the socialism he fashioned—and understand it very profoundly. Besides he was a brilliant Normalian and that is something we cannot help but admire.

I'm reading a few works on ancient Greece and especially on music in the Greek language; I have made some surprising discoveries. I admire you for your erudite readings. As for me, I'm still reading Anatole France, *La Vie littéraire* (where there is the famous article on the Normalian mind), *Le Vie en fleur*, *Thaïs*, and I reread *L'Île [des] pingouins* and the *Contes de Jacques Tournebroche*.[10] I have also reread nearly all of Racine's plays, who is to me as Voltaire is to you (am I wrong?). I reread *L'Introduction à la vie dévote*; it's not as boring as I thought. Believe it or not, I have taken a liking to Baudelaire (but not to make Valéry jealous). And last, a writer I must tell you about is Marcel Proust. First let me tell you I like him, to avoid ambiguities. Many people find him boring because his sentences are very long. Proust is at heart a prose poet, which is to say, from a simple prosaic act, he analyzes all the sensations and memories that this act awakens in him, as an observer might study all the successive circles emanating from a stone thrown into water. He makes this analysis with much feeling, sadness, sometimes with spirit; there are descriptions of the life in the provinces (in *Du Côte de chez Swann*) that—I assure you, I who am there—are startlingly true. That whole part of his work is very interesting and touching to me. I liked the second volume less, which contains the actual affair, and for which I think I'm a little too young.[11] A final word, you must not be surprised at failing to find the correspondence between Mallarmé's poem and Debussy's music, *Prélude à l'après-midi d'un faune*. I simply wanted to say that Debussy's work, which is foremost an evocation of Mallarmé's poetry, illuminates it, in its entirety, with much art. Besides, as you say, the work of Debussy is very beautiful, and so this true bond appears between Music and Poetry. Speaking of music and poetry, the other night in the casino in Biarritz I saw a Spanish dancer—La Tersina—who completely thrilled me.[12] I rank her, for dance, with my great gods of music and poetry: Beethoven and Valéry.

My dear friend, I must apologize again for my excessively long letter and my inveterate egoism; I only talk about myself. Nonetheless I wish you all good things. Write to me, please, as you were willing to do this first time, because, if I haven't already said so, your letter made me infinitely happy.

In waiting for your response, please accept, my dear friend, the assurance of my sincere friendship.

R. Barthes

While writing to you, I have received two books that I will thus add to the readings I've mentioned: two works translated from Russian, *De la dignité du christianisme et de l'indignité des chrétiens* and *Le Christianisme et la lutte des classes*.[13]

*   *   *

Bayonne, January 1, 1934

My very dear friend,

Your letter was as welcome as ever, and excuse me for not having answered it immediately. I'm happy to know that far, far from Paris, you have once again become the physical body that, before all else, we are (this is an idea developed in the first part of *Diodore ou la journée antique*).[14]

But let's take a look at the ideas your letter suggested to me:

Despite the fact that I'm in Bayonne, I am no longer thinking about my novel at all.[15] I am absolutely sure that I will not continue with it; I've made that decision and my reasons are many. First, there is too much that pleases me about my life here, the sweet pleasures of this house where I'm pampered like a true cloistered Anatole France, for my potential novel to be colored with the same bitterness, the same acerbic rancor that I may have imagined a few months ago.[16] At my age, one does not yet say, "I am getting older," but finally one has to admit that we evolve and our virile indignation finds objects deeper than the turpitudes of a certain social class. I mean that now my grandmother's stories, told with much spirit, amuse me and disarm my anger.[17] That is, I think, the practical reason. The theoretical reason is that, personally, if I had to write something, that something would always strive to be within the framework, within the "tonality" of Art, whereas the novel is, by definition, an antiartistic genre. Form is basically secondary to it and psychology necessarily overpowers aesthetics in it. I'm not blaming the novel for this, let me add; everything has its place. But I myself seem to have a certain concept of the literary work of art that still remains unconfirmed. I tried to give an example of it in "La Journée antique."[18] Sadly, it's childish, already outdated, and unfinished. You can read it anyway, if you'd like. Thus, for the moment, I have only a few projects: I'm in the process of composing a light divertissement for piano, which I will play for you, if you'd like.[19] Then I want to write a sonata. But what would make me especially happy is if you would write me something that I can put to music. Accept, don't duck out of it, you are more than capable of it; and if you shrink from extracurricular intellectual endeavors, to whom can I turn, I ask you? So think about it, please, and we'll talk about it as soon as school starts again; I would really like to attempt an actual intellectual partnership between us.

You see, for the moment, I'm taken up with music; nonetheless I'm thinking of (which is to say, I would like to be) writing something on Art, which, in my mind, I used to called "The Birth of Orpheus." But the greatest temptation for me is to address my famous question—the division of Christian and Pagan. I must bore you with this refrain. Imagine, after being all on fire over paganism because of reading Nietzsche on Apollo and Dionysus, I am now caught up in the Christian wave, under the influence of Pascal, whom I'm reading.[20] He is a wonderful man, and I believe that he has really captured me. I'm beginning to have deep, urgent ideas on the Christian virtues that I have often condemned. I see real grandeur and high philosophical meaning in humility (although my letter is no example of it), and humans seem to me so inane that charity seems like an act of heroism that is certainly not easily accomplished. Most of all, in Christianity I see something like the highest form of effort, of struggle. For my part, I would not advise seeking peace or consolation in it, but rather the torment that cannot be pacified, the thirst that cannot be quenched, etc. Thus, one arrives (does this make sense?) at a sort of Christian Pyrrhonism that is obviously paradoxical. Which is to say that what you say about Puritanism and Catholicism is very interesting to me; I find it very accurate. But since my heresy has bordered on indifference for some time, I have lost touch a bit with the Protestants. And certainly someone like Monod must know more about these questions than I do.[21]

Finally, I have some plans for this term: to continue with German and English very seriously, to set to work with you on music, to discuss things with you, certainly more than last term; finally, I'm always thinking about finding intelligent friends with whom to play music, say, or to voice one's thought. I ask only one thing of them:

to be "nonconformists," "companions of David, *Davidsbündler*."[22] But to explain that would take me too long.

Excuse me for having talked only about myself; feel free not to read my letter to the very end. Goodbye, my dear friend, see you soon (I am returning to school Friday afternoon!).

Best to you,
R. Barthes

*   *   *

Bayonne, July 23, [1934]

My very dear friend,

You must not be annoyed with me for not writing. It is not that I'm not thinking of you; on the contrary I miss you very much and the thoughts that I subject you to in my imagination are hardly "literary." But I cannot express to you how difficult it is for me to write right now. My thinking is not dulled, just the opposite. Since I have been sick, my life has become much more intense, much sharper.[23] I'm becoming more aware of myself, if you will. Thus I have in mind many ideas for novels. But I cannot bring myself to write. I think it's simply because it wears me out. So, do not be annoyed with me. We must let this phase pass; all I ask is that you write as often as you can because I look forward to your letters, and that you don't require a regular correspondence from me at the moment. Make that very Christian effort of giving without the hope of receiving. I would like for us to be above the conventions of correspondences and for us both to be aware of these small crises that make it impossible to accomplish minor acts even with major effort. There is certainly a very rare grandeur in respecting these mysterious caprices of being.

I don't believe I ever thanked you for collecting my books from Mme. Guex. Well, I'm thanking you now because you certainly were brave. I'm going to get back to work in August; you're so kind to offer to send me those papers about the baccalaureate. But send me only those you consider truly indispensable.

Of course I'm much better than when I left. Still I am not very happy with my health. I have to say that my discontent comes especially from the terrible uncertainty I have about my actual condition. I've fallen into the psychology of the sick person; the smallest thing frightens me, the smallest thing reassures me. I spend the day making inferences, looking for correlations between symptoms and external causes. You have no idea of all the thoughts that come into my head. Tuberculosis is a serious condition that leads very quickly to death, either in fact or in one's imagination. Then on top of that, all those who don't have it, and who do not show the least regard for the one who does, assign to it all kinds of mysterious powers and create a real panic in and around the one who is sick. Although it's not in the least a shameful disease (and in truth, are there shameful diseases?), it is treated that way. I think that's stupid and dangerous.

And now that my prospects of leaving grow so distant, my desire to leave is greatest, especially to go abroad. I am not ungrateful or an anarchist, but I am beginning to tire of French conformism. I'm passing through a wave of anticonformism. You cannot imagine what disgust I now have for politics, especially the politics of "President Doumergue" and all the fine words written on this subject.[24] It is grotesque. Moreover the Socialists and Communists do not escape conformism. As for the radicals, in this regard they deserve a good beating.

In literature and in music, conformism is less irritating to me, because it only involves a small minority and because, for the moment, I tremble with horror at the endless stupidity of the masses.

I have not yet left for England where I would like to live for many years if possible. In the meantime, I hope to see you very soon, in September in any case, if you don't come for a short visit in August, as I may ask you to do, later.

Affectionately, your friend,
Roland Barthes

*   *   *

[Bedous,] Thursday, [December 28, 1934]

Dear Rebeyrol,

Although I sent you a fairly long letter just yesterday, I'm answering your letter today. As you say, letters are tangible evidence of affectionate and ever-present thought; I'm becoming very aware of that through the negative form of the proposition. I'm very, very happy that you were thinking of me during a time when someone other than you so easily and justifiably had forgotten me. Everything you tell me I well know, despite being several hundred meters south of you. I know the quality of your exhilaration, I've seen what you are seeing, the snow in the blue sky. Here I cannot praise the air's clarity so much as its softness. Today I returned from Osse about five o'clock and the evening was like an evening in June, very clear, the Spanish wind, our god, making the already mild air even milder still. I tell you, along the deserted road I had the mad desire to stretch out in the grass, to dissolve into the earth, that solemn inert thing that is really the most illustrious example of fertility, of life. In that moment, I hated humans. I would have been happier as tree or dust, any participant in the communism of nature. I would have given anything not to feel excluded from that vast organism, at the gates of which I weep as before a forbidden—or lost—paradise. (On this subject, I'm surprised that literature has not explored further the clear ties between love of nature and splenetic Romanticism.)

Christianity was the source of many paradoxes; among the most dazzling and hateful is the one you note: that revelers celebrate the nativity. I see no greater Christian crime than the celebration of Christmas; we see the extravagant success of that institution just as much among the hypocritical and indifferent. As for me, would you believe it? I had a very orthodox, sweet, and peaceful Christmas. What in much of the world is only drunkenness and Gallic behavior was for me a sweet dream, the benefits of which I will feel long after. The night of December 24, I went to bed at nine thirty, I read a little Saint-Évremond[25] (a man of good sense and subtle wit if there ever was one) and a little Luke.[26] Tuesday morning I went to the pretty little church in Osse, which is very old and very rustic. The pastor I like very much, M. Bost, who is a fanatic supporter of the SDN.[27] I was welcomed there in a touching manner. I received communion. Surely you do not know this, my dear Rebeyrol, but Protestant communion has a beauty and grandeur that truly compensate for the errors of that religion. That evening we had a small Christmas tree at home as is the custom each year. At least God will have nothing very much to blame me for that day and the following one. I decorated the church Christmas tree and you should have seen me balancing on a ladder a good part of the time, hanging shiny garlands on the branches of the "king of the forest" or measuring the cotton powder. Bost, his hat askew, passed me the candles. I leave for Bayonne on Saturday.

Our letters crossed; you cannot have seen in mine that I reminded you of the music, and you told me you could do without my warnings. Now that you went to the concert all alone, you no longer need me; as soon as one enters that enchanted forest, all paths are good and the guide is nothing but a hindrance. I am sad to be releasing a victim simultaneously so docile and so intelligent.

Write to me, please; consider my pleasure at hearing from you about such a fine symphonic piece.

Very affectionately,
Barthes

In the attached photos you see: 1. The village of Bedous and the valley, in the heart of the Thermopyles (below, narrow pass).[28] You can see the main road that goes to Spain. 2. The house you see at the end of the road is Maison Larricq, where we live.[29] The third window is my mother's room, where I have my piano.

My writing is better than Clément Vautel's.[30] My apologies nevertheless.

*   *   *

Bedous, Monday, August 13, 1935[31]

Dear friend,

If I haven't written to you, it's because I am in love, madly in love with a charming girl, sixteen years old, named Mima. Mima has very brown hair, skin, and eyes. Perhaps it's because I am blond and have blue eyes. She has a little something about her that might be called "comical" or "funny" or "amusing," which I myself find adorable. It is exactly the "je ne sais quel charme" that Corneille talks about.[32] We have still not spoken very much and I do not want to say much more about her. Sometimes I run into her, with her family, at the Bousquet's grocery, and it makes me happy for two days. Sunday evening there was a public dance at the square and we danced together. She does not know how to dance and neither do I—absolutely delightful regardless. We certainly make a charming couple. But I see that I haven't told you enough about her grace, and nevertheless I can't tell you more. I would have to represent to you—and what art would be sufficient—the exact proportions in which her lightness, harmony, seriousness, and childishness are combined, her voice, a bit deep, the voice of a child who is no longer one, her little surprised air, etc., etc. (I'm not ashamed of the Romantic cliché). She has the loveliest little white hat that she wears tilted back a bit over her very dark hair, which contributed greatly to her conquest.

I have long thought of her, the little Musset heroine circa 1935, who has worked her way into my life—oh so little and so much—with a whole parade of such poetic things: the dance, the hat, a few trite words exchanged at the pelota party, and then she appeared to me in the path full of flowers and sunlight. . . . All this tremendously Romantic imagery. All these little repeated Faustian incidents and other adventures that prompt in me the charm and suffering that all love distills. Why tell you all this? Is it in earnest or literary or ironic? A bit of each. I don't know, I don't know; I'm letting myself be swept up in this wave of poetry, this wave of beauty, this wave of banality as well.

But here is where things become Cornelian. Alas, Mima's family is as unpleasant as she is adorable. It's the old story. Mima has a cousin, Annie who is a very pretty young woman, more classically beautiful but lacking Mima's charm. I cannot stand Annie. Vain, affected, scornful, she has all the exasperating faults of a pretty girl. Annie feigns great affection for Mima, who is a few years younger than she is. Mima, good girl that she is, cannot escape it. And it's already inconvenient enough that Annie is always by Mima's side, chaperoning her, monopolizing her, never letting her answer, not even letting her make an appearance. Mima has a cousin Jean, who is Annie's brother. I cannot set eyes on this fellow without wanting to hit him a few times. Ill-bred, extremely arrogant, proud, but a bit less intelligent than Pascal's man, he's a distillate of everything I detest in life. All my hatreds, phobias, dislikes, indignations, stupefactions I find in him, hideously alive and breathing. This feeling of repulsion translates into a physical urge to smack him. Now the worst of it, my friend, is that just at the time when I am occasionally reawakening to antifascism and socialism, this fellow takes it upon himself to be fanatical burning cross, a rabid militarist. And I am coming to the actual facts behind this business. On Saturday there was an open (and public) meeting here against fascism in which a communist professor, Verdier, spoke. At this speaker's first words, young Jean began shouting; he had a serious fit of hysterics; his father and mother got mixed up in it and in the midst of the shouts and insults, you could hear them calling the audience imbeciles and idiots. You understand that after this debacle they're not viewed very well in these parts.

You understand too that it's sad to fall in love in such a family.

All this is as tragic as one of Corneille's third acts. So much poetic lightness balanced by so much hideousness. . . .

Poor Mima, so true and so innocent—"oh so charming, charming"—in this tangle of pride, fanaticism, idiocy, and spite. She's like one of those medieval princesses locked up in a faraway castle among dark demons. All that's missing are the two braids flying in the wind from the top of her tower, a sign that makes the noble knight's heart pound as he speeds across the plain to rescue her.

Dear friend, excuse your friend who so shamelessly tells you things that are not worth your trouble, that perhaps he never thought about this way, and perhaps he invented so as not always to be telling you the same thing.

Very affectionately,
Barthes
I'm thinking of you and will write to you more intelligently very soon. Because this letter must have been such a disappointment to you.

I'm attaching a note to give to Brissaud, please.[33]

*   *   *

Paris, March 1, [1939]

My dear Philippe,

I haven't forgotten you and think of you very often, but if I haven't written it's because I don't have the heart to send a few lines offering a bit of trivial news. With you, I always want very full letters and I often feel distressed at not being able to provide you nearly so many of them as I used to, because it's almost as though I don't know how to write any longer, having lost the power to truly ponder, as I really could to some extent in my early youth, at the time of our wonderful correspondence. I always have the impression that since that time of relative strength, I've continually been in a state of crisis, unresolved crisis, without the beautiful aspects of the crises of heroes in novels. What's more, you have registered this each time you've seen me and you no doubt understand that my instability and inner weakness must be allowed to ripen until a path emerges in one direction or another.

All this became very clear to me through a visit I made to a Benedictine monastery near Bruges, where we went with the Théophiliens.[34]

I was extremely affected by this twenty-four-hour visit. I'm still disoriented and disconcerted by it; I have yet to come back to my senses and I have the impression that my friends here find me bizarre. To them I must seem to be in a bad mood, a bit short-tempered, and tired (as you see, nothing very good!), whereas in reality and from within, it's more that I am dumbfounded (that is the word for it) by the revelation of this monastic world that moreover—I do myself this justice—I have never ridiculed or underestimated because I have always had infinite respect and secret envy for everything Catholic.

You understand of course that this is not in the least a religious revelation because God and Christ are—for the moment—a whole other discussion. So it's not at all one of those sudden mystical flights toward God, which must be hard because the fall, so likely to follow, is unpleasant. What truly disoriented—more than moved—me is the vision of such a perfect, fruitful stability for which all the daily means and materials for nurturing it seemed to me supremely intelligent and effective. I think that any humanist can feel the weight and incomparable transcendent value of Catholic ceremonies; but finally among these monks—who are so compatible as well—one feels real contact with the absolute, in every moment of every day. Whether it's through the very beautiful practices of daily life, or through the day's thousand religious formalities, or through the actual worship in which it seemed to me that, except for the catechism, I amazingly grasped the most profound spirit. I must tell you that we lived the life of these Benedictines for twenty-four hours, eating in their refectory, attending services, sleeping in cells. Naturally I will forgo the usual clichés about the peace, serenity, joy, and certitude that emanate from those men and from that monastery, even though all that is absolutely true.

But I confess that these lines, more or less expressing what that visit meant to me, do not explain in the least the bizarre revolution that took place in me, coming in contact—however strained it was in that moment—with this monastic world. The fact is that I feel everything. Is this more than superficial? I really do not know. I'm waiting to see. I can say that deep down I fear so. Whatever happens, I believe I have experienced a very beautiful emotion. But what primarily intrigues me is that this expression, "beautiful emotion," does not satisfy me. It's something else entirely that I felt, that I am feeling, an emotion that is not qualitative, and that absolutely does not happen on the level of the emotions I've experienced until now.

But maybe I'm exaggerating all this. Who can say?

Send me your news soon, dear Philippe. Everything is going well here, I'm a bit tired, that's all.

I send you all my faithful and affectionate thoughts.

Your friend,
Roland

Basically, what I really feel is a great emptiness inside me; I have no taste for anything, and I feel as though this is mysteriously tied to my visit with those Benedictines. It's an extremely peculiar kind of depression. At any moment, I strongly grasp this within myself.

*   *   *

Biarritz, Thursday, [March] 7, [1940]

My dear Philippe,

Your letter made me very happy and I'm glad to sense your calm. It takes so much for me to be at peace. It's difficult for me to speak of all this in a letter, but I am thinking so much of everything that's happening in our country and in the world, and I am frequently seized with fear, not for the physical future of our race but for our moral future. When I read the newspapers, when I listen to the radio, when I hear the news, I'm routinely appalled by the stupidity, the self-important vanity, and the shortsighted miscalculations of our fellow citizens. Yes, I tell you, I'm alternately angry or sad; both. I think that mine is the country of La Bruyère and Napoleon and in the final count, nothing, it seems, remains of all those games of great and victorious intelligence that make us so proud of being French. I cannot say anything; I must speak and especially with you, that would do me good. My heart is heavy because I have been struck dumb until now by the onset of this inevitable war, but now I'm more and more struck by cruel flashes of lucidity. Me, whose thinking has never been tied to the problems of the world, who understood nothing about it, my eyes are gradually opening and I have the impression that I can see just how everything is happening and even how everything will happen. And my powerlessness, my silence, that of others, make me suffer cruelly. At times I truly feel as though the harsh truth is burning me, and frantic, I stop short at the edge of an abyss.

Where will you be for Easter? Could I see you, if only for a day or two? I would make the trip just to be able to talk with you; and what good that would do me, because either you'll share my opinion or you'll be able to find the words to calm me down. And you could also help me bear the weight of my personal troubles, the lonely present, the dark and vertiginous future, all those perfectly natural small selfish thoughts that superimpose themselves over the large general distress.

Of course all that does not prevent spring from lighting up the luxurious gardens of Biarritz and the waves along the shore. And you must believe that I am steeping myself in this spring, this country, this peace, in all these beautiful things that are so close, so kind, and so sure. You know that, because you tell me of your walks along the bright, deserted beach. As for me, I often go to the lighthouse, two minutes from the house, sometimes even at night. Yesterday I went up there after coming back from the cinema. The night was so very strange, very still, almost dead still, and filled with mild, stagnant air. At the edge of a terrace very high above the sea, right in front of me, was an unbelievable crescent moon, golden yellow, thin, curved, tapered, truly a sickle. And with a feeling of cosmic dread I could make out that immense unmoving movement of the sea in the rocky depths. And right next to me, gradually revealing themselves to my unreliable senses: benches, the crunch of gravel. I perceived couples and you have no idea what a terrifying feeling I had about the universe, as if in a lightning flash I understood everything without being able to express anything: love, the stars, the flowers, humans, and *Questo enorme mister de l'universo!*[35]

Because you know that I feel such acute longing for this palpable knowledge. It's this truly metaphysical perception of the universe that I am endlessly seeking, that I experience daily, humbly, prosaically, and that I re-create at times in music.

Have I told you that for a long time now I've been haunted by a work I would like to create, an essay I would call "Love, Music, and Death"? But I'm having a very hard time writing because of the war. First we must win it, then we can think about writing. What do you think? If I wrote a few bits, would you let me send them to you? While waiting for "Love, Music, and Death" (no doubt it will be a long wait!), I've begun a meditation on a portrait by El Greco, and if I finish it, I will send it to you.

Dear Philippe, of all the horrible things about this war, the most depressing for me is not having seen you for nine months now. That's why you must not hold it against me if sometimes I've remained silent. We have been apart far too long and it's too sad. We must find a way to see each other, or else things will continue like this even longer.

Write to me, please. I think of you with the deepest and most faithful affection.

Roland
Les Sirènes, Rue Lavigerie, Biarritz

*　　*　　*

Paris, December 13, [1941]

Received your long letter today with all your news. What a pleasure to hear some of your thoughts, but I had already guessed everything about the examination. Finally you are saved.[36] But everything you tell me makes me so long to see you again that I've become morose. Ah well, that will happen soon in any case. As for the examination, I too have so much to discuss with you. I feel exactly as you do, I don't know if I will take it; I have to tell you what Séchan told me at my thesis defense.[37] As always for me, there is a conflict between the path of work and the path of life, and they both tempt me. My dear friend, I am as always very full of conflicts. At the moment, I am enormously tormented within; sometimes I sink to the bottom of the deepest abyss, sometimes I rise to the heights. If you want to understand the intense atmosphere in which I live, read Dostoevsky. This is a man who has defined me entirely, and for the past two months, thanks to him, I feel I'm at the base of a mountain about to begin an ascent. Please, I beg you, read *The Idiot* and you will discover the extraordinary Muichkine.[38] I'm also thinking about many other things and I absolutely must tell you everything. I'm very excited to see you again and if my illness allows me to see you sooner, I am grateful to it.[39] Moreover, basically it's doing me much good. At any moment, I have the kind attentions of your mother and your uncle. Thank you! Write.

Your friend,
Roland

*   *   *

Saint-Hilaire, Thursday, March 26, 1942

My dear Philippe,

I received your letter, by way of Vichy, this morning. Our long separation is coming to an end and I would like to tell you the practical details of your visit. But first, I have some misgivings about taking you from your mother, you'll be with her for such a short time; I'm afraid that this trip, which is quite long after all, will wear you out; and then I'm especially worried that coming here will not be very cheerful for you in this sad place for those in good health. Do not protest. Two years ago I spent three days with Michel Delacroix, who was in a sanatorium on the Assy plateau.[40] I was consumed with fear and sadness there, despite all my fondness for him; I don't want you to

17   **FROM ADOLESCENCE TO THE ROMANCE OF THE SANATORIUM**

experience similar feelings because of me. I will tell you more about the sanatorium; you find the best and the worst here, it seems to me. But the fact remains that it will be a difficult trip for you, unless you are insensitive, which I do not believe. So, dear Philippe, if you feel that practically you cannot come, don't hesitate to extend our separation a bit, I will understand completely. Although I am, quite literally, consumed by the desire to see you and it has been a long time since I've envisioned such joy in the future close at hand.

If you are coming, you must let me know as soon as possible, because it's very difficult to find lodging here and it would be a big waste of time—of our precious time, yours overshadowed by your departure, mine eaten up by cures—if you had to stay in Grenoble. At the moment, connections to Saint-Hilaire are not very easy; there are two systems: either a direct bus; or bus, then cable car, and then taxi. I will send you the schedules. So as soon as you receive my letter, please let me know your plans.

Two weeks ago I could have written that I had a thousand personal, self-involved things to tell you. But the sanatorium has changed all that. It is such a displacement—although not a sad one—that I'm all befuddled and numbed by it, having lost myself, having lost that heightened self, to whom five months of bed, reading, and solitude had given such intensity.[41] You see, to be able to bear the shock of this new life, the ground had to be prepared, a certain space had to be made; all pain here comes from the degree to which one feels one's separation from something. Here, the state of perfect happiness is the state of perfect availability. Inner memories must be abolished, those habits of the soul that form the continuity of a being. Every point of comparison must be suppressed between the past—house, mother, friends, Paris streets, the living world where everything is possible—and the present—those beings with whom one is going to live for a long time, bound to them only through a disease that moreover varies widely in its intensity and subtleties—the present, with accordions in the bedrooms and exuberant moments of warm camaraderie. Each moment of the present here, if one literally and rigorously abstracts it from the delightful past and the undoubtedly difficult future, each moment can be very intense and very full! You may well think it impossible that it would offer much, this life so physically involved with all these fellows who are often cheerful and pleasant, even rowdy, but who all bear within their hearts the heavy weight of suffering, if not a horrible fear of death (for the worst stricken), that it would constitute a present that is vigorous and rich and not the least bit sad. What is played out here does not, for a moment, fall into the domain of drama. In any case, one must concentrate on what it is not. But sometimes there are glimpses of tragedy. I will relate all that to you, all the specific cases, all those Shakespearean situations that have stripped me of all my previous preoccupations, and captured my curiosity exclusively. All this, dear Philippe, to explain what? That since I've been here, I no longer read, I no longer write; my intellectual life, which I had enriched fairly well in Paris, fled me within two days, is depleted, deflated. Before arriving here, what pleasure I took in telling you of my reading, my great ideas, the passionate discoveries I had made within the realm of thought. For the moment, I no longer experience this. It will return, intermixed with my life here, if we are lucky enough to meet again before too long, and are not afraid of wasting time in silence and in apparently useless talk.

Arriving here, I found your long letter sent by airmail. How I wished to see you at that moment, to talk with you, to respond in your presence to everything you said in it. The time has come when our friendship is completely laid bare, that is, it becomes something inexpressible, I would say almost animal, because a taste for sharing ideas and experiences is no longer the only part of it. Now there is also the desire to actually be together physically, beyond what we could say or not say of interest to each other, the desire to sit side by side and tell each other many useless things about the essentials. If you are coming, I will give you a short list of small things to bring me that I can't find here—example: shoe polish! But I can talk to you about this again.

My health is good; that is something else we must discuss. I must say that here one gets vertigo from the medical explanations, partly because of the atrocious vocabulary, a kind of moribund medical student slang that has a genius for making metaphors out of surgical realities and the almighty presence of death.

There's the bell for the five-thirty cure. I will leave you, dear Philippe. Write to me on your arrival. What a joy to bring this great stack of paper to a close. Emotion has me putting it to poor use today! But we'll make up for it. To think that we may be able to see each other in two weeks!

Write soon.

Your friend,
Roland
Sanatorium des Étudiants
Saint-Hilaire-du-Touvet
Telephone: n° 9 at Saint-Hilaire, except during 1:30–4:00 treatments

*　*　*

Sunday, August 2, 1942

My dear Philippe,

Are you still in France? I received your letter and I can gauge more accurately now what I had guessed, the trouble that this unjust ordeal has caused you. How are you now? How is your family?

Don't be surprised to find nothing in my last letters or even in this one. I can no longer think, I can no longer write, I can't even think about myself anymore. There is no longer any strength for contemplation or silence in me; I no longer read and only write letters in great fits and starts, entire mornings when I fill ten inter-zone cards with the same story. In between I no longer think about anything. So what is happening? A fresh wave of what I will call the desire for glory, which makes me live intensely and makes me relive completely the years when I assembled the Groupe Antique at the Sorbonne. I feel that is the part of me that most demands expla-nation, that perhaps you understand the least.

Let me first offer the facts: during the first months of my stay here, when you saw me, I was still lost in the haze of nostalgia for the people and the life I had left behind in Paris and everything here was odious to me: not the hint of a comrade, not the hint of any-thing interesting, and as always when I'm deeply dissatisfied I could not even read. These are the most terrible periods in my existence, those in which I'm not suffering but nothing makes me happy nev-ertheless. I felt I lacked what destiny required of me, contrary to the great law that accommodates and manages our fates.

Then came a month in bed, of which I have absolutely no mem-ory. But that month of bed rest was like a baptism—unconscious like any baptism—into a new life through a thousand little tempo-ral facts of which I then became conscious.[42] I was part of the house, I had become ensconced there, and when I got up, I had an enormous thirst for activity, for life, and especially—a major fact I would like to make clear—*that my actions, among others, would begin to in-crease rapidly.* Which you will take to mean that what I was basically seeking from all this activity was the company and acquaintance of new people, as many as possible. That was always the case, I have never thought of anything but that, in an almost compulsive fash-ion. You will not refute me, you who have known me for so long. I have no curiosity about facts, I am only curious—but fanatically so—about humans.

When I say that my actions have increased, I mean that I'm beginning to exert a certain charm over others, which is most fascinating until the moment when, because it slackens, it becomes very painful. I wondered about that and I, who have such a need for others, I wondered if I was particularly lovable, if others found they loved me easily, deeply, enduringly, according to which mode. I had a wonderful period when I felt appreciated, admired, and valued by a whole group here, no doubt by virtue of what Girodon called my Atticism and my desire—however weak—to be lovable and simple, which, here, bore excellent fruit.[43] And as this respectable (!) popularity grew and expanded, it won me a seat at the Bureau de l'Association, by a big majority and without propaganda (wait, do not call me conceited before having read the end of my letter). Meanwhile, amid a small circle of friends, I also enjoyed a kind of domination that was dear to me because it developed among equals and seemed based on that part of me which is lightest, my incurable instinct for comedy, which, by merging with my serious and nostalgic depths, constitutes my misfortune.

The moment of conquest was exquisite, but soon my dark, insatiable nature seized control of the situation, an entirely happy and even glorious one for someone less exacting than me. And the suffering that I feel at not being sufficiently loved returned. I am attached to certain fellows here and after having conquered them I have somehow become their slave. This thing has become even more painful because feelings of friendship in me are always extremely fluid; nearly all my friendships with boys began as love. Of course, time has almost always clarified them, even while leaving a certain flavor I hold dear. On the other hand, the rare times I have loved a woman (why not admit that, in fact, it has only happened to me once), that began as what everyone calls friendship.

In short, you must understand that the affairs I have are mostly with men (by which I mean all that an affair includes of play, strategy, passion—intellectual? Making that qualification would be idiotic, as, for that matter, would be getting more specific). All this to tell you that my heart, if I may say that, no longer knows which way to turn in this place. There's the whole worldly, conscientious part of me constantly plagued by worries about the little public office that I hold here (you know how easily I worry). And then there's the amorous part, constantly on alert here, always very daring, because my passion stops at nothing, so that the lively image of an ideal never attained and its correlative, the phobia of opportunities lost, plunge me into the worst stupidities, obstruct conscious behavior, without dulling my consciousness in the least, only my will. In short, once more, I bleed, I weep, I discharge (as Stendhal would say).[44] For me it's always a question of fluids (the fluent being something purely Romantic).

My dear Philippe, I know too well that you will understand this crazy, abstract letter, as you have each time that a sharp torment grips us in the depths of ourselves. Do not hold it against me, you are the only one to whom I can write like this, and for me there's no greater grief than to think that tomorrow, if I want to, I can take up another blank page and write to you in greater detail and clearer words all that I have only sketched out here.

Write soon.

Your friend,
Roland

*   *   *

Clinique Alexandre, Leysin, Vaud, July 12, 1945[45]

My dear Philippe,

Your letter brought me great joy. It's true that your silence was beginning to worry me, not that I ever doubt you, but because I quite simply needed you. I can say without exaggeration and as literal actual fact that I think of you every day. My desire to see you again is mixed up with my present life and its problems, and everything I could tell you of myself would only be a way of saying how much I would like to have the benefit of your friendship near at hand again.

There are two new facts in my life: the intellectual death of these last three years has ended; my lack of affection for others, my indifference, my inertia are reviving. In the six months since I've been here, since my general health has improved, I have begun to work again. But it's under fairly curious conditions; it's fairly mechanical, almost disinterested work, because I have not resolved anything with regard to humanism, and matters of the intelligence are not at all enough to reconcile me with the world. But all metaphysics are slowly abandoning me; I long to possess a skill that would allow me to live in society. So I'm trying to make certain literary acquisitions in a carefully considered way (at first, my plan was tied to the idea of a thesis, but I'm still too ignorant to choose a subject). For the last three months, I've been reading Michelet. This choice is fairly odd; it's largely a matter of chance and to a lesser extent an old predilection. It's a bad choice in that Michelet is huge, and I'm making it a point of honor not to give up until I really know his work. It's a good choice in that this writer is a kind of ultrahumanist who fully represents the drama of encyclopedic knowledge, toward which a part of me has always leaned, in that with him one can study in vivo the formidable problem of great words, and in that some of his absurdities—which achieve the grotesque—produce a healthy rage in me and are exorcising for good the Micheletian part of me. In short, studying Michelet, I really do have a general idea forming in the back of my head:[46] to exorcise Romanticism, separate the stupid from the intelligent, completely exhaust the misfortunes of Faust, before turning to poetry. I think that after the anti-poet Michelet, it will be a lovely necessity to study—I mean really read—someone like Baudelaire. Since my graduate degree, I have been pursuing some vague but powerful ideas on the mythological value of the word.[47] It seems to me that literature could be considered from this perspective. There's an imperceptible and uniform movement from magic to art, to poetry, to rhetoric; that is what my thesis demonstrated. That marvelous thread could set us free from the idea, the content, to grasp literature in its creative—that is to say, organic—phase where it is most pure, as nascent oxygen is the strongest. Basically, everything holds together and I anticipate exciting connections: a history of literary art on the surface—that is, at greatest depths—captured in samples, cuts taken from the purest episodes in the continual drama of the word: the Greek lyric, sophistry, scholasticism, euphuism, classical rhetoric, Romantic illusion (where the desire was to fuse magic and truth, to criminally suppress the sacred distance between the word and the idea, to socialize, Christianize, authenticate the magic, which immediately resulted in depreciating the truths treated thus: the problem of Michelet's great hollow words), and finally symbolism and what follows, the purest examples of this attempt: Valéry or Michaux and the contemporaries in general when they are not stupidly mysticizing or confusing prayer and poetry. That's the plan I would like to follow; I'm very ill-prepared for it given my deficiencies: a weakness of intelligence; the very cancer of the word (precisely what I want to study would eat away at me, my discoveries would disintegrate the moment they solidify into words); philosophical incompetence in a time when you can no longer do literature without a degree in philosophy; and the frequent feeling of having an intelligence—at its best moments—that dates back about fifty years and would be scorned by those more strictly in tune with the present times.

But I am waking up to these times; not that my amphibological nature has stopped torturing me, since I always find myself disoriented by a single truth and political discussion are a true ordeal for me from which I emerge infinitely sad and discouraged, absolutely sure of my fundamental inadequacy for experiencing the happiness or ordinary troubles that others do. But the country in which I live—and because I'm living at the time when the great wave of war recedes, and after the cruelty of the storm, the ugliness of the mud appears and the muddy eddies, everywhere triumphant stupidity and the sacrifice useless, withering when it ought to flower—this country has awakened in me a feeling so unknown to me in my past life: hatred. I finally have a clear image of society that I do not want because it makes me sick, because it offends everything in me: the humans, morals, customs surrounding me—and this includes the majority of my stupid French companions—nearly all make me burn with indignation. I have become so impatient, so easily offended, even nasty, a purist for the human dignity that is so thoroughly trampled here. I am starting a file on our hosts and I assure you it will be a thick one. Flagrant stupidity makes me suffer horribly, stirs my bile, and overwhelms me. There are some gatherings, meetings, and meals that I leave physically ill, livid with anger, and wishing that I had less self-control and could be calculatingly insolent instead of just displaying my aggressive or embittered distress. And so, as Michelet says, I am sick with France; I would like to be there, to know what is happening. I suffer from its loneliness, from the evil said about it, from the ignoble pursuit of the wounded beast. I need to see the young men of my generation again, to hear what they're thinking, to take comfort in feeling and knowing that I think as they do.

That would be a reason for me to return in the fall if my health permits it. My dream would be to spend a peaceful year at home taking care of myself. For four years I have been in this funeral parlor, cut off from those I love. I want to live with my mother for a little while and—I would not say this immediately out of modesty but you know it very well—I would consider the joy of spending a year near you a major reason to return. What joy after so much misery! It would surprise me if I resisted the temptation. Just think that this winter we may be able to see each other and not just for a brief time. I would like to be free of any occupation in order to work and to rest for another year. That is a very serious issue. I will decide in August.

Thank you, my friend, for your offers of clothing and money. For the moment, there's no hurry. Simply see if you can find a way to let me access money through the "clearing."[48] There are excellent things to buy here; and given the situation in France, it would be bad business to leave with nothing. Check with Maman. But you know that is only of minor importance. All the same, why not try to take home from this country the one good thing it has to offer.

My affectionate respects to your mother. Write soon.

Your friend,
Roland

2. Roland Barthes to Jacques Veil

Jacques Veil (1917–44) cofounded with Roland Barthes the Groupe de Théâtre Antique de la Sorbonne in 1936.[49] A member of the French Resistance under the name of Gustave Nutte, he was killed by the Gestapo in Marseille the night of January 10–11, 1944.

* * *

Paris, March 16, [1940 or 1941?]

My dear friend,

A word in haste to tell you that never could I express the pleasure and emotion that your last letter brought me. It's a comfort to witness friendships like yours that can be all these things at the same time: sensitive, deep, active, and faithful. But I have never been worthy of it and you are too indulgent with me. But I hope to be able to talk about all that with you very soon. I'm going to Bayonne for Easter. Would it be all right with you if I stopped briefly in Arcachon on the way there? I would be so happy to see you. But I have some misgivings. Maybe you follow a strict regime and my coming would disturb and tire you. So you must be frank with me. I was planning to arrive in the morning and leave again in the afternoon. But it's important that this does not disrupt whatever schedule you keep. Don't worry for my sake and simply tell me where I might see you briefly if I stop in Arcachon.

Until very soon, I hope, unless my visit will bother you!

I send you my best wishes. Please give my regards to Doctor and Madame Monod, whom I had the pleasure of seeing at the Brissauds, if they remember me.

Until soon,
R. Barthes
Everyone here sends you warm greetings.

* * *

My dear Jacques,

I'm happy to take up a large sheet of paper to write to you. I've been here for about a week. My journey and settling in went well and I have already adopted the monotonous rhythm of sanatorium life. For the moment my health is excellent. I still have not decided anything with regard to my studies. I have to look at the possibilities.

But it's mostly about you that I would like to hear word. I'm delighted to feel closer to my dear friends in the free zone and I look forward to getting the details on your life and plans. In Paris, all those I left send along their warmest wishes to you. We have gone for so long without exchanging letters that I seem to have too much and too little to say. Above all I would like this letter—which does not really count as one—to carry with it all my affection and to be an opportunity to answer me at length and tell me everything about you and yours. For the moment, I cannot write much because I must—like all new arrivals—do most things in bed where one can hardly even read and then only when the accordions and visits from the other fellows do not prevent it!

I'm here with Jacqueline Mazon's brother, and we speak of you often.[50]

My dear friend, write to me very soon. Faithfully yours with best wishes.

Roland Barthes
Sana des Étudiants
Saint-Hilaire-du-Touvet
Isère

*　　*　　*

My dear friend,

Your letter made me so happy, but we must be able to see each other. Perhaps if I'm doing well this summer I may get a few days' leave, and I want to take a short trip to the Midi if possible, in which case I'll come by to see you briefly. These are nothing more than plans, but I assure you that it would be a great joy for me to see all of you again and have a long chat with you.

I didn't answer you sooner because I've just been ill. I had pleurisy and pneumonia that brought on a fever, fatigue, weight loss, and pain in my side for the month that I just spent in bed. This is quite vexing since I had gotten through a particularly hard winter in Paris with serious restrictions but with no incidents, thanks especially to Brissaud and maternal care. It's likely that the change of climate and altitude gave me the pleurisy. I promise you that I was angry about catching it here, especially since I had a fine case of pneumonia that was coming along beautifully. I'm doing much better now; I can get up for meals and I'm a little more active. Let us hope no problems develop when the fluid is resorbed.

I'm telling you my troubles without forgetting yours of course, the anxious life you must lead. And yet it seems to me that given your nature, so attuned to all new experiences, you must find great joy in that deep, genuine contact with the land. I'm sure you'll have a thousand things to tell me, and I can't wait for the chance to see you since we are already closer to each other than before.

Please give my regards to your parents. And to your brother and you, my faithful friendship.

Barthes
Sana des Étudiants
Saint-Hilaire-du-Touvet
Isère

*   *   *

Roland Barthes to Jacques Veil's Parents and to His Sister Hélène Veil

[Saint-Hilaire-du-Touvet,] July 5, 1944

Dear Madame, dear Monsieur,

My dear Hélène,

Thus what I had feared and have not stopped thinking about since the letter from Claude is really true; Hélène's letter received this morning informs me so. I am not afraid of rekindling your pain in mingling it with my own through these words, because nothing can lessen it, console you, or make you forget. I will never forget the one whom you mourn; I have always thought and spoken of him as a very beautiful soul who had all the highest virtues and whose keen divination of the Good and the Just was always instantly accompanied by total engagement of his whole being in his chosen cause. His death makes him greater still. He is irreplaceable not only in the hearts of his family and his friends—needless even to say this—but also in that small army of just men so necessary to the dignity of the world, and for whose friendship and respect we truly do live. I am saying this very badly, helter-skelter, but with seriousness and conviction. We must speak of him now and forever. Through his life and his death, he has earned a place beyond forgetting, beyond death. That is certainly no consolation for our hearts, but it is an obligation, an example for our living souls. I am there with you and share all my sorrow. I will not forget you.

Roland Barthes

3. Roland Barthes to Georges Canetti

Georges Canetti (1911–71), the brother of Elias and Jacques Canetti, and a tuberculosis victim, stayed at Saint-Hilaire-du-Touvet many times in 1934, in 1941–42, and when he had a relapse between 1944–47. Already a doctor and researcher at the Institut Pasteur when he met Roland Barthes in the sanatorium, he was a specialist in tuberculosis and went on to become one of the great innovators in the discovery of protocols for modern care.

*   *   *

[Saint-Hilaire-du-Touvet,] Wednesday, March 24, 1944[51]

My dear Canetti,

You will have guessed that I haven't written to you sooner because of this bleeding that Vincent must have told you about and that came on the day after my return; it was not very much but it started again eight days later, which made it nearly two weeks that I was immobilized almost without eating—and I am very hungry. For two days now it seems to be completely over and I'm reviving. I had no fever or fatigue, and the radioscopy indicates nothing more than before. I'm awaiting the results from an X-ray and will keep you posted.

I arrived to a very unpleasant concern: Caron must have an extrapleural in a month, right here with Bonniot, because any scheme with D. Lefoyer is impossible, as you know. Given Bonniot's reputation with extrapleurals, this operation is truly worrisome and I am quite morose, I would even say—you will understand—in anguish. As for Caron, he is optimistic; he draws much from the fact that Bonniot's unfortunate record is old news and that he might have performed successful surgeries since at Rhône or Mines. But it seems to me you can't deny that his chances might be better with a surgeon in Paris rather than here. And I'll also admit to you that despite all my affection and respect for the doctors here I worry that they are a bit new to the postoperative care that's said to be so critical for extrapleurals. What is your opinion, my dear Canetti? I feel that it's a very delicate thing for you to tell me and surely very indelicate of me to ask you. I am troubling you again by mail and you must be assailed with these kinds of little medical consultations. But I cannot bear doing nothing and remaining passive without getting information. It's a very delicate thing for me to be continually drawing Caron's attention to the risks he runs with Bonniot, because it's likely that it will be Bonniot. On the other hand, there is a kind of duty that affection requires of me, no matter what.

I will tell you that these apprehensions, which I very much believe to be heartfelt, are nevertheless without self-interest. I hope for nothing more from Caron and if I continue to worry about him as I would a loved one it's because, of all the times when I could abandon him, this is the only truly impossible one. But my trip changed many small things, broke a few habits, overturned the mirror of love, as it were. I am beginning to be unjust in the opposite direction, getting exasperated by his faults, which are great and many, contradicting him continually, and finding irritating what used to enchant me. I watch this love dissipating without being able to do anything about it, without even really wanting to stop it, because I'm hoping that at the end will come the positive benefit of freedom. But I am annoyed with him and with myself. I find it ridiculous that rejection, frustrated hope, can corrupt and ruin what was progressing quite beautifully. I must tell you that meeting the whole family together, which happened in Paris—I had lunch there—left me strangely moved and, frankly, irked. I must tell you about that house; there, for the length of a proper Sunday meal, that is, a good couple of hours, I had the intense experience of a thousand amusing or poignant sensations watching this large and hierarchical bourgeois family eat. Each member exhibited a familiar but distorted or caricatured trait (but really? that's when the doubts began), and between Uncle Jean, Aunt Rosine, and the great goose of a sister, there was only Caron's delightful younger brother, who will no doubt make many futile conquests among those ten years younger than me. But I'm impenitent; what happened to me doesn't keep me from envying them, those others.

My dear Canetti, in one sense I very much regret getting to know you during this strange period in my life—oh, I admit they occur frequently—because, completely tied up in this love affair, I haven't been able to offer you anything by way of distraction, interest, or visible and palpable affection, all of which I had wanted for us in that vibrant and truly intimate obscurity of ourselves, that secret, sincere place where the passions hide, retreat, founder, but from which true pleasures and true progress come. I was thinking that through letters we could speak more freely but I see that I'm beginning to talk only about myself; don't hold it against me, don't focus on me when you respond, but tell me about yourself as I've told you about myself, only better, because I hope that you are less unhappy.

Believe, my dear friend, in my very strong and faithful friendship. I miss you very much, and I am certainly not the only one.

R. Barthes

*   *   *

[Saint-Hilaire-du-Touvet,] Sunday, April 23, 1944

My dear friend,

I am writing to you from the terrace where I have a very beautiful view; the weather is splendid and I've never seen anything more calming than this Sunday afternoon. Nearly everyone is at the cinema; they don't know what they're missing. After my last letter, I felt such remorse at having told you all my troubles, thinking of the troubles that threaten you continually, the precariousness of your work, of your situation. I was very self-involved, but you must be so used to people wanting you to listen.

I also felt some remorse at having asked you for a medical assessment for Caron, but your response was so wise and so obvious that I really do not regret it. It is exactly what, as a layman—but not indifferent—I thought. I explained your response to him patiently, going over it many times without insisting too much—I have no right to. But his mind was already made up; he wants to have the operation immediately and is waiting to leave very shortly for Paris to put himself in the hands of Bourgeois. His arguments are plausible but, in my opinion, not entirely in good faith, since he has never really given the basic reasons for his decision. Well, I don't blame him, he is exposed to enough risks and problems. Thank you, my dear Canetti, for answering me regarding his situation; Caron attached much importance to your opinion, but his impatience prevailed. Moreover, isn't it true that in this matter you and I can only judge from a certain distance, a certain silence? No doubt you will see him in Paris because the questions concerning file transfers will bring him to postcure. Besides, he may think his departure will be easier and quicker than it is.

This month we have grown apart considerably. From the day that I could no longer love him with any hope, I could only very rapidly fall out of love with him. If he has the makings of a lover, he does not have those for becoming a friend; too many essential things divide us and in truth I do not respect him enough. Naturally this aversion is a very painful feeling because it draws much from the tiresome, ugly impulses of anger, jealousy, contempt, and sensitivity, all blended with passions, regrets, and hopes. But on the whole you could say that this affair is ending very quickly and leaving me much calmer than I would have thought. In the last two days I briefly decided to change rooms, but since his departure seems imminent and certain, I'm going to wait. (I must say also that I'm being careful because Hillairet, in quite a bad way himself, is about to drop in on me.)

As for my health, the situation is not clear and for the moment very uncertain. Outwardly I'm doing fine, I have regained weight, I look well, and my general state is good. Internally, the doctors are of two minds; first, after an X-ray, they decided that the cavity of my right lung (the one where a pneumothorax is impossible) was once again dehydrated and even if it's a very small area and the rest is very clear, it might be necessary to wait to be able to do a thoracoplasty there eventually.[52] But they said there was no hurry and would wait at least two months to discuss it again. Then in the last few days, during a [medical] exam, they seemed to hear noises on the left side, where the old pneumonia was. They're going to do tomographies and I will let you know the results.[53]

Personally, I think that everything is [. . .][54] and I'm not in a hurry to conclude anything; moreover I'm becoming, if not fatalistic, at least a little hardened. I understand that there will be no normal future for a very long time, for much longer than I would ever have imagined, and I would like get myself organized according to this idea.

At the moment, I'm not unhappy since I have a certain energy related to a certain pessimism. Thus I'm reading a lot (on the eighteenth century, related to a possible thesis), but I'm finding the method, rhythm, and progress of this reading more interesting than the content. I'm not leaving a single moment of my day empty, so as to avoid any vague melancholy, as it were. My reading is very methodical, but I do not have a single idea; that is the price of no imagination, of keeping idleness at bay, and at the moment I'm interested in this attitude. I have been asked to write a few pages for

Existences, on the short trip I made to Greece.[55] I still take pleasure in putting sentences together, but feel incommensurable nausea at rereading, rethinking, and submitting them. The important thing finally is to keep going, not to give up, not to be afraid. I have to stay in bed except at noon; no music; that is a big annoyance.

I'm doing English regularly with the delightful Grünwald, an excellent teacher, full of passion and thoughtfulness. He's trying to teach me a host of everyday words, with an intense enthusiasm that's conveyed through brisk comings and goings into his room to draw me the objects in question. I am not at all unhappy with the progress I've made in the last month.

I think I have about covered my thoughts, feelings, and occupations. I can tell you again how very dull all that is, and how I realize that your presence, your friendship, your life, your example, in fact a thousand essential and extraneous things about you, would add an irreplaceable brilliance to it.

Believe, my dear friend, in my faithful and very strong friendship,

R. Barthes

*   *   *

[Saint-Hilaire-du-Touvet,] Monday, July 31, 1944

My dear friend,

I have learned from Caron that you have health problems. What exactly is happening? Is it an actual relapse? Where are you in it? What do you plan to do? Can you send me some word about all this? I'm anxious to hear from you. You know that despite my silence I have not forgotten you. I have thought of you very often, always missing your presence and your friendship. But I was not hoping that you would write to me, knowing how torn you are between so many occupations. If you're not too tired, send me a short note, please, if only just a few lines to tell me how you are.

You know that since my relapse in March, the state of my health has not changed. I do not feel ill, but I confess that at the moment I can hardly get out of bed. I'm obliged to stay there until four when everyone goes for a walk. They'll have to do a new set of X rays in a month; I am mesmerized that date, as if it should be a kind of liberation, even though in fact there's little chance my regime will change.

Sometimes I see no harm in people and distract myself with the pleasures of conversation; sometimes I want to weep with loneliness and I read passionately. As Brissaud has me inclined, I cannot write without breaking the rules, as I sometimes do with remorse.[56] And above all I have one crazy desire, a real need to leave the sanatorium.

Please write, and believe in my very faithful friendship.

R. Barthes

*   *   *

[Saint-Hilaire-du-Touvet,] Sunday, January 14, 1945

My dear Canetti,

You well know how the life one leads here makes periods of long silence very natural and they mean nothing more than that one is very lazy, even though one loves one's friends as much as ever. After mail was interrupted during the Liberation, I didn't have the heart to start writing again to anyone and yet I was always thinking of you with so much affection. In September I received a long letter from you written before the events of August and it moved me and made me think. I really wanted to answer it, naturally, and then I was consumed by the monotony of the days, little personal affairs, everything that absorbs a weak nature like mine (weak but nonetheless faithful). Now I learn from M. Cohen that you have had a relapse.[57] But I have also learned that your book is finished and you have found a publisher.[58] I imagine you're thinking more about the latter than the former. But I wonder what you will do now. Why not write something less medical? I have thought again and again, seriously and admiringly, about the notes you read me. Why not write something like that? One is so used to seeing you cheering others, and you give the impression of needing it so little yourself that when some kind of health problem strikes you, there's nothing to say, except how loved you are and how your friends are affected by everything that happens to you, good or bad (I thought of you so much during the Liberation). That is the reason for this short note.

My health is not bad; I'm endlessly doing the cure and will be for a long time still. I feel fairly well. I must leave for Switzerland with the mob (ten times more numerous than I would like) that is going to Leysin. But that departure seems to be increasingly problematic; they said just today that the trains are canceled.

The material output of my life for the last six months has been slim; I successfully completed a few music classes, but that is about all. On the other hand, I am very busy spiritually (!) with one or two fellows, which has taken up the better part of my time and strength.

But I think that's where I give the best of myself; I have no regrets, I have lived well, I would like to say nobly. And to learn the value of what I've done, it's better to ask them rather than me. At the moment, it is a wasteland.

My dear Canetti, I think of you with most sincere affection and hope to see you again.

R. Barthes

* * *

[Saint-Hilaire-du-Touvet,] Saturday, February 3, 1945

My dear Canetti,

A brief note before leaving because I need to tell you what a pleasure it was to see you again. I found it all too short and I remain hungry for more. No doubt embarrassed by the good sister's presence, I didn't know how to say to you, in parting, that I hoped very much for your quick and good recovery—I think of it often—and generally I wanted to thank you for everything that a friend like you always brings of strength and clarity into the life of a man like me, when so many loves basically bring us nothing and are capable of nothing. I'm going away more peaceful because of what you said, although I do not have the impression that it will be a long separation. We will see each other soon and we will finish healing together.

Your friend,
Roland Barthes

* * *

Clinique Alexandre, Leysin, Vaud, March 16, 1945

My dear Canetti,

I have no idea if and when this letter will reach you; mail is extremely slow and unreliable, correspondences practically impossible. I have received only one letter from my mother, but alas there's a god—or a devil—for such things, and those at Saint-Hilaire have been luckier; from there I've received very embarrassing letters and cards (if not for my virtue, at least for my answers).

Perhaps you already know through the rumor mill that we have been wonderfully received here, taking those couple words literally and implying all the details you could imagine. Food, lodging, cleanliness, and care are almost perfect, of a standard incomparable to that of France—which is to be expected—but particularly to that of

Saint-Hilaire. After a month of this comfortable life—and I think our illness excuses us from denying ourselves comforts—it's impossible to think of Saint-Hilaire without distaste and perhaps even without harshness. I'm doing well, despite having caught a nasty flu upon my arrival. The doctors are extremely cautious; I cannot go out and will not be going out for a long time, no doubt. But that doesn't stop me from having access to all the cigarettes, cigars, cake, etc. that I want. For three years, my cure had only ever given me the impression that there was no change; here they know the positive, truly reorienting value of rest. The climate—spring all day long for a month of the cure—as well as the silence and the meticulous cleanliness of our living quarters produce a deep rest and everything relaxes, really seems colored with the happiness of nothing to do, of living, and of healing. If I'm dwelling on this tableau, my dear Canetti, it's because ever since I observed the difference between here and Saint-Hilaire I am tormented by the idea that it is absolutely necessary for you to come here. I truly feel it as a very grave necessity; I know nothing about your disease, and it's impossible, of course, for my opinion to weigh much against the considerations for your care and comfort from all the eminent doctors looking after you—and you yourself. But I believe that a friend can truly feel what is necessary—from a strictly practical perspective—for another friend. If you really must have an operation, why not consider that it may go better for you here? I'm not speaking of the medical question, which you know and I do not. There is a surgeon here, de Rham, who, it seems, is a great star.[59] But more importantly there is abundant, fortifying food, generally providing all that we have lacked for the last five years. There are all the medications and products you could want. I tell you that one gradually—and unfortunately—gets used to all the restrictions, imperfections, miseries, and shortages, basically vital to survival in France. When you come here and reestablish a normal routine, it's frightening to think how you endured it, and it's especially frightening to think that others you love are enduring it. My dear Canetti, please, I beg you to try and come here as quickly as possible. This is not just a polite request, I am actually begging you, and forgive me for insisting and for wanting this once to interfere in plans and decisions that are not my business. I, who am resistant by nature to any even slightly categorical opinion, this time I am too convinced of the good that it will do you not to try to get you here as quickly as possible.

My morale is not bad although I'm lazy, but in the last six days I've taken heart and I'm studying languages every morning fairly seriously. In the evenings I read—always for that famous thesis—without making any decisions. Right now I'm researching—without getting bored—Michelet. I'm sharing a room with David—I've told you about him.[60] I am going through a lot with him, joys and suffering as always. I can no longer bear Caron—and no longer see him. His enormous faults dazzle me, each time he speaks—a specialist in stupid, empty sentences blurted out with conviction—and each time he eats—he makes a pig of himself and impudently bullies others—and each time he makes a gesture—he has a conceited way of rolling a cigarette and puts on snobbish airs about smoking only bad tobacco, here where excellent tobacco abounds, as a sort of pretense of manliness—and every time—and this is the last straw—he makes an appearance. He combs his hair carefully into a quiff that looks horrible on him and fills me with contempt. Your turn to laugh at my vehemence. But at least we are basically in agreement now.

I wonder very much about your health. Have you already left? Is there improvement? What operation is it exactly? What is it similar to? You must come here as soon as possible, please.

Believe in my most affectionate and faithful friendship.

Roland Barthes

There are thirty of us here alone in a very good clinic in Leysin-Village. One or two per room. Two nurses and a resident physician, Dr. Bruno Klein, an Austrian. Weekly checkups by an excellent Belgian doctor, Dr. Van Roleghem, and cardiology supervision. Perfect individual care, unknown at Saint-Hilaire.

*   *   *

Clinique Alexandre, Leysin-Village, Vaud,
Switzerland, June 8, 1945

My dear friend,

I wrote you a long letter when I arrived, but perhaps you didn't receive it since you haven't answered me. I will not write at length today, I would simply like to ask you to send me your news. I worry about you often. I want so much for you to be able to come here and take care of yourself. Please answer me and bring me up to date on your health.

Mine is good. My general state is much improved and I want to stay here as long as possible in order to heal. For the first time in a long time, I have a taste for work; I'm doing Michelet and that will help me find a working method. I have some other projects, and patience and perseverance for the first time.

I would like the pleasure of writing to you at greater length, but above all I would like you to write to me. I await your letter.

Very affectionately and faithfully,
Roland Barthes

*   *   *

Clinique Alexandre, Leysin, July 12, 1945

My dear friend,

Great joy and emotion at receiving your long letter. I love you very much and I often think of you (the other night I had a long dream in which you were mixed up and many pleasant things happened to us). Your intelligence and your friendship do me much good, although the first often intimidates me and the second I am always a little afraid of not deserving. I understand very well that you are not coming and I will even tell you that I will no longer be so insistent with you. You would find appreciable material advantages here, but if you get less worked up than I do, even so, the stupidity of this country would drive you mad and you would think only of leaving, as I do. My very dear friend, I would love to write you at greater length, but I don't have the heart to make small talk so long as I think my letter could arrive at the time of your operation. I earnestly ask you to send me word as soon as you possibly can to give me details on your health, or even have someone write to me if your operation has worn you out. Don't take my request lightly and don't be slow to answer out of modesty, fill a letter with your news and all the practical details of yourself. You cannot know my exact feelings, you cannot know how attached I am to you; don't let me go without news.

No, truly, my dear friend, I don't want to tell you all my inner troubles when I think that when you receive this letter you may be suffering from a thousand troubles and worries before or after surgery. How I would like to receive word that would free and calm my mind on your account. I'm doing much better, my morale is good, very full of hatred against the stench of this country. I have a mad hope of reviving, of rediscovering the intelligence, beauty, spirit, and passion of human beings and of knowledge. And I also have a mad desire to be your friend, without either of us being ill anymore. Please, recover quickly, come find me again so that we can rediscover each other and taste the world together, which you light up for me with your intelligence, your solicitude, and your affection.

Forgive me this letter of effusive feelings. It's a bit loose because I'm always afraid of words that are too crafted, but I ask you, Canetti, to feel in it the warmth of my friendship and my concern. It is not out of laziness that I'm not writing more to you today. I simply want to say only this. Write, I am waiting impatiently.

Roland Barthes

*   *   *

Leysin, August 17, 1945

My dear friend,

I was already reassured about your operation by word from Mme. Lardanchet; after your letter, I am filled with joy. All the same, that thoracoplasty was a kind of barrier beyond which life lay. And now you have crossed the bar, you are fully alive, you are moving forward again toward more life, more pleasures, more thoughts, more generosity, more friendship, more work, etc. And that is why I'm happy. I am incapable of not being selfish and of not rejoicing for myself. Moreover I think it's better for you to know that your existence and your vitality are precious to me personally. The lift, the elation, the emotion that your letters, your inspiration, your advice, or the simple thought of you always give me add and will add to my own joy in life, my own security, and will continue to add to my temperament (that is, all of me) what they have always added.

All this month I've been worried about my health and only since yesterday when I had the results of an X-ray have I been reassured and regained a taste for life. I have been very tired, but it seems that it was nothing. Not that my X-rays show any progress; it's nothing much, but something is always there. As to what it is hiding, we will know in a few days when the slow Swiss doctors will have done a tomography for which I have been asking for eight months. My plans will depend a bit upon the results; maybe I will be able to return to my own country (what a sweet weakness, not in the least jingoistic, to be able to say one's own country!) next spring. It would be wonderful to meet in Paris then, almost healed, and both of us equally hungry for life and work.

I don't know how to explain to you the complex conflict that dominates my work in Switzerland: I am working, and I am working quite a lot. How much time? Hours and hours each day, with exquisite pleasure and, in moments, with an intensity and such a strained impatience that it torments and tires me to be taking so long. I've developed the mind-set of an athlete of work. I'm setting a record for productivity and I top it every week, every month, increasing my pace, etc. What am I working on? That's what I cannot explain to you completely, and not without a certain fear of surprise and perhaps ridicule—no, let us at least count on your friendship—or judgment. I have a consuming desire for knowledge (even as I know that is not the essential thing in life, even as I consider with utter despair this itch, this temptation, this vertigo, this impenitent humanistic nature of mine to be a vice). So for the last six months, with a will I've never before experienced, I have abandoned myself to all the powers of Faust. And the thirst for life and the thirst for knowledge are superimposed so that I'm unable to extricate myself from this contradiction. But at the same time, I feel sick over what is poorly known, what is known only from books and is said with assurance only at the cost of huge lies, deception, bluffing, etc. I no longer can or want to talk about anything other than what I know. And that is where the drama begins. One must know the technicalities of the things one talks about; and that is an infinitely long, infinitely tiring process; but I'm not renouncing it, I'm forging ahead. Although my interest in literature is, in short, only *secondary*, I'm passionately filling my present life with it, since everything else is refused me (and also because perhaps everything else will be increased tenfold later on). Three months ago I began a very careful inquiry into Michelet. Why Michelet? Largely through chance, a little through reflection (I wanted to see up close what that bizarre thing, the Romantic, was, that kilometric verbiage that happens to catch a few scintillating truths; I wanted to exorcise Romanticism, and then too, I am obsessed with a desire for research—an intuition of certain problems that appear to be entirely formal, which I will call for now the magnetism of the word, the mythology of the word). And ever since, I've been reading and annotating Michelet at a terrific pace. Disappointed by the good fellow, to put it mildly, but he is not really what continues to interest me, it's all that magnetism attached to discourse, all that mythological fauna that a writer—even a Romantic—carries within himself, that makes me work my way through those indigestible books (in this case, I burn through them, I race through them in a day—without losing anything). It goes without saying that after Michelet I have other, much more interesting research projects. But I cannot bungle what I have begun. Often the vision of a Micheletian wilderness overwhelms me; once in a while I discover exciting things; but I have indomitable courage; I entered literature through the most thankless writer, and through him I must exit, I must produce something. I'm sticking to my plan, my grand plan, in which Michelet is only a marginal point, but a wonderful testing ground and a way to sharpen my spiritual tools.

I will never be a man of letters, because I have neither the talent nor the taste for it (or rather I have a distaste for it). But, for want of love, one has [. . .].[61] At the same time, I love matters of the intellect, I love the substance of knowledge, as unreasonable, intellectual, and conventional as that is. Even knowing Michelet well (and I am smiling at myself, saying something so blatantly laughable) offers a kind of freedom, joy, and justice when, taking a break between *La Sorcière* and *Les Jésuites*, you go for a walk, all sense of the animal and superiorly ignorant life aside, in search of a beautiful face, or you play—with much feeling, as you know, believe me, you have told me so yourself—on the admiration or curiosity of someone you could desire, as you please, depending on your momentary wish for risk or for rest.

In this regard, I've led a more or less conjugal life (you understand that "more or less") with my roommate, the exquisite being I told you about in Paris.[62] Entirely occupied with the problems of method (no, I'm not playing Valéry), but I need a method for escaping the intellectual mire, the sniveling where so many unfulfilled desires held me for three years. I think that gradually I'm arriving at it. That does not mean that I'm happier, as you know. What one seeks is only a feeling of strength, fate, toughness, unity. If I'm telling you this, it is for a reason that involves you very specifically, because your example and your advice about the necessity of work (all proportions strictly maintained between the significance of your work and the uselessness—except personally—of mine) have aided me enormously. And why not say that they got me moving again?

But the counterpart of all this is the birth of a feeling a bit foreign to me, and which is not far from being called hatred. Many things in life and in people fundamentally revolt me; it's beginning to show and since I am very inept about it, this is leading to major changes in my everyday life. I live in a state of revolt, nausea, and a constant desire for revenge. The ugliness of the landscape, the lack of physical beauty (nothing is beautiful here, I swear this to you with no pessimism), the dullness and mediocrity of my comrades, the stench of the Swiss, the baseness of nations, all that sickens me, gets me worked up, sharpens my wit, my anger, my repartees. With a few exceptions, I am no longer very well liked among my comrades, whom I antagonized with a few outbursts (I have to say most of them are stupid); I am absolutely not appreciated by the Swiss, unlike that unfortunate Deschoux and his emasculated philosophy, but I congratulate myself on that. I delight in my obscurity, from where I judge them in all their horror. I am amassing unbelievable examples of stupidity and self-importance, two vices that you know make a person ridiculous. I will tell you all about that. There are a few exceptions—but not in Leysin—a charming fellow from Zurich who is writing to me, a socialist and unfortunately a citizen of such a stupid country.

I see no one here; the native fauna is colorless and therefore invisible. As for the French fauna, sputtering noncoms with cigarette butts, or your colleague Rist, stupid optimist, I absolutely do not see them.

My dear friend, do not assume from my virulence—disagreeable perhaps because it's not my style—that there is nothing in me but bile. Hating certain people, enduring other people and things, you know, that's what gives flight and purity to our images of those we truly love, the things we respect and love.

Don't hold it against me if my letter is not what you would wish; but you cannot deny me the deep friendship I have for you. I need you deeply. Write to me.

Your friend,
R. Barthes
Continue to give me news of your health.

*   *   *

Clinique Alexandre, Leysin, Vaud, October 8, 1945

My dear friend,

I would be happy to have news of you; besides your letters always giving me so much, I always wonder if you are doing well when I have no letters from you.

I'm writing you a brief note in much haste for the following reason: they are performing an extrapleural on me next Wednesday.[63] My tomographies showed that my cavity was not closing up by itself. This has been the story of my life, compelled to struggle along, to loaf around, not allowed to do anything I want to do in life, etc. I have accepted it: my general state of health is excellent and so is the surgeon here. If everything goes as usual, it should be fine.

Before those worrisome days I will have to go through, I am thinking especially about my life; I tell myself—and I am telling you—that if I'm fighting for it, it is in fact for the pleasure and—let us assume—the fullness of knowing certain beings now or to come, among them you, my dear Canetti. There it is, good-bye, my dear friend, write to me, do not forget, you know that I'm thinking of you.

R. Barthes

Would you be good enough to inform M. Cohen and add to this news my faithful regards. I don't want to write right now, but I haven't forgotten.

Write to me by airmail, that takes two days.

*   *   *

[Leysin,] Friday, [October 26, 1945]

My dear friend,

I received your last letter two days after my operation. That did not prevent me from savoring it fully and taking much pleasure in it. I felt in it a little more sadness than usual, but personally I like it better when you are not eternally optimistic because I'm so often unhappy that I feel alone when I see you so full of spirit.

My operation was very successful, exceptionally well performed by Rham. I have the impression that it resembles nothing that is done in France. Now I have the inevitable complication of fluid, which is giving me a bit of a fever and fatigue. There's nothing to do but wait for it to pass. I was only in discomfort for eight hours (I will not say in pain, but a thousand miseries: nausea, shortness of breath, sleepless nights, etc.). None of that is unexpected, as you know, and life slowly resumes.

But I experienced a strange mental suffering: my brain did not go to sleep. There was no break, no drowsiness, no absorption in the pain, none of those gestures of healthy and profound egoism by which one sends the world away and asks only not to suffer. The more my discomfort grew, the higher my brain soared,

[. . .][64]

present are very great since the departure of my friend David. I feel a terrible clarity. It seems to me I am the type to feel everything right up to the moment of death. Everything affects me, nothing ever knocks me out. I was counting on this operation to distract me for a few days from the pain of existing as I am. I only succeeded in superimposing two kinds of suffering. You will certainly understand me, Canetti, and you will understand how the discovery of this strange power—or powerlessness—is major for me; it's a bit like a path to damnation, especially since you know what unhappiness— and what beauty—bracket my life.

My dear one, I learned yesterday through the horrible wave of arrivals from Saint-Hilaire among which—aside from your news that this girl

[. . .]⁶⁵

truly odious. I learned that you entered the little kitchen of initials. The CED has you!⁶⁶ Luckily I saw you were joking about your schemes to get me mixed up in that kind of thing! But they will not have me. I am counting on leaving here as soon as I can put one foot in front of the other.

As to my inner state, as they say, maybe that will be for another letter. Today is for giving you my news.

And to ask you for yours, as a friend. Not only is it so important to me that you are recovering, but also I do not want you to be suffering too much in your present life. It is much more serious for you than for me to be ill, because you are following a path in society and you are needed. I would very much need [. . .]⁶⁷

*　　*　　*

[Leysin,] November 12, [1945]

My dear friend,

Your letter annoys me, your advice is the opposite of what I want; to take my health seriously, which I do not care about a bit, and not to be serious about the rest, which is much closer to my heart.

First of all, you can be sure that, if my arrangements do not change, I will be leaving Leysin as soon as I can (what is more, it's ridiculous to talk about it now when I am still worn out). I have never thought of going to Saint-Hilaire, even if there were ten Canettis there! Your CED philosophy does not persuade me one bit. And then, I'm very sure you're embellishing it, with much art, I can see, but with even more [. . .].⁶⁸ Making a witty lesbian⁶⁹

[. . .]⁷⁰

that will never make me smile. And then, seeing M. Cohen again, the first floor mess tins, the medical care, etc., I would rather kick the bucket in a hospital. No, Canetti, I repeat, you must leave that Saint-Hilaire, which pleases you so and gives you a worrisome philosophy that I do not like at all. You must come to Leysin. It is understood, the French group is a complete failure because M. Cohen dumped all the Saint-Hilaire ruminants here, the Deschoux, the Seinteins, the Fressanges, the Hulots, etc., who are once again making France into an odious, lamentable subject. But there are the Belgians, heavy, puerile, but some of whom have such tragically pale eyes; there are the Swiss, uninteresting of course, but some with skin that is—or at least, alas, seems—as fresh and innocent as that of scouts; there are the Yugoslavians

[. . .]71

paths, trees, tramway, patisseries, where all that passes, stops, meets. If I were not in love elsewhere, I would stay here.

I will not go into a Douady house either.72 And in any case, I will surely not go to Neufmoutiers, with its poisoned air, to play Rudolphe between an innocent priest and a Bovary household.

What I would like is to return home, to my old room, my friends, and my friend. Swear to me that you yourself never did anything as mad as this. Well, mad anyway, let us not exaggerate; and here at the moment, I am living filled with bile, impatience, rage, and constraints.

You tell me that I am no longer twenty; that I know, even better because just today, November 12, I turned thirty. You see that in your own way you wished me happy birthday. But, my dear friend, that kick in the pants no longer works. I am fully of age to love

[. . .]73

to talk about all these things, in theory. All I can say is that love's power of *anarchy* is the only thing that allows me to live in world. As for the rest, we are the ones who see most clearly the grandeur of all that, everything you say so well and accurately, on all that I agree with you. I've still been thinking about it these last few days with regard to Michelet, who revealed to me some grand ideas. Not that he was a homosexual, the poor man. But I discovered—listen to this—that he was a lesbian. I will prove all that, if I ever write something on Michelet and the Woman-World.74

No, Canetti, my very dear friend, who knows how to write me such beautiful and such *useful* letters, do not write me any more like the last one. You are not yet sixty years and able to look at the world without being burned. The flame is immeasurable. You find my "sadness" ridiculous; you say that I am discreet and my sadness is only the outer reflection of my passion. [. . .]75

*   *   *

[Leysin,] Wednesday, November 21, [1945]

I had gotten as far as the Recovation of the Edit of Nantes when I received your letter. I had a bad conscience after mine and you were good to write to me immediately. I have one specific regret: having spoken ill of M. Cohen and risking upsetting you. You know that I don't think at all badly of M. Cohen; you know that I think all the good things you say about him. You must not hold it against me if I inserted him into a wave of impassioned oratory. His (poetic) image is associated with bad memories for me. As is all of Saint-Hilaire. At the moment I share a room with a fellow who, historically, temporally, realistically, if you will, I would have no reason to dislike, and nevertheless I would speak of him in the darkest terms. Must I condemn myself to silence? M. Cohen is sometimes the victim of an unfortunate extension of depression. Does this explanation seem contrived to you? No, it's true. And it's an excuse. Do not forget that Géo—always very kind to me, of course—never left the legend, unlike me, never went outside the walls of Saint-Hilaire. You know the man, you can reconcile his reality and his poetry. As for me, like anyone at Saint-Hilaire, I only knew the second—and through you, no doubt, had glimpses of the first. Even so, that's why I'm afraid of having saddened you and mainly why I'm writing you, and why I'm acknowledging that I was wrong.

What good does it do to drag out the Socratic debate on Love? I do not deny any of what you tell me. I am even very sympathetic to it because it's appealing. Perhaps that even troubles me. But truly, is it so opposed to what I do? You only see the sadness in my attitude, the stupor, as you say. Really, isn't a total passion only that? Perhaps the surrounding darkness serves to better protect its flame. I mean that the beloved must be questioned; maybe he would say to you—without sharing anything—that the spectacle of so total a passion to which one attributes, *even while lying*, the ring of eternity is one of the strongest, most agile, most alive things that he has ever seen; that the pressure, the heat, the transport of a passion that is logical to the end stupefies him, forces him, and obliges him to yield, that for the first time in his life, through this contact with what you call an absurd illusion, he has experienced what was only theater, and perhaps what was only a man. If you accuse me of sadness, exhaustion, stupor, he will laugh. That is exactly the opposite of what he knows of me: ecstasy, hope, despair, revolt, the implacable domination of physical events like the elimination of others, separations, etc., an agile and subtle intelligence that analyzes and explains all situations, draws consequences from them, violates cold logic and substitutes for it the superior logic of passion, and forces him, the healthy one, to yield to the mad one, the possessed one (because how could we be so vain as to believe that this transformation is not the effect of a possession?).

Can one play the game halfway? For me that makes no sense. It is and it is not an act. One must risk everything and at the same time one risks nothing. It is an extraordinary sleight of hand and I'm sure the Greeks offered us an example similar to it in their way of believing—and not believing—in the gods. We know very well that through love we enter a universe where the concepts are no longer the same, where truth itself becomes amphibologic, etc., and what troubles us is finding in history, civilizations, literature, religion, etc., reflections of this reversed world that therefore no longer seems to us completely illusory; and that comforts us and confirms our thinking, our surmising that Love is only a myth in a system of fraternal myths pursued for so long by the historical world, and which return very often to tempt it through the impetuousness of their dream, through their truth, if you like.

This is becoming philosophy and not very good philosophy, no doubt. My excuse is that I am living it. For me there is no possibility and no sense whatever in not committing myself to the utmost. I do not see the dangers you point out. And I am stubborn to the point of saying to you: maybe you see them, you, looking at me— you see me sad, on the path to stupor, to exhaustion, a victim of illusion. Well, even if you see me that way, I do not believe I am that way. Only the being I love can see me. To the judgment of others, I grant only one point of truth: I am suffering. But what good is discussing it? There's no need to argue over a point so natural and necessary from both perspectives.

Moreover this is all idiotic. It's one of thousands of possible defenses. I let myself be dragged into it even though I really feel that what divides us has no meaning, neither actually nor rightfully. It should be enough that I'll complain a little less—even if I'm suffering just as much—so that we don't feel we're in conflict. It's a question of discipline that divides us. I was wrong to be strident— verbally. A false—and lazy—dialectic always convinces me that bravery is a very pharisaical virtue. I feel no shame at bemoaning what I lack. It's not the desire for comfort that leads me to air my feelings, but rather a compulsive mistrust of striking a pose, and the illusion that one will see through my weakness—which is irresponsible of me—to what I feel to be there of strength and grandeur.

But I know—I have experienced it—that is a mistake. One must not complain—ever. Except to you, maybe, since if that earns me the expression of a difference of opinion that leaves me even more lonely, it also earns me very beautiful letters and the example of a firm, affectionate tone—which I so stupidly abandoned in my last letter and which you call me back to with all the greatness of your nature.

There, my dear Canetti; those are very *grand siècle* compliments. How else to write true things? Those who are ill only have speech for expressing themselves. If we were healthy and free, we could experience friendship in silence, as in certain American novels. I truly believe that as long as I'm sick, I will inevitably be saddled with this academicism that weighs on me so heavily that sometimes I go for weeks without writing to avoid assuming the burden of the only habit I have at the moment.

You speak to me of speleostomy.[76] Basically—I mean despite the disproportionate paragraphs in my letter—that is what interested me most in your own. I have heard talk of miracles resulting from this method: Hillairet and Rocheblase regaining weight and occupations again, etc.* But what concerned me is if you'll be going to Châteaubriant and will have to remain there for some time. In which case, it will be a long time before we see each other again.

And then, less selfishly, I am also thinking of you. No, my old man, you do me wrong to imagine I'm thinking better of Saint-Hilaire. It is not true. First of all, do you think I feel I am healed? I have never considered it a privilege to be here. There are often many open spots. Surely there still are. But you know that certain people didn't want to come here. . . .

Don't force yourself to answer me immediately, but do not let me down. I think of you often and I need you.

Your friend,
Roland Barthes
Do not do it, I'm not leaving here yet. I will talk to you about it when the time really comes.

*   *   *

[Leysin,] Thursday, December 20, [1945]

My dear friend,

I take such pleasure in receiving your letter, and moreover it comes at exactly the moment when all other work bores me, so I'm responding immediately that I would like to be with you. Let's not speak of the good it would do me, that is all too clear. But also it

---

*Regaining weight, but not good looks, I am afraid, at least in one case.

would *distract* me. I have never known anyone as diverting as you; there's never a dull moment either with you or with your letters. You always lead one toward conviction, so that one ends up seeing the world as you do, shedding tons of bad thoughts, and telling oneself that, before sinking into some small stupidity or misery, one must always consult you, you alone. It may wound one's pride a bit, but the benefit is one's salvation.

Michelet has been going for badly for two days due to the combined effects of three random events: reading Sartre's manifesto in the first issue of *Temps présents*;*[77] rereading my little pieces in *Existences*;[78] and reading (all day yesterday) Sartre's latest novel.[79] Don't worry, I am not turning to Sartrism—although the talent of this man is enormous and truly penetrating. But admit it, given the strange roundabout ways for approaching Michelet—and I make use of them—to bring Sartre and Michelet together in the same week, that's a funny sort of chemistry; the second loses many of his properties there. (Surely chemistry could provide a good image here, but I know that you categorically disapprove.) Thus I left him in the lurch again today. Nevertheless, before this, it was going fairly well. I have quite a lot of ideas on this surprising man whose portrait you may not know. Maybe you see him as only the slightly foolish apostle of democracy and secularism. On this point his face is reassuring: no lips, the face of a tough, wicked old witch, and in those hard, crooked, haggard features a kind of black flame, a hell fire that lights up the eyes with unbearable pleasure. Here's an extraordinary man with furious intelligence, an *intelligence with errors* that I love. His work, which is truly modern through its *mythological,* anti–nineteenth century, *anti-Romantic* nature (anti-Taine, Renan, Guizot, and other nuisance scientists), includes strange pockets that are exhilarating to discover and assemble. If I come to believe a little in the interest of these discoveries, perhaps I will be able to do something not too boring on Michelet. Of the men of the past, this one suits me very well. It's not a passion (because he makes shameful slips) but a very fertile alliance of reason. Moreover, in a marriage of reason, one can still get carried away with certain qualities in one's wife, at least I assume.

Michelet is right for being different from me, opposed, surely, but not symmetrically, and that's the great thing. He represents an almost perfect degree of otherness. And then, as one says half fool-

---

*Silly mistake: I mean *Les Temps modernes* (confusing Sartre and the Dominicans!)

ishly, half rightly, it is too much! All the same, there's less resounding inanity in the study of a powerful humanist than in that of a poet or novelist. Michelet the Romantic historian is, by all evidence, neither historian nor Romantic and, I would add, hardly French. This erroneous labeling is already an excellent starting point. The big question that's worrying me right now is this: Is he (that is to say, is studying him) modern? Can one work on Michelet and remain in our world of 1945? That is essential. It's no good leaving our epoch out, it's the only one we have to live in. For two days I have been a bit deflated. If reconciliation is not possible—or too artificial—I will mercilessly drop the old goat. But that would make me sad, especially since, despite everything, it is not light-heartedly that all alone one enters the hard flame of "today." Yes, it's really true, two thousand years of Christianity (and more, Plato was already corrupted) must be recovered. And not by retracing our steps. The terrible thing is the *necessary* destruction of the Church—of the Churches—because the Church is the world's vice and it is exactly the kind of condenser and revealer of all moral vices that creates instincts for vices. The annihilation of the Church still means nothing more today than a sort of secular, communist crusade of the Chevalier de La Barre. Where would you like us to stand in this debate? We must be very careful. Thus we must declare aloud that we are not taking sides, neither one nor the other. Atheistic materialism is just as nauseating as Catholicism. What we must create is a pagan world, neither theist nor rationalist. After all, this could be a very fine task for the men of our epoch. I am more and more set on it. You yourself see how much that Christian poison is still active in the veins of this world, of this France: MRP;[80] Messiaen at Saint-Hilaire (as I surmise and understand from you!);[81] here the blundering clergy, the very caricatures of Jesuits, lurking around confessions, turning youth into morons, shamelessly clinging to the most puerile—and unpoetic—state of childhood through boy scout rubbish, the appearance of principles, etc. I can no longer have any relationship with those beings, with that corrupt world. And believe me, it's a blight that infects even the so-called independent minded. There's a way of thinking, of reasoning, that even without being sectarian is Christian (Socratic) and is nauseating because of its emasculation of passion, its slack objectivity (Jesuit perfidy, what Michelet calls—brilliantly, admit it—the vaccine of truth,)[82] that way of constructing all human fact on the "undoubtedly. . . . but nevertheless." We have good examples of that rot here.

Your lectures on Greece make me envious. Here we have the same old thing: Pierre Emmanuel, Siegfried (not stupid though).[83] Moreover, I am in bed and the lectures are not held here. I have not heard any for a long time. I live between the radio and Michelet. Two or three intelligent fellows, that's it. No one handsome, without lowering one's standards. No friend here. Solitude is often fortifying, sometimes it overwhelms me. All these spineless, mediocre boys with their old flesh that I have known for two or three years, from every angle (so to speak!), what game would you like me to play with them? There are thirty-five of us, replenished every six months. This is not a nursery like Saint-Hilaire, it is deadwood. Never so poor an environment for affairs.

No news from the California fruit.[84] He must be secretly fretting over some failed exam among five or six other misfortunes. Here there are not even any California fruits; there are only good little French apples, a bit wrinkled, worm-eaten, and very bland, the kind that desserts are made from during the six months of winter.

You did not even mention your health to me. Maybe it's not a problem for you at the moment, but don't forget that it's always a question for me, dear friend.

Mine is not bad. They want me to go out a little. But I cannot be bothered. And I hate snow and empty roads where you run into some filthy old peasant every fifteen minutes. And my Athenian tableau from the other day, shall I tell you about it? First a little overrated, and then you know what happens. After having salivated for three bedridden months over some lavish feast, only to go out and meet a sly seminarian and a fat, bloated soldier. It's crazy that it takes so much trouble, so many relationships, outings, intrigues, to connect with one or two slightly desirable people. What a stupid waste, what rubbish and dross! The danger is compromising the quality of one's desire; not being able to match desire and beauty, creating the illusion of the second in order to experience the first all the same. It must remain very lofty.

Don't wait too long to write. Because I am really in need of your letters. I am never quite strong enough to get along without them. A terrible victim of Mood. Why haven't our famous psychologists studied this queen of all the faculties yet, instead of wasting their time on Will, Attention, etc.?

Do not forget me, my friend. With all my affection,
Roland Barthes

* * *

My dear friend,

I know that you're about to leave. In fact you may have already left. Doctor Bernou came to see me when he passed through Leysin, sent by Brissaud. It is a true prizewinner, this speleostomy. Tell me soon how you have settled in and where you are.

I'm returning to France in eight days. I've been caught up lately in this departure and have not been able to write to you. Now I'm just sending you a quick note to tell you that I'm thinking of you. I will write you a real letter from Paris.

I am returning to France:

1) for the reason you know;
2) because Brissaud agrees;[85]
3) because in a few weeks those from the first convoy that arrived a year ago are going to be sent back to make room for others.[86] This is very serious; I should have been sent back in April.

I'm going to spend a few months at home resting. After that, I will see. My health has much improved in the last month.

That is the main news. But naturally there's an infrastructure of feelings. Well, for the moment, I am profoundly happy to be returning home.

I tell myself that if I'm well enough this summer, which is very possible, I'll come to Châteaubriant for a few days to see you. I hope that by then you too will be on the other side of all your worries.

Send me quick word of your news. With my faithful and deep affection,
R. Barthes
11, rue Servandoni, Paris VIᵉ
Danton 95–85
And if you're passing through Paris when I arrive? That would be great. I get there February 28.

4. Roland Barthes to Robert David

Little is known about Robert David, with whom Barthes was passionately in love. Born in Rennes on March 3, 1923, David was twenty years old when they met at the Saint-Hilaire-du-Touvet sanatorium in 1943. David left Saint-Hilaire for a first postcure Paris at the very beginning of December 1944; he rejoined Barthes in Leysin in February 1945 when a certain number of patients from Saint-Hilaire were transferred to Switzerland. But he returned to Paris for postcure on September 17, 1945, where he began his studies in political economics. He later taught history. They reconnected in Paris when Barthes returned in February 1946. The bond between Barthes and David continued after the war, as is evident by the appearance of his name as a "student" enrolled in Barthes's seminar at the École Pratique des Hautes Études in 1962–63.[87] The letters from Roland Barthes arrived to us through Bertrand Poirot-Delpech, to whom Robert David had entrusted a very large bundle of photocopies of letters from Barthes that he had saved. The poor quality of the photocopies often makes it impossible to reproduce them in full. The ones published here represent a fairly limited selection.

*   *   *

[Saint-Hilaire-du-Touvet,] Thursday, December 8, 1944[88]

My dear friend,

I still have a fever; I'm very tired and I'm worried about not being able to write you the letter I would like and that you are no doubt waiting for; just as you came to my room hoping for some spiritual nourishment and you found only vague thoughts and a very weak heart; just as you undoubtedly imagine I'm going to write to you of beautiful things, ethics, systems that will make you think, and you are going to be very disappointed. I have had a fever since you left, I live in darkness and only come to you as a weak man who has lost even the use of beautiful language.

Since Sunday my soul has suffered much, and never has the feeling of a noble cause and the impossibility of really serving it weighed so heavily upon me. I struggle in the night, thinking of you, because it is always the David of the day that I believe I will find; I imagine that he will renounce the David of the night and that he will confront me with his coldness, his morals, his certitude, as in this little quote from Pascal that the David of the evening sent me.
[. . .][89]
Since all the requirements for a predetermined confession seem empty to me, incomprehensible beside the deep life of my soul, I would even say beside the truth of a certain absence (at least of words) where finally I sense no deception—if I weren't afraid of being misunderstood by your honest heart, your avid intelligence for

formulated truths, because your extremely straightforward and delicate soul has something Hegelian about it that tells it the ineffable is nothing but the imaginary, and even if you acknowledged the mystery, you would only do so within the framework of your own confession.

Only if you love me—or when you will love me or if you have loved me—you will be able to understand that my consciousness can only breathe beyond all theology, in that place where God himself is unformulated. [. . .][90]

Love illuminates for us our imperfection. It is nothing other than the uncanny movement of our consciousness comparing two unequal terms—on the one hand, all the perfection and plentitude of the beloved; on the other hand, all the misery, thirst, and destitution of ourselves—and the fierce desire to unite these two such disparate terms and to fill the void of one with the plentitude of the other. The miracle happens, perfection descends upon us when the beloved gives himself, lets his plentitude freely, generously, answer the thirst of the lover. Lovers consider denying one another out of humility, not understanding what is being asked of them. They do not see that it's much more arrogant to bring up questions of value; the value of a being is an extremely fiduciary notion. Without playing on words, it is a market value: your worth is that I love you; that's what must be understood. Only love truly creates; a being who is not loved is worth nothing, has no existence, is an element in the scenery and that scenery is a desert. I believe that a being's moral progress means understanding that and consenting—if only timidly at first—and entering the flaming circle of love in order finally, truly, to be born. And then, how distant grow all the intellectual and moral values of character, etc., how they shrink and shrivel up! How many intelligent beings are nevertheless dead, useless, cold, hard, etc. There is a miracle, there is a life, there is a flame that struggles to emerge between us, a sign that, once raised, would endow us both with our true value, our eternal value, would shower us both with serious things. Having consented to the ultimate weakness of love, we will find ourselves truly strong. But you still do not really see all that; you see it sometimes with the eyes—always so penetrating—of night. At night, when we looked at one another and our hearts swelled, we were truly worth something. You were ecstatic over the miracle that there was no more of the intellectual pontiff in me, and yet, at seeing your joy, your joyous surprise, wasn't that when my value was the greatest? And you too, wasn't it in that nocturnal fire that you were worth the most? Did you have a single moment of doubt about your own value? As though we left all of that far behind! But, come day, I could see in the way you would not look at me that you had gone back to those things that, not being part of love, can only be part of pride. Infernal self-pride, and that's why I suffer, even as I am sure of being right, even having already been enriched a thousandfold, just as Pascal suffered and yet. . . . But neither for you nor for me can I continue this comparison.

I have no news about leaving for Switzerland. I am basically staying in bed, my fever is not going away, although it's nothing serious, do not worry. I'm longing to know if you are home and if you are happy there. Please let me know about your projects and your plans. Write to me, my friend, my life took refuge with you. As I go on, the more I feel that I love you without deception, the more I sense my salvation in this feeling. Do not be too severe. My joy is in you, relent a little.

Your friend,
Roland Barthes

*   *   *

[Leysin], Friday evening, [September 28, 1945]

My friend,

I received your letter from the 25th. Thank you for writing to me, for thinking of me. I am not just saying these things, we are beyond all that now, you know what I think. I am moved by what you are to me.

Let's see what I have to tell you.

First of all, so I don't forget it, I received the 96 francs from the Red Cross; I paid Morand and that leaves me 6 francs.

As for Leroux, don't be fooled by his coolness, all the same. Be extremely careful. At the first small warning, charge, defend yourself to the hilt. I'm going to send you everything that I have on him, put it into the file.

Do not talk too much, even to make small talk. Please, David, control yourself on this point, curb your tongue. It's your first and last weakness. Overcome it and you'll be worth ten times more than all the fellows who might impress you. (The more I see of them—the Mossers, charming but cold;[91] the Villiers, immodest; the Poulains, idiotic; the Urbains, childish, etc.—the more I appreciate—judging not with my heart but with the steel of my intellect—how much more you have to offer than they do *in every respect*.) So,

David my friend, do not talk too much, do not get carried away, do not lose your bearings, endure the silence, the weapon of the strong. Besides, in talking there's always the risk of spilling secrets or making gaffes (I shudder when I think of everything you told me the first nights at Saint-Hilaire). For those who have known you to be more quiet, this excess draws attention to you, which flusters you, etc. (Difficult to write between the records Van Humbeeck and the general's daughter are playing while they pass the time talking as you know; she just asked me for news of you, like everyone does here, and they all speak so kindly of you.) You don't want me to lecture you and tell you to do this or not to do that; I'm doing what I would do if you were here beside me (a sentence I cannot write without getting those butterflies in my stomach, you know what I mean).

Your letter arrived just at the right time to comfort Mosser. He is now radiant and infinitely grateful to you. Since your next-to-last letter, he has only written drafts of letters to his uncle and has only talked about that to me. He read them to me, but I am frightened. It's the kind of paranoid dialectic that's found in Leroux. Oddly, that has left me thinking about Mosser for the last two days.

You must have received my letter by now in which I told you that my operation is to be decided. I hope I didn't cause you too much worry, my friend. You must excuse me when I'm a bit cold; it's because if I get emotional I'm afraid I'll lose my courage. God knows that I think of you at the very moments when anything directly affecting me occurs. You know that I live with this disease by virtue of Maman and you. You must have also received my

[. . .]92

excuse me for leaning on you in these moments. I don't do this with anyone else, you know, and you know that I take a certain pride in not showing my distress, but the unique mark of our friendship is that I cannot put on an act for you. To bolster my courage, I have adopted a kind of method (you will recognize me there, of course). I begin with this principle: one's intelligence must be in proportion to one's sensitivity; when one is not sure of the first, the second must be decreased. If my intelligence doesn't allow me to overcome a difficult situation, I'm going to try to lessen my sensitivity a bit, reduce the flame. This is all to let the mind retain control; to do that I must avoid certain temptations so they do not destroy me: the image of the Mother and the image of the Lover. I'm trying hard not to be forever thinking of you both. I know that you are always extraordinarily present, but I'm trying not to let myself be monopolized by your images. It's simply because otherwise I lose control and that results in days like last Wednesday. You will understand, David. I am expressing myself badly today. This is a bit of a girlish, slapdash letter I'm writing you; it makes me think of the letters from M. L. Translate everything I say into my usual form and you will see what I mean.

I stayed in bed for two days because of an insufflation reaction (which may be the reason for my depression). It does me good to walk, to go for strolls alone. There are moments of splendid nostalgia this fall. The other day I played piano duets with Perlemuter.[93] Yesterday Mosser and I went to see a stupid play at the theater and stopped at the patisserie on the way back. You see, the same routines but without you, my friend, and I suffer a thousand times a day. I am absolutely cold to Van Humbeeck; he must be disappointed but he has certain traits that get on my nerves. I'm having a lot of trouble working. In short, my friend, I am *bored* [. . .][94]

*   *   *

[Leysin,] Thursday evening, [October 25, 1945]

My friend,

This morning I returned to Alexandre. This afternoon listened to a Bach concerto. From my emotion at hearing this first music, I could measure the shock of that operation and these last two weeks.[95] It was amazing the effect that music had on me; my soul was carried away. I had played that concerto arranged for four hands with Perlemuter six days before entering Miremont.[96] I recall so well that icy autumn day, my loneliness on the Leysin road in the wind, dreaming of that music and thinking of you.

[. . .][97]

Otherwise, I got a warm welcome.[98] The sisters bustling about the very sick ones, Mother Morel breaking through with a bottle, a can of sardines, and a pack of cigarettes, Klein truly overjoyed and charming.[99]

As for my health, basically I think that you no longer need to worry. So I can tell you, my friend, that I still feel terribly tired, absolutely not relaxed, my stomach hurts, I can't sleep, my head aches and my heart is as clenched and heavy as ever with my wounded love. I still have a slight fever because of that nasty fluid. But my friend, you are not allowed to worry. You know that all that is normal two weeks after the operation and if I tell you about it, it's to keep you up to date on my condition, my coenesthesia. And anyway it's more nervousness than weakness. *Do not worry.* (My hand-writing is bad because these famous tables that I always envied are too high and of course *not adjustable*.)

My friend, I'm sending you this short note, despite having received nothing from you since your letter and my letter of Tuesday, *just* because you must know that I'm thinking of you with courage and faith. Don't worry too much about my letters and my suffering; there's nothing more authentic and the substance always remains there, unchanged. But always ends in lingering over the feeling of your friendship and the certainty that you will come to my aid. That will help me until I can see you again.

I think of you as you can imagine, afraid of your next letter and even more afraid of receiving no letter at all. Don't give up on me; life is unstable at the moment. I am summoning all my willpower. Write.

Roland

*   *   *

[Leysin,] Thursday noon, December 20, [1945]

My friend,

Why do our famous psychologists waste their time on contrived topics like Will, Attention, etc., instead of studying the only important thing in modern psychology: Mood? Mood is basically the contemporary form of ancient Fate, that irrepressible power that makes someone different from one day to the next, that turns one day's gain into the next day's loss, that makes one night sufficient to reduce what was enthusiastically created into something nauseating, that for a succession of such days makes it impossible for us to use certain words, of [. . .]¹⁰⁰ the treachery that approaches, even though deep within our hearts we have not changed: (this *we* is a polite form of *you*?), so that finally our depressions, our changes, our entire inner coenesthesia no longer resemble a clavier with its very limited, very even and mechanical notes by which one can shift very clearly from willingness to laziness, from gaiety to melancholy, etc., but rather a ramp with no steps, a cottony cloud in which minuscule external variations create *subito* opacities, flights, knots (oh, these "knotted" natures of the modern age!), or clarifications. All that is Mood. Mood, the new deity, the new psychology of Modern Man, a kind of symbol in opposition to classical Passion, the engine of contemporary philosophies, Sartre's novels, Barthes's days (although, even through his discouragement, he risks the unique and totally classical permanence of passion), the engine of David's letters, which, although now arriving in regular and frequent convoys (profound thanks to him for this reliable happiness), still cross in groups of three or four (not more, I hope) small lifeless deserts, not horribly dry, but without tenderness, without interest, if you will, for the one who thinks of you with so much ardor and esteem. Oh, my friend David, you see Mood is sometimes good; today it allows me to do what I did not have the strength to do yesterday, to implore you in all friendship and in a wholly precautionary way to pay attention to those little letters that you send me (ever since you have been writing to me more often), I beg you, my friend, with all my affection—and all my own failings—let us avoid the dramas and catastrophes, let us hold out until my return (because no catastrophe will ever be possible between us in person), let us fight to remain in this fertile happiness, you knowing me to be brave, me knowing you to be affectionate, attentive, impatient to see me again. Hear me this once while there's still time, my friend. In practice, I tell you, it's very simple: write to me only when you want to, when your heart is full with something to share with me. You see, I will renounce very frequent letters because I want no servitude for you.

I'm shaken by many things these days. But I feel a certain discouragement in telling you all about that with any excitement. Always the vertigo of these letters that do not really connect, from this person who talks less about himself.

I have so many things to tell you; my letters do not suffice; and no, a one-way correspondence, very heavy and full of confidences on one side, very light and receptive on the other, is not possible. You can understand that I do not dare, that it is unbearable for me, given my genuine humility, to go on about myself for eight pages every two days without knowing what effect it has on you. I'm going through a few very hard days. Sartre's manifesto taught me nothing but articulated it well.[101] Then I reread my little pieces in *Existences*, so quaint, so bad, and then Sartre's latest novel (which I read in one day).[102] All of this threw me into violent thoughts about my life and my character, not encouraging thoughts, as you can imagine. Why aren't you here, my old man? How much good you would do me. I feel that basically, each according to his own temperament, we're at the same point and we're suffering from the same thing. You can understand how distressing these thoughts— let's call them anarchistic—are at this moment. They are raising grave questions about my work on Michelet.

[. . .][103]

*   *   *

[Leysin,] Wednesday noon, January 9, 1946

My friend,

Here is my faithful little midday note, the house being almost quiet, the others having lunch. I don't know why today especially I longed for a letter from you. Last night I could not sleep, I thought of certain memories involving you, and I tried to re-create your image exactly. I managed it, but in a truly uncanny way, not so much through memory, which *absolutely refuses*, as you know, to return to us the loved one's features in full, but more through a kind of reviviscence of certain complete moments, of certain total seconds, that is to say face + bearing + walk, etc. I wonderfully recalled some of your expressions, your gait, not slow but meandering, each part of which has a very determined air, but the whole of which nevertheless has a charming imprecision above all, a dreamlike quality.

The weather is superb, flawless sunshine, but you'll be surprised to learn that I no longer want to go outside for the cure, for fear of confronting the memory of the long, long days we spent outdoors, in which I was happy.[104] You never talk to me of the past, never of the future, and I still wonder what it is you are made of, what goes on inside your brain and heart. What are you thinking? That harmless question, generally asked without waiting for a response, takes on, in your case, the dimensions of an essential interrogation into nature, and you both answer through the same cloud of mystery.

I'm spending some fairly bad days preoccupied with my health, with that feverishness returning as it did two months ago. I think I will have to go for an X-ray today. Health is stupid. It is essential and yet we can only talk about it in a dull way. And others also are very bad at talking about it to us. For me, it has been four years and I am still not resigned to being sick.

I'm also having difficulties related to my work. Not with Michelet strictly speaking, but those two or three articles that I faithfully attempted (on this subject, send me back the one on Camus)[105] showed absolutely clearly that I'm incapable of writing. That has not affected me deeply because I have known for a long time that I'm not a writer, but it bothers me with regard to my practical life because it jeopardizes a potential source of income. My only hope is to be able to write on what I know well, regardless. Thus, more than ever, I must forge ahead with Michelet. I came to a stop these last few days, before tackling—with no great courage—the six volumes on the Middle Ages. How long all that is! Never has life been so long for me, in all its forms.

My dear, I will leave you with only four pages. Believe me, it's not from lack of subject matter. I would like to tell you about Michelet's good page on Rousseau, *tied in knots* and then *unraveled* by women, I would like to harp again about this separation that tortures me, the reunion that I live for each second, but I am literally worn out, my friend. You can see by my handwriting, my arm hurts. No doubt I will have a letter from you tomorrow, and you will have your eight pages in response. I know that you cannot hold it against me. I am writing you almost every day and I think of you all the time. It's just that today I ask your pardon for my bad shoulder. My friend, let me tell you of my joy at having you for a friend.

Until tomorrow,
Roland

*   *   *

[Leysin,] Wednesday morning, January 23, 1946

My friend,

I had a day yesterday that broke up the monotony a bit. Mosser returned to spend the evening with Villiers and me. We had quite a good dinner in my room. Mosser slept in Van Humbeeck's bed, who left for good that morning. Today I'm writing to you in the messiness and hubbub of changing rooms. No doubt I'm going to be cursed in the daytime with a sturdy Dutchman, ugly, fat, thickset, who loves the cold and laughs too loudly. That will add to my ingratitude for the life here and will make me more eager, if that is possible, to extend my wings and fly. But in that regard, I can say nothing. Alas, besides my inner fears, which I told you about in my last letter, I feel so weak when I stand up and when I walk. It worries me to be so very feeble, and, I must say, without making progress. Well, all that is really of no importance.

I digressed. I wanted to continue with last evening, as I am doing now. During the conversation, which was painful as long as Solliers was there because of his growing mythomania (vanity), then more relaxed when I was alone with Mosser, I thought of you intensely many times. I talked to Mosser about passion (in an absolutely general way, adopting that proverbial tone I love). I surprised myself with the power of the hypothesis on love that I constructed. I reconsidered, reexperienced, and reaffirmed that vocation of passion which is my own and which I understand better and better—without knowing where it is leading me—this is part of it. Some elements that I have often mentioned to you appeared forcefully to me: the dialectical logic of Love, which is one of the most astonishing things I know.[106] One is taken with a surge of emotion at seeing this power of *thought* that makes no act indifferent, that makes a telegram or letter an eternal *sign*, transforming *everything*, absolutely *everything* into the absolute. It's exhausting, but it is undeniably great, this sacredness upon which, in Love, one bases each movement, like a gold medal in a foundation (Michelet). I thought again—but I've already explained this to you—precisely of that discovery of the *sacred* (I cannot find a better word) that prompts passion. I sense the degree to which, for example, the vocation of passion and that of revolution are identical. It is an engagement of the same nature. Through that similarity, one can easily understand the chemical formula of the absolute, the eternal. It would be a kind of indissoluble compound—indissoluble for having become a truly living body—of *suffering* and of *loving-suffering*, of the horror and the love of love. *Amori et dolori sacrum.*[107] That chemical formula of the absolute, that theoretical body of the eternal, has isomers, so to speak: love itself—as I experience it— the gift of self for an idea, a nation, etc. But in all these acts there are: 1. A *beyond*, efficacy, a kind of practical disinterest, a moral force—and thus, if you will, a despair. To be revolutionary or in love basically entails being in despair—or without hope, which is better. 2. A *sacrificial*, almost ritual element that acts both contradictory and authentic and, thus essential to the true man, that plunges him into what he fears, the fear and love of torture, which pushed generations of men toward the guillotine during the Revolution. And that is why Revolution remains a unique mystery that will eternally set men on fire—certainly not through its political or even ideological content—almost depleted—but through that collective sacrifice that is truly an *example*, the example of a society that, for four years, was perhaps closest to the heart of Nature (men/things/history) in all of History. That is how it is with passion—if it is truly followed to its end—because even as a man who is content with having political *ideas* without being wholly on fire knows nothing of the sacred in revolution, so a man who tries to elude the suffering of love, either by not loving completely, or by abandoning love (the most frequent case), or by sublimating it (perhaps the most contemptible case), will know nothing of the sacred in love, and for him there will be only losses, whereas, for the other, only gains of an essential order. To make this understandable, but carefully avoiding any inference of identity—David, you who wish that I would sometimes talk like Bossuet—the best analogy might be that of religious salvation. A man who follows his passion to the end—and I don't mean to degrade this in the least—also fulfills a kind of Law; he is redeemed in the sense that he exists in *essence* and no longer only in existence. But alas I understand full well that one could say just the opposite.

I was also thinking—in my efforts toward intelligence and wisdom—that one can say all this only when it is a friend whom one loves. I imagine that, with regard to a woman, a whole other metaphysics applies, not at all inferior, that was not my thought. Because the degree of otherness one finds in a woman is entirely different, and that leads to experiencing the issue in an entirely different way. But that, my poor David, is a dangerous direction for the moment.

In the end it was impossible not to assign our names to these thoughts, which are only variations on a theme deeply and truly embodied by our friendship. You can consider this to be one of the most intimate letters I have written you. You know that well enough. Never until now have I felt in my life such a sensation of *solemnity*; but one could write a whole new letter on that essential feeling, so essentially tied to the existence of David. I live forever lost in the desire to see you again. I am hoping—trembling—to have a *good* letter from you very soon. Do not tire yourself, be happy, do not be uneasy on my account.

[. . .][108] of the friendship of your friend.

Roland

*   *   *

[Lausanne?,] Friday, February 15, [1946]

My friend,

I'm writing you a note from the Milhits' house in this room where I even find traces of you since you have been here.[109] I came down this morning in absolutely Greek weather (I believe that is your expression, and this morning confirmed how true it is). Today I am happy. This may be the first time since your departure. It's because I am rediscovering life in all its splendor, knowing that I will see you again in two weeks. Before this, I willingly made myself the theorist of the Greek ethic that consists of savoring life's rhythm of purifications after sensual pleasures, of asceticism after festivities. And it's true that complete asceticism these last five months, dominated by the essential grief of your absence, gives a particular purity to this return to civilization. I left a Leysin ablaze with sunlight, it's true, but from a coarse, inhuman sun that burns without melting the ice. Below, coming through the sunlight, there is a kind of humid caress; I feel ten times better. Also, my friend, I understand very well your deep happiness in looking forward to the walks we will be able to take together. This earthly life must be recognized as the splendor it is—especially when one knows he is going to see his friend in a few days. Otherwise the sun would only be grief. My coenesthesia has for [. . .][110] nervousness. But here, below, it becomes less so, more like vitality. I feel stronger, and at the same time my back hurts and I am short of breath. But nothing serious, it seems to me. It was a bit like I was rediscovering my youth this morning, when I was less hardened, when I sensed so strongly the ineffable and the sacred in life. I rediscovered in myself the source of contemplation and sensibility—and curiosity as well. Perhaps that will remain true with these two blessings so close at hand: recovery and my friend.

I thought again about our last twenty-four hours together. What weighed on me then was stupor and an almost paradoxical impatience to leave you—as one is impatient for an operation—and the weight of the separation from Maman the day before when I took the little train from Vallorbe while you were waiting for me at the café, which had been so hard, an image of heartbreak that I had promised myself to erase as quickly as possible.

And you, what are you doing while I am writing this? I'm thinking of you, my old man, as you would wish. Having left that artificial place above, it seems to me the depth of my love has already regained the apparent moderation you wish for it. Or is this the euphoria of seeing you again soon? No matter, my friend, have faith; I will do my best to make sure you get something out of this reunion. Have faith in it. I think of you with the best of myself. And the happier I am, the more I think of you. Tomorrow I'm going to Berne and I'll send you a note from there. Until soon, my friend, my dear Robert, do not worry, it won't be long now. I will be there soon, I will shake you up!

Impatiently, your friend,
Roland

*   *   *

Sketch of a Sanatorium Society*

The facsimile of this text was published in the catalog for the Roland Barthes exhibit at the Centre Georges-Pompidou in 2002 (Seuil-Centre Georges-Pompidou-IMEC, 2002). The original belongs to the Barthes collection at the BNF.

*   *   *

In a sanatorium society everything conspires to return one to a situation defined and embellished with the attributes of an authentic society. The costs of this accumulation of artifice hardly matter, but first among them is considering as sufficient a society that is, alas, only parasitic. It is above all a matter of dissociating the consciousness of the ill person from the memory of not having been one; the junction of these two states would result in an intolerable strabismus. Hence the cheerful naturalization of the state of disease, and the creation of a triumphant sanatorium society where the consciousness of exile no longer has a place. The malaise of not being social is exhausted through social exercises re-created in the image of those from which one has just been excluded. The appearance of inner freedom is reestablished within a new social conformism imitating the old one. A sanatorium code is postulated; what goes by the name of freedom, what goes by the name of responsibility, restrained by very real chains, is the very means of escape. We know that irresponsibility is never so fully achieved as it is in the innocent process of oversocialization.

The bourgeois sanatorium fosters a puerile society. In the first place, medical authority establishes the rules of paternalism here. We know the ambiguous status of medicine in social consciousness: mocked, disputed, and always obeyed. That contradiction, elsewhere attenuated, makes its full weight felt here at every moment. As both miracle worker and hotelkeeper, the sanatorium doctor, despite himself and his patients, has final authority here, unrelated to pity and independent of the esteem or contempt elicited by the one who holds that authority. The hierarchy of sanatorium society is fixed in a way that seems truly absolute and eternal because its apex is immutable. No play of power, no shift in responsibilities, no change in values is possible here. It would be an understatement to say a patient confronts his disease at every turn; in short, he confronts a certain general, natural, human condition. The doctor is the one

---

*The analysis focuses on society in a private sanatorium. It involves intentional sociability of course and not natural sociability.

who reveals his disease, and, at the same time, is the only one with the power to save him from it. As in any given religious society, the deity both condemns and absolves the sinner. The point is that, between nature and man, there must be a living, conscious, omniscient element that, despite oneself, one must take for omnipotent. Here we can recognize a providentialist state of society; we can say that sanatorium society is a theocratic structure. Obviously this structure bears no relation to the individual doctor and the degree to which he uses his authority. It is enough that the patient's irresponsibility is justified by the inevitable existence of a being who knows and does not suffer, whereas he suffers and does not know.

In the second place, there is the gang, the band, the team, whatever you want to call it. One can imagine how common this almost-feudal social condition is in the sanatorium. The homogenous, hierarchized, exclusive company formed within an already-closed environment is solidly sealed in a very different way. Here, the weakest ones look to the strongest ones to defend them against their freedom, and all together they surround and defend one another against the exterior that defines them. The pranks that are the favorite diversion of gangs serve as pretext here for additional warmth and oversocialization in human relationships. Each member of a club accumulates what he knows to be the most winning, most rewarding social attributes; by molding his actions, initiatives, reactions, and opinions according to watchwords of the group (watchwords that are often diffuse, barely verbalized, reduced to a certain esoteric spirit), he saves himself the trouble of adapting. Others create for him, in relation to a "public" that represents the necessary otherness, this salutary automatism. Here again, ritual serves as the standard expedient. We know the liturgical function of laughter among gangs whose profession is the prank. For nothing in the world does a member desert such a group; the joy of being admitted overcomes the illusion of supersociability.

"Always together as much as possible," that secret slogan of every sanatorium society clearly formulates the normative image of the patient who looks after himself, essential to the sanatorium and not to be undermined. In general, sanatorium society is horrified by anything that seems to contest the seriousness or usefulness of its own social structure. Any society closed in upon itself is hostile to friendship. In a manner very much belonging to entities that see themselves as multiple, it condemns the couple for intolerably negating its own usefulness, and is scandalized that one could be happy outside of it. It testifies to the contempt felt by any moral system supposedly based on the common good when it must confront the single and the whole, without questioning whether the asocial nature of sanatorium society does not justify one's right to act freely there and to reserve the full exercise of one's sociability for the time when one returns to authentic society. As for the solitary patient, he is a kind of libertine who denies the laws of sanatorium-human-nature. Thus he is banished and, without flinching before the contradiction, organized sanatorium society excludes him, so that he himself wants to renounce it.

The most liberal form of the sanatorium gang is the cultural club whose guiding principle involves grouping together a certain number of shared noble tastes. Here, the illusion of social interaction is embellished with disinterested motives that can justify any humanist ideology. Sanatorium society thus aims for a philosophical, Platonic structure. Clubs, art and discussion groups, circles, and so-called work teams are endlessly created (because they are endlessly dissolving). The social illusion achieves its height. A gang of pranksters acknowledges a certain self-serving structure through its declared goal, which is diversion; a cultural club claims to be exercising an eternal truth, that is, the natural superiority of culture, a notion that is most often only empty talk here. These clubs compensate for the instability of their purpose and the insufficiency of their means by appealing to the cooperative mystique. But here the sentimental humanist ethic is an empty exercise; aid and benefits are expected more from the method than the purpose, so that idealism too can confuse ends and means (art for art's sake, action for action's sake, choice for the sake of choice, etc.). That is because sanatorium society develops more as a community than as a true society. Its members find it enormously helpful to view their time here within a teleological order and not simply a causal one. There is a constant shift from the contingent to transcendent, and interested parties endlessly disguise what is very difficult—because very useless—as providential and finally beneficial. Thus meditation, which may—or may not—result from idleness, is usually presented as the mystical meeting of suffering and truth and not as the conditional result of disease, as a revelation and not as a contingent operation. Or even, inversely (but we can see it is the same thing), the patient will be invited to profit from this interruption by making it a salutary cure for his frivolity. From two sides, *physis* and *antiphysis*, there is great pressure to give disease meaning; according to a well-known mechanism, a causality is turned into a finality because the mind finds the idea of meaningless catastrophe intolerable. At all costs, the disease must contribute to the notion of destiny and it must be acknowledged that such a contribution is very generous, capable of dignifying the destiny of an infinite number of "spiritual families."

Paternalist, feudal, or liberal, bourgeois sanatorium society, through various pretenses, always tends to revert to the irresponsibility of childhood. It is an essentially puerile society, corresponding in its various facets to the bourgeois image of childhood. We know that for most French writers over the last century nothing is as perfect, nothing is as happy, as childhood and there is no human mission more vital than recovering it. This is not the place to recount the history of that myth, from the moment when Descartes and Pascal declared childhood to be a time lost to reason, up until its most baroque expression (Cocteau's *Les Enfants terribles*)[111] and perhaps beyond. Suffice it to say that the bourgeoisie spontaneously use the sanatorium as a substitute for rediscovered childhood. Once again, here is a place cut off at the roots from the world of serious people. This place lives for itself; it is given over to those who inhabit it, even as it still belongs to an external presence that justifies it (the Doctor). Playing in the hayloft, playing war, playing high society: transposed, all the elements of childhood revisited (a particularly bourgeois myth) are the very ones of sanatorium society. One can object that collectives and clubs are, after all, accidents belonging to any human group. The point is that nowhere else but in childhood and the bourgeois sanatorium does one witness the pretense of such groups attributing to themselves the elements of a complete society, within which the *social* supposedly has the same restrictive value as in actual society.

Sanatoriums can be *great families*, no doubt about it. But if one is obliged to spend time there, must he be complicit in such a cheerful familiarization with disease?

June 25, 1947

2

The First Barthes

1. Return to the World of Institutions

Roland Barthes to Philippe Rebeyrol

[Alexandria, Egypt,][1] April 1, 1950

My dear Philippe,

Maman told me that you're in Barcelona. What are you doing there? Are you there for a long time? And most importantly how is your health? I'm afraid that you may not have been feeling very well for some time after that illness this winter. Please, give me a few actual details; tell me how you're feeling and what your plans are. For me, this year is offering no satisfaction and a few bitter subjects. I'm not speaking of thankless Alexandrian social life, which is base, conformist, vain, hostile to all intelligence and sensitivity, where any contact results only in injuries and indignation; or of nonexistent employment, because that is rather a good thing. I live intensely with the Singevins, where I take my meals, occupying two rooms with the family close by.[2] I reflect after a fashion on the problems of my work through the grand portal of laziness, even of sleep, due to the climate that everyone acknowledges to be harmful, difficult, not unhealthy but lulling and injurious for those who like having many activities. It's very hard to fit into twenty-four hours one's occupation, rest, small pleasures, and work. Everyone experiences this problem here, and there's no question of considering an extended stay in this bleak country; all the same I would like to remain for another year. That is not at all guaranteed. In December I was summoned before a medical board regarding my civil servant post and was rejected because of a formality, that is, because I had had a pneumothorax. This is all the more ridiculous since it's not a question for them of hiring me long term or of having any financial responsibility in the case of a relapse (the contract specifically covers them); but their law is retrograde—at least compared to France—you'll remember that I was trained last year, despite the very same pneumothorax—and they bring to it an incredibly literal and formalist spirit. The matter has dragged on since then; I am paid—fortunately!—but I have yet to be appointed and no decision has been made for next year. I thought that it could easily be settled through some administrative decision, and surely that's so. The trouble is that in this country where obvious formalities are only overcome by pulling strings, which goes on incessantly, I have no one supporting me, no one really pulling strings for me. Langlade, the department head, who could surely obtain a quick and favorable solution, does nothing. And I'm afraid that even if his inaction is not concealing his actual opposition, which I cannot rule out, it may end up costing me my post. I don't want to condemn the fellow and blame him for all the low political maneuvers and intrigues of the Egyptians. This is the first time I've seen that and, naively, I'm surprised by it. My only other experience was in Bucharest, and everyday I see more clearly the price I'm paying. Finally Langlade directed at me all his rancor against the Vichy, spending a nasty fifteen minutes on the Liberation. He felt me to be an enemy, not because of my ideas—he has no idea what they are or what they are about, since I have never opened my mouth here. Are they even clear to me? But because he instinctively hates any mind that believes in History, philosophy, the sciences, nonacademic criticism, etc., everything I try to be much more than I really am.* That all seems unbelievable but each day I see more clearly that it's true. I will not give details; they are of limited interest. The important thing is that the fellow does no harm. I don't really know anymore how to start sorting out the situation. No one here—with influence—has any reason to back me: the consulate remains empty or indifferent; a cultural attaché greeted me in a hallway and doesn't do anything. Of course if you knew the situation here, you could give me good advice, dear Philippe. You see, basically, since that first year when you let me stand on my own two feet, I miss you. I still need you and this disease pursues me like a *fatum* and there are not enough of those who love me to conspire against it. Must I notify Cultural Relations, and according to what procedures? Can they do anything in a situation that only involves the Egyptians? Yves Régnier, the cultural attaché, is backing out because the minister just denied him something. And in the case, which is ultimately possible, that I couldn't come back here next year, do you think that Cultural Relations would get involved again

---

*And also because, like Singevin and Régnier, whom he hates, we were sent by Cultural Relations.

with such a questionable candidate? I'm thinking about all this, dear Philippe, and I think that if I can't get an assistantship, that is, a work schedule compatible with my thesis (the only reason I want to stay here), then, for work, I'd rather be a pawn in some Paris lycée, and give my heart and mind some rest at least, if not my body—in my own country.

You're seeing a certain collection of my daily thoughts that revolve around the immediate and practical future. Another subject of sometimes more distressing thoughts is my thesis itself. I've organized all my notes into the form of a very detailed plan, or even a draft that can serve as a general and quite necessary way to focus after the irregular work of these last years. Now, so far the work developed along these lines would hardly be worth an essay. It's the entire academic—and thus historic, literary—dimension that must still be added; and for that I have no books. So I risk getting stuck very quickly. But that's not all; at this point in my work, the relationship itself between the historical method and the structural method is the issue. For me, there's no question of conceiving the structural criticism (which corresponds to the present part of my work) as anything other than a necessary but not sufficient introduction to the historical criticism; conjoining the two in a single work, in a single sweep, takes an immense effort that I don't think I can make, at least not quickly enough. And the academics will never accept a thesis that's only a vast explanation of the texts in an opus; and what use is a thesis to me if it doesn't give me hope of someday, somehow, teaching at the university level in France? I'm not going spend my whole life wandering from one fascist country to another without the means for a critical work that corresponds to that life—already well advanced. You see the connection between the theoretical and the practical. A young Lithuanian, a professor here, Greimas, who has a doctorate, insists that I can convert my thesis—without difficulty, he says—into lexicological work.[3] That way, I could do all the research I want, but it would take me longer to secure a position in France since the philological disciplines have considerably fewer candidates.[4] On a deeper level, this would be to finally find a framework for constructive research, a nonhypothetical way to do sociology through language. . . .

Old nostalgia. I talk with him a lot about all this. This crisis takes on a critical aspect in light of my age. But will my work ever stop being a path? And toward what? For two weeks I have been strangely drawn to Cartesianism. Maybe I have to accept working for truths that, if not partial, are at least singular. . . . We may be finding ourselves at a similar point but on different paths. I need an answer from you. Be careful of the censors. Better to write through Maman.

Your friend,
R.

*   *   *

Paris, Thursday, May 15, 1952[5]

My dear Philippe,

I have a brief break and I'm taking advantage of it to write you this note. I have much to do here right now and not a minute for my own work. Thus I am surer than ever of my decision to find a position when school begins. I still don't know what; nothing will be perfect, but at least I'll be able to recover a zone of quiet, of absolutely essential freedom, because the lack of time amounts to an actual wasting away for me that affects everything: my own work, culture (I no longer read), intelligence (I no longer have ideas), faith (I have no system, method, or even interest anymore), friendships (I neglect everyone), music, ethics (I do not even have that kind of Gideian fervor and freedom that made me love Paris, for example, or be happy taking some little stroll). The picture is very bleak. Not only am I always worried, tense—and at the same time exhausted—but also my ability to "plan," which has always been so indestructible, suffers finally; I have no more confidence, I condemn myself for being indecisive, and I *am afraid* of making any decisions whatsoever about my future, as though that were necessary. Having poured all my humanism into intellectual research, and not being able to practice it, I feel myself becoming truly "inhuman." And in moments, in flashes, I feel the deepest part of myself to be affected, the part that, exposed or ravaged, makes a man into an unrecognizable being.

This time with Cultural Relations is a fundamentally disappointing experience; I am creating nothing here. For me, who sustains myself only on principle, it's the one place on earth where the word *culture* lacks all meaning. And how disappointing Baillon, for example, turns out to be as well; never is a general idea passed along to give you the least motivation to understand and execute it well. In reality, his endless scrambling only hides endless evasion, a total lack of interest in his colleagues. I don't think he's capable of doing a basic favor or understanding the basic situation of anyone he works with. And this amid what is called "the greatest kindness." And I'm not speaking of that unwritten, unstated but unquestioned taboo that determines rank according to academic degrees and that makes it absolutely impossible for me to have any sort of real future, here or abroad. And since I lack the health for adventure (there was an Opportunity with Basic Education),[6] I come back to that idea, that need for a thesis, even while I'm now afraid of succumbing under the burden of the enterprise, and of having a very difficult time accomplishing it abroad. At least I've decided to try again. I am really struggling anxiously with all these thoughts, and increasingly so. Sometimes I berate myself for being so susceptible to worry, even though I went through the ordeal of a disease, so much more terrible than anything else. But that is easily explained, because what is finally undermined by this Cultural Relations detour, these two years in Paris, is the very meaning of the life that I risk watching collapse, all in trying to sustain it unfulfilled and in a void—and that produces this vertigo.

Nothing is lost since, in any case, I will leave here this summer. Finding a little time, catching up a bit on reading, allowing myself to be lazy, and a job I like will let me regain that mental strength without which my present—but temporary—life is so anguished and sad.

Do not hold this too-lucid "point" against me, and most of all, do not worry about me. For now and until soon.

Your friend,
Roland

*   *   *

[Paris,] December 9, 1956

My dear Philippe,

Even so we have been a little worried about you and your note is reassuring. But what sinister buffoonery all that is![7] You must be very annoyed, it's appalling.

Here, obviously, especially in the leftist circles where I move, it's Hungary that was the big event.[8]

That was an enormous shake-up and it's not over. How many heartbroken, disoriented friends! I have always thought that Stalinism was a sinister deviation from socialism with which socialism itself must compromise only under very specific conditions, so this has only confirmed my pessimism. I believe socialism is very ill! and I don't see how it can survive between those two massive capitalisms, the State and the American-West, that surround it. There are colonial wars everywhere now. What's happening in Poland only gives the image of a last revolutionary *correction*.[9] I have a hard time working with all this going on. I am getting started again now; I'm finally making headway in my sociology of clothing, and it's not boring, quite soothing in fact.

Nothing much new besides that. Paris weighs on me more and more, but, without gasoline, we can no longer look for a house. What a mess France is! You can believe that my patriotism is deteriorating. Basically, what I cannot forgive France for is not how it's so clearly leaning to the right, but its damned stupidity.

Have you no news for me? Write, if only just a note.

With all my affection, my dear Philippe.
Roland

2. Author of *Le Degré zéro de l'écriture*

Roland Barthes with Éditions Gallimard, Raymond Queneau, Jean Paulhan, and Marcel Arland

This group of letters with Queneau, Paulhan, and Arland offers a good summary of the Barthes's relations with Gallimard. First, there is Gallimard's rejection of *Le Degré zéro de l'écriture*, despite the support of Raymond Queneau (1903–76). Then comes Seuil's publication of that book thanks to the support of Albert Béguin and Jean Cayrol.[10] Successive solicitations follow from Jean Paulhan (1884–1968) and Marcel Arland (1899–1986), codirectors of *La NRF* from the time it reappeared in 1953.[11] They tried to persuade Barthes to publish in the review and he systematically refused. We have included letters dating well beyond the publication of *Degré zéro* because even in 1972 Barthes continued to turn down requests from Gallimard. It took the intercession of *Les Cahiers du cinema* to convince Barthes to publish *La Chambre claire* with Gallimard in 1980, copublished with Seuil.

Raymond Queneau to Roland Barthes

November 9, 1950

Dear Sir,

I see, according to the "lead" in your article, that your research is only represented here in a schematic fashion.[12] Have you ever considered proposing a more extensive account (quantitatively of course) to a publisher? "Established" as I am with Gallimard (see the *Billet doux* return address), I would be very happy to promote your cause in the publishing house.

I look forward to the rest of your articles. Could you send me the complete manuscript?

Please accept, dear sir, my best wishes.

Queneau
Lit. 28.91

*   *   *

February 8, 1952

Dear Sir,

Purely from the publishing perspective, there is little chance of publishing such a short work here. Distribution is difficult (bookstores have no interest). However, I would like (nevertheless) to bring it up here and pursue that "little chance." Would you be so good as to send me your manuscript?

In any case, this will not prevent you from publishing the unpublished part of it in *Les Temps modernes*.

Please accept, dear sir, the expression of my best wishes.

Queneau

*   *   *

March 28, 1952

Dear Sir,

I am dismayed. I realize that your manuscript is stuck here under a pile of other ones.[13] I read it more than a month ago and I would like to discuss it further with you. In short (because I am leaving tomorrow for a month and a half), I find it extremely important, and personal. I gave it a very favorable reading. But the same objection remains: the length (or rather, the opposite). It would have to be published in the Essais series, and even "inflated," it would still need a few more pages.

I would like to reread the text and discuss it with you, but I have a thousand things to take care of before I leave.

During my absence, you could telephone Robert Gallimard regarding the fate of this book.

Again, I am so sorry, do forgive me, I follow everything you write with the greatest interest.

Very cordially,
Queneau

*   *   *

October 30, 1952

Dear Sir

Permit me to tell you how *excellent* I found your article "Le Monde où l'on catche."[14]

    I repeat: *excellent.*

Very cordially,
Queneau

*   *   *

March 4, 1955

Dear Sir,

I would be very happy to meet you one of these days. I have an honest proposition to make you (honest and encyclopedic).[15] Could you come by Rue Sébastien-Bottin one of these days? I am there every afternoon but sometimes I am not. . . . The best thing would be to arrange a meeting. In any case, Tuesday between 2:30 and 4:30, you can certainly get hold of me (Lit. 28.91).

    Please accept, dear sir, the expression of my best wishes.

Queneau

*   *   *

November 4, 1955

Dear Sir,

How is Tuesday at 4? If not, can you telephone me now so we can arrange another meeting time?

Very cordially,
Queneau

Jean Paulhan to Roland Barthes

July 12, [1953]

Dear Sir,

The news that I hear from Marcel Arland gives me great pleasure.[16] Would you really accept 2000 francs per page? That would come to (approximately) 10,000 francs for each column, and 500 francs for each note that you would submit to us in the same way each month.

Yours very cordially,
Jean Paulhan
This is just between us, please.

*   *   *

November 29, 1953

It has been a long time, dear sir, and I owe you thanks for *Degré zéro* (although Maurice Blanchot had meant to thank you for all of us) and would like to ask you for an article and notes for *La NRF*. Alain Robbe-Grillet assures me that you will be coming to see us on Wednesday, and I am delighted.

Yours,
Jean Paulhan

*   *   *

December 20, 1953

Dear Sir,

Would you give us the study on Marcel Jouhandeau that I have been told you just completed?[17] We would very much like to have it.

Is it too early to make New Year wishes? My wish is for your name to appear often in the coming year in *La NRF* briefs.

Yours very cordially,
Jean Paulhan

Roland Barthes to Marcel Arland (BLJD)

December 28, 1953

Dear Sir,

I am very touched by your kindness toward me and I thank you with all my heart. But, as you know, I have a grant from the CNRS and I must provide an annual report on my thesis work.[18] And the time is approaching when I must present that report this year. So I must devote myself entirely to it, especially since I usually work very slowly and with much difficulty.

Please do not hold it against me that, for the moment, I must decline your request for work—I know the cost. And please accept my deep and humble gratitude.

R. Barthes

*   *   *

Hendaye, September 4, 1954

Dear Sir,

I have not forgotten your kind offer to make me a regular contributor to *La Nouvelle NRF* through a column of my own. I had told you I was moved by this offer and I would have liked to accept, but my answer had to wait until my situation at the CNRS became clear. I thought that would all be settled this autumn. Unfortunately it is not, and I must wait until spring 1955 to find out if I can be part of the Sociology division.[19] At that time I must present a sufficient quantity of convincing work and, alas, it would be unrealistic to add a new obligation to this essential task, given how anxious I would be to achieve a level of perfection in fulfilling it, which would not leave me free to write the columns for *Esprit* and *L'Observateur* that I rashly promised them some time ago. May I ask for your patience for a few months longer?

I know how irritating my procrastination may seem, but it is because I am putting my desire to tackle a true sociological study before all other tasks and all other satisfactions, and for that I need the support of the CNRS. I cannot feel truly free until I have done everything possible to obtain it.

I do not presume to ask for a response, but I would nevertheless be very relieved if I knew that you understood my reasons and did not hold it against me too much. You know how much importance I attach to your esteem and support.

Please accept, dear sir, the assurance of my respectful and deep admiration.

Roland Barthes

Marcel Arland to Roland Barthes

September 10, 1954

Dear Sir,

Of course we are disappointed, Paulhan and me, not to be able to publish at present the columns we had discussed. But since those columns would hamper the work you must do, let us wait until spring. . . . Unless, between now and then, you write some article that you would like to give us.

Please accept, dear sir, my very deep and cordial respect.

Marcel Arland

Roland Barthes to Marcel Arland (BLJD)

September 24, 1954

Dear Sir,

I am sincerely moved by your understanding of my unintentional procrastination. I was concerned about annoying you. I promise to give you an essay for the Revue this year, while you await a more regular column.[20]

Please accept my feelings of deep and respectful friendship.

R. Barthes
11, rue Servandoni, Paris VIᵉ

*　　*　　*

Paris, November 17, 1966

Dear Marcel Arland,

Forgive me for taking so long to answer your letter in which you asked me to contribute to the issue of *La Nouvelle Revue française* on Breton. I was in the USA and only discovered your letter when I returned.[21] I am very sympathetic to your idea but sadly, for purely practical reasons, I will not be able to be part of this issue. I have an enormous backlog of work and I am not able or willing to take on a single new commitment. Please do not hold it against me; I am very touched by your faith in me and thank you for it.

Please accept, dear Marcel Arland, my warm regards.

Roland Barthes

*　　*　　*

January 9, 1972

Dear Marcel Arland,

I was very touched by your note (forgive me for taking so long to respond). I would like very much to give something to *La NRF*, the prestigious fulfillment of an adolescent dream! And I thank you for the invitation, but I am overloaded with professional (teaching) work, I have nothing ready, and I must wait for my life to slow down to fit in a bit of my own writing.

Thank you in any case,
With all my heart,
Warmly and faithfully,
Roland Barthes

Roland Barthes with Éditions du Seuil, Albert Béguin, and Jean Cayrol

Albert Béguin (1901–57), originally from Switzerland, was an intellectual and author of *L'Âme romantique* and *Le Rêve*, which so influenced Michel Foucault. He was undoubtedly Barthes's first great reader and editor, along with Jean Cayrol and Maurice Nadeau. He became the editor of *Esprit* in 1950, the review where Barthes published his first piece on Michelet in April 1951. With Claude-Edmonde Magny, he directed the "Pierres vives" series at Seuil, in which Barthes's works appeared, until the publication of *Sur Racine* in 1963.

Albert Béguin to Roland Barthes

Esprit, October 2, 1950

Dear Sir,

I would like very much to contact you and, if possible, convince you to contribute to *Esprit*. Your article last year on degree zero really struck me, and since then I have wanted to meet you.[22]

Excuse me for not voicing this desire until today, and for making this request.

Albert Béguin

*   *   *

January 16, 1951

Dear Sir,

I am very late in responding, but I would very much like to see those pages on Michelet that you spoke of. And then I would also like, over the long or short term, to initiate in the review an ongoing discussion on the crisis of language (not only literary but common language as well) and for that I would really need you.

So be sure to come see me, call in advance.

Yours faithfully,
Albert Béguin

*   *   *

January 31, 1951

Dear Sir,

Your pages on Michelet are simply wonderful, for their thought, vision, and, I must say, for the writing. I will be more than happy, *proud*, to publish them in *Esprit*. I hope to have a spot for them in April.[23] They will make evident, to the best readers, my desire to raise the review to a new level, which only a very few contributors help me demonstrate. Thus I vow, more strongly than before, to win you as a frequent contributor.

I was counting on seeing you this week. But thrown off by my chief editor, Domenach, taking ill, I will not have a minute before I leave for Italy.[24] But, as soon as I return, I hope to see you—that will be about February 15.

Yours faithfully,
Albert Béguin

*   *   *

[End of 1951]

Dear friend,

Sorry to be so long in writing. I've been overwhelmed. But I am anxious to talk with you before leaving for a week (Bayonne, Pau, Dax, etc.) because I think so highly of your essay on Cayrol. From beginning to end these pages are so solid and so deeply analytical without ever seeming anything like the result of a gratuitous intellectual exercise. It's so rare to see in a commentary on a body of work the kind of seriousness you bring to it! One could not ask for more in the way of insight, accuracy, and also in that tone of authority that only necessary writing possesses. Cayrol was deeply moved and entirely approving. He will tell you himself because I hope all three of us will get together when I return. I plan on publishing your pages in December unless questions of space in that issue make it necessary to wait until January.[25]

Thanks again, see you soon, and my best wishes,
Albert Béguin

*   *   *

September 7, 1952

Dear friend,

Jean Cayrol passed along to me your "Catch." Thank you for giving it to us. It is completely exceptional in quality and this essay is exactly the kind of literary text that I would like to publish in *Esprit*, that is, pages in which the surest writing expresses reflections on human phenomena extracted from their banality, deepened, located. I admire your method very much; everything you write is impeccable. I would like it very much if you could give me reflections like this regularly, or whatever you wish, as a sort of column without a title that would limit it. Maybe, for example, every two months, you might be tempted to respond to this request?

Domenach read these pages as soon as he returned and shares my opinion.

Just one question: A title for your essay? I propose "Moralité du catch" but it's your decision.[26] And you can just indicate it on the page proofs.

Yours kindly,
Albert Béguin

Jean Cayrol to Roland Barthes

[January 1951][27]

Dear Sir,

Allow me to write to you in the name of my friend Albert Béguin to ask if you could possibly lend me for four or five days the articles that you published in *Combat* and that mean so much to me.

I am doing a lecture tour in England and I would like to talk about language and its power in the world of poetry. I will also be talking about the philosophy of Brice Parain and Queneau's spoken language.

If it is no inconvenience for you, could you have the printed texts sent to me immediately at Éditions du Seuil?

How are you doing, Roland Barthes, in this night that pretends to be day? Me? I am buried under that card deck that authors are always stacking.

Jean Cayrol

Roland Barthes to Jean Cayrol

February 7, 1951

Dear Sir,

I am happy to send the *Combat* articles to you. Unfortunately I am sure they will offer you nothing because they are based not on actual inquiry but on a simple feeling. I will get them back from Albert Béguin when you are through with them.

I hope your time in England goes well and send this with my kind regards and admiration.

R. Barthes

3. The Period of *Michelet* and *Mythologies*

Readers of *Michelet*

Jean Genet to Roland Barthes

Isba, Cortina d'Ampezzo,[28] [1955]

My dear Barthes,

This is my third draft, but I am more at ease before a face than a blank page. And I had set out to speak with you—through letters—about the fantastical metamorphoses (you see, this is a start!) of historical facts and figures. Your *Michelet* (which was waiting for me in Cortina for more than a year and I knew nothing about it) interested me immensely. Because of it I went back and reread passages—cast in such a new light that I truly had the impression of swimming upstream in the humors and blood of Michelet but also in the humors and blood of History. At the same time, I received an issue of a review (*NRF Lettres nouvelles*)[29] where you talk about

Childhood, the Child, and the toy.[30] All that makes me want to have a long talk with you. If it's not too much trouble, could we have dinner when I return to Paris? I am so slow to respond to your book because I had not returned to Cortina—and frankly I thought you had forgotten our meeting at Margot Mascolo's.[31] In about two weeks I'll be in Paris. Could you let me know? My address in Paris is: J. G., Hôtel Royal Fromentin, 11, rue Fromentin, Paris, Tri 85.93. That's it.

Best wishes,
Jean Genet

As for your dedication, it makes me very proud. It's the first time a writer has written me anything like that.

Jacques Audiberti to Roland Barthes

[1954]

Dear Sir,

A huge, huge bravo for your book. It's first-rate. It's very, very good, and I'm grateful to you for having drawn so well this extraordinary portrait of lyric humanism, so inspired and so blind a figure, so cut off from everything and starved for any response despite his genius.

Let me express my great admiration for this fine book on Michelet.

Jacques Audiberti

Gaston Bachelard to Roland Barthes

April 8, 1954

Dear Sir,

Your book astonishes me and fills me with wonder. I am only on page 82, but already I know that after having read it, I will read it again. But I cannot wait to tell you what passion it inspires in me. With you, Detail becomes Depth. Your technique of illuminating through beams of light penetrates into the depth of being. You need no story line to maintain the continuity of being. The themes are so well chosen that the contours reveal the underlying pressures. You have just quietly made a great work. I am telling you this myself, just as quietly.

I am so looking forward to reading Michelet's journal. I hope that nothing will be omitted from it, that we will be given all his "humors." Then we will have to leave you, your tables, your snap-shots, your nourishment, to read fruitfully the confidences of a great Living Being.

I was very moved to find a reference to my obscure work on the elements. I thank you for that.

Accept, dear sir, my very warm wishes.

Bachelard

Jean Guéhenno to Roland Barthes

Paris, April 19, 1954

Dear Sir,

Thank you for having thought to send me your book. I read it with lively interest. It represents an admirable effort to attend to Michelet, in his entirety. That idea of "themes" around which you structured your essay is, I think, a very appropriate one in the case of Michelet.

I am thinking of rewriting my little book.[32] I now see all its short-comings. I only traced a single line in considering Michelet. I am sure that your book will be very useful to me.

Please find here, with my thanks, the expression of my warm regards.

Guéhenno

*   *   *

Readers of *Mythologies*

Roland Barthes to André Frénaud (BLJD)

Monday, [May 1957?][33]

My dear Frénaud,

I am *very touched* by your letter; it is important to me. Don't consider these empty words; someday I'll be able to tell you in person the precise reasons why, for me, your reaction goes beyond the question of personal value; I mean that my final text is, *for me*, important—morally, if you will—and *acknowledging* this text is, to my mind, an act on the part of a friend that affects my life at the deepest level.[34] On the content, we can talk more later, when I will have read yours—which I'm starting—finally!

Be in touch soon, dear Frénaud, for a drink. Yours in gratitude and friendship.

R. Barthes

Roland Barthes to Jean Lacroix (Bibliothèque de l'Université Catholique de Lyon)

[Paris,] May 11, 1957[35]

Dear Jean Lacroix,

A big, big *thank you* from the bottom of my heart for your article in *Le Monde* on my *Mythologies*. What a wonderful introduction, fluent, sure, coherent, too fine for this book that has many rough spots, much dross. You have wonderfully *Hegelized* me, much more than I deserve. It is a very beautiful review, in a class by itself, to which we're no longer accustomed. Everyone has said this to me, admiring that unique sense of *the other*, which is not, for you, mere assertion but truly penetrates the very fiber of intellectuality, its very life. I envy your students, I would like to be one of them, I have such a hunger for doing philosophy seriously.

I will add that on a practical level (one also writes for others), your article will do me immense good. Coiplet is happily demolished.[36]

I send you all my gratitude and admiration.

Roland Barthes

Dedication of *Mythologies* to Jean Paulhan, 1957

Dear Jean Paulhan, we have had enough heated arguments over these *Mythologies*[37] so that today I can express to you my feelings of deep respect and affection.[38] R. Barthes

Other Letters

Roland Barthes to Robert Pinget (BLJD)

December 9, 1953

Dear Sir,

I found your note when I returned from England. I am very touched that you thought of sending me your book and I thank you in advance.[39] Please do send it to me, you will make me very happy. I plan to see Alain Robbe-Grillet one of these days, and I intend to arrange with him a way for all three of us to meet.

Thank you again and please accept my warm regards.

R. Barthes
1, place du Panthéon, Paris V[e40]
Odéon 44–24

Albert Camus to Roland Barthes Regarding *La Peste*

Paris, January 13, 1955[41]

Dear Sir,

I told M. Carlier that I do not agree with your thesis on *La Peste* even as I appreciate the way in which you defend it, and he suggested that I publish my point of view in conjunction with yours.[42] I told him I could not do that without being sure it would not displease you. He informed me of your consent and I want to thank you for your fair-mindedness, a trait I know, by experience, is hard to find.

That said, I do not want to let M. Carlier publish my response without knowing if you have any objections to it. I am enclosing it here; please send it back to me with your approval or your comments.

Please accept, dear sir, my very warm regards.

Albert Camus

Roland Barthes to Jean-Paul Sartre

December 7, 1955

Dear Sir,

Last summer you suggested that I write a regular column for *Les Temps modernes*. Unfortunately, I have since been named attaché to the CNRS (at least for this year) and that precludes me, both administratively and practically, from taking on any new tasks besides Research. I am just barely continuing my column for Nadeau's review, which I cannot let go, but I do not dare take on anything else.[43]

I would like to express to you my deep regrets, and my deep gratitude as well for your confidence, which is very important to me. Moreover I told Péju that occasionally, on specific topics related to my research, I will try to give *Les Temps modernes* some texts.[44] In this way I would like to assure you of my total solidarity with your review.

Please accept, dear sir, my feelings of deep friendship and admiration.

[Roland Barthes]

Roland Barthes to Marcel Arland (BLJD)

March 28, 1957

Dear Sir,

I am writing to you for the following reason: L'École de Préparation des Professeurs de Français à l'Étranger, where I sometimes teach, organizes meetings between students and a French writer two or three times a year. I am acting on behalf of my colleagues and my students—and myself, if I may say so—in relaying to you how happy we would be if you would agree to be one of our writers this year. I am told that some years ago you spoke of giving a lecture at the school, but this time, it involves nothing of the kind and the protocol is very simple. We all gather on a Friday evening (probably in May) about six o'clock; you do not have to prepare anything; the students ask you questions about your work and French literature; you answer as you please. It is a matter of a perfectly informal conversation. If I cannot vouch for the students' knowledge and insight, at least I can assure you of their absolute goodwill and sincere curiosity. Will you let yourself be persuaded?[45] We are very excited about having you visit. I would like to add that I personally would be very happy to welcome you to our school. Through a few remarks in a simple conversation, you can give our students a *luminous and just* image of our literature, which they greatly need, and I sincerely believe that you alone can offer them that particular quality of tone today.

If, in principle, you accept this invitation—which on the most basic practical level is, sadly, purely Platonic!—I will call you to discuss the question of the date.

Please accept, dear sir, my warm regards.

R. Barthes
11, rue Servandoni, Paris VIe

Roland Barthes to Michel Leiris (BLJD)

April 5, 1957

Dear Sir,

I hardly dare bother you again by phone, but I would like to give you one or two details on the conference on the ethnography of the spectacle, which we would so much like you to participate in. Of course this is an event that, given its audience, exceeds the size of a simple seminar (especially if word spreads that you will be speaking). So I believe, in terms of numbers, we must not delude ourselves and we should plan for about two hundred people. But in terms of quality, it is not a matter of the general public; essentially it will be researchers from CNRS, students in sociology and ethnology. Moreover, if the *discussion* aspect of the meeting bothers you, why not limit yourself to your statement and ask Claude Lévi-Strauss, for example, to direct the rest of the debate?

Please consider my insistence only a sign of my desire to have you join us; we really need you. But if, despite everything, I have not been able to persuade you, I only have to put myself in your place to be able to tell you that I perfectly understand.

Please accept this expression of my deep admiration and respect.

R. Barthes
11, rue Servandoni, Paris VIᵉ
Dan. 95–85

Roland Barthes to Nathalie Sarraute (BNF)

June 12, [1959?]

Dear friend,

I'm leaving for Hendaye and will read your book there.[46] Thank you for sending it to me, that makes me happy—and gives me the opportunity to tell you how much I already like the few pages I could not resist sampling in haste—because there is no true reading for me except in Hendaye.

I hope to see you soon and send this with deep respect and warm regards.

R. Barthes

4. Two Letters to Charles Panzéra

We know how important the singer Charles Panzéra (1896–1976) was to Roland Barthes. In an interview with Claude Maupomé, Barthes said the classes he took with Panzéra in the company of his friend Michel Delacroix happened before the war. Here, in the first of two letters from 1956, he says they took place in 1941, just before the relapse of his tuberculosis. That date is undoubtedly more reliable. Along with Pierre Bernac (1889–1979), with whom Barthes had been tempted to take classes, Charles Panzéra served as model for what French singing could be (Fauré, Duparc, Debussy, Ravel . . .), although he also sang the great Romantic German lieder. Barthes devoted many texts to the art of Panzéra's singing, which he established as one of the paradigms for his vision of written and spoken language.[47]

*   *   *

[Paris,] January 10, 1956

Dear Sir,

I do not know if you still remember that you had agreed to give me lessons in 1941, along with my friend Michel Delacroix. Perhaps you recall that I had to interrupt them because I fell ill and then left to spend many years in a sanatorium.

I have been completely well now for more than ten years and I have the greatest desire to start singing again—just for myself, of course. I am afraid that my age (I am almost forty) may be an obstacle. So I would like to ask your advice: Do you think that I can hope to work in an interesting way—naturally, you cannot judge the condition of my voice, given my disease and my impaired breathing—and, in the case where you would have no initial objections in principle, would you agree to giving me regular lessons again? You know what great memories your teaching left with me and what steadfast admiration I have for your art.

In any case, dear Master, please accept my deep and faithful admiration.

R. Barthes
11, rue Servandoni, Paris VIe
Danton 95–85

*   *   *

[Paris,] Saturday, April 21, 1956

Dear Sir,

I have thought about it, and I believe I must give up the singing lesson that I began a few months ago. It was an experiment; we knew that from the start. I think I see clearly that the results are insufficient. I accept this without bitterness, in the same objective spirit that I undertook it. Moreover, I still have music, most of all singing, which I think I understand all the more deeply because of what I have gained from your lessons, if not empirically, at least spiritually. Please believe in my most sincere gratitude; even without immediate results, these lessons have meant so much to me, as you know.

And I must also tell you once again how much I admire you, because I have never felt such admiration for any musician.

I do not think there is any point in my coming on Friday, since the situation is clear to me and you had the goodness to let me be the judge of that.

Once again, let me express my feelings of gratitude and admiration.

R. Barthes
11, rue Servandoni, Paris VIᵉ

5. Author of the Theater

The *Théâtre populaire* review was founded in 1953 by Robert Voisin (1918–2008) who was also the director of Éditions de l'Arche, created in 1949 with Roland Barthes, Morvan Lebesque, Guy Dumur, Jean Duvignaud. . . .[48] Originally it had strong ties to Jean Vilar's Théâtre National Populaire (TNP) before falling under the influence of Barthes and Bernard Dort in 1954 and becoming the mouthpiece for Brechtism.

Roland Barthes to Robert Voisin

[Groningen,] Sunday, July 19, 1953

Dear friend,

Here is the article, on time I hope and on target (of that I'm less sure).[49] I'm sending a copy directly to Dumur to whom I addressed it, stipulating that he gives you his approval as quickly as possible.[50] I'm including an extra copy with yours that you may want to send to Morvan Lebesque.[51]

I have concerns about the play you may have found for our second issue. I'm annoyed with myself for not speaking up enough before leaving, I have real doubts, a priori, I know, about Jules Roy, whose latest "Rizières" are very disturbing.[52] I am very suspicious of a play about airplane engines, all that boy-scoutism of war that always ends in fascism.[53] The time of Vauvenargues is over.[54] But I'll let you see if you have the same reactions as I do. No doubt you've already made a decision.

The atmosphere here is extraordinarily relaxing and slightly dull.[55] But that was needed. I come back about August 15 and hope to find you completely rested from Normandy. Write or telephone if you need me long distance.

Warm regards to you,
R. Barthes
Teleph. Groningen 32.588

* * *

Tuesday morning, [July 1953]

Dear friend,

I have no objections to publishing the play by Adamov, which is very well done.[56] Personally, I find Adamov's drama fairly *démodé* already, because the ideas very quickly become myths, and the myth of the hunted or mad man (phenomenologically, it's the same thing) already belongs to the past in literature. You said as much by citing Kafka, who is a great fellow who prophesied our times wonderfully; but that's precisely why it's our job to prophesy something else. Nevertheless, Adamov's is certainly authentic drama, ideologically very sound, and consequently worthy of publication. So we have objective reasons for justifying this necessity. In the fall we can try to be less improvisational with our issues. Duvignaud wrote to me suggesting there were some very interesting submissions.[57] At least according to him we will have a choice. The important thing is that these first two issues serve as a good springboard; better to rise than to fall, etc.!

Since Adamov is proposing it, I personally am completely behind taking his short preface, on the condition that he doesn't rack his brains too much over the term "popular theater," which none of us

know the meaning of yet, that he doesn't involve us in a local definition that will encumber us later on. But again that's a useless
qualm, because basically he has the right to say whatever he wants
under his own name.

Thanks for submitting this text to me despite the rush.

Yours ever,
R. Barthes

* * *

Saturday, [July 1953]

Dear friend,

Actually I had anticipated the question of illustrations for my next
article.[58] And I've written to the Groupe Antique to send me photos.[59] Naturally, they haven't done so, probably on vacation.

I'm annoyed that I can only give you these instructions and not
the completed work as I wanted to.

There are two ways of illustrating the article:

1) Contact the president of the Groupe Théâtral Antique de la
   Sorbonne, Daniel Bernet, Maison des lettres, 6, rue Férou.[60]
2) Track down the following reproductions at the Bibliothèque
   Nationale, which, moreover, has a photography department:
   1. In Baumeister: *Denkmäler des Klassischen Altertums* (1885–
      1888), fig. 1637. Caption: "Tragic actor (feminine mask)."[61]
   2. In Margarete Bieber: *Denkmäler zum Theaterwesen in
      Altertum* (1920), plate 53, subtitle "Andromeda in tragic
      costume."[62]
3) Last resort: ask either at Bulloz, 26, rue Bonaparte, or at Doc-
   umentation Photographique, 4 or 6, rue de Seine, for a good
   photo of the Epidaurus Theater, for example, with the caption
   "Epidaurus: theatrical site."

Don't think I release myself lightly from this task. I hadn't anticipated that we would need the second issue by the end of July, and I
counted on a response from the Groupe Antique.

Warm regards to you,
Barthes

* * *

Dear Voisin,

I've been busy with our issue 6, but with limited results:

1. Ghelderode: He should send his text to the review directly.[63] As of Saturday, there was still nothing. Mme [. . .][64] will provide the address and I think we must wire him.

2. Duvignaud: Columns and articles should be sent to you Monday.[65] Duvignaud was doing his lectures until Saturday. But that's a promise.

3. Laude: You have everything now.[66] The article, a little scholarly in form, is, in its serious way, excellent, and there's no reason to have any reservations about publishing it.

4. Adamov. His contributions are attached: *Cruche cassée* proofs.[67] First page. Note on Adamov. Foreword on Kleist, and correction regarding the article by Duvignaud.

5. Barthes. Here's my "Ruy Blas."[68] Impossible to do more with this Avignon speech to prepare.[69] If this isn't enough, I'll throw something together next Wednesday. Then you'll have it April 10, the deadline, I believe?

6. Miscellaneous items: To tell the truth, too overwhelmed with Avignon (Duvignaud with his lecture, Paris with his bad mood) to have found anything.[70] I'll help you Wednesday, I promise.

7. The editorial. Impossible to lay hands on the Paris text, left on the table in the small office at our last meeting. In my opinion, if we take it, we must 1) have him tone down the judgments on the French considerably, 2) not simply let pass what might seem like an attack against the USSR, which could *objectively* be unwarranted, given our present state of knowledge on the case.[71]

There's another possibility: do another editorial. I was thinking of a subject with necessary candor: the ties between the Review and Vilar, a good opportunity to put an end to latent maneuvers. But that can wait for our meeting on Wednesday at 6 when we have to root out the Rouvet-Vilar evil.[72] Not only on the ATP level but on the Review level.[73] I will explain.[74]

I would much prefer if my trip to Avignon were taking place *after* our meeting because I'm leaving full of doubt. No matter, I will do my best.

I plan to return Tuesday evening.

Until Wednesday morning,
Yours,
R. Barthes

* * *

Avignon, Saturday, [July 1955]

My dear Voisin,

I just saw Zéraffa, who tells me that he left you worn out and that you worked all day July 14.[75] I'm all the more ashamed of pampering myself in this lazy South. The trip went perfectly well. Nîmes was fairly interesting, however well paid![76] Last evening was *Marie Tudor*, which everyone was waiting for: remarkable production, Casarès impressive, the play totally stupid. People here who saw it wondered what Vilar was thinking, and what was the point of wasting so much talent on such stupid crap.

Tomorrow I'm going to Marseille for two days, staying with the Richards.[77] I think I'll be back Tuesday or Wednesday evening.

So, in haste and with best wishes,
R. Barthes

* * *

Hendaye, Sunday, [1956?]

My dear Voisin,

Yes, I'm guilty—fortunately, in a way, I'm not the only one. Here, finally, are the papers, one for the *Théâtre populaire*, the other for the Hungarians, if there's still time; you can still try sending it.[78]

I hardly stopped in Paris this time. I'm here for three week, a month. If I work as I intend to, it's possible that at the end of my stay I can do something fairly comprehensive on the theater; I need to do that for myself, get ideas a bit in order and clarify plans. I'm making you no promises, but I really feel it's necessary for us to take stock.

Good summer to all and my best wishes always,
Barthes
Etchetoa[79]
Hendaye-Plage

* * *

Zurich, September 28, 1956

My dear Voisin,

I just saw a young fellow who is involved with the theater and who had spoken to me in Geneva last year. He's proposing that we do a review of the play by Schehade that Barrault is going to present in Zurich in a couple weeks.[80] I don't know if it's worthwhile, but we can give it a try. Could you send him by return post two lines on Revue letterhead (if you're alright with this) to this effect: the *Théâtre populaire* review would be grateful to Monsieur l'Administrateur du Théâtre de Zurich for authorizing M . . . to attend the opening performance of . . . and thanks him for taking care of this matter.

Name of fellow: Philippe Deriaz, Trittligasse 5, Zurich
Thanks.

I'll tell you about contacts here with the Russians; fairly meaningless of course, with fairly futile efforts, but I believe that in practical terms exchanges will be possible.[81] They may possibly extend to *Théâtre populaire* (which we always speak of stipulating that its future will have to be analyzed). Duvignaud was here, but I haven't seen him alone, and I regret that, because I would still like to come to some clarity about the situation going forward.[82]

Until soon and faithfully yours,
R. Barthes

*   *   *

Saturday, [April 1958]

My dear Voisin,

Yes, of course, for *Ubu*.[83] I had not said anything to you about it because I find it a bit annoying that I'm always the one who does the reviews for the TNP, and since they are always unfavorable. . . . It's true that I do not attend plays anywhere else! Only, I'm asking you to give me until April 22; but absolutely without fail (I do not want to give up on my plan, and one stage of it will be done April 20).[84]

My stay here is already settling into a routine: peaceful, weather very changeable but always very mild, work respectable (I'm making great progress on Racine—until that infamous April 20).[85] I'm thinking of returning to Paris at the very beginning of May.

Faithfully yours, both of you,
R. Barthes

I just remembered: very important! Can you send me the issue of *Théâtre populaire* (or the page cut out from it) where I discussed Monnet's *Ubu* (toward the end of 1955?)?[86]

*   *   *

Friday, [summer 1959]

My dear Voisin,

Thank you very much again for your second money order, invaluable.[87] I enjoyed seeing Pic, he must have told you about it.[88] I am not working furiously anymore; it seems I'm always a little depressed, but at least I'm still working on *Mère Courage*, a little each day, that is. Thanks to the two texts you sent me, I'm in the process, for the moment, of writing a very detailed commentary on the text itself, without yet approaching the photos really. It is decidedly a very rich text; I almost regret that we cannot bring together text, photos, and commentary in a kind of comprehensive edition. For the moment, my commentary has no editorial value, and I have no idea what will happen in the final version; I have no new ideas on this subject. The commentary on the text is going to take me some time still; then I'll comment *myself* in the same way on the photos. Only after completing these two steps can I give you a specific proposal for organizing the whole thing. In short, my aim right now is to know the work by heart.

I am absolutely convinced of the necessity and the novelty of the work that we're doing here. As I said to Pic, this will not be just an essay. We're getting serious here and trying to move the photography of the theater beyond the realm of luxury, leisure, and mystification. I would like you to be pleased with me about this; we're very much in agreement about the seriousness of our effort, its complexity, and its comprehensiveness (it's not a matter of adding a preface, even a Brechtian one, to an album of beautiful photos).

Remind Pic that he must make me a contact sheet for *all* his film; that will be indispensible to us, he himself proposed it, and it really is his job. I'll be here at least until October 3, the date of the sale.[89] I'll be in touch as soon as I get back or if I have to stay longer. It has been stormy here since yesterday, very beautiful.

Your friend,
R. Barthes
I skimmed the Willett very carefully.[90] It is extremely valuable, a very good study in the manner of Robichez.[91] I learned much specific

information from it. This suggests three things to me: 1. A sort of quick, typed translation for Brechtians; 2. Printing the chapter on theory in the review; 3. Assembling a general Brechtian archive.

* * *

Hendaye, Tuesday, August 9, [1960]

Dear Voisin,

I was happy to hear your news and that everything is going well for all of you. Here are the proofs for *Mère Courage*. For the note on page 8, please add a reference to the specific issue of *Théâtre populaire* in which the article I mention by W. Benjamin appeared; it's impossible for me to verify it from here.[92] Please don't forget.

As for my paper on *La Mère*, I am backing off a bit, *formally*, on my proposition that the subject of *La Mère* is not Marxism, etc. (I'll do it in the proofs).[93] Otherwise I'll have the whole left wing of *Théâtre populaire* on my tail. Actually, I would like to make it clearer that the *object* of *La Mère* is Marxism, but the *subject* is motherhood. So much for business.

Otherwise? Well, just this morning I sat down to begin drafting this thing on Fashion.[94] I panicked, especially facing that first blank page. I don't know when I'll be returning; that depends on work.

Send me your news from time to time, a note.

Faithfully yours,
R. Barthes

* * *

Urt, September 3, 1961

Dear Voisin,

Now that I've finished with Fashion,[95] I'm getting back to thinking a bit about all that I let drop for the sake of this "formalist" initiation, and of course what comes first is *Théâtre populaire*. It was always agreed that I would do it, and I'm very grateful to you (without going on about it) for retaining your confidence in me during this lapse (at least until our last evening together?!).[96] So, this is how I see things—first setting aside my own problem.

It seems to me there are three solutions: the first is dropping the effort, the action, the enterprise, but by saying so, that is, by taking stock—in the form of a general assessment—of the impasse our theater has reached (assuming we believe this) which would thus be the impasse our review has also reached, as well as our society. Or at least—because in History there are no impasses—the powerlessness of our thinking—creative or critical—to grasp the exact nature of our society in such a way as to offer or propose to it the progressive theater it needs—or more precisely, that it does not seem to need. To tell the truth, I'm only offering this solution for the record. Because first of all, the feeling that old explanatory patterns are no longer relevant to the world's situation and we must understand this world in a new way may well be a mistaken feeling, too quickly accepted, lazy, etc.; and second, even if that feeling were justified, it doesn't necessarily follow that we must abandon this instrument of thought and combat that a review like ours serves as. This solution—along with its alibi—has tempted me a bit, but now that I've written the Fashion thing, I'm rethinking it. For me, the full direction of things was precisely to write Fashion and not to lose *Théâtre populaire*, but for this dialectic not to be rigged, it was necessary, obviously, to write *only* Fashion, for a time. . . .

The second solution (*I am still talking as though there were a crisis*) would be—and we have already discussed this—to expand the parameters of *Théâtre populaire* by making it a review for every kind of spectacle, I do not dare say popular, because that could include the weird or quaint but, let us say, *unsophisticated*. This, I believe, would be new and well justified; it would allow us to tie the theater to the whole economy of the spectacle in modern society. It would allow us to apply nonculturist, nonaestheticizing criticism to the cinema, and maybe there we could convey in an exciting way what Brecht has taught us. Let me add that, for us, this would be *new* and consequently fairly dynamic, and then there are all the other kinds of spectacles: music halls, sports. There is *meaning* to draw from all of that, no one draws it, we would be the first to do so. But this solution, I can see already, is also for the record. Because basically you believe the theater is autonomous and sufficient, and you love it; you will not willingly abandon that "popular aristocracy" that is the basis for *Théâtre populaire* and Arche, especially in favor of a profile that closely resembles that notion of *mass culture* you condemn. You're afraid that expanding the project would not meet with approval in the world *as is*, and that enlarging the vision would entail *a suspension of judgment*, as I don't know which English poet said, quoted by Vinaver.[97]

And that brings us to the third solution. This would be quite simply to continue, let's say, with a simple reviving "jolt": new papers, new contributors (?), or at least newly solicited, and maybe a new editorial committee—not for show, it doesn't matter what appears on the cover, but so we can have regular meetings to share our thoughts a bit about the theater. We have said this often: we cannot continue in the same fashion. But really, that doesn't mean we must not continue at all; only to continue with things arranged differently, and without forcing them, they will come around on their own. Because if there is a theatrical void right now, that's not *necessarily* a reason to keep quiet. We can try to *speak again* of Vilar, Planchon, and others.

I myself cannot resolve this all alone. That wouldn't make any sense, and basically I don't really know what I think or what I want. That depends on all of us, and very much on you; we need to talk. All that I can tell you now—and this is the main reason I'm writing to you—is that I am—as I have basically always expected to be—fundamentally inclined to contribute in a very real way to whatever you do, whether it is *Théâtre populaire* or Arche; I will do it, of course, as I am now—and not as I was—assuming there is a difference, which I myself do not believe in the least. No need to answer, I've written you (even though I don't like "long-distance" letters) simply so we can discuss it when I return (about September 20), and so you have my assurance of real support* from me from now on, whatever we decide.

With faithful affection to you and Geneviève both,
R. Barthes

With Michel Vinaver

Michel Vinaver, whose real name was Michel Grinberg, was born in 1927. After writing two novels published by Gallimard, he went on to become a very important playwright while pursuing a parallel career in industry (at Gillette, where he was chairman and chief executive officer for France). He is best known for *Les Coréens*, a play produced by Roger Planchon in Lyon in 1956. His last play, *Bettencourt boulevard ou une histoire de France*, was published in 2014 by Éditions de l'Arche.

---

*By which I mean: financial support in *praxis*, that is to say—the fate of the intellectual!—essentially in *works*.

Michel Vinaver to Roland Barthes

All Saints' Day, [November 1, 1956]

Dear Roland,

I welcome the news your letter brings as one welcomes the unexpected. For me it is an event, a "victory" (in Conrad's sense)[98] more than a reward.

And your paper that I just read is the very one that will allow the play to find its place in the general movement.[99] It propels, but it also guides, and criticism here becomes conductor. That is an invaluable service.

I was glad you weren't there Saturday.[100] The evening was successful as an operation is successful. It was a victory in the ordinary sense, thus followed by a house depression—that Planchon and I shared: the reality of the performance was obliterated by that of an enormous "machination." I'll fill in the details for you this weekend. Tomorrow evening, Friday, I'm going to Lyon and will take a night train to Paris, where I'll spend Saturday and Sunday seeing what Serreau is doing.[101]

Michel

Roland Barthes to Michel Vinaver

Thursday, [late 1957 or early 1958]

Michel, I've finally read *Les Huissiers* and I really enjoyed it.[102] I am very much *for* it; I see many things in it that are simultaneously very simple and very interesting. It is much more relaxed than *Les Coréens*, without losing anything.

The part of the *Huissiers* is so *right* that I have already copied passages for my courses on France this summer. I have only one objection to discuss with you: the political palaver, offered as palaver, as empty talk, is too long. You must find a way to render the Algerian *hole* (in relation to the barbers' positivity) without inflating the language too much. I'm expressing this badly, but you see what I mean.

I'll arrive in Annecy next Saturday, coming from Lyon, at 3:19 PM.

Don't worry about me. I'll take the bus and will get to Menthon about 5 PM; find a way for me to get into the house. And don't hurry back from skiing.

Until Saturday,
Roland

I'm leaving Paris Friday at noon, staying with Jean Lacroix, 107, cours Lafayette, Lyon. I'll have to return Sunday evening. But it's better than nothing.

*   *   *

January 5, 1961

Michel, since I have your Brussels address, I can tell you how your play has dazzled me.[103] Me, for whom reading is such an effort, such an obligation, I spontaneously read this text on a whole other level, that of pleasure, of seduction. I've never seen such sure *mastery* combined with such profound *correctness* of thought, of judgment on the world. I hope, yes, I hope that Planchon will produce it—I don't meaning the *staging*, because that he does fairly well—but *without vulgarity* (not his, but his actors . . .). Yes, this play seems good to me, the best I've read of yours. In our generation, I find only you inclined toward an explosive mixture of *ambiguity and correctness*. The others are either muddleheads (that is to say, bastards) or ideologues.

Happy new year to all the family,
R. Barthes

Michel Vinaver to Roland Barthes

January 15, 1961

Roland,

That's something I myself feel, the effort of reading, the sense of obligation. And from time to time, like you with the Mycéniens,[104] a break in the clouds, a feeling of pleasure. Recently, *Le Bel été* by Pavese. It's true that I had the strange sensation of writing what I was reading. Recently as well, the *Contes de pluie et de lune*,[105] which are the opposite of what I could write. But why this resistance to *embark upon* some new reading? When it ought to be no problem, like a child popping his thumb into his mouth.

Ten years ago, three things seemed equally necessary and equally verging on impossible for me: writing, earning a living, and creating a family. Three things available to others, closed to me who wanted them not separately but together. Today I feel I've hardly progressed.

Maybe because I've grown too many branches, not enough leaves. Because I haven't paid enough attention to pleasure.

Your friend,
Michel

*   *   *

November 21, 1961

Roland,

I read, this morning, "Savoir et folie."[106] Good to hear from you *there*.

You don't publish very much, and what you do publish I rarely come across. Each time, reading you brings with it a physical sensation, the sensation of having my hand grasped by a very sure hand feeling its way. I read you and it is simultaneously with recognition and surprise.

Feeling one's way toward what? In any case, what I seem to read constantly between your lines is "One cannot escape." Your curse and your privilege to feel and express that with such force. Nothing of what is written offers simultaneously (I keep coming back to that) such an impression of stillness and movement, of the urge to move out from a center.

I tell myself that in my friendship with you there is that scandalous certainty that I can, at any time, set off on vacation; as long as you're there, I cannot help but—at one time or another—come back.

Michel

The Future of Rhetoric

This unpublished text, drawn from the BNF archives, is one of the very first critical essays written by Roland Barthes, which can be dated to the spring of 1946, as is evident from Barthes's final note for this essay, which alludes to the January 1946 issue of *Contrepoints*. Thus it was written upon Barthes's return from the sanatorium in Leysin, one year before the publication in *Combat* of the sketches from *Le Degré zéro de l'écriture*, the first of which appeared under that title on August 1, 1947.

*   *   *

We know the principle of the historical method applied to literature (Lanson): to present the text as within History and to require that it be understood historically.* Lanson cared very much about the scientific spirit of his method; nevertheless, that is its most debatable feature. A scientific attitude too often authorized in these matters the triumph of the letter over the spirit, the secondary over the essential, collation over organized explanation.† Still it is true that after Lanson the literary text no longer belonged to a supernatural and unknowable order; it became the product of precise determination, historical in nature. It appeared as an object, if not concrete, at least observable. A certain portion of the taboo was lifted that had shielded, behind the name of inspiration, the various processes of verbal creation. Criticism began to comprehend; it no longer simply commented. It claims to mark the limits of subjective opinion, the lack of which, despite the appeal, leads to nothing. In short, by helping to eliminate the supernatural from the work of art, Lansonian criticism remains an available method, that is to say, from the moment when the text is presented as an object, it is possible to supplement the pure historical method with an instant set of observations, descriptions, and what could almost be called experiments that link literary criticism to the general and shared movement of the other sciences.

*   *   *

But before moving beyond Lansonian criticism, we must say how its applications leave us—justifiably—unsatisfied. First of all, it is criticism that relies on false psychology. In its explanations and conclusions, it continually resorts to a certain philosophical view of the world and ontological view of man. If that view is weak and unconsidered, it nonetheless exists; it is the one quite naturally colored by the philosophical trend of the moment. By virtue of the apparently objective division of domains, classical literary criticism never addressed questions that seemed beyond the immediate goal of its method. But to be objective in this way is simply to adopt the slogans, that is, the clichés, within the tradition. However innocently

---

*We know the method: to gather all useful documents for illuminating the writings—works by predecessors, contemporaries, and successors, letters, satires, journals, official papers, etc.—in short, to control the subjective reaction of taste through contact with documents. Gustave Lanson, *Méthode de l'histoire littéraire* (Paris: Les Belles Lettres, 1925), first notebook.
†We now begin to see that the traditional skills of the scholar can become part of the historical process; it is less clear that the discoveries of science are consistently due to the strict application of scientific scruples as understood by Hippolyte Taine, Charles Seignobos, or Gustave Lanson.

and without thinking of the great responsibility involved, Lanson-ism will thus base its criticism on a certain dualism in man, the separation of reason and temperament, ideas and feelings, thoughts and words, in short on the existence of an absolute mental order. One of the doctors of pure history, Gabriel Monod, thought that he had explained all of Michelet when he reduced him to a *homo duplex*, in whom the imagination struggles against realism, sensuality, ideal aspirations, etc. Contradiction is for him an avant-garde explanation. Everyone knows that in French literature it is forbidden for a poet to be intelligent and for a cerebral type to be an artist. In this kind of psychological analytics, there is no concern for the total human. Once presented in a great daring gesture, the contradiction is never afterward traced to its roots. One considers oneself too fortunate in having discovered it, in having presented it in the antithetical form as an element of balance. Whereas there is no true explanation without dialectical reduction to unity. Lanson and those who followed him were not at all bothered by using the results of a historical method to develop an arbitrary kind of psychology. They did not believe they had to make a distinction for humans; it was enough for them to adopt the perspective of their time, considered to be eternal. With complete ingenuousness, chapters resolved into paragraphs on the sensibility, the imagination, the ideas, and eventually the form of the writer. But no one considered the degree to which the least writing itself is engaging, and no one foresaw how profoundly damaging erroneous psychology could be to a writer's work.

That is not all. Plekhanov praised Lanson for returning Descartes's ideas to their historical milieu.[107] That was, in fact, an important critical operation. But could it be decisive insofar as no one had precisely defined this notion of "milieu"? The ideological determinants of a work are not merely secondary. If one gets involved in doing historical criticism, it is important not to stop midway; one cannot avoid calling into question the fundamental structure of society. And here again, an apparent paradox holds that the theory of pure history, the profession of a method free of any social motive, would in fact lead to more superficial results than would an objective, but partisan, critique, framed within a comprehensive explanation of History and society. One can simultaneously want to subjugate everything to History, and claim to dominate it. Lanson did not resolve that contradiction. Thus the same distance separates him from the possibilities for a sociological critique of literature as separates Taine from materialist historians.

Since the milieu can only determine the work through the intermediary of the author, classical criticism gave precedence to the writer's biography. That means that time was given an all-consuming place in the development of works of art. Through dating crises, movements, reversals, and influences, critics subjected the intelligence of the work to an emotional conception of duration; they considered the written text as a pure succession of moments, and they turned away from the static, even stubborn, elements, the habits one could say, that the text includes. Despite the method's scientific basis, the results conform more closely to a conception of personal, incommunicable time that dominates the period. Beneath an apparent coolness, beneath the apparatus of objective chronology, slips a totally subjective view of man. Here, alone and definitively, emotional time is creator; works are only accidents of substance: duration. It was after Lanson that many literary hacks began writing biographical novels, whose distinctive feature is to make a writer's works entirely dependent upon the chance events of his life, and to organize the *lifetime* into a providentially significant drama. Thus the highly decorative but false notion of destiny was introduced into criticism, where it serves no purpose. Ingenuity vied with arbitrariness in organizing the lives of great writers into dramas. Almost every year the lives of Racine, Pascal, Voltaire, Chateaubriand, Pushkin, Mallarmé, Péguy, etc. submit to the easy unity of the novel, and their works are reduced to the state of personal messages and secrets. No one comes close to caring about analyzing actual content, the verbal substance of the written thought. By wanting to define the work through its widest and most lively context, critics neglect the work itself. It is no longer a set of concrete operations, it is an emanation, a quasi-spiritual and inessential vapor, from a single reality: the author. And that reality is rarely examined for what it, like the human body, can offer of the solidly observable; the author here is most often only the geometric location for a certain number of adventures, crises, passions, and influences. He is a character in a setting, the milieu itself being no more than material for a picturesque resurrection.

It is because of too great a desire to explain that one neglects to describe. Explanation loses sight of its object, because it relies upon a spiritual conception of the work. Wanting to elucidate *Le Misanthrope*, classical criticism will explain in depth comedy before Molière, and even the life of Molière, but the play itself? Not at all. Such effort is necessary, but can only be preliminary. The Lansonians fell somewhat into the error of a more mechanical than dialectical view of causality. Critics did consider the determination of the author over the work; but did they try hard enough to discover the inverse action of the work on the author, the mental categories, verbal reflexes, rhetorical automatisms that the work creates and establishes as latent habits, powerful enough perhaps to shape in advance, as it were, the writer's future thinking? The danger is mistaking the literary text for a pure summation of influences. One thus abandons, gradually and despite the best, most objective intentions, the sound and necessary idea according to which the text, the writing, always remains a concretely observable subject, requiring description and not just explanation. To tell the truth, the historical method alone can only, in the final analysis, refer to an absolute mental order. The Lansonian tyranny of *influence, milieu, rapprochement* is only possible within the framework of idealism, where ideas exist independently of words, where what is directly observable in the text, that is, the verbal substance, is relegated to the last chapter on style, a sort of impalpable magic powder thrown over the all-powerful ideas, a final moment of poetic chemistry. And it is, in fact, very much within the framework of Lansonism that the traditional distinction between *le fond* and *la forme*—content and form—blossomed; along with Flaubert, all classical literature considered style to be the flesh on a skeleton, the outward appearance of a hidden vital essence. Criticism maintained the old scholastic dualism of mind and body, mental and physical, intelligible and sensible. Our literary handbooks are still burdened with this division. It goes without saying that in these analyses, form is always the poor cousin; it prompts only a short, vague commentary, a kind of false window for symmetry. Philology, which nevertheless has the merit of rigor and historic spirit, restricts itself to the chronology of forms and does not try to penetrate the verbal automatisms belonging to a writer.

The preceding discussion may make it clear that we must now take the desupernaturalization of literature to its limits and try to construct, through trial and error, the framework for comprehensive and objective criticism of literary texts. The reduction of the written work to an observable subject, which is the path to follow, is certainly not new; it is in the air. From what appear to be very different approaches, writers have tried to reduce inspiration to a set of concrete, technical operations; that was a fruitful attitude to adopt, since it moved us from the metaphysical to the natural. All these questions were then rendered familiar through Valéry and the Surrealists; under the rebellious work of the latter and the aristocratic work of the former, poetic chemistry lost its magical character. Abandoning the supernatural, we have sanely turned toward a technology of creation.

*　　*　　*

There will be no materialist history of literature so long as literature is not restored to the practice of a language.

Saying that the milieu acts upon the writer is nothing. Because what is the writer in this case? An organism that adapts through language alone, and not through action. Thus it is to the level of language that literary criticism, if it wants to be entirely historical, must attend.* And here, it must be said, literary criticism can reasonably find hope in the developments of experimental psychology. The future of criticism, an open, nondogmatic future, can only exist where the mechanisms of language, and thus of thought, will be elucidated in accordance with a gradual synthesis of other sciences. For a long time still, criticism will have to remain only partly objective; it will have to be content with hypotheses and approximations. It must be patient, except in immediately linking to the historical method the study of the written text considered as verbal behavior, a set of spoken reactions. Written thought must be reduced to an order of verbal processes, that is to say, to rhetoric. It is, in fact, to a resurrection of rhetoric that we will sooner or later be led, not, of course, as the art of persuasion through the means of formulas and formal classifications, but very much as the science of written language, taking into account all that experimental psychology will have to teach us about the acquisition of verbal habits, the conditioning of speech, the construction, conclusion, and use of word groups, all of which, under the name of expressions or even themes, we will learn to recognize and appreciate for their importance. From now on, criticism must be able to make certain lists, certain calculations and observations of this order. Even without first moving to the verbal level, but remaining for now on the hypothetical level of a pure mental order, we can say that criticism, oriented until now toward the problems of chronology, neglected to inquire into certain *constants* in the work of a writer. The stubborn and almost involuntary nature of a few ideas and processes, which constitute the very unity in tone and style specific to an author, must arouse suspicions. We soon see that the work of a writer nearly always involves a set of themes, more or less

---

*Largely by putting to good use the eminent work of Ferdinand Brunot [1860–1938, French linguist and author especially of the very important *Histoire de la langue française*, published by Armand Colin in 1925].

complex, more or less evident, according to the author and the period. This set of themes—and this is its remarkable feature—usually resists apparent variations in ideas. To tell the truth, even in the case of an obvious change in beliefs, like the transition from Christianity to non-Christianity in Michelet, there is much more inversion than transformation. That is to say, ideas change but remain within the same stubborn framework, the incorrigible signs in this case, for example, being Michelet's religiosity and apocalyptic view of History. It is not that criticism can discover something outside of time; it is simply that time does not act only as a succession of different and differently determined historical situations, but also, inversely, as creator and then preserver of automatisms of thought that contribute to the specific image we have of a writer and that form part of his talent and genius. At this point, time is no longer the place where a soul evolves emotionally; it resumes its solely physical function, that is to say, it helps to establish certain repeated processes within an organism that is always simultaneously seeking economy and efficiency. Time preserves because it accuses the figures of its own rhetoric within which a writer thinks first with happiness, and then with ease, and outside of which he is soon no longer able or willing to think. It is not unusual to see, in a great writer's old age, these grooves become ruts; beyond maturity, the written work is no more than a collection of habits, a rehearsal of cherished themes. Hence the monstrous nature of those grand old men of literature, among whom genius has the blind force of habit. Because thanks to the pathological distortion of time, this set of themes, taken initially for more than convenience in its classical mental aspect, reveals its essentially verbal nature. The themes are initially alive enough, that is, the organism does not use a word without searching a little, without choosing the best adaptation from among many; but soon the reflex is created. If it is a matter of a lyric writer, that is, if he believes in inspiration, he will continue playing to the very end. We know that the last books of Michelet, Hugo, Claudel, etc. are thick condensations of their specific natures, running on empty here, with the perfect imbecilic efficiency of a machine. This is not to say exactly that the word has triumphed over the idea, nor is it a matter of describing classical verbalism, because initially as finally the writer is only words, as is everyone who speaks or who writes. Rather, it is that verbal automatisms have invaded all discourse, whereas the balanced work is the product of a subtly unstable and not overwhelmingly immediate oral adaptation.

In short, in many cases, these verbal categories—images, themes, allusions, analogies, metaphors, antitheses, couples, figures, cadences—whose formal aspect was considered until now to be pure product, pure clothing for thought, seem in reality to be a driving force. They are first induced as responses to the demands of some situation of thought, and then come to act as stimulants; the writer is led by his rhetoric as much as he leads it. The literary text is like a gathering of reversible links. An incessant dialectic, enormously complex and of which we see only the most stable elements, agitates the written thought, which is created as it goes along by the action and reaction of figures and cadences, through whatever other words are being organized less immediately, filling, in a more laborious fashion, the voids left between the ready-made forms. In this sense, the writer's text is like a sequence of sure, rapid, original gestures (that he possesses exclusively, alone or with his era, as a species possesses its specific means of adaptation) and efforts that are more difficult because they are unlearned, but finally more precise because they are more supple and new.

Thus some trite figure like antithesis can first be the most natural means for adapting to situations of thought that effectively involve antinomies. But what was initially only response comes to play the role of stimulus; the *figure* of antithesis creates in turn the antithetical *situation*. We know that, in romantic eloquence, the object of discourse comes to organize itself in the form of a permanent couple, according to processes that are basically only a matter of rhetoric.* The importance of antonomasia in Balzac (Curtius)[108] and catachresis in Baudelaire has already been noted. We could equally point to the pleonastic structure of discourse in Molière (from which he draws comic effects when he is aware of it), the driving force of metaphor in highly mannered language or of the symbol in romantic eloquence, etc.

And again, the alexandrine, as a given rhetorical cadence, absolutely shapes thought, forever acting as a driving and conditioning force. We may foresee all that criticism may one day discover about the rhetoric of Racine or Molière the poet (hasn't an attempt of this order been made with regard to the verse of Corneille?), that is to say, about precisely what is called their thought. That will be at least as fruitful as pondering over the portion of angel and devil in the soul of Racine or Molière's relationship

---

*A given social class here functions exactly like geniuses. We know the importance of the cliché in language; each group has its clichés (its rhetorical figures); no one will dispute that the active thinking of many people is reduced to a series of formulas. The commonplace acts as a driving force; it leads to others. This is what Prévert, for example, remarkably observed and parodied.

with Madeleine Béjart. Imagination, symbolism, realism, sensibility, ideas, etc. cannot have true critical significance outside of an objective rhetoric that must study the development of the literary text at its surface level, in the verbal accidents that it offers to show us, before studying it in the "soul" or the "psychology" of the writer. The point is not to arrive at a static description. The verbal structure of discourse must be seized in its creative aspect; the way rhetorical figures act as a driving force must be brought to light.

*　　*　　*

We may wonder if these verbal categories, these rhetorical figures, are so obvious among all writers and, in each case, where they originate. This is where History must be reintroduced. It is clearly essential to a writer's rhetoric that he be born in one era and not some other. The age, or more precisely whatever society is in a given age, determines not only the historical state of the language, which is the business of philology; through the play of constraints and deliberations, motives acknowledged or not, it also allows or defends a general rhetorical orientation, within which each writer lets his automatisms function more or less unrestrained. One can say that in general, an *aim* exists for writing, shared by the writers of the same period. Hence the famous French clarity, the myth of enlightened philosophy (a myth still very much alive since we are forever hearing about the eternal virtue of our language in diplomatic discussions, as if the use of a language could miraculously be the cause and not the expression of a relationship between political powers: see the complaints and hopes of Duhamel in *Le Figaro*.)[109] The myth of French clarity is the product of history, the history of a very well-defined class that, in its ascending phase, aspired to universal power and forged the means for itself. But why should this clarity belong to the French bourgeoisie in the eighteenth century? Here we must allow for new, more technical, historical explanations. We must be able to offer a verbal description of that language, completely elucidate its spoken origin, and really consider that, in the past, French literature followed conversation very closely. The articulations and rhetorical structures of the classical language possess that general character, no doubt, because they are the substitute for actual gestures and developed much more from the requirements of communication in a very homogenous society than from a psychoanalysis specific to each writer. On the other hand, in the Romantic period, under the influence of multiple social and ideological causes, literature abandoned conversation and tended toward prophesy. The rhetorical revolution claimed by Hugo (its social significance is undeniable) replaced persuasion with intimidation, and writers, abandoning a shared set of verbal gestures and universal rhetorical figures (for their class, of course), let themselves get entangled in entirely personal verbal chains that, some fifty years later (Symbolism), they would be the only ones to understand. Abandoning conversation, rhetoric, that is to say, literature, moved to solemnity and then to mystery, and that movement can be seen even more clearly in the historical usage of words than in the profession of ideas. Inquiry into rhetorical processes in literature must thus adapt its means to the period under study. It may be more difficult to understand the genesis of some Romantic enterprise without resorting to psychoanalysis. For a figure employed in very diverse intellectual usages, we may find a single common latent emotion, a single common organic reaction to some natural stimulus like light, the void, the feminine, etc.* The texts most suited to analysis will be those in which general History and personal history (understanding, of course, that the latter is, in fact, a matter of general History) are not absolutely merged. Also it will be easier to bring verbal critique to bear on so-called lyric works. This notion must be emptied of its classical content to receive an entirely formal one. Between Lautréamont and Voltaire, it is not subject matter that sets them in opposition; it is above all verbal behavior. At the extreme, one is all biophysical, the other all historical. And if the first is more available to an immediate rhetorical critique, that is because the personal automatisms there are more numerous, while for the second, verbal adaptation, aiming simply at communication (the social stages of *conversation* need to be studied closely as well), is grounded in the general history of the language of the period. Resurrecting rhetoric may thus involve old scholastic notions like genre, language, style, etc., but understood in a certain spirit. It is not interesting, for example, to contrast the subject matters of political eloquence and noir fiction. And nevertheless, what an instructive distance there is between the processes of expression in someone like Félix Gouin

---

*The text is the product of a functioning organism; indisputably, that organism is located in a given society, in which History determines our role (which still happens only very imperfectly). But it also has functions according to its own determinations, and individuation is the determination of the body, that is to say, of the biologically closed and unified being. Thus the text cannot present only a historical problem, in the mental sense of the word. There are also problems of verbal technology and kinematics for each writer, as for each human there are personal biochemical problems.

and someone like Sade.* For the novelist, precise writing, that is to say, writing that was searching, writing that did not adapt automatically to ready-made situations, but intelligently created its own adaptations to new problems and was not content with purely automatic formulations; for the politician on the other hand, vague writing, that is to say, a weave of standard phrases arising spontaneously like an instinctive gesture, an unreasoning and almost animal adaptation to old problems. What constitutes the talent of the first is that, by not adapting through purely rhetorical automatisms, he can thereby adapt to a much greater number of situations; from his most primitive imperfection he draws a final superiority, which is precisely the superiority—not in the least moral, let it be understood—of man over animal. This apparent paradox, which is not now recognized, must be accepted: the precision, the securities of ready-made phrases, the very perfection of their play, represent an almost animal organization of language; and inversely, it is the instability of verbal adaptation that is the distinctive feature of exactitude. By which certain authors have been able to propose the anteriority of poetry over prose. Poetry, to the extent that historically it issues from strict formulations, is an entirely animal construction. Thus Valéry did not become a poet because he was interested in the origin of spoken ideas; he believed that in poetry the questions of verbal genetics could better be asked, and the mechanisms of formulation better grasped, which he sensed to be the very mechanisms of thought. (It would be strange to rediscover the constraint of History in what Valéry made into *beautiful* poetry.) Everything comes back to poetry, rarely so experimental, and conveys through the means of rhetoric a nostalgia for animality (which poets call innocence), by which man would be released from *thought*, that is to say, from adapting beyond verbal automatisms. This is not the place to wonder if all poetic† (in the loose and not the normative sense of the word) awakening does not correspond to a general refusal of

---

*Sade is chosen here for the remarkable density of his writing. [Félix Gouin (1884–1977), socialist political figure in the Third and Fourth Republic.]

†Some day we must come to consider poetry itself as historical, and except for the myth that focuses only on the poet, we must put an end to the theories of poetry as pure and immediate knowledge, as spiritual exercise, etc. Objectively being nothing other than a certain kind of language, poetry must reenter History, which is to say that at any given moment, language has complex but precise social and historical determinations. The history of poetry would make the relationship between history and literature as language very clear. Modern poetry has lost its apparently formulary (sacerdotal) nature, but through its theoretical clairvoyance and intuitive truth, it has maintained the same purpose and, in fact, the same function. History can make sense of both this transformation and this consistency.

responsibility and does not flourish especially in periods when a given social group, either tormented and disgusted or alternatively content with the image of its idleness or misfortune, seeks to justify this situation through a sort of verbal fatalism and return to the original conditions of language.* (Here we come back to the modern myth of the poetic childhood.)

* * *

While awaiting the developments of a precise psychological science, the first tool of rhetorical criticism is the statistical method. We recognize the barbarism involved in listing the accidents of language for a given writer, and that nothing could appear to be further removed from the spirit of refinement, the customary, glorious tool of literary criticism. And nevertheless rhetoric must use statistical information. If a rhetorical figure occurs twenty times or more in the work of a writer, it must signify something important; thus we must go through the numbers. Of course this detailed, often useless research, primarily involving limited observations and uncertain results, cannot be the work of a single individual. Here we must overcome the stubborn prejudice that holds literary criticism to be the individual activity par excellence. In the parascientific operation that criticism must be, collective work is imperative. That would mean accepting a form of research that completely violates the strongest taboo in intellectual activity, the one requiring solitary effort, individual organization of the work, undivided glory for the results. Nevertheless, henceforth the scientific laboratory must fully correspond to the notion of institute and seminar. The Sorbonne must play a role here, because it alone can easily establish indispensable connections between the various sciences of language.

Some day, with all possible delicacy, criticism will have to transform the problems of expression into problems of adaptation and in this way settle the question of genius. This involves a mindset, materials, and aid that have yet to appear. So why this effort, why revive rhetoric, why prolong the life of literary criticism at all? Well,

---

*Though some have found it so, there is nothing surprising about the dormancy of poetry in the eighteenth century when that era was occupied with something else, or about the awakening of that same poetry from 1940 to 1945. It is worth noting that this apparently attentive form of literature actually falls within the framework of a poetics overwhelmed with the supernatural. (Popular expressions like poetic message, testimony, poetry as spiritual exercise, visitation of the poet, etc.) Transposing Marx's remark (with its context), we could say that poetry (and in a sense all of literature) is the opium of the empowered class, suffering not from the evils that it endures but from those that it sees. (A possible definition for philosophy as well, the esotericism of philosophical language.)

simply for the sake of understanding. To understand is to create a kind of freedom, and that aim is not immaterial. The most subjective disciplines arising from the cultural practices and the art of a limited society, like aesthetics, psychology, or literary criticism, will eventually become part of the gradual synthesis of the sciences; and it is necessary for that to happen. At that time, exact knowledge of these matters will in itself create a kind of freedom, if it is true that freedom is born the day one recognizes a necessity. Thus we have the right to work toward a recognition of the necessity of poetics.

It would be ridiculous to prescribe or predict what freedom would produce in this domain.* It is enough to know that it is on the level of language, of social language, that the fate of Belles Lettres will be played out in order to bring light into that taboo world of verbal creation,† even if this must contribute to the death of all that we now call literature.

Two Romanian Texts by Roland Barthes

Roland Barthes arrived in Bucharest in November 1947 as an assistant librarian. He soon began teaching there, and then when the Institut Français closed in November 1948 and following the departure of his friend Philippe Rebeyrol in November 1948, he became a cultural attaché. He returned to Paris in September 1949. Two

---

*The concrete function of literature is finally to manifest (or, in the best-case scenario, to aid) a certain transformation of language. That transformation can be conceived in an anarchic, byzantine form by attaching it to the irrational and uncanny, as the Surrealists do. We can also conceive of it in a more *natural* form, that is, primarily as the irruption of spoken forms in a language, with conventional automatisms (various examples: Prévert, Queneau, a certain *blank* style in Camus, *The Stranger*). That transformation is certainly more revolutionary, because it can end in the death of Belles Lettres. In short, must literature continue? That is a question belonging to ethics, for which the course of events must provide the answer.
†And musical creation, for example, where criticism exists at present only in the form of paraphrase. Historical criticism is manifestly powerless with regard to music as long as one is not objectively informed about the mechanisms of aesthetic creation (no doubt analogous to those of thought and language). Here more than elsewhere, the materials provided by present analysis are, in general, essentially scholastic and tendentious; classical analysis of forms (conceptions of theme, phrase, construction, etc.) is based on a purely static and mechanical view of musical discourse (in accordance with the image of a fixed human nature). Musical criticism is essentialist. Half of musicians themselves attribute their operations to the supernatural. (See a recent study by *Contrepoints*, responses by Fumer, Joliver, Migot, Capdevielle, Messiaen.) The others keep quiet, with good reason. [*Contrepoints* 1 (January 1946), articles by Dynam-Victor Fumet, André Joliver, Georges Migot, Pierre Capdevielle, and Olivier Messiaen, review edited by Fred Goldbeck of Éditions de Minuit.]

documents attest to this time. The first is from a lecture on French song, "Popular Songs of Paris Today," probably written in 1948; the second is the report Barthes sent to the Ministry of Foreign Affairs just before his departure in July 1949.

Popular Songs of Paris Today

In 1948, Barthes gave many lectures for the "general public," a francophone audience that gathered on Saturday afternoons in the main hall of the Institut Français at 77 Boulevard Dacia in Bucharest. They covered such topics as the French tune, Ravel, *Pelléas et Mélisande....* Among these lectures was one on the French song, which addressed Charles Trenet, Yves Montand, and especially Edith Piaf; it is now part of the Roland Barthes collection at the BNF. Barthes would later recall his admiration for Piaf in *Fragments d'un discours amoureux*, citing "Mylord."[110]

*   *   *

[...]

Music for a class that lives in a special environment: *the city*. Hence daily encounters, constant pressure of other classes: the boundaries not always very clear. Pressure from the petite bourgeoisie or the underclass: hence a *composite style*. No barrier against a certain potential vulgarity. This is not *pure music*. It cannot be. Example: that music for the poor often originates in chic, expensive cabarets: proletariat elements, rise or fall in class through money but not through taste.

Proletariat: a fluid class with regard to its content. It is, by definition, *the class without property*; hence, migrations, dispersions, rises, falls. Brownian movement of the working population of the great urban areas (as opposed to rural farmworkers); hence the fragility of the repertoire. Creation of a special element: a kind of *popular mode*, rapid, very pronounced; outburst whose future is sometimes hard to predict from its beginnings.

Hence the special role of the performer: *the star*. Role of a medium, magic role; she reveals the music.

Also role as object of transference, the individual, humble, poor, powerless, sees herself in the image of the star: glorious, rich, omnipotent; the ugly feel beautifully alive, the lovesick imagine they are happy, etc. Through the great popular star, music becomes "the heart of a heartless world, the soul of a soulless world."[111]

Role of the star: *total*.

Looks + voice + art + poem + music.

Urban folklore is strongly centralized: Paris.

a. Specificity of Paris as urban complex: the height of luxury, the strongest commerce, the intellectual pinnacle, plus the factory belts. Very strong attraction, special conditions: the poor are in frequent and obvious contact with outward signs of luxury, wealth, power, happiness.

b. Very rich popular history. Great tradition of intelligence and liveliness among Paris workers; the industrial proletariat of the suburbs is grafted onto a very active and enlightened stock of old artisans, a special mix of factory workers and Proudhonian lower-middle-class artisans: that is what you find in the Bobino and Alhambra music halls. Special intellectual resourcefulness. A taste for irony, for fate; imaginative hearts and critical minds, mythological and fabular powers.

c. Role of the Parisian *rue*—street. Paris: narrow city, extreme density of the street; heightened street-sense; points of general sensitization: the Bastille, the République, the Chapelle, the Étoile (the smart set); points of particular sensitization: metro stations.

Common sight: metro station, for example, Barbès-Rochechouart. Three fellows wearing fedoras, sitting on stools, with a mandolin, an accordion, drums; all around them, a dense semicircle of Parisians; in the middle a man with a megaphone sings an old song ("Y'a pas de printemps"),[112] a woman with no hat sells the printed text of the song with the music! And the audience? Characteristic phenomenon, paradoxical and touching: they do not sing. Or at most they sing to themselves, but these people, otherwise so cocky, do not dare sing all together. The onlooker's complex: not to perform. Moving: they remain a long time, a compact quiet circle; they are collectively singing *in silence*.

[. . .]

Édith Piaf, Piaf "la môme."

Tradition of realist singers + *something*. What?

A small woman, not very young, not very pretty, with a wicked little black dress; voice a bit raspy, not at all sweet, a little harsh and bitter. Enormous success, represents a deep enormous wave of people who want to sing. Why?

a. Direct poetry, language of the people, but without excess, without caricature; simplicity. Other realists (Damia)[113] faking it: embody the people, realism, for the purposes of the rich. Piaf: a small woman like all the small women who take the metro four times a day and who, on Sundays, *wash, iron, and resume* their poverty.

b. Guts, courage. No softness, no sweet cooing after love. Other singers: the mentality of kept women, flatter the people's desire to be rich: beautiful affairs, beautiful naive fairytales, a bit too easy, without character.

She: fully assumes her poverty, prefers love to money; does not believe in fairytales. Faces facts, serious.

c. Goodness: sings of the weak, the oppressed, the unfortunate; sings of the great inevitability of injustice. Sings of: the abandoned, the Negro, the poor daughters of the common people.

d. Sense of destiny, but with moderation, depth, truth. Direct realism with a strange harmonic, a kind of veil of dream. *Tragic sense of fate*. Other singers: melodrama, flatter the people's ignorance. She: often rises to the level of tragedy. Expresses the tragic sadness of the people fallen victim to a fate that transcends them.

("Voyage du pauvre nègre")[114]
[. . .]
"L'accordéoniste"
Set: underclass living quarters; red-light district. Emotional theme: a prostitute's love; wonderful success of this innocent story through rough, direct language. All that comes from the beloved is conveyed through his music, all that comes from her is conveyed by her gaze. "She listens, she looks." There is an impulse, there is no contact.
"Y'a pas de printemps"
For the very poor (Piaf): no springtime, that is, the most vital of elements, the rhythm and cycle of Nature, that affects the slightest grass, the smallest creature, is denied to the man oppressed by work. Work cancels Nature.

But one thing triumphs over the City, over Work, one thing is equivalent to the Season and reintroduces nature into the city. One thing erases injustice, oppression, slavery: love (love always encountered by chance).
[. . .]
"Un monsieur me suit dans la rue"
Here is one of the strangest and most disorienting stories. A complete and tragic fate is expressed through this banal act: "I am followed on the street." The image becomes the center of a strange reverie for this woman who reviews her life through the steps of those who followed her; the theme develops in a suffocating, almost

epic way: first, it is a little street urchin that an old man follows down the street (but this is not just a dirty old man), then a second episode with the intrusion of a specifically urban element, a modern myth of terror: the Police: I am followed on the street. And finally, it is my funeral that someone follows down the street.

"Tout fout l'camp"

This is a kind of half-philosophic, half-realistic meditation on the insignificance of human fates. Viewed from above, we are nothing. Viewed from below, we are nothing; nothing remains stable; a kind of cry, paraphrase of an almost existential feeling about life, the heart's justifiable compensation in a heartless world.

[. . .]

"C'est lui qu'mon coeur a choisi"

For example [love] compensates for the whole world, nature; it establishes an equivalence between the world and the beloved; it re-creates a world with all its dimensions and does so through absolutely direct eloquence, without metaphor: "He doesn't need to speak, he only has to look at me, in his caressing eyes, I see the sky that's falling apart, it's good, it's amazing."

"From the other side of the street"

[Love] also compensates for money; and for the common people, that is the greatest victory. In the literature of the upper classes, there is an entire, very beautiful, fabulist tradition that shows us how love conquers death, for example; and this theme can be found again in the popular poetry of the Middle Ages when death actually was the harshest Master. But now, it is Money that is the harshest master; therefore there is no victory more beautiful for Love than to be stronger than Money.

[. . .]

The Politicization of Science in Romania

Cultural attaché for the France legation in Romania
to
The Minister of Foreign Affairs (Department of Cultural Relations)
c/o The Minister of France in Romania[115]

After a few months' delay, Romania has just fallen into line with Soviet Russia with regard to an area that was relatively independent until now, science. This alignment conforms to taking the position adopted by the Soviet Union concerning the recent Mitchourine affair.[116] In its structure and terminology, the campaign of the Romanian press faithfully reproduces the campaign of the Soviet press.

The Romanian press recently published (June 29–30, 1949) two reports from the Academy of the Romanian People's Republic on scientific activity and trends in the RPR.[117] The first report was written by the Department of Medical Sciences at the RPR Academy; it contains eighteen typed pages. The second report is simply a commentary on the first; it was written by the president of the Academy, Professor Trajan Savulescu, and contains twenty-two typed pages.

The reports take as their subject two issues of the Romanian ophthalmology review edited by a well-known university professor, Dr. Blatt. The review is accused of containing "the poisoned vestiges of the ideology of the former exploiting classes." More precisely, it ignores Romanian medical science and only publishes the texts of specialists "in Western capitalist countries." It ignores the use of the national language and prefers English and French; it passes over the works of Soviet scientists. This last grievance is expanded upon the most. One of the reports explains at length Filasiev's role in the discoveries of cornea grafts and therapeutic tissue; the ophthalmology review made the mistake of contrasting Filasiev to the Swiss scientist Franceshetti, whose works, according to the report, are much superior to those of Felasiev. The ophthalmology review also published an article by the "Western" professor Biett on trachoma, without mentioning the Soviet scientists K. Trapenzentzeva and Tchirkovski. This offensive attitude toward Russian science, moreover, has earned the implicated review encouragement from the "imperialist circles of the West," in the form of an approving article by the *American Journal of Ophthalmology*. The individual responsible for such reprehensible deviation is Doctor Blatt, "false man of science," servile lackey of American imperialism, upstart who conceived of his review only to attract clients.

*   *   *

It is obvious that for those behind these reports, such an unnecessary attack on Doctor Blatt's review is only of interest because it allows certain general themes to be established and presented for general circulation.

The first of these themes is apparently simply a matter of principle: it maintains that there is no universal science. Believing in science with no homeland is "a prejudice spread like a virus by bourgeois education." It is even worse; it is "heresy," "falsehood." In fact, the "cosmopolitan" theory of universal science conceals the interests of the bourgeois class in its efforts to subjugate the countries of the people's democracy.

Thus one can replace the theme of universal science with that of class science (as there is class justice and class culture). It goes without saying that such a distinction inevitably sets Soviet science in opposition to Western science in the minds of the report writers.

This first theme, then, is only a simple introduction to the second theme, much less ideological than political: the real motive for these reports is, in fact, to affirm the preeminence of Soviet science, which is, it seems, the "most advanced science." Soviet scientific production "dominates and exceeds that of the most advanced capitalist countries." "It occupies first place today, vibrant, healthy, bold, in contrast to the decadent bourgeois science pledged to capitalist interests." Russian scientists of the past and Soviet scientists of the present were and are innovators and forerunners in all areas: in the eighteenth century, M. V. Lomonossov discovered the law of the conservation of matter; V. V. Petrov established the bases for modern electrotechnology; A. S. Popov invented radio long before Marconi; N. N. Jukovski is the creator of modern aerodynamics; M. Butlerov founded modern organic chemistry; D. C. Tchernov created metallography. "Physics in the USSR has experienced progress unknown in other countries." "Soviet scientists are playing a decisive role in answering the important questions in nuclear physics." Mitchourine and his students have raised biology to a superior level of knowledge, interpretation, and application. Soviet biology is clearly superior to Western science. In short, "Soviet scientists have indisputable priority when it comes to the most important scientific discoveries in recent times."

If the question of the relationship between science and the State seems at first to be treated in an abstract, conceptual, and ideological way, we can see that the solution is hardly disinterested dogma. Claims for the Marxist method are presented here in a fleeting and cursory way. The report writers consider themselves in line with those principles when they maintain that only Marxist-Leninist science combines theory and practice and only such science understands that "there where death is imminent, life is born" (cornea graft). Marxist ideology is superficially present in the vocabulary; it is not at the core, which is, in reality, only an entirely political matter of Romanian scientists following orders, their turn having come to place themselves under the yoke of Soviet State science.

*   *   *

It is useful to list the processes brought to light by these two reports because they constitute the invariable elements of all Stalinist writing.

The first of these processes is to "stuff" the report with all the official clichés, tried and true in propaganda, that must appear word for word (transposing a single word constitutes a deviation) in all written output, whatever the subject. Thus we find in these texts on science all the phrases, the bits of phrases, and the terms that together constitute the "basic" language of communism: construction of socialism—historical task—to guide the people—reactionary and antipatriotic tendencies—the working class armed with the reliable weapon of Marxism-Leninism—the realities of life—heresy—deviation—nations targeted by Anglo-American aggression—the struggle for peace—national independence and socialism—decadent cosmopolitanism—decline of bourgeois society in decay—warmongers—deep socialist content—the camp of peace and progress, the camp of war and reaction—noble patriotic spirit—Tito's Trotskyist clique, etc. These clichés are present at every turn of phrase, without any logical necessity, as so many clausulae in this new rhetoric. But we should not underestimate the incantatory power of this process, meant to gradually impose upon the reader's critical thinking the desired automatisms.

The second process is made up of a kind of nominalism in which each word implies both its subject and the judgment brought to bear on it; the history of the words "nationalism" and "cosmopolitanism" are good examples. These two pejorative words are reserved for "Western" feelings; when the same feelings become "eastern," they change names, are assigned a euphemistic meaning, and become "patriotism" and "internationalism." Thus each word constitutes an abuse of trust because it is the vehicle for a deliberate equivocation meant to confuse any critical reaction.

Another process, related to the preceding one, lies in the use of crude tautologies. Thus, one passage in the text states that true scientists, like Joliot, are fighting on the side of the people; but the authenticity of these scientists does not need to be demonstrated independent of their political convictions—since there is only politicized science. It must therefore be understood that the true scientists are precisely the ones who fight on the side of the people. In other words, scientists who fight on the side of the people fight on the side of the people. The absurdity here hardly matters as long as the reader yields to the text and accepts the desired blurring of scientific value and communist conviction.

Moreover, these processes are only one aspect of a more general mechanism, which is the basic process of all Stalinist statements: petitio principii. The reasoning is always stated, the terms are always chosen beginning from an initial postulate that transcends all criticism and initially separates the world into Good and Evil: Soviet Good, Western Evil. The most frequent example of this attitude is the notion of "Western decay." That decay, so often mentioned, is never described or analyzed; its obviousness comes solely from the—theoretical—existence of its causes. A hypothetical etiology replaces positive investigation. Clearly it is a matter of a combat position that believes it possesses a universal truth and does not back down in the face of partial defects. Again, the pervasiveness of this process must be noted, and the extent to which it stamps all thinking and all art with Soviet obedience, so that it is no exaggeration to speak of the East as a veritable civilization of the Postulate.

Finally there is an obligatory process that gives the text thus constructed a kind of publicity that develops according to a systematic design: sudden and simultaneous publication of texts throughout the press on the same day; daily commentaries taken up by each newspaper over many weeks (the campaign connected to this business has still not ended); organized meetings in the Institutes and Universities, where resolutions adopt, with the same violence, the terms of the initial reports and become basic texts for this vast campaign. Stalinist propaganda proceeds deliberately through the launching of a "theme" signified by a word-type and imprinted in minds, nonstop, through all possible means. Positions for critical thinking are thus taken through successive campaigns, true tactical operations, each of which has a name. There was, for example, a "principality" campaign; here it is a matter of a "cosmopolitanism" campaign. This word is now in fashion; proposed as the subject of newspaper articles, repeated in all the exposés, it becomes—through this deliberately spectacular process—the new term that has just increased the lexicon of orthodox communism.

*   *   *

The very wide campaign against the ophthalmology review and "cosmopolitanism" in science is affecting, or is going to affect, Romanian scientists. Already the linguistics review edited by Rosetti, the rector at the University of Bucharest, had been the object of similar reproaches.[118] But the case of these scientists is, in the end, less tragic than that of Romanian intellectuals who subjugate themselves to Soviet imperatives and go beyond the slogans imposed upon them. That is the case with the author of the second report, the president of the Academy of the Romanian Republic, Trajan Savulescu. This academic, who owes all his training to French scholarship, does not hesitate to utter an indictment against Western scholars just as shameful as the endless blatant fawning addressed to Soviet science.

That part of the Romanian intelligentsia so embroiled in servility is, in the end, the saddest element of this whole affair. Trajan Savulescu's fate recalls the words of Vauvenargues: "Servitude debases men to the point of making them love it."

3

The Great Ties

1. Roland Barthes to Maurice Nadeau

Roland Barthes met Maurice Nadeau (1911–2013) in June 1947 through the intermediary of Georges Fournié.[1] Fournié was a Trotskyite like Nadeau, whom Barthes met in Leysin, where he was treated for tuberculosis resulting from his deportation to Buchenwald for resisting. Nadeau then edited the literary pages of *Combat*, where he would soon publish Barthes's first texts ("Le Degré zéro de l'écriture," which appeared on August 1, 1947). Nadeau would continue to publish Barthes's texts and speeches in *France Observateur* (precursor to *Nouvel Observateur*) as well as *Les Lettres nouvelles* (created in 1953) and *La Quinzaine littéraire*, the first issue of which appeared in 1966.

*　　*　　*

Wednesday evening, [1952]

My dear Maurice, I received your book this evening and, since I spent the evening at home, I have already almost finished reading it, because it reads itself, it holds together wonderfully, and I assure you that it has a *continuum* that will be a revelation for all your readers who are accustomed to reading you week after week.[2] For me, this book makes me happy because basically there is not a single point where I don't agree with you and I feel the same as you do about all these authors. With regard to substance, how easy it would have been to do a weekly! There's a potential instinctual unity, and your book conveys that to me very well, with great clarity—you know that I don't use that word lightly—and power that gives me deep pleasure and definite *confidence*—if that word doesn't shock you too much coming from me, who has done nothing or almost nothing, and directed toward you, who has already done so much.

It was only after my reading that I saw your group dedication in which I appear: let me tell you I was moved by it and I thought what a great fellow you really are, and that I would love to be able to work for you and with you again.

I'm saying this all badly of course, because it's coming from emotion and euphoria, but better than in person—which won't stop me from coming to see you very soon.

I didn't think this book was due out so soon and really, from every perspective, I was happy and delighted to see it appear.

Thanks again for having thought of me in the two dedications and for sending it to me.

Faithfully and affectionately yours,
R. Barthes

*   *   *

Saturday evening, [1954]

Dear Maurice,

I should have sent this text along to you some time ago, which Robbe-Grillet would very much like to see published in *Les Lettres nouvelles*.³
    Here is Robbe-Grillet's address:
    24, plaine de Kerangoff
    Brest, Saint-Pierre

In haste,
Best wishes,
R. Barthes

*   *   *

Thursday evening, [September 9, 1954]

Dear Maurice,

As you can imagine, Koupernik's article today in *L'Observateur* on Le Grand Robert will absolutely prevent me from publishing mine next week.⁴ First of all, it's a matter of too obvious and too close a duplication, bothersome because of the particularity of the subject, and then because what I say about theatrical hypnotism is too much at odds with the paper by this psychiatrist. I absolutely do not want to expose myself to "competent" refutations.

So I had to come up with a new paper, which I earnestly beg you to substitute for the first one. Dear Maurice, I am *absolutely* counting on you to make this substitution despite your likely indulgence for the repeats and my papers. If you have nothing better, I even think that this second paper could go first; it's a good subject, half-topical, half-general, as I would really like to do more often.

This Koupernik incident confirms for me the need to take precautions to avoid duplications. I'm more determined than ever to stay with you at *L'Observateur*, and you can count on me; but I think certain tendencies of the journal overall must come to an end. I'll make specific proposals to you on this subject when I return.

I'm going to try to telephone you this evening, because I'd like to be sure that you can stop my first article and replace it with the second. But, for now, forgive me all the countermands this fall. I hope I haven't made your job too complicated.

I'll revise the first paper and you can run it in *Les Lettres nouvelles* in October if you like.[5] Does that work for you?

In haste (until Tuesday),
Your friend,
Roland

*　　*　　*

Valence, August 21, [1955]

My dear Maurice, what a fuss over this article![6] You must have worried yourself sick about it (if you're in Paris), but let me assure you that I did too! I was all tied up with my courses until Friday, August 12, literally from morning till night, impossible to write a line.[7] We left on August 13; I couldn't make the family wait and, naturally as soon as the trip began, was barraged by major obstacles that kept me from finding the few necessary hours for work each day: upsets, hotels full, noise, etc. We had to land in Valence for me to find the two necessary days. The outcome isn't very good. It's a bit heavy and I botched the subject. Well, it's done. I assure you I was very worried about it. The family can tell you so. I know that I'm holding up the issue. And that was driving me mad. Please don't hold it against me too much.

Apart from that, a magnificent trip for what I saw of it through the Tour de France! We're continuing south. I return about the tenth, but I'm going to get to work now on the next mythology.[8] Trust me and don't worry.

If you have time, send me a note, general delivery Madrid, to tell me there are no hard feelings and where you're spending your vacation.

Faithful affection to you both, your old friend,
Roland

I'm sending the manuscript to Chantenay early tomorrow morning.

*   *   *

Hendaye, September 22, 1957

My dear Maurice,

Some fellow sent me this text to pass along to you, which I'm doing. It has certain qualities, I think, but is there something hiding behind this good rural realism? I can't decide.

I'll be returning to Paris soon; Hendaye has still not succeeded in obliterating the summer I had; that is to say, I'm working very badly, without enthusiasm or ideas. I'm drawing a blank.

Don't get angry, Maurice, but I'd like for us to talk about my participation on the editorial board.[9] Of course, it's not a burden, given my lamentably lazy way of participating, nor is it a responsibility, since I have absolute confidence in everything you do at the review. Rather it's a more general question for me. For a long time now I have wanted to withdraw formally from all such commitments that my laziness and my fits of solipsism, in fact, render illusory (Prix de Mai, *Arguments*, *Théâtre populaire*).[10] And if I do this, it must be for all of them. Tell me what you think. For nothing in the world would I want to upset you or cut myself off from you; you can count on me completely. But, how to say this, I'd like to set up this year for myself as a "sabbatical year," like American university professors get every seven years, twelve months "without responsibilities." Maybe leave Paris often, for example (for this reason I'm not going to resume my classes at the Sorbonne).[11] Basically, it would almost be easier for me to give you a new text sometimes than to provide a "Parisian" presence. This is probably a bout of subjectivity, not very pretty from an "engaged" perspective; but basically I prefer trying to let it run its course. Well, nothing dramatic or urgent here. Answer me from the general perspective of the review.

In haste, your friend,
Roland
Etchetoa
Hendaye-Plage

*   *   *

Urt, June 21, 1965

My dear Maurice,

It has been a long time since I've seen you—for the stupid reasons you know, being overwhelmed with work, with Parisian dissipation. But I think of you affectionately, faithfully, in solidarity as well now when everything you do, everything you have done is threatened (I know nothing more about it than what *Le Monde* said, but enough to infuriate and disgust me).[12] Please know that, as a friend from the beginning, I'm at your side and if you need me in any way at all, you must let me know. I won't be in Paris anymore during the summer, except for quickly passing through, but you can write to me. And in the fall we'll have a long chat.

Best to Marthe and you,
Your friend, Roland
Urt, Basses-Pyrénées

*   *   *

Urt, April 13, [1966]

Dear Maurice,

I'm sending you my note on Benveniste right away.[13] I would have liked it to be much better because the book is important, but it's very difficult to do. I only saw a way to approach the book once I was completely finished and sadly I'm too swamped with work to start over. At least these few lines, if you approve them, will highlight the book. I won't read the Revel or the Finas piece on me until I return to Paris next week.[14] I'm anxious to work quietly here and I have a good method of doing a whole block of reading from time to time; otherwise I waste time fretting. I'm leaving it to you, Maurice, to decide if there's some incompatibility between the Revel and my work with *La Quinzaine*.[15] You tell me no, and I trust you, but please, consider the problem one last time.* We can telephone when I return.

Very best,
Roland

*   *   *

---

*As if it were you and not me.

Friday, [April? 1967]

My dear Maurice,

Here's the short text on Severo Sarduy.[16] I'm afraid it may be a bit abstruse and that Erval will be livid.[17] But I don't have time to make it better and I would still like very much to help Sevoro, with your help. I'm leaving tomorrow for a week in Urt. If there's anything urgent, you could telephone me (47 at Urt, Basses-Pyrénées).

Your faithful friend,
Roland

*   *   *

January 21, 1969

My dear Maurice, I would really like to see you again soon, but in the meantime, would you agree to letting me talk about Jean-Louis Schefer's book, *Scénographie d'un tableau*, in *La Quinzaine*?[18] I've known J.-L. Schefer since he was very young; I like him, I admire him, I know he needs money, and I would like to help him, especially because his book, I know, is not easy to read or to critique, although, in my opinion, it is, fundamentally, remarkable. What do you think?

Your friend,
Roland

*   *   *

February 15, 1969

My dear Maurice,

Here's my text on Schefer. I realize that it's very elliptical. This is not, as I see it, a true review but only a sort of *alert*. I hope that it will do and I thank you for accommodating it. You know, you must be sure, that I would like to write for *La Quinzaine*, but you must also see that I'm hardly writing any articles anymore; l'École des Hautes Études has become a real job, very burdensome, and I'm endlessly struggling to retain at least the possibility of writing a book from time to time; and even that's in question. I'd like to talk to you about all this. For Marthe and for you, the affection of your old friend, Roland.

*   *   *

October 7, 1971

My dear Maurice,

You put me in an awkward position, because I don't have the heart to refuse you anything no matter what it is (to say nothing of my ongoing attachment to Michelet), but at the same time, those three months of the year are now beginning when I can do nothing but prepare my seminar. I have to provide two hours of new discussion each week, and I don't manage it very well.

  I don't have a block for continuous work before me. Thus, this Michelet appears at a very bad time.[19] So as not to be completely negative, could you combine something I could give you—say two pages, more an account than a critique—with another article? That I could do, if need be, as long as I don't have to read too much in advance and get weighed down with the Superego of a "review." What do you think?

  Try to call me some morning.

Your friend,
Roland

*   *   *

March 15, 1973

Dear Maurice,

Thank you again from the bottom of my heart for your article in *La Quinzaine*.[20] It made me so happy to feel all the freshness you bring to your reading, as you did for me more than twenty years ago.[21]

Your friend,
Roland

*   *   *

January 25, 1975

Dear Maurice,

It's a good idea and I'm going to try it.[22] As quickly as possible. Thanks for this proposal.

In haste but yours truly, both of you,
R. Barthes

*   *   *

October 26, 1975

Dear Maurice,

My deep sympathy, of course. I will give you the "paintings" you want—if that's not too ridiculous.[23] Just tell me when you need them and where to send them. As for the debate, no, I'm sorry; I no longer have any heart for these things. I handle them poorly, as I please, and that, as far as I'm concerned, benefits no one. It's partly a question of temperament; mine is hardly profitable at this point—and not a bit brilliant!

Your faithful friend,
Roland

*   *   *

December 23, 1976

Dear Maurice,

Thank you for asking me for this lesson.[24] I'm touched and would be touched to have the last "exam" of my life published by you who were my first examiner: confident and efficient. Of course it has already been requested, not only by Seuil, but also by Nora.[25] In fact, there's no decision to make, because the College—this is the rule—first publishes the text in a small volume, and it cannot be published (commercially) until six months after the copyright registration. What I can tell you is that I'm going to try very hard to give it to you—arguing from the emotional and symbolic factor that I mentioned at the start.[26]

Your friend,
Roland

*   *   *

February 21, 1977

Dear Maurice,

I do understand your plan, but as far as I'm concerned it won't be possible. I'm overworked, harried, swamped, and I desire only one thing: to withdraw from all "appearances." I can hardly bear anything involving public debate and I have decided as I get older not to force myself to do what makes me uncomfortable any more. All these reasons made me turn down Bernard-Henri Lévy despite his insistence in wanting me to participate in a debate with Attali at this same Beaubourg. I can't accept your request now having just refused that one. Really, it's not all that serious; I'm not a good debater and the theme of power belongs much more to Foucault and Deleuze than to me.[27] Please excuse me, Maurice, good luck, I wish you success.

Your faithful friend,
Roland

*   *   *

[February, 1979]

Maurice, a sign of my negligence, I can no longer find your telephone number, I don't have one for *La Quinzaine*, and my phone books are out of date! Thus this note: I'd like to ask you if we can change our Wednesday, February 21 appointment. I was able to get out of two meetings (on Thursday and Friday) in such a way that I have a few free days to go away a bit, a miracle during the term because I can no longer do that. If I reclaim Wednesday, I would be able to leave Tuesday evening and come back the following Monday. Can you call me (just not Friday morning) so we can arrange another time? And then I can get your telephone number.

Thanks.

Your friend,
Roland

2. Roland Barthes to Jean Cayrol

Jean Cayrol (1911–2005) is undoubtedly the contemporary writer on whom Barthes wrote the most. Their first contact was in January 1951, regarding texts from *Le Degré zéro de l'écriture* that Barthes had published in *Combat* in 1950 and that Cayrol had read.[28] But Barthes had already written his first article on Cayrol, which also appeared in *Combat*, a review of *Lazare parmi nous* (La Baconnière, 1950), regarding Lazarian man brought back from the dead, returned from Nazi concentration camps—Cayrol had been deported to the Mauthausen camp in 1942. Barthes's last significant text on Cayrol dates from 1964, a postscript to *Les Corps étrangers* (Seuil, 1959) titled "La Rature."

*   *   *

Monday, [July 1953] c/o [Pierre Guiraud,][29] Groningen, Netherlands

Dear Jean, having just arrived I had the chore of writing a hurried article for Voisin's theater review (biannual obligation, monthly check) and I am now emerging.[30] We're very happy with our stay here; I think we're all getting a good rest and I have the impression that Maman is happy, my brother is in excellent spirits, Lux the dog very busy. The car is serving us well; we take little outings in the afternoon. Yesterday we drifted along in the wind and sky toward the fantastic North Sea, leaden and cold, something like Van Gogh's bisters, with no more sun. For me, it's only in the evening that I feel caged in, because the very rural town discourages roving about, at least the superurban kind that's of any use to me. Intellectually, I'm completely blocked; I had a terrible time writing my ten pages on tragedy (absolutely cranked out in this happy country without spirituality) and I watched with horror as my sentences took on the density of Dutch cheese or a peaty polder.[31] So I'm afraid of starting on Michelet; I'm afraid of seeing it develop a red rind despite my efforts, whereas in Paris it might be more effervescent.[32] But all that is probably an illusion and I must shake it off. I have only been reading *Le Monde* and the Hachette guidebook here. I think that you're just about to leave Seuil and I hope these last days haven't been too difficult.[33] Let me repeat, you may come here whenever you like, on the condition that you understand the place can only offer you rest and nothing else, except perhaps, thanks to the auto, this sky, which is truly very beautiful, very big, very human, not vertical as in the East, but amply circular like large, loose folds.

I'm thinking of making the short trip to Hamburg or Amsterdam, but not for too long and I don't know when. For a weekend no doubt. The weather is not very good and I still have not executed my plans to exercise and lose weight.

Send my news of your vacation and Saint-Chéron.[34] In any case see you soon.

Your friend,
Roland
Come if you can.
c/o Guiraud, Van Ketwich Verschuurlaan
Groningen, Netherlands
Tel: 32–588

*   *   *

My dear friend,

First of all I must thank you for your book and for what you added there in your own hand, which touched me and made me happy.[35] I read it quite quickly because, as I told you, despite the "ingratitude" of your creatures—as in "ingrate," at an awkward age—there is in everything you do a kind of incantation, that gift for the continuous, pressure, tempo, "momentum" as Sainte-Beuve called it.[36] So that even before the reader wonders about their content, these books succeed, and one reads quickly, carried by the tension of an actual duration. I don't want to do a standard critique of your new book; I'm only formulating ideas slowly. I think that if I had to speak of it in the same vein—both thematically and genetically—as I spoke of your earlier novels in *Esprit*, I would try to show how this time you have organized material specific to the novel with a duration that comes close to the kind of concentration and then explosion in Time specific to the stream-of-consciousness novel.[37] I'm expressing myself badly, but it's certain that, whereas in *Je vivrais . . .*, as I said and as you had mentioned on the cover, the duration was a unilateral given, still incapable of concentration and superimposition, which was tragically striving toward the easier, more constructed, and thus more social Time of the Novel, here we have this specifically novelistic or historic Time, the definition of which is always the organization of a past beginning from a present.[38] Moreover I think that, on this level, if the novel is assumed from the first, it is to obey the main line of your work in general, work past and probably to come, which is to begin from a Vertigo-Time to discover the problem of the other. As Time is organizing, creatures reveal themselves; you must make this double movement felt, which is both the uneasiness and the glory of man (you know that in the Gospel, to glorify means to manifest in essence, at least according to Karl Barth).[39] I'm jumping around here and in bad philosophical form, but finally, if I actually had to talk about your novel, I think I would talk this time, more explicitly than the first time, about sociability or charity. I'm struck—even affected—by the *ingrate* nature—I'm repeating this word—of your characters; they are not *amiable*, and I think that is essential. All novels generally think of humans as a source of appeal; the novel chooses desirable, successful, interesting, passionate creatures, models of Evil or Good, in short, select human material that makes us dream. Thus, in other novels, there is generally no human problem other than the one of passion, which is basically erotic. Here, there are whole other relationships; beings are neither ugly nor beautiful. This is not a human anthology, a preparation for that apotheosis of sensual delight that crowns every novel. The human material of your novels introduces a sociology or a theology, that is to say, an order in which *the human* entirely absorbs *the person*. There's an almost monastic gaze, in any case one that is very absolute—if that word can take the superlative. That's why, despite the extraordinary everyday matter of your account, despite that specific sensitivity to phenomena that so often approaches irony, your novel—even more clearly than earlier ones—points to a kind of transcendence. I'm sure it's full of symbols, understanding the symbol to be a *naturally* figurative form of thought, "never being a translation, neither can it ever be translated" (this is Jean Baruzi speaking of Saint John of the Cross.)[40]

[. . .][41]

Saint-Chéron; the train arrives at 12:16. Till Saturday, then (a week from Saturday).

Warmly and faithfully,
R. Barthes
11, rue Servadoni, Paris VIᵉ

*   *   *

Saturday, Bordeaux, [early April 1956]

Yes, my dear Jean, I'm sending this note from Bordeaux, where I've come for two days with a friend, Olivier de Meslon, whom you saw once outside the [Deux] Magots, and who is from the area.[42] You're wondering if I may have forgotten you here. I wasn't able to call you before I left, and it seems to me, too, that it has been a very long time since I've seen you. I'm spending a night in Paris but leaving again immediately for a week in Annecy at Vinaver's to try finally to write that famous mythological preface there—which, for the moment, is all the more mythic.[43] I'll be in touch immediately when I return, about April 13. Dear Jean, can you rest a bit during this vacation? I'm thinking of you with all my affection and finally want to say—because this is why I began writing to you—how touched I was by your words in *L'Express*, touched and overwhelmed, because I feel so weak. All your responses were very beautiful; only you can be direct and nevertheless so reticent.

In much haste, dear Jean,
Your friend,
Roland
My kind regards to your mother.

Thursday morning, [January 14, 1965]

My dear Jean, I'm taking the train in a minute but how not to tell you that we (François B[raunschweig] and me) were *overwhelmed* by your film.[44] What power, what beauty, what mystery, and what clarity as well; it's heartrending and nevertheless I left it with the courage to live; it's ambiguous but without compromise. With what joy, we are profoundly *for*; I will say this wherever you want. Convey all this as well to Claude Durand, who I really feel gave the Cayrolian voice—inalienable, recognizable throughout—a place all its own. I'd like to talk to you about it, as soon as I return.

To you Jean with my *gratitude*—and my affection,
Love to you,
Roland
The acting is remarkable. No comparison to the latest "nouveau" films; finally a *serious* work that says what matters to *us*, and not only what matters to the history of the cinema.

* * *

[After 1977][45]

Jean, your book is very beautiful (I just finished it).[46] What writing, smooth, noble, shimmering—fragile as well, so much the opposite of the rising wave of vulgarity. Thank goodness you're writing! And I was happy and moved by our lunch. I'm less deaf now; my ear is getting better. To be continued soon. Call me before coming.

Your faithful friend,
Roland

3. Roland Barthes to Alain Robbe-Grillet

In his conversation with Roland Barthes during the Cerisy Collo-quium in 1977, Alain Robbe-Grillet (1922–2008) portrayed Barthes as a novelist and a writer, and, moreover, he revealed that his film *Glissements progressifs du plaisir* (1974) was an adaptation of Barthes's commentary on *La Sorcière* by Michelet. That appreciation is no doubt indicative of their relationship, in which Robbe-Grillet considered Barthes's important talks on his novels to be less commentaries or critiques than a work in progress, parallel to his own.

*   *   *

June 8, 1953

Dear Sir,

Please forgive me if I've been slow to thank you for having sent me your book.[47] Jean Cayrol told me about it; moreover I'd been alerted in passing by a certain type of critic (Coiplet) whose incomprehension is almost always the sign of an important work, which proves the critic serves some purpose after all.[48] For my part, I believe I recognize in your book the major themes (I'm using this word because I'm writing very quickly) of a new literature: time as destiny (that is, as tragedy); the absorbing power of the object (which is also a very new, still very clandestine form of tragedy); and finally, space itself as destiny, in the form of the circular-city, the city moreover representing symmetrically the *circulus* of time. I'm saying all this very badly, but if I had had to do a critique of *Gommes*, I would certainly have not talked about Simenon but rather Greek Tragedy.[49] One word more on the writing in your book, which seems to me wonderfully aware of the problems of contemporary literary language, and which resolves them—almost (this "almost" not dependent on you and perhaps constituting a sort of fourth tragedy, diacritical to your work).

I myself would be very happy to meet you. If you live in Paris, maybe we could get together sometime with Cayrol at Seuil.

Let me repeat that I have the very highest regard for your book, what confidence it gives me, and how sure I am that this is an *important* book, avant-garde, in a word *successful* (and I'd like to give that word a deeper meaning than that of success, a kind of historical meaning).

Please accept my cordial admiration.

R. Barthes
11, rue Servandoni, Paris VIe

*   *   *

June 12, [1953]

Dear Sir,

I wrote to you yesterday at Éditions de Minuit, but today I was given your Paris address. I believe Cayrol has spoken to you about our plan for a quarterly publication at Seuil, and we would be very happy to have you as a contributor.[50] Could we meet with you soon to discuss it? Would you be good enough to call me—or Cayrol—so that we can arrange a time for the three of us? As soon as possible would be best.

With warm and cordial wishes,
R. Barthes
11, rue Servandoni, Paris VIᵉ
Danton 95–85

*　*　*

Thursday, [June 1953]

Dear Sir,

Thank you for your letter. I'm sorry that you left Paris before we were able to see you, especially since I don't anticipate a visit to your area.[51] But please let me insist that you send us those short texts you mentioned as soon as you possibly can, which, according to what I know of you and what you yourself told me in one sentence, would correspond exactly to what I'm seeking for the part of the publication that falls to me.[52] As for the rest, it seems to me that, despite your misgivings, you must send them to Cayrol.

No one understands better than I do your need to write slowly and not very much. That rhythm of sedimentation is part of the very nature of what you say. I'm simply asking you to think of it positively, no longer as just a plan, but as something we are expecting from you and for which we are counting on you for the first or second issue.

I thank you in advance and ask you to accept my warm and cordial wishes.

R. Barthes

It's not because I write for *Les Lettres nouvelles* that I know about the critical notes they get, as you may imagine. As for giving them one myself on your book, that's very feasible, but in terms of timing I read your book too late. But *Les Gommes* is not going to vanish like that. . . .

*　*　*

Henday, September 23, 1953

My dear friend,

I read the texts that you sent to Cayrol. As with everything that comes from you, I found them *important*, and by definition the object of criticism, that is to say, literature in question. I don't know yet how we will present them in the review—where there are still structural issues to settle. What I do know is that your texts correspond *ideally* to the idea we have for this publication, and we thank you for them very much.

Moreover we can discuss all this if you're coming to Paris. I'm returning there in a few days. May we see you as soon as you arrive?

I'd like to talk to you about that critique of *Les Gommes* that Piel, of *Critique*, had me write.[53] I'd like to explain to you my reasons for hesitating to undertake it; it's because *I am not a critic*. In criticism I see only impasses, and the question for me would be finding a method. Also I feel I'm only authorized to speak of criticism but not books. Any criticism involves a method and that goes a long way.

We need to think about it, to talk. So, I repeat, let's get together.

And thank you for what you took the trouble to write about my book.[54] It was very nice of you to respond.

Until soon, I hope, and kind regards to you,
R. Barthes
11, rue Servandoni, Paris VIe
Danton 95–85

* * *

[Paris, October 14, 1955]

Dear Alain, thank you for your note, it was really a relief to me. Everyone is in such disagreement with me over this subject that you remain my only hope that this paper was at least written for someone. How lucky that person is the author in question.[55] But we'll talk about all this again.

Your travels are very mysterious. Let me know when they'll be over. And try to go to the Moulin Rouge some Thursday evening about 11 o'clock (entrance 300 francs, coat and tie required + 500 francs food and drink) to *see* (make no mistake about this!) an amateur strip-tease competition, infinitely richer than the Apollo![56] There you'll see the relationship between *awkwardness* and eroticism.

Warmest wishes and until soon,
R. Barthes

* * *

Hendaye, Friday, [March 20, 1959]

My dear Alain,

I've devoted the mythology that will appear in *Les Lettres nouvelles* on Wednesday, March 25, to the Round Tables and particularly those that the Nouveau Roman tirelessly holds.[57] Nothing new for you, since we've already talked about it. All the same, I think you're going too far! You're burning through your cards too quickly and increasingly so, I tell you. The next time, this will be a *letter to Robbe-Grillet*! Well, what, more publicity! That said, I'm looking forward to reading your opening, as promised.

Your friend,
Roland

*　　*　　*

[Paris,] December 20, 1961

My dear Alain,

I've been wanting to see you for a long time—and you too, I think—first and generally, out of friendship, second and specifically out of my concern to set right the kind of extended dispute that has mutually distanced us, from Velan's *Je* to *Marienbad*.[58] Weeks have gone by and I haven't gotten in touch with you because I'm tied up in a university affair (regarding a thesis) and because I only want to return to your work really fully and at depths; wanting to do it well, for the moment, I can do nothing. But that shouldn't stop us from seeing each other again. If you'd like, it could be after the holidays, in January, after the fifteenth. I'll call you then and you can invite me some Sunday afternoon for a cup of tea! How does that sound?

In the meantime, happy New Year, my old man, and my warm and faithful wishes,
R. Barthes

*　　*　　*

Paris, December 7, 1970

My dear Alain,

We are passed the time for complimenting one another (and moreover I never paid you any insincere ones!), but nevertheless I have to tell you what admiration I have for your *Projet de Rév* . . . .[59] It's so perfect a construction that there is in that perfection a kind of very beautiful fidelity to yourself, to what you have always wanted to do, a kind of *theoretic* secret to your art. In some way you've created the model (in Leibniz's sense) for your whole opus; hence the great power of the *swarm* (you're going to be widely copied, if that's not happening already). A movable model: what a beautiful idea. In short, I thank you for this work (even if Freud is absent from it, which distinguishes me a bit from you).

Faithfully yours,
Roland

4. With Michel Butor

Barthes's friendship with Butor (born in 1926) was less public than his ties to Robbe-Grillet or Philippe Sollers, yet their letter exchange reflects an almost familial intimacy between them. To get an even more concrete idea of their ties, one must read the very beautiful correspondences between Michel Butor, Georges Perros, and Pierre Klossowski, because this friendship was first of all that of a "band": Barthes, Butor, Klossowski, Perros, a band that formed around the years 1954–55.[60] What knitted them together was the piano (music for four hands with Barthes and Denise Klossowski or Georges Perros), writing, the theater. . . . Another way of assessing the ties between Barthes and Butor is to read Barthes's very important text on *Mobile* in which he outlines—notably through the notion of work-model—the first categories of a "conceptual" vision of literary work, developed in his last course at the Collège de France, "The Preparation of the Novel."[61]

Roland Barthes to Michel Butor (BNF)

Sunday, [late 1956]

My dear Michel,

I think that the major question that must be highlighted in everyone's awareness by our latest political traumas is this one: What exactly is the nature of the USSR?[62] I want to say that only a response of the deepest order, concrete, economic, and historic, would allow us to go beyond this unappeasing movement of convictions, choices, declarations, and signatures that is like a fluttering veil thrown modestly over that question in which hangs the whole future—or the death—of socialism. I'm reading much political writing all the time now; I dozed off a little on ideology and suddenly politics wakes us up—which is its cruel function. As it happens, I still know nothing, but all the same I believe that by applying oneself to learning about the political reality, some taboos—at least—collapse.

Send me something, if only a few words, like that; it makes me happy. And stay well in barbaric Helvetia.[63]

Yours,
R. Barthes

*　　*　　*

Monday, [March 1957]

Dear Michel,

I should have thought to send you *Mythologies* in Switzerland.

The term drags on, I see. Hang in there, by Easter the fight will be won. I don't think I'll be able to come to Switzerland: I'm giving a talk on clothing with Friedmann on April 3.[64]

I would love to see you, to talk with you—I'll admit it—about myself!

Yours,
Roland

*　　*　　*

May 21, [1957]

My dear Michel,

Poulot[65] tells me that you are making a quick trip to Paris for Pentecost: you'll get in touch with me, won't you?

I'm thinking of leaving for vacation on June 15 and coming to Geneva to spend part of a day with you. We'll talk about it.

Could you also exchange some money for me, as we discussed? About twenty thousand francs, is that within the realm of possibility?

I am doing—all affairs coming to a close—philosophy, that is to say, more modestly—or more superbly?—I'm reading philosophy, the existentialists. We'll talk about it.

Till soon,
Your friend,
Roland

Hendaye, Friday, [April 1958?]

I have only this souvenir from Holland[66] to offer in contrast to your beautiful card from Greece, which made me happy because you seem to be happy there.[67] The weather is dreadful here. I'm working well enough, half on Racine, half on my American course.[68] The dean of Middlebury, M. Bourcier, who is in Paris, would like to see you, with the intention of inviting you for next year.[69] He's asking me for a note of introduction: here it is! You would be able to work well here; why not come for a short time in May? I'll be in Paris for a few days early next month and will get in touch.

Yours faithfully,
R. Barthes

* * *

Middlebury College, Monday, [summer 1958][70]

A fascinating visit of course, but not without some distress. I'll tell you all about it. I'm thinking of you, both of you, with all my faithful affection. I think I'll spend my final month mostly in New York, which is an absolutely sensational city.[71]

Yours,
R. B.

* * *

Friday, [late 1958—early 1959?]

Michel,

In the end, I'll be spending the night tomorrow, Saturday, in Menthon, at Michel Vinaver's,[72] because I'm taking his son George there (and my American!).[73]

Don't expect me Saturday, but surely Sunday; I'll call you around noon (but be patient).

You can call me at Vinaver's if something comes up: no. 94 at Menthon-Saint-Bernard (Haute-Savoie).

Until Sunday,
Roland

* * *

Hendaye, August 3, [1959]

My dear Michel,

I blame myself for not being able to see you during my last trip to Paris—and for not knowing a better way to tell you I understand your worries—your weariness because here the singularity of the seventeenth century would better account for that body of small contingencies that reveal to our subjectivity the very unity of what's not going well in the world, in human relationships. All I can tell you—but you know this—is that such troubles are only left behind in the work, in that ongoing creation that we all await from you. It's easy for me to preach, although I assure you I'm not blind to my own frailty.

How many times I've stopped working for days at a time because of some injury, worry, indignity, etc.

I hope the whole family is well.

Work well,
Your friend,
Roland
Etchetoa
Hendaye-Plage

*   *   *

Hendaye, February 14, 1960

My dear Michel,

I'm in the process of reading *Degrés* but I don't think I need to wait to tell you how deeply this book affects me.[74] In my view it's your most beautiful novel, in any case the one I myself feel closest to; let me say that it's as complete as one of Plato's dialogues! I'm swimming in it like a fish in water, in the Ocean—perhaps also because I've been a teacher and teaching is basically the only *technique* that I like—and that I've been frustrated by. I also felt very close to your last text, *Répertoire*, the one in which you discuss how you came to the novel.[75] That is *me*! (except I never wrote poetry or—yet—a novel!). Besides, I would really like to write—not novels but *Tales*. In short, all of this work of yours gives me profound pleasure.

How are you, all of you? New York? The college? You *yourself*? Here, really nothing new—except Algerian anguish, which isn't new. I'm here for a few days to write a paper for the *Annales* on literary History.[76] After which, I will put my coat back on. Nothing of note,

I believe, not on the literary front or regarding friends. Work is long, subterranean, that's it.

Yours in faithful friendship,
R. Barthes

Michel Butor to Roland Barthes

Bryn Mawr, February 16, 1960[77]

Opening catalogues, glancing at magazines, deciphering labels, I think of you. If ever there was a country overrun by pulverulent micromythology, surely it's this one. What prodigious material for your criticism! Which sometimes offers ludicrous glimpses that return to us.

We're beginning to get acclimated. We were extremely tired the first few days, but now we're bouncing back and everything is going very well, provided that Marie-Jo gets some rest.[78] As for Cécile, she's flourishing and is a great success.[79] Marie M. was kind enough to rent us her car while she's away. Marie-Jo drives very well, and that's changing her life because even the smallest errand means going some distance. I'm setting to work on it, and also on getting a Pennsylvania driver's license (eighty-six questions and answers to learn by heart). Since the car has an automatic transmission, I hope that I won't have too much trouble. Moving again from Bryn Mawr to Middlebury with the second baby will probably not be uneventful. Our audacity takes people aback; they look on us like Martians.

At the end of the month I'm going to go and do a lecture almost every week until May (then, my family responsibilities . . .), which will take me as far as Los Angeles, and you can be sure that I'll arrange to make a detour through San Francisco.

Philadelphia is a fascinating city that I find intoxicating to explore. Like all my friends, you tell me, compared to New York. . . . But I'm lucky enough not to know New York yet. We only passed through it, heading immediately for Bryn Mawr to rest and get settled. I have to say, that first contact was electrifying. I'll come back full of things to say. That will allow me to bear the peace and quiet of Middlebury.

I haven't yet begun to work. There are so many pressing issues to settle. I'm beginning to get news about *Degrés*, and that's encouraging.

We're buried under snow, with a brilliant sun. Write to us. Is everything going better for you? We have news from Georges; he seems more relaxed.[80]

Warm wishes,
Michel Butor
Low Buildings
Bryn Mawr College
Bryn Mawr, Pennsylvania
USA
I'll no doubt end my class on the French essayists with you. Be prepared.

Roland Barthes to Michel Butor (BNF)

Hendaye, April 11, 1960

My dear Michel,

A note, however brief, to tell you I'm thinking of you faithfully. I hope this year is progressing well, that you're amassing your America—and preparing for your Middlebury—morally, of course.

What news here? Georges's book, you must have received it.[81] Piano with Denise, that's becoming more relaxed, it seems to me.[82] Le Nouveau Roman be damned; I'm not thinking about anything but sociology anymore, not even structuralism. I'm absorbed in various tasks. I'm going to start writing the essay on Fashion. I'm nervous. I wonder if *writing it* will even be possible. And nevertheless I must exorcize that. No traveling in sight. Peaceful, subterranean work (the optimistic assessment).

I hope the whole family is well.

Faithfully yours,
R. Barthes

Michel Butor to Roland Barthes

Bryn Mawr, April 17, 1960

My dear Roland,

Yes, everything is working out unbelievably well, but what acrobatics! Housing in particular this June, with the birth,[83] and moving, and "practical" preparation for Middlebury. That's beginning to take shape. We'll have Marie-Jo's sister come to help us. She'll be there June 17.

I'm bombarded with letters from Bourcier and Guilloton asking me for a great many notes, book lists, an hour-by-hour schedule for my class, etc.[84] You experienced that. There's no end to it. It's making me quite miserable because I have absolutely no time to think about it and I can't get out of it. However much one is used to doing ten things at once, there is a limit. . . .

As for America, I'm filtering enormous quantities of it. I leave for Los Angeles Thursday, two lectures; Saturday morning I arrive in San Francisco, where I'll wander about Sunday without a thought in my head. Returning here Monday, with a connection in Chicago.

I did receive Georges's book; it's very beautiful.[85] Marcel Arland asked me to discuss it in *La NRF*. Unfortunately, I can't at the moment. Do you know that Tania is expecting a baby?[86] Our problems are nothing compared to theirs.

As for the essay on fashion, you know how I'm looking forward to it. The writing will be [. . .],[87] except that what you'll have written will probably be quite different from what you're thinking at the moment. But isn't that the rule for any work worthy of the name?

Good luck. Send me your news soon.

Very best,
Michel Butor

Roland Barthes to Michel Butor (BNF)

June 6, 1960

My dear Michel,

A note, as always a bit hurried, life being as disappointing in Paris as in the USA. I imagine you're about to reach Middlebury; at least you'll be able to rest there (except for always having to change places at meals, which is mentally exhausting). And afterward, we'll have the pleasure of seeing you again. Here everything goes on, everything perseveres as ever. In principle, I've finished the preparation for my Fashion.[88] I'm going to write it up over the summer in Hendaye; first, I'm taking a very classical two-week vacation in Italy. Nothing on the literary front, at least to my knowledge (which is very limited), except the very beautiful, very important Kafka by

Marthe Robert.[89] We had the Prix de Mai and I deserted the Nouveau Roman for Velan's *Je*, which earned me R.Grilletist wrath.[90] I'm focusing only on this essay on Fashion, putting aside other work and even other interests for later; I can only ever be involved in one thing at a time: once more, a lack of openness! My ecumenicalism may only be diachronic.

Our friends are going their own sweet ways, from Poulot to Pierre.[91] Pierre really seems to be working on his third *Roberte*.[92] Poulot is always the one to whom I owe a letter![93] It has been a very long time since I've seen him. And there you have it.

This is only to say you're always in my thoughts. We're waiting for you.

Roland

*　　*　　*

[Hendaye,] Friday, [December 30, 1960]

My dear Michel, I'm wishing you all a good, happy, productive year. I'm sorry not to have seen you at all this term, but you were traveling and so was I; and work took up the rest of it. Until soon—although I'm leaving again for Canada until the beginning of February.[94]

Faithfully yours,
R. Barthes

*　　*　　*

March 2, 1962

My dear Michel,

A quick glance at the article by Kanters in *Le Figaro littéraire* puts an end to my laziness and prompts me to thank you for *Mobile*.[95] And to tell you that I myself love it.[96] You can well imagine, of course; you know there's nothing better, to my mind, than that very beautiful "dossier" that turns on itself, that epic catalogue whose ancestor (but you see it's a distant one) might be the wonderful descriptions from Greek tragedy or those of the Dutch painters I love so much; you've known how *to say* how full the world is, and I consider your work to be very novel for that. Kanters is an idiot; he believes that literature is meant to *express* something, there are "rules" for books, etc. He doesn't know that, on the contrary, literature consists of struggling with language and it's always right to carry that struggle to its extremes. He writes what Sarcey undoubtedly would have written on Mallarmé's *Le Coup de dés*.[97] Basically it's all very good, because it's very clear.

Until soon?

Warm wishes to all of you,
Roland

*   *   *

Sunday, November 25, 1962

My dear Michel,

Your card made me happy. Happy as well that your exile's coming to an end and that you'll be among us once again.[98] Of course you'll find Paris in its usual state: the intellectuals (like me) overworked, literature quite lifeless, it seems, the "Revue internationale" on the (delicious) edge of the abyss.[99] All the same, the essential thing for me once again this term is my seminar.[100] It's very unwieldy, it's a lot of work for me, but the work pleases me. If I only had that, life would be fine all in all; but there is all *the rest* of it, the maintenance activities, all that kills you, like the people of Antiquity, "for lack of knowing how to say no."[101]

Come home with an American novel. We're waiting for you.

Yours,
Roland

*   *   *

Wednesday, February 19, [1964]

Dear Michel,

I was happy to have word from you on your arrival.[102] I hope that you're now settled in and already at work; tell me a bit about what you're doing. For over two months I've been more removed from life than ever, not just my social life, but my relationships. I'm working hard, although on nothing important, piles of old things to finish up, but nevertheless I'm going to get through them and I think I'm finally going to have a free summer, free to do something *for myself* (maybe for the first time in my life). That's my big plan. Michelet had his *vita nuova* at about fifty; I'm approaching fifty and I have the same desire. I'm thinking, I'm resolving that I haven't yet written—that I'm going to write.[103]

Don't forget me in my Paris retreat, as I don't forget you in yours.

Faithful affection to you both,
Roland Barthes

Michel Butor to Roland Barthes

Berlin, March 8, 1964

My dear Roland,

Many thanks for your letter and your book.[104] I'm going to make a quick trip to Paris from March 16 to 20, and I would love to see you. You're going to receive an invitation from M. Jean-Pierre Delarge, director of Éditions Universitaires, for cocktails on the nineteenth, a party to celebrate the publication of a small work that R. M. Albérès wrote on me.[105] If you come to it, you'll make many people happy who are excited to meet you, but I'd much rather see you quietly if you have time, for example, for dinner the evening before, Wednesday March 18. Send me word *in Paris* to let me know if that's possible.

I saw Georges Poulot during my last trip through, around February 15.[106] He was going to [. . .][107] to see his father before quite a serious operation. I received a very worried letter. He moved to Douarnenez.

As for me, I'm immersed in Montaigne. I hope to have outlined a three-part preface before the sixteenth, and hand in the written manuscript by the first.[108]

Best wishes,
Michel Butor

＊　　＊　　＊

Berlin, June 2, 1964

My dear Roland,

It has been a very long time since we've had news from you, and we miss it.

I'll be making a short trip to Paris at the end of the month, from June 25 to July 1. Will you be there or already in Urt? I'd like to waste a friendly half-hour with you.

I see from Seuil's advertising bulletin that you're giving a lecture. On what? On the "Nouveau Nouveau Roman" as in the "Nouvelle Nouvelle Revue française"? You must tell me about it.

No doubt you've heard that G[eorges] P[erros]'s father died. With his mother coming as well as his stepdaughter Élisabeth, and with the baby they're expecting any day now, he's going to find himself at the head of a seven-person family![109] What an adventure!

Send me word to tell me where I'll have the pleasure of greeting you.

Best wishes,
Michel Butor

Roland Barthes to Michel Butor (BNF)

Urt, August 16, [1964]

My dear Michel,

We'll miss each other in Venice, sadly, because I'm not going until the end of September, about the twenty-seventh. And it would have been perfect to see each other—and to see each other there. When are you coming to Paris? I'll be there for three days at the beginning of September, but otherwise not until October, that is, after Venice. I'm immersed in "vacation," that is, over a month of travel (Morocco and Italy), and now here in Urt, in that bizarre rest that comes of relentless work. I'm catching up on things and mostly I'm working on this Rhetoric, which will be my next seminar.[110] I'm reading the Ancients, and am so fascinated by the coherence of their system that I don't really know anymore how I'm going to connect that to our literature—and yet that was my great idea at the beginning. I'd so like to talk with you about this—if we haven't already, because I know, I feel that you would share my interest. Some of them get on my nerves, like Cicero and even Plato; others delight me, like Aristotle and Quintilian: an unexpected division for a structuralist! The "heart" and "soul" are more powerless, more agitated than ever, "understanding nothing," but fortunately there's Quintilian and the classification of the *status causae*.[111] I'd love to see you, to rediscover that mixture of "heart" and "intelligence" for which I have such great need, given my solitude here, my problems.

Write to me,
Yours,
Roland

Michel Butor to Roland Barthes

Berlin, August 24, 1964

My dear Roland,

Really, I'm very interested in what you're going to tell us about Aristotle and Quintilian.

Our life is going to change a bit because we've decided to move to Paris at the beginning of the school year. We're buying a house in the south suburb of Sainte-Geneviève-des-Bois. The apartment on Rue Saint-Charles has grown too small and is for sale.

So you'll not be coming there anymore (at least not to our place). I hope you'll find the time to come to Sainte-Geneviève.

Marie-Jo left for Paris this morning to take care of all that. I have two sisters-in-law with me for the girls. I'll go to Paris myself in September, for that important business, but after Venice. Then I won't be returning there until November, but I still don't know which days; that will depend on my *Illustrations* collection.[112]

So I'll save you a few moments for three months from now.

Best wishes,
Michel Butor

Roland Barthes to Michel Butor

November 21, 1965

My dear Michel,

Thank you for your support in the Picard business.[113] I've been overwhelmed by it in all sorts of ways, and it has taken on something of the shape of a *crisis* (not internally of course, because the debate is a sham) that has exposed all kinds of ill will (literature, what a crystallizer for hatred! a truly magical object) but also friendships like yours. I'm struggling with an enormous workload, increased by this incident that I did not need. Dear Michel, I'd like to ask if you could come speak to one of my seminars in the second term. This year I'm pursuing a kind of investigation into Rhetoric and I've reached the contemporary period, that is to say, our literature, inquiring into either authors of the past like Mallarmé, or authors of the present, like you. If you accept, you are free (I insist on this freedom, knowing from experience that an author doesn't always want to assume the image attributed to him) either to talk about an experience of language that is not directly yours (that of the Surrealists, for example), or to talk about yourself, faced with the *art* of writing, and you can do this as you please, through a statement, followed by questions from the audience and from me, or directly through questions that I would submit to you. The seminar seems to be going well, friendly, informal. It would be a joy for me personally to welcome you to it. It's held on Thursdays, from 6 to 8 PM and the dates I can offer you are January 20, January 27, February 10, February 17, February 24, March 10.[114] Can you drop me a note before your return to let me know what you decide?

I wanted to call Marie-Jo before she left and then time got away from me, especially because I made a (very successful) trip to Morocco. Both of you please send news. I am yours in faithful friendship.

Roland

Michel Butor to Roland Barthes

Sainte-Geneviève-des-Bois, March 17, 1966

My dear Roland,

Much joy in the family on receiving your essay.[115] The three girls are delighted with the dedication. As for me, I want to tell you how I admire the text. When responding to attacks, it's very difficult not to descend to the level of your adversaries. You did a perfect job of making Picard simply the pretext, a microorganism among so many others in a drop of the Parisian broth. How all those quotes swarm about in the notes of your first part!

Now people are going to regret not coming to your defense. They're going to see how beautiful the struggle was, what nobility and intelligence there would have been! Too bad for them.

As for the second part, I hear it as profoundly right. Yes, many passages complete—by giving them a surer form—countless thoughts that I have had or with which I still contend. What strides you take! How much ground you've already covered! And let me congratulate you on having the courage to refer so often to those younger than you, something I'm hardly capable of.

So thank you with all my heart. Marie-Jo asks me to remember us to your mother with our best wishes. We're hoping to see you both soon.

Yours,
Michel Butor

Roland Barthes to Michel Butor (BNF)

Monday, [March 1966]

My dear Michel, your letter gave me immense pleasure. I need to know that emotionally I'm by your side and so I'm deeply touched to find you at mine. Thank you for taking the trouble to say this so well, and thank you for those very beautiful "cross-outs."[116] They transcend their own name furthermore by revealing that any "cross-out" is only superimposition, layered "ruins," sedimentation of meaning; and what shows through the surface is very beautiful. To all that must again be added one more very big thank-you for the seminar that you gave us and that we've talked about again often, with gratitude—I'll be in touch in April.

My best to you both,
Roland

*   *   *

Tokyo, May 26, 1966

Dear friends, you can imagine that no postcard in the world bears any relationship to what can really be seen here, which is, for me, incredible.[117] Notably, there is no postcard of faces, and I've never seen more beautiful people. I'm delighted for you that you're coming here, for all that you will get out of this country.

Until soon, your faithful friend,
Roland

*   *   *

Tokyo, Wednesday, March 29, [1967]

Delighted to learn here of the arrival of the fourth daughter.[118] I hope that Marie-Jo isn't too tired and that everything is going well. We've often spoken of you with Pinguet.[119] My second visit is outdoing the first in intensity, pleasure, and discoveries. I'm all perception and no writing. I return in eight days and will be in touch.

R. B.

*   *   *

My dear Michel,

I was happy to get your card. I'm in the midst of settling in, worries exactly parallel to yours, and I have not yet been able to work (although classes have not yet begun).[120] I can't talk about my stay yet; I have only a practical perception of all this and I don't yet know if my new life will fulfill the function (of work) that I've assigned to it. Before leaving Paris, I nevertheless had time to be absolutely *enchanted* by your Fourier.[121] It's the greatest of successes. You've produced a text homogeneous to its subject and that consequently destroys the antimony of the text and its critique. I'd like very much to see you, so that will be in June in Paris, when both of us return from our own latitudes (it's almost out of Jules Verne).

Best wishes, love to the whole family and to you,
Roland
11, rue Pierre-Sémard, Rabat

*   *   *

Paris, October 20, 1970

My dear Michel,

I was happy to hear your news, and what you said about Fourier touched me (I've had hardly any response, except for yours).[122] Of course I wanted to dedicate it to you, but I was afraid that might seem too predetermined by your own dedication; we'll have to wait for the next text. I've just returned for good from Morocco. I'm deeply depressed, overloaded, that goes without saying, but in a way that cuts me off from that *laziness in writing* that basically makes all writing strong somehow; thus I'm cut off from my desire. I hope to see you without fail when you return to Paris; try to save a little time for me.

Love to all,
Your faithful friend,
Roland

*   *   *

My dear Michel,

I was happy to hear your news but a little saddened by your practical difficulties, which I can well imagine.[123] As for the troubles with the University, I have the same kind of problem; it's a question of modifying the statute of the École des Hautes Études, and then this would raise the problem of the thesis, which I've always tried and been able to avoid.[124] I'm finished in Geneva, and despite the fatigue (due, above all, to the fact that I had never prepared classes in advance), I'm retaining the best memories from the experience.[125] Everyone was extremely kind, I liked Geneva . . . and I would happily do it again (at least I had that alibi for all those meetings that bore me to death here).

Now I can resume my own work a bit; I'm starting on Sade again—but I'm buried under everything else.[126]

I'm looking forward to seeing you again, dear Michel.

Love to all the family and all my faithful warm wishes,
Roland

*　　*　　*

Paris, October 20, 1977

Michel, my mother is very, very sick; practically all I do is take care of her and that keeps me from other activities. I haven't even been able to think about resigning from the Médicis, as I announced to you.[127] So I will vote in November, but without being able to attend the meetings no doubt. For the moment, I don't have any names, except maybe for the foreign prize, Goytisolo or Bianciotti.[128]

Thank you for having written to me, dear Michel,
Your friend,
Roland

5. Roland Barthes to Jean Piel

The first contact between *Critique* and Roland Barthes goes back to the year 1954, when, in the January issue, Jean Piel[129] paid homage to *Le Degré zéro de l'écriture*.[130] That same year, Barthes published his first article in the review started by Georges Bataille with his famous text "Littérature objective," devoted to *Gommes* by Alain Robbe-Grillet. In 1962, shortly after Georges Bataille's death, Jean Piel put together a new team that included Roland Barthes on the editorial committee with Michel Deguy and Michel Foucault.

*　　*　　*

[June 24, 1959]

Dear friend,

Here is my text on *Zazie*.[131] I'm afraid it may not be very clear, but I was pressed for time. Do you have something planned on the work of Edgar Morin?[132] If not, I have the idea of starting on that project—but I haven't spoken to him yet, I don't trust myself.

Best to you,
R. Barthes
I don't need an offprint.

*　　*　　*

August 24, 1961

Dear friend,

Don't apologize; it was up to me to write to you, to give you an answer, I recall that very well, but what can we do. To finish *La Mode*, I have to resume so many tasks that I'm still very tied up. Still, I want to try to do something for you quickly. There are three possibilities; choose according to your own plans:

1) The Foucault.[133] It's a possibility, but Michel Foucault told me that Bélavel asked for the book, maybe to pair it with the Michaux?[134] When in doubt I prefer to back off, not to deprive anyone of it, especially because I'm not qualified to discuss it.

2) The Girard remains a possibility but my copy is in Paris, so that will delay things again.[135]

3) I have my own idea for an article, but drawing its components from the books you've already mentioned—or probably already reserved. It would be something on description in literature. It could include:

—Ricardou: *Observatoire de Cannes*;—Leiris: *Nuits sans nuit*;—Brosse: *Ordre des choses*;[136]—Robbe-Grillet: *Été dernier à Marienbad*[137] (the text appeared in *Tel Quel*, which unfortunately I only have in Paris).*It could be called something like "Description, space, language."

Tell me your choice soon. Warmly and faithfully yours,
R. Barthes
Urt, Basses-Pyrénées
I don't think I'll return to Paris before September 20.

*　　*　　*

[September 3, 1961]

Dear friend,

Thank you for your letter and your mailing. I'll hurry and read the Foucault carefully (it's undoubtedly a very good book) and the Girard, and I'll let you know very soon what I decide, since you're leaving the choice to me. I'm really leaning toward the Foucault because I want to write an essay on literature and I don't like burning through my cards! (I don't have that many of them); but maybe the Girard, who verges a bit on my own formulation of things. . . . Well, in three or four days, I'll write to you and start to work.

Yours ever,
R. Barthes

*　　*　　*

September 17, 1961

Dear friend,

I decided in the end to discuss Michel Foucault (here's the text).[138] I know you would have preferred something on literature, because you no doubt have plenty of philosophers to discuss a philosopher. But not only does this book present me with an exciting problem (that unfortunately I didn't succeed very well in making clear in my text, but it's done), but neither Girard nor *Marienbad* prompted enough ideas for me to write about them, not without spinning them out. The Girard is very strong, but for me fairly irritating and I don't like getting involved in controversy, as least not in *Critique*.[139] And *Marienbad* is beautiful but it would require taking up

---

*Thinking about it, this text wouldn't work very well for this article. I can imagine a fourth article on this text alone (but it only appeared in the journal), a way of taking stock of Robbe-Grillet. [In 1954 Roland Barthes published "Le Point sur Robbe-Grillet?," which was reprinted in *Essais critiques* (*OC*, vol. 2, 452–59).—Ed.]

the whole question of Robbe-Grillet again, and for the moment I can't be bothered with that. So there you have it. I hope there will be much less time between the texts I give you in the future. Forgive this long silence, the brevity of my text, and know I am faithfully yours.

R. Barthes
I'm returning this week.

*　　*　　*

[late 1963–early 1964]

Dear friend,

I received your note. As you know, I'm in Urt for a few days. I'm thinking of returning Wednesday and will then be available for the meeting you discuss; please telephone me as early as Thursday. I'd like to help you more than I do (which is, alas, none at all), but I can't. Everything comes down to this: my life is too busy given the inherent slowness of my work; my output is too low in relation to demand, as modest as it is, and as much as I control it. A part of my life goes to Hautes Études and I can't reduce that share: a weekly seminar to prepare and re-create each year (unlike university courses), articles for specialized reviews like *Communications*, theses to finish. And as minimal as it is, a part of my life goes to "literature"; and from time to time I have to write a preface here or there, each time (and it's rare, I assure you) that I need my writing to be transformed into a bit of money. And with all that, I have the increasingly urgent—and oppressive—feeling that I'm missing the essential part, which is for me to write something that I will crudely call my work. I don't have pretensions; I admit that my personal dilemma lies in how slowly I write. I can't do otherwise because it's wisdom and maturity that bring me into alignment with this slowness. I must honestly tell you that I can't promise you anything for *Critique*. I have a backlog of several months, which is absolutely imperative, and I can't blindly add to it with promises that I can only honor by never undertaking. That situation must come to an end for me, because I feel like I'm exhausting myself in the inauthentic (I've just gone forty-eight hours, which may explain this language). I love *Critique* and I love you; that's why I came to you. I don't have to go on here, but there's no question of me accepting in this agreement (which, alas, is not a competition) the least obligation (of an annual nature, as you mentioned). I admit (I do more than admit, I positively believe) that position is unsustainable; the uselessness of someone is never justified. Thus I think sooner or later I'll have to consider stepping down, so that the reality of the committee coincides with its form, which is the just end of any enterprise! You'll see, we'll see when this can be done with as little fanfare as possible so as not to disrupt an already-diminished group. I want to avoid any upheaval at *Critique*, but basically there can be no ambiguity: any editorial participation exceeds what I can or want to do, and nevertheless, let's be clear, that's really the only way to help you.

Once more, I'm not dramatizing or even resolving anything. We have time to rethink this and discuss it again. But I believe that the future of my participation is ineluctably negative.

Until very soon, with all my faithful best wishes,
R. Barthes

*   *   *

Paris, October 24, 1965

Dear friend,

Sollers asked me to propose to you this short text by him on Pleynet.[140] Since the text is excellent, that makes it all the easier for me to do so. What do you think? Also, Wahl (François) is after me to find out where the Verstraeten is.[141] Have you talked to him about corrections to make? And finally, I really must see you to discuss the Picard business with you.[142] Without wanting to escalate it, I've almost decided to respond, but don't know yet in what form or where. I'd love to get your advice on this. Could we see each other soon?

Yours faithfully. I received the Queneau.[143]
R. Barthes

*   *   *

November 10, 1965

Dear friend,

In very great haste, before leaving for Morocco. I don't want you to have the impression that I'm neglecting *Critique*'s hospitality toward my response. God knows it's as important to me as our friendship. But as I'm anxious to respond to Picard in a tract, as a way of having a bookstore presence, I can't issue multiple responses (that would be to make the opposite mistake!). If we could find someone to show *Critique*'s solidarity with regard to the *attempt* of Racine, that would be perfect, but you see I can't be the one to do it.[144] This note is especially to tell you (better to write this than to say it) how deeply comforted I was by your kindness.

Until soon,
R. B.

*   *   *

[August 27, 1966]

Dear friend,

I add to my guilt by being so slow to respond to your letter. My summer is more proletarian than the rest of the year because all my deadlines come now and I can't stop working. I read your wonderfully tantalizing list; many upcoming items are appealing: the Wetherill (who is this?)[145], the Todorov,[146] the Kempf, the Lourau,[147] the Batany, [148] the Deguy,[149] the Attal,[150] the Le Bot,[151] the Bleman[152] (I'm naming my "first choices"). You see I would be an excellent subscriber to the *Critique*. It all looks very good to me and I admire your ingenuity in eliciting the necessary texts. As far as I'm concerned, I beg you with all my heart not to be discouraged. For about two years now I've been trying to resolve a much-too-busy work situation, to deal with very old commitments, complicated—although I can't do anything about it—by professional (Hautes Études) or money-making (like Enquêtes) tasks. I'm patiently working away at it. You have no idea all the things I turned down in the last six months; I'm no longer accepting anything. When my accounts are settled, four or five months from now, I'll adopt a new rhythm, which I absolutely need at this time in my life, and then I assure you that: first, I'll give you texts regularly; and second, I'll give you more help with editing. What I'm telling you here is not some kind of trite—or thoughtless—stalling tactic. My connection with *Critique* is tied for me to more freedom to work—and so it shall be done!

You know my whole summer; I'm doing nothing but work, which fortunately I can do very quietly here. I don't think I'll return before the end of September and we should be able to see each other then (I'm going to the USA from October 15 to 30).[153]

I hope you're doing well. With regard to everything I just wrote to you, I send you my faithful affection.

R. Barthes

* * *

Monday, [early 1967]

Dear friend,

In thanking you again for the lovely evening the other day, I'm sending you Badiou's text.[154] It's long and difficult and unappealing to me personally.[155] But the exceptional quality of the thinking is clear and it seems to me beyond doubt that it must be published—with the reservation about the note on Foucault, which, for me, would present no problem but for which the imprimatur of the affected party must be obtained.[156] If Foucault doesn't respond, really doesn't, I think the text must be published all the same.

All my best wishes,
R. Barthes

* * *

Paris, May 11, 1967

Dear friend,

On rereading it, I really find Girard's text remarkable, not only worthy of publication, but requiring it.[157] So the only problems are the ones you saw: its length (but Girard, I believe, is willing to shorten it) and its relationship to Lacan, which is too vague for it to pass as a review of his book—a review nevertheless necessary. An issue loosely centered on psychoanalysis (Lacan) would clearly be an excellent solution; or else putting Girard in that anticipated issue on criticism . . . ? (an issue on something a little broader than criticism would be better: the theory of literature, literature and symbolism, etc.). I return from Italy May 20. Let's get together then?

Yours,
R. Barthes

* * *

[June 27, 1968]

Dear friend,

Thanks for your note. I understand the idea of doing an issue on the university. I agree but, if I may say so, under very specific conditions: that it's not an analysis of events and even less a body of testimony (every review is taking this route these days and I've been asked ten times to give . . . the same text—which can only be the same text; and again: very difficult to do, lacking distance), but truly imagining what the desired university would be. Because this much is clear: in everything that's done and written, the incompetence is the most distressing thing (for my part, I'm convinced that this incompetence is not improvised: in fact, the "movement" aims, profoundly, to eliminate any university, and targeted by both the "revolutionaries" and the "technocrats," there's little chance that it will survive!).

I'll be in Paris for three days beginning Monday, the first. Can you call me (maybe Monday about noon)? Let's try to see each other—maybe with the others; that would make me happy.

Best to you,
R. Barthes

*   *   *

[July 25, 1968]

Dear friend,

Allow me to send you, for *Critique*, an excellent text by Todorov on Benjamin Constant.[158] It was first anticipated for the *Langages* review, but it didn't fit with the whole; it's not linguistic enough—which would be an asset for *Critique*, on the other hand. See what you think; of course, ask the others; but I think it would be good, it would be a text on literature, which is always invaluable. And I believe Todorov would agree to it.

My health is forever unstable, fragile, and sometimes that's depressing. I hope you at least are enjoying a few days of vacation as you said you'd planned.

Yours faithfully,
R. Barthes

*   *   *

[March 19, 1969]

Dear friend,

The fellow who wrote me the good (in my opinion) text on Cocteau-Derrida would like to do an article—for *Critique*—on the Buñuel film *Le Voie lactée*.[159] Maybe this offer would be an opportunity to introduce a text on film from time to time—so as to abolish, at least in principle, the traditional separation between text and film? What do you think? I didn't give him the go-ahead before getting your opinion. Write me a quick note on this, if you can.

Yours friend,
R. Barthes

6. With Claude Lévi-Strauss

Relations between Roland Barthes and Claude Lévi-Strauss (1908–2009) were complicated: Lévi-Strauss's refusal to direct Barthes's thesis, his bittersweet mocking tone with regard to *S/Z*,[160] but in contrast, Lévi-Strauss's support during the violent attacks in *Le Monde* at the time of the quarrel with Picard regarding *Sur Racine*, and especially, even more essentially, his support during Barthes's election to the Collège de France. For his part, even while constantly paying homage to one of the founders of structuralism in France, Barthes was able to distinguish himself from Lévi-Strauss, and especially from the tendency toward positivism in Lévi-Strauss's work and toward binarism with which he is associated, through Barthes's thinking on degree zero and the neutral.

Roland Barthes to Claude Lévi-Strauss (BNF)

Paris, October 3, 1961

Dear Sir,

When you agreed to meet with me a few months ago, I spoke to you of my work on Fashion.[161] I have now finished that work, at least a certain form of that work, because I can still see many corrections and additions to make.[162] At least I have a sufficiently coherent manuscript to offer now for criticism. I would like very much to show it to you. I am worried about taking up your time, but it seems to me that it is precisely your perspective it now requires. If you agree, I could deliver the manuscript to you.

Please forgive my indiscretion and accept my expression of respectful and deep friendship.

R. Barthes
11, rue Servandoni, Paris VIᵉ
Dan. 95–85

Claude Lévi-Strauss to Roland Barthes

October 4, 1961

Dear Sir,

I am ashamed to answer you with an equivocation, but it is not a quick, casual glance that you want from me, and in the present circumstances, it would be impossible for me to offer any more than that. I have just returned a small book to the printer, I have to finish another more important one before the end of October, and then I have to concentrate on preparing my classes....[163] All that leaves me without respite. I regret this all the more because I very much look forward to your book. The study that you published in a recent issue of *Annales* shows you in full possession of a method that I find promising, especially as you apply it to unexplored subjects.[164]

Please accept, dear sir, my most cordial wishes.

Claude Lévi-Strauss

Roland Barthes to Claude Lévi-Strauss (BNF)

Urt, December 24, 1965

Dear friend,

Returning from traveling, I found both the page from *Le Monde* and the clarification, of which you sent me a copy.[165] I find ample consolation in the second for the first, and I am deeply touched that you took the trouble to write these lines to J. Piatier.[166] Although, to tell you the truth, I do not know if she will publish them. Their relentlessness in this affair is both so incomprehensible and so implacable. But what matters to me is not being wrongfully separated from what you do; wrongfully: I mean, by someone other than you or me. That is why your intervention is so important to me.

I thank you for it and convey my warmest wishes.

Roland Barthes

Claude Lévi-Strauss to Roland Barthes

January 16, 1966

Dear friend,

I have launched into *Critique et vérité*, in all innocence moreover, having not read Picard's pamphlet. To be frank, I am not at all sure I completely agree with you. First, because in defending "nouvelle critique" in general you seem to cover many things that hardly warrant it, in my view. And then, because of an eclecticism that is demonstrated in too much indulgence for subjectivity, affectivity, and, let us use the word, a certain mysticism with regard to literature. For me, the work is not open (a conception that opens it to the worst philosophy: that of metaphysical desire, of the subject justly denied, but in order to hypostatize its metaphor, etc.); it is closed, and it is precisely that closure that allows an objective study to be done on it. In other words, I do not distinguish the work from its intelligibility; structural analysis consists, on the contrary, of turning intelligibility in on the work. And, unless you want to fall into a Ricoeurian kind of hermeneutics, it seems to me you must distinguish, more radically than you do, the inherently and objectively determinable forms (which are the only ones that interest me) from the insignificant content that humans and centuries may pour into them. Please see in these quick thoughts only the effect of an immediate reaction that leaves me not in the least insensible to your always-impeccable form and to so many profound and accurate remarks. I will be thinking about your text for a long time and I am grateful to you for raising these questions.

Very cordially,
Lévi-Strauss

Roland Barthes to Claude Lévi-Strauss (BNF)

Paris, January 14, 1967

Dear friend,

I have two big thank-yous for you: for being kind enough to send me your second *Mythologiques*[167]—which I have begun with great impatience and already very great joy—and for agreeing to accept me into your research laboratory, as Greimas has just informed me, which makes me very happy and will facilitate many things, I believe.

Thanks again and best wishes,
R. Barthes

Claude Lévi-Strauss to Roland Barthes

January 17, 1967

Dear friend,

You have always had a rightful place in the research lab—a reserved pew like the manor lord at his village church!—and please know, if I have never mentioned it, it is solely out of respect for a certain idea of your independence that you have been able to create. I say "a certain idea," because that independence itself cannot be questioned. Moreover, what the laboratory can do to assist you amounts to hardly anything, as you know, but by agreeing to add your name to our staff, you bring us additional prestige, and I am the one who should be thanking you. At least this mystical union gives me hope that we will have a few additional occasions to chat.

Warm wishes,
Claude Lévi-Strauss

*   *   *

Paris, April 5, 1970[168]

Dear friend,

Returning from the country, I find your letter and *L'Empire des signes*, and I do not want to be slow in thanking you. The book produced by your fertile pen touched me all the more deeply because at the age of six I was transformed into a Japanese art fanatic by a gift I received of a Hiroshige print. I spent my whole childhood and adolescence playing the little collector to the point that I became almost an expert for a time. And perhaps it is to preserve Japan as a myth that I have never been able to bring myself to go there. So I was delighted to visit it with you as a guide, since you declare your intention from page one to treat Japan as a myth. . . .

Since my last letter, I have come up with a bundle of additional arguments.[169] Zambinella being physically present in the story in the guise of an old man, the symbolic genealogy is read from the bottom up, the actual genealogy from the top down. So only the second level remains invariant. Now, par[agraph] 433, Mme de Lanty inverts Zambinella, and Mme de Lanty is "brotherless" whereas (407) Zambinella asks Sarrasine to come fill that position, left empty in actual genealogy. Following the same logic, the first level of the symbolic genealogy must correspond to the third level of the actual genealogy, that is to say that (sarrasin—"Sarrasine") < (Filippo—Marianina). Now it is remarkable that the lexical item (sarrasin = Arab from Spain), totally absent in the text and that I postulated to balance the system, is implied in the patrilineal filiation of Filippo, who can only get from his father, "dark as a Spaniard," (24) his "olive complexion, thick eyebrows, fiery velvet eyes" (22). The system is thus closed by the transformation of the maximum space (Filippo—Marianina), that is an oblique 1st/3rd level relationship, into a minimum space (sarrasin—Sarrasine) where, subject to inflexion, the space becomes minimum ("Incestuous") between two terms rendered perfectly "horizontal."

No need to respond to these last remarks, to which I attach no more importance than they merit.

Cordially,
Lévi-Strauss
P.S. On the subject of inversion (Zambinella/Mme de Lanty), there would also be something to say about the endogamy of the first (who can accept a brother, not a husband) and the exogamy of the second, who has no brother, but does have a husband whose exotic-exogamic nature is stressed by the text and reinforced by the story of Jaucourt, the type of lover coming from outside "to a strong woman, full of energy and passion," comp. (21) and (443).

*   *   *

Paris, January 5, 1972

Dear friend,

Thank you for your note, but there was nothing to worry about. The mail has not been reliable these last few months, especially in my neighborhood . . . and many letters did not reach me. I was only asking because I wanted to make sure the distribution of review copies had been done correctly.

During the last vacation, I read and really liked your *Sade, Fourier, Loyola*. Unfamiliar with the last one (and already knowing the text), I am more taken with the other two and especially with Sade, about whom you speak excellently, it seems to me. I have always thought that it was by way of logic and the combinatory that he could best be approached. And you demonstrate that with incomparable perception and grace.

Warmest wishes,
Claude Lévi-Strauss

Roland Barthes to Claude Lévi-Strauss

Paris, June 10, 1973

Dear friend,

Only yesterday I received the card from Plon inviting me to the June 4 reception.[170] I am sorry; if I had received it sooner, you know, of course, that I would have come to give you my best wishes and tell you how delighted I am with this (ritual) "passage" of your book into a new milieu.

Please forgive my involuntary absence and accept my faithful friendship.

Roland Barthes

*   *   *

Paris, November 9, 1975

Dear friend,

In thanking you for your double book on Masks, I promise you that I am not simply performing a gesture of gratitude, however sincere.[171] In reading you, I found a kind of exhilarating pleasure; for the first time I think, something is truly revealed about that enigmatic and fascinating object, because the illustrations take one's breath away. I experienced this book as an extraordinary structuralist lesson *in the presence of the object itself*. It achieves a perfect balance, which the Skira collection makes possible.

So I thank you for sending this book that I cherish—and assure you of my respectful and faithful friendship.

Roland Barthes

*   *   *

Dear friend,

I have learned that the Literary Semiology chair has just been declared vacant at the Collège de France. I am applying for the position and would like to thank you again for your support.

Yours ever,
Roland Barthes

*   *   *

[Paris,] December 3, 1975 (*sic*! 1976)

Dear friend,

I was going to send you a note to convey to you my deep gratitude for your support and your friendship. My presence at the Collège, in many respects, would have been unthinkable for me, without you.

Thus thank you with all my heart.

R. B.

7. With Maurice Blanchot

Maurice Blanchot (1907–2003) devoted two major texts to Roland Barthes. As early as 1953, he was one of the first to recognize the importance of *Le Degré zéro de l'écriture*, which may have provided him with the missing signifier for his own thinking—the Neutral. He paid just as much tribute to *Mythologies* in 1957.[172] The period when they saw each other most often was in the early 1960s during the "Revue internationale" venture in which Blanchot enlisted Barthes. Political differences must have played a role in their growing apart beginning in the 1970s, but the extreme proximity of their thinking no doubt separated them as well. Blanchot powerfully reentered Barthes's thoughts during his last course at the Collège de France on the preparation of the novel.

The letters we found between Barthes and Blanchot mainly involve the "Revue internationale" project, begun in 1960 and reaching its height between summer 1961 and summer 1963. This review, with its provisionary title of *Gulliver*, and its very ambitious plans for revitalizing writing practices and bringing together writers and intellectuals, especially Germans, Italians, and French ones, failed.

Barthes evokes the memory of it in an interview in 1979, speaking very warmly of Blanchot.[173]

Roland Barthes to Maurice Blanchot

May 12, 1962

Dear friend, thank you for your book and the personal words you included with it.[174] The work I'm doing at the moment on this semiology of Fashion, which I've madly embarked upon, sometimes makes me so unhappy (even though it's a necessary enterprise for me nevertheless) that your book arrived as a true consolation; each time I read a "dose" of it, it's as though I'm rediscovering a *true* language, of which I'm very much deprived right now. I'd like to talk to you about all this some day soon. I don't know if you're usually in Paris, and if you would agree to it, but it would make me happy.

Yours,
Roland Barthes

*   *   *

Thursday, [June 18, 1962]

Dear friend,

Could we see each other briefly before my departure (I think I'll leave Wednesday)? On the off chance, let me propose next Monday, June 25, at 7 PM to you, at the Café de la Mairie, on the corner of Rue des Canettes and Place Saint-Sulpice. If that doesn't work for you, could you call me (Danton 95–85); otherwise, until Monday?
    I'm looking forward to seeing you.

Yours,
R. Barthes

*   *   *

Tuesday, [1962?]

Dear friend,

Thank you for your note. I'm leaving for a slightly extended weekend but I think I'll be here toward the middle of next week. I'll drop you a line immediately to suggest a date.

Until soon, then, yours,
R. Barthes

Arguments

Saturday, [July 1962][175]

Dear friend,

I tried to call you, without success. Maybe you're not in Paris? I simply wanted to tell you that I'm back and would be happy to see you again.

Yours,
R. Barthes

Maurice Blanchot to Roland Barthes

Paris, 48 rue Madame, July 31, [1962]

Dear Roland,

I called you several times, I myself having been gone several times. I'll be back again sometime during the month of September. If, at that time, I mean when you return, you could let me know, I would appreciate that, as I'd like to see you, if only for disinterested conversation.

This note, then, only to express to you kind regards.

M.

*   *   *

Paris, 48 rue Madame, Bab. 14–12, September 28, [1962]

Dear friend,

You'll recall our conversation and how happy I was that you agreed to take part in the organization and development of the planned review.[176] The German and Italian editorial staffs are ready to begin work, so we must get ready to begin our own.[177] And we've decided, as least as long as we don't have our own office, to meet every Wednesday at 2 PM at Dionys Mascolo's (5, rue Saint Benoît, third on the left).

We all hope very much that you can participate in these work sessions and each of us (all of those to whom I've spoken) appreciate how useful your presence would be, particularly in these early stages when a plan is ready to take shape but remains malleable and modifiable.

The editorial difficulties are, in principle, resolved (with Galli-mard as the sole publisher of the French edition, as Suhrkamp will be in Germany and Einaudi in Italy).[178] Budgetary negotiations are still underway.

I hope to see you. Let me express to you my strong feelings of friendship.

Maurice Blanchot
It's true, I don't know if you're in Paris at the moment.

Roland Barthes to Maurice Blanchot

Monday, [October 1, 1962]

Dear friend,

I've just returned. I'm still very much on board with your venture. The problem is that I'm not sure I can attend your sessions each week. In any case, this Wednesday (October 3) is unfortunately not possible. Let me know if there's definitely a meeting the following Wednesday, October 10. What can we do to maintain regular contact without these weekly meetings, on my part? I'll have a clearer picture in November when the schedule for my Hautes Études seminar will be determined.

Faithfully yours,
R. Barthes

*   *   *

Sunday, [November 1962]

Dear friend,

What to do about these Wednesdays. It's now certain, with the academic year being organized, that I will be tied up *every* Wednes-day, since that's the day the Centre des Communications de Masse, which I am part of, meets. And that begins next Wednesday, which means I can't meet with you even once, as I had hoped. It would be best, I think, if we could see each other, just the two of us one day (when you wish); you could explain to me where we stand and later, when we have an office, I could join you in a more improvised way, as you suggest.

Kind regards,
R. Barthes
Dan. 95–85

According to Roland Barthes's diary, he participated in many meetings in fall and winter 1962 at the home of Dionys Mascolo, Rue Saint-Benoît, which was also the home of Marguerite Duras: Tuesday, October 16; Friday, October 26; Thursday, November 8; Friday, November 16; Tuesday, November 27; Tuesday, December 4; Friday, December 14. On December 2, 1962, he wrote the fragment on the "dialogue" ("Les Trois dialogues") for the "Revue internationale."[179]

Roland Barthes was present at the big meeting in Zurich, Saturday, January 19, to Sunday, January 20, 1963, with the German, Italian, and French participants.

Then he participated in many meetings at Mascolo's apartment in 1963: Thursday, April 18; Friday afternoon, April 19, and Saturday morning, April 20; as well as Friday, May 17. There were a few more meetings in 1963, one on Wednesday, October 23, and one on Friday, December 13, which is the last to be noted by Barthes in his diary.

During that year, he met alone with Maurice Blanchot twice: Friday, June 14, 1963, and Wednesday, July 17, 1963.

Maurice Blanchot to Roland Barthes

Paris, 28 rue Madame, Thursday, [May 1963]

Dear Roland,

I believe Dionys told you that I was going away for a few days (a week at least). Before leaving, however, I wanted to thank you for your book.[180] It was a friendly greeting I much needed after those hours that were hard for me, why hide it?[181] What is your feeling at present? Do you think something may still be possible and in what direction? You know that, for me as well as my close friends, your opinion will be a deciding factor. I don't say that to burden you with an unpleasant responsibility, but rather to invite you to share your thoughts in complete freedom and without hesitation.

Yours with all my heart,
Maurice

*   *   *

Dear Roland,

With Dionys about to make a weeklong trip to Italy, mainly to Milan, it seems that through his intermediary, we must examine one last time with Vittorini, Leonetti, and Calvino the possibilities for an international effort, albeit reduced to our two languages, envisioning a Franco-Italian review with an editorial committee that could include, besides French and Italians, a German writer, an English writer, and a Spanish-American writer. If the Italians turn down the project or even accept it reluctantly, because they are tempted by Enzensberger's solution[183] or for other reasons, then we would be free—both in heart and mind—to turn to the Other project. That one, which I think involves radically questioning all forms of publication and writing envisaged until now, needs to be considered completely by itself.

I believe it's now clear that Maurice Nadeau 1) will agree to participate in a French-Italian review, if it comes about; 2) if that's impossible, he'll return to Enzensberger's solution, which we would not be part of, just as he would not be part of the other project that's unfamiliar to him, I think, and, moreover, difficult to discuss at present except in ambiguous terms.

I'm leaving for a couple weeks and then I hope we can see each other sometime. Not long ago I caught a glimpse of you on Rue de Rennes a few steps away from me, but separated by a stream of cars. It was touching to see you like that, so close and completely inaccessible.

I am sending you, dear Roland, all my best wishes,
M.

Roland Barthes to Maurice Blanchot

Postcard showing a painting by Caravaggio, *Saint John the Baptist* (Kunstmuseum, Basel, 1609)

Urt, September 4, [1965]

Dear Maurice, your note touched me deeply. I'm worried about your health. As soon as I return toward the end of September, I'd like to telephone you—or at least Dionys, to get your news. I wasn't able to see Leonetti in Italy; he seems inexhaustible.[184]

Until soon, I hope, dear Maurice,
Your friend,
Roland B.

Maurice Blanchot to Roland Barthes

Saturday, [March or April 1966]

Dear friend,

I'd like to thank you for the happiness that reading your book gave me, through the truth of its language and its constant invitation to us to call things into question.[185] It seems that this disruption—the disruption that precedes a new form—despite your infinite discretion in proposing it must be, for some, a kind of personal wound. It must be that research applied to "writing," in whatever form, thwarts our ease, disturbs our complacency, and threatens our safety. Already we have seen the violent manner in which our poor project was received. It's beginning again. There's something very instructive in this, I think.

And nevertheless, knowing that a deep inquiry is underway, feeling linked to it and aided by it, how that lightens life.

To you, with all my heart, dear Roland,
M. B.

*　　*　　*

Paris, May 11, [1967]

Dear Roland,

For such a long time now I've been thinking of you continually, regardless of the circumstances or because your writings bring me back to the center of my thinking. They have often aided me, not just as intellectual resources but by maintaining their orientation in those obscure regions where the somber mind governs.

For all that, thank you.

For some time now as well, having half returned to the real world, I've been thinking it would be good if we could reconnect. But when communication no longer corresponds with daily events, that's difficult. There must be a medium. Please forgive me for sending you the attached text partly as pretext for providing the possible occasion.

One word on this text. It was prepared with friends whom you know. But in submitting it to you, I'm not simply or exactly asking for your approval, but rather to consult a kindred spirit on this issue of rupture. Naturally we all know how intellectual and aesthetic activities in all our societies are continually and necessarily threatened by the play of cultural powers. But the general problem cannot serve as an alibi for the other, more present one, evoked by the text. But is this text *possible*? Would you like to think about it and consider what could be changed or added here to make it more accurate? And when you have the time, would you like to share your thoughts with me?

Yours, dear Roland, with warm regards,
Maurice Blanchot

The attached text by Maurice Blanchot:

Brought into power by a military coup, claiming historical legitimacy that he holds according to his judgment alone, and appealing to the populace only if it reinforces his designs, having imposed a Constitution that is monarchic in nature, having imposed it in a period of unrest when events offered him Algerian colonels for allies, that is to say, the repeated threat of civil war, and then not even caring about respecting that Constitution, but making it more authoritarian year after year, to the point that it exists only through him and to legalize his individual intentions, de Gaulle has established a regime that bears his name and signifies that name only, bearing no relationship at all to the democratic tradition of this country!

A regime of social regression, serving the privileged class, with equal participation for all in restoring "grandeur" as the only measure of justice, that grandeur being nothing but a nationalist aberration here. A regime of political repression whose entire philosophy consists of this: first, to put an end to parliamentary democracy, then to suspend all meaningful civic life, political decisions belonging only to one individual and the law itself embodied in one individual.

Like all dictatorships, this strangely regressive regime has lasted only by linking itself with danger and exalting danger. But the time has come when that very power appears to be the true danger. No longer passing for a power that saves, it reveals itself to be the expression of the most unjust violence, which is the essence of all nationalism and which prevails every time popular sovereignty finally fails to express itself through the institutions and the laws.

That is where we are: at this turning point. The recent elections are evidence of it. And the result of those elections is that, far from speaking as he always has—wrongly—for an entity called "France," dangerously glorified to enhance his own glory, de Gaulle is only in a position to respond to the demands of the wealthy powers, finding his support only in them, as a group plainly determined to unite political power with financial power. This is now abundantly clear, and it is clear that this regime must vanish. First of all, the circumstances are favorable, and the citizens of this country have the means to hasten this end.

In our position, the moment has come for us as well, through our own powers, to take an actual part in a decision now pending. We could not exercise those powers any better, with any more rigorous exactitude, than by implementing the possibility inherent in them for rupture, which goes much further than protest. Our power lies in this possibility for rupture, and it is the only power that we can still exercise freely.

We must face the truth: to maintain appearances, necessary for concealing its true nature, the Gaullist regime needs the intellectual class. It cannot do without it and has continually relied on it, flattered it moreover, and used it for its own gains through the honorable means of cultural events. How to end this relationship that, if we accept it, cannot help but become a form of complicity? What to do so that this power no longer succeeds in diverting and using for its own ends even our criticism, even our rejection, which is always too indeterminate? Maintaining a distance is not enough. We are in its society, we live among institutions that it controls, and, however much we have behaved as a foreign body there, it has treated us as its possession, its national possession, it goes without saying, and, however subversive, as material for "national" prestige. Any words already uttered, even a single word, can therefore reinforce the state of things that we want to end.

In order to terminate these relationships that make us allies of the regime, we call on all men of thought, writers, scholars, journalists, to refuse to support the services, organizations, institutions, and forums controlled by the government and lacking true autonomy, such as ORTF, and to forbid them the use of their words, writing, works, and names. These institutions are not public services; no citizen maintains the illusion of communicating through their intermediary with other citizens. Having become the property of power, they serve it, they serve it alone, and they serve it all the more by occasionally letting a few words of protest be heard.

Let the truth, so constantly duped about the actions and real needs of men (those of workers, to cite only the most striking example, never mentioned, or, worse, minimized, misrepresented), at least become perfectly obvious as a complete lie. When not one of us will let some semblance of discourse enter into the game of real propaganda, that propaganda will have to reveal itself for what it is and, in losing its liberal appearance, will lose the essence of its authority that it owes entirely to its adversaries' caution. Let us cease to be accomplices. The principal means: rupture. Rupture with all of Gaullist society, throughout and in all circumstances in which that society might try to appeal, calling on them as intellectuals, to the support of writers, thinkers, and scholars. Rejecting the alibi that would allow it to circulate work. Refusing to mix true words with official deceits. Maintaining no relationship with either the institutions or the individuals of the regime.

Even though it is already in effect for some of us, this rupture must now be declared openly. We are doing so here. And we are inviting all intellectuals to declare it with us.

Roland Barthes to Maurice Blanchot

May 22, 1967[186]

I found your letter when I returned from Italy and I'm responding to you with a word on the text that you sent me. The political analysis that it implies does not seem very accurate to me. It makes everything dependent on De Gaulle whereas, it seems to me, it is the opposite accusation that must be made, beginning with the classes, the economy, the state, the technocracy.[187] And if the analysis is not accurate, it inevitably involves false gestures. It seems to me that in wanting to treat Gaullism as a dictatorship pure and simple, without nuance (as if there were some advantage in entering a stereotyped intellectual situation), there is the risk of denying oneself the means to combat it. I confess moreover that I'm a bit shocked that this text totally ignores the global situation, although henceforth it is, to my mind, the only *political* matter that concerns us and everything must *already* be related to the United States' future war against China. And finally, given my disposition, which you are aware of since it has already come between us, once, at a more serious moment than this one, I always feel repugnance toward anything that could resemble a *gesture* in the life of a writer.[188] Such gestures occur outside one's writing but nevertheless give credence to the idea that writing, independent of its actual substance and somehow institutionally, is capital that lends weight to extraliterary choices. How does one *sign*, in the name of a work, at the very moment when we are attacking from all sides the idea that a work can be signed?

Valéry and Rhetoric

For two years (1964–65 and 1965–66), Roland Barthes devoted his seminar at the École Pratique des Hautes Études to rhetoric.[189] That seminar responds to a theoretical and genealogical inquiry beginning with literary structuralism and a return, from within that framework, to old questions posed to discourse through all types of rhetoric.[190] But it also responds perhaps to the very first steps taken by Barthes as early as 1946, a bit before "Le Degré zéro de l'écriture," in his first text "L'Avenir de la rhétorique," unpublished and reproduced here.[191] Georges Perec, Severo Sarduy, Gérard Genette, Tzvetan Todorov, Phillippe Sollers, Michel Butor, and others attended or played a part in these seminars. In 1970, Barthes published a major text, "L'Ancienne rhétorique: Aide-mémoire," in the review *Communications*.[192] This work on Valéry and rhetoric appears to be a significant supplement to it.

Session of the "Rhetoric Today" Seminar, 1965–66

What writer today, except without a good dose of provocation, would call upon the support of a rhetorical art?

We are only familiar with a degraded, narrow, strongly pejorative sense of the word *Rhetoric*: pompous, cold, conventional, ornate writing. Nevertheless for almost two centuries, rhetoric had a much vaster scope; from the sophists to the Renaissance, by way of Aristotle, Cicero, Quintilian, and the arts of the Middle Ages, Rhetoric was both a philosophy and a technique of language, the subject of incessant, profound, original thinking, the truth of which we are now beginning to rediscover with astonished admiration.

Nevertheless, before it collapsed in the nineteenth century, this very old empire saw itself seriously weakened as early as the seventeenth century by the assaults of the modern mind. It had two formidable enemies with very different styles, Descartes and Pascal, one in the name of mathematical reason, the other in the name of the truth of the heart, which had to impose its living order on discourse. That last name ought to make us prick up our ears. As an enemy of rhetoric, Pascal is also an enemy of Valéry and what comes between Pascal and Valéry is, in the final analysis, precisely a certain usage of language, that is to say, Rhetoric. Here is how Valéry attacks Pascal, using as the occasion one of his most famous Pensées: *The eternal silence of these infinite spaces frightens me.*

> I cannot help but think that there is some system and some work in this perfectly sad attitude and in this absolute disgust. A well-tuned sentence excludes total renunciation.
>
> Well-written distress is not so complete that it cannot save from the shipwreck some freedom of mind, some feeling of number, some logic, and some symbolism that contradict what they say. . . .
>
> Moreover, even though the intentions may be pure, the concern for writing alone and the care brought to it have the same natural effect as an afterthought. Inevitably, what was moderate is rendered extreme; and what was rare, dense; and more complete what was partial; and emotional what was only animated. . . . Blind windows take shape. The artist can hardly help but increase the intensity of his observed impression, and he makes symmetrical the developments of his first idea, a bit like the nervous system does when it generalizes and extends to an entire being some local modification. That is not an objection against the artist, but a warning never to confuse the true man who made the work with the man that the work makes us imagine.*

We can see that Valéry is reproaching Pascal for not knowing—or rather for pretending not to know—what I will call the fatal theater of language. Language is a theater to which man is condemned. Rhetoric is the discipline that transforms that condemnation into freedom. It is a technique of responsibility. And it is not nothing.

Thus Valéry's conception of Rhetoric is profound, serious. It is not a simple pastiche of classical conceptions, even if it does not have their scope, because Valéry completely despised the Rhetoric of the *dispositio*. This conception rests on three principles:

I. The first affirms—and endlessly reaffirms—the verbal condition of literature: literature is language; there is a universe of words.

---

*"Variation sur une 'pensée,' " in *Variété* (Paris: Gallimard, 1924), 143–44.

"Literature is and can be nothing other than a kind of extension and application of certain properties of Language."* The equation literature = language is so strong in the eyes of Paul Valéry that he sees through a very striking sort of paradox a veritable circularity between literature and language. Literature is language but language itself is literature: "Moreover, in considering quite elevated things, can we not consider Language itself as the masterpiece of literary masterpieces, since every creation of this order is reduced to a combination of the powers of a given vocabulary, according to forms established once and for all?"† That may seem trite today, but we must not forget that Valéry was still very close to Mallarmé, even to Hugo, to Flaubert, who established in our Literature an empire of language.

> In Racine, perpetual ornament seems drawn from discourse, and that is the means and the secret of his prodigious continuity, whereas, among the moderns, ornament breaks discourse."
>
> Racine's discourse comes out of the mouth of a living, although always quite pompous, person.
>
> The same is true of La Fontaine, but the person is familiar, and sometimes quite neglected.
>
> On the contrary, with Hugo, Mallarmé, and a few others, there seems to be a kind of tendency to form nonhuman, and in some way *absolute*, discourse, discourse that suggests some sort of being independent of any person—a divinity of language—illuminated by the All-Powerful of the Ensemble of Words. It is this faculty of speaking that speaks and, in speaking, gets drunk and, drunk, dances.‡

Nor must we forget that the total identification of literature with language, however banal, is still hotly contested by all those, traditionalists and realists alike, who see form simply as the garb of content, which remains, they believe, the principal matter of literary art (Valéry, by the way, hotly contested the content/form opposition, following Flaubert and Mallarmé). Finally, we must not forget that the verbal nature of literature has still not been exploited by criticism. If literature is a language, then it is, in some way, a matter for linguistics, and from this perspective, we are only at the very beginning of inquiries and explanations in which Valéry is al-

---

*"L'Enseignement de la poétique au Collège de France," in *Variété V* (Paris: Gallimard, 1944), 289.
†"L'Enseignement de la poétique au Collège de France," 290.
‡*Rhumbs* [in *Oeuvres*, ed. Jean Hytier (Paris: Gallimard, 1960), 2:635].

ready considered a predecessor. Haven't some of his texts on the sign just been taken up again in the review of pure linguistics, *Cahiers Ferdinand de Saussure*?

II. The second principle underlying Valéry's Rhetoric is in some way an explanation of the first. If literature is a language, it is because in fact the very function of the language inevitably divides in two. There is a practical language, meant to transform reality and thereby be abolished as soon as it achieves its goal. This is basically the language of prose that Valéry always vigorously distinguished from poetry—too vigorously for our tastes because there is, of course, very literary prose, Valery's itself. And then there is *poetic* language (let us say more generally, *literary* language), which is essentially speculation on palpable properties of language; there is an opacity and an independence from the form. Literature is a second language.

> Poetry is an art of language. Language, however, is a practical creation. Let us note first of all that all communication between humans only has some certainty in practice, and through the verification that practice offers us. *I ask you for a light. You give me a light*: you have understood me.
>
> But, in asking me for a light, you were able to utter a few unimportant words in a certain timbre and tone of voice—with a certain inflection and with a certain slowness or haste that I was able to notice. I understood your words since, without even thinking about it, I offered you what you were asking for, this little bit of fire. And yet the business is not over. A strange thing: the sound, and something like the figure of your little sentence comes back to me, repeats in me, as if it took pleasure in me; and as for me, I like hearing myself repeat it, that little sentence that has almost lost its meaning, that has ceased to be useful, and that wants to live on all the same, but in a whole other life. It has taken on value, and it has taken it *at the expense of its finite signification*. It has created the need to still be heard. . . . Here we are on the very edge of the state of poetry. This tiny experiment will be enough for us to discover more than one truth.
>
> It has shown us that language can produce two entirely different kinds of effects. One kind has the tendency to provoke what is necessary to nullify entirely the language itself. I speak to you, and if you understand my words, those very words are abolished. If you have understood, that means that those words have disappeared from your mind, they are replaced by a counterpart, by images, relations, impulses. And you will

then possess what retransmits those ideas and images into a language that can be very different from the one you received. *To understand* consists of the more or less rapid replacement of a system of sonorities, durations, and signs by something entirely different, which is basically an internal modification or reorganization by the person to whom one is speaking. And here is the counterproof of this proposition: the person who has not understood *repeats* or *has repeated to him* the words.

Consequently, the perfection of discourse whose single object is comprehension obviously inheres in the ease with which the words that constitute it are transformed into something else entirely, and the *language*, first, into *nonlanguage* and then, if we wish, into a form of language different from the primitive form.

In other words, in practical or abstract uses of language, the form, that is to say, the physical, the palpable, the very act of discourse, is not retained. It does not survive comprehension; it is dissolved into clarity. It has acted, it has done its job, it has been understood: it has lived.

But on the contrary, as soon as that palpable form takes on an importance through its own effect, so that it asserts itself, somehow demands respect, and not only notice and respect, but desire, and thus repetition—then something new declares itself. We are imperceptibly transformed, and available to live, to breathe, to think according to a regime and under laws that are no longer of a practical order—that is to say that nothing of what happens in this state will be resolved, finished, abolished by a predetermined act. We will enter into the poetic universe.*

A very important view since it justifies on the part of the writer a certain right to obscurity (he does not write solely to *communicate* but also to *speculate*). A very modern view since it allies literature with a *secondary* language. Like all social institutions (sociology emphasizes this more and more), language has return effects (feedback, boomerang effect); literature in some way is the development field for language turning back on itself. Finally, quite a pessimistic view. Valérian theory assigns the writer a nonpractical activity, refused any sanction from reality. The writer is the technician of a useless language.

The occupation of intellectuals is to move all things around beneath their signs, names, or symbols, without the counter-

---

* "Poésie et pensée abstraite," in *Variété V*, 142–44.

weight of real acts. As a result, their words are astonishing, their politics dangerous, their pleasures superficial.

These are social stimulants with the advantages and the dangers of stimulants in general.*

We might ask, then what purpose does the writer serve? Valéry would answer: to make of the language of a nation a few perfect applications. Sociologically, the writer would be essentially a puppeteer of language, and it is as such that society would consume him.

III. The third principle advances even further into the literature-language theory because it offers it both a psychological and a moral foundation. This principle answers the question: Why attribute some glorious value to the work of form? Valéry responds, in short, like this: the form has preeminent value because the content does not.

For Valéry, the content is *Ideas* (always plural because Valérian atomistic psychology sees the Self essentially as divided, any unity only fleeting). *Ideas*: not only intellectual sparks, brainwaves, but also sensations, images, dreams: mental flux in its anarchic succession of states. This is not the signified; it is before meaning (*inventio*).

The mode of production of Ideas (fundamental in Valérian theory) is *irresponsible*. Ideas come to humans for no reason. In short, [their] mode of production is *Chance*; one has ideas by chance (let us stress the paradox of this for an intellectualist). Chance is the great provider of ideas; and since, for Valéry, Nature is all that is *given*, we could say that, for him, Ideas are *natural*—but therefore ambiguous: cherished emotionally because they are the first contact humans have with the world (upon awakening, for example); discredited intellectually because man cannot claim his freedom in this. In a word, Ideas are accidents (a very Valérian word).

Form is precisely the labor that transforms the chance of an idea into a resistant work; the work is an *accident redeemed*, circumstance transformed into intention. In short, form is the *deferred action of the idea*.

> I enter an office where some business calls me. I must write and I am given a pen, ink, paper, which are marvelously well suited. I write easily some trivial thing. My handwriting pleases me. It leaves me with a desire *to write*. I go out. I leave. I bring with me the excitement to write that is search-

---

*Rhumbs, 619.

ing for something to write. Words come, a rhythm, lines, and this will result in a poem for which the motive, the music, the charms, all of it will proceed from the material incident of which they will retain no trace. What criticism would suspect that origin? Is criticism possible? I mean criticism that would serve ourselves, and would make us imagine a bit how we do what we do.*

In modern terms, we could say that form, the labor of form, consists of giving meaning to the insignificant, thought to the futile; form consists of *thinking*. It is the field exclusive to humans where they wrest free their ideas from nature. Everything that amplifies that wrenching (the Rules, for example, of Poetry, of style . . .) is Form. It is what justifies writing:

> *Writing* was for me already an operation entirely distinct from the instantaneous expression of some "idea" through immediately stimulated language. Ideas count for nothing, no more than facts or sensations. The ones that seem the most precious, the images, analogies, words, and rhythms that arise in us, are more or less frequent accidents in our inventive existence. Humans do hardly anything but invent. But the one who becomes aware of the ease, fragility, and incoherence of that generation opposes to it the effort of the mind. This results in the marvelous consequence that the most powerful "creations," the most august monuments of thought, have been obtained through the thoughtful use of voluntary means of *resistance* to our immediate and continual "creation" of words, relations, and impulses that are unconditionally replaced. Completely spontaneous production very easily accommodates, for example, contradictions and "vicious circles"; logic obstructs them. Logic is the best known and the most important of all the explicit, formal conventions against which the mind rebels. Methods, well-defined poetics, norms and proportions, rules of harmony, precepts of composition, fixed forms: these are not (as is commonly believed) formulas for restricted creation. Their deep purpose is to call upon the complete, organized man, *the being made to act, and whose very action in turn perfects*, to assert himself in the mind's productions.†

Let us summarize again: form is the freedom that content lacks.

Rhumbs, [628–29].
†"Mémoires d'un poème," in *Variété V*, 86–87.

I do mean that Mallarmé is obscure, sterile, and precious; but if at the cost of those *faults*—and even by means of all those faults, by means of the efforts that they imply in the author and that they require from the reader—they make me imagine and locate *beyond all the works* the conscious possession of the function of language and the feeling of a higher freedom of expression compared to which all thought is only an incident, a particular event, then that consequence that I have drawn from my reading and meditation on his writings remains for me an incomparable good and a greater one than any easy, transparent work has offered me.*

Conclusion

This is a theory that makes Valéry's place very ambiguous. On the one hand, insofar as Art for him is essentially counterchance, counterinspiration, Valéry is a classicist; but to the extent that he recognizes chance's role as a provider of ideas (and thus creator of content), he is a romantic (to adopt a convenient mythical opposition). That ambiguity is expressed very well in Valéry's conception of dream: dream is the touchstone of modern literature, ever since Romanticism. Contrary to what one might imagine of an intellectualist writer, Valéry often spoke of Dream—and he described several dreams in a very beautiful way, like this one for example:

> Tale (jotted down upon waking in the residue of a dream)
> *The treasure is guarded by a dragon (or by some other kind of monster) at the First Door.*
> *If you manage to infuriate it, it will be at your mercy,*
> *It will reveal its heart and you will pierce it.*
> *The Second Door is guarded by perfectly beautiful woman, a magician.*
> *If you manage to charm her, she will be at your mercy. She will open her arms to you and you will bind her in chains.*
> *The Third Threshold is guarded by a small, sad child. If you manage to make him smile . . .*
> Here the tale stopped and I felt very distinctly that to continue *would be to invent it.*†

But Valéry cannot remain with Dream, not because of reason, but because humans are condemned to speak of dream in the waking

---

*"Je disais quelquefois à Stéphane Mallarmé . . ." in *Variété III* (Paris: Gallimard, 1936), 32.
†*Mauvaises pensées* [in *Mauvaises pensées et autres*, in *Oeuvres*, 2:855].

state: "The very one who wants to write his dream must be infinitely awake."* In other words, writing is a fatal counterdream. We come back to the contradiction denounced in Pascal: to write is to renounce the dream inasmuch as it is to use it. Waking, the privileged moment of the Valérian dietetic, is precisely that fragile friction between the dream and writing, the passage from Dream-adherence to Writing-separation: "In the dream, thought is not distinguished from living and does not slow down for it. It adheres to living; it adheres entirely to the simplicity of living."†

---

* *Variété*, 56.
†"Études et fragments sur le rêve" in *Variété*, in addition to an unpublished chapter (Paris: Gallimard, 1925) [*Oeuvres*, 1:936].

Divertissement en fa majeur

A. Philippe Rebeyrol.

C'est quand sans l'oser, quand de telle sorte
Qu'avant que tu l'aies lu, j'ai repassé la porte,
Qu', Illustrissime, je dépose dans ta main,
Cet inamusant et bi pauvre parchemin,
Mais qui, non point ingrat, d'un dévouement que j'eusse
Voulu plus éclatant, t'assurera — ne fût-ce
Que par les mille ~~excuses~~ et mille excuses qu'humblement,
Ton serviteur joint à ce divertissement.

Cher Jean Paulhan,
nous avons assez
librement disputé
autour de ces
MYTHOLOGIES
pour que je vous
dise aujourd'hui
un sentiment
qui est fait de
beaucoup de
respect et d'af-
fection,

R Barthes.

à Sartre   7 Déc 55

Cher Monsieur,

Vous avez bien voulu, l'été dernier, me proposer une chronique littéraire régulière des les Temps Modernes. Malheureusement, j'ai été nommé depuis attaché au CNRS (du moins pour cette année), et cela à la fois par administrativement et matériellement, m'interdit de prendre de nouvelles tâches en dehors de la Recherche : je garde à grand peine ma collaboration à la Revue de Nadeau, que je ne puis laisser, mais je n'ose prendre rien d'autre : ~~je n'y arriverais pas.~~

Je voudrais vous dire tous mes regrets, toute ma gratitude de aussi pour votre confiance, qui est importante à mes yeux. J'ai dit d'ailleurs à Péju que occasionnellement, sur des sujets précis en rapport avec la Recherche, je tâcherai de donner aux TM des textes; je voudrais par là vous assurer de ~~mon entière~~ mon intime profonde solidarité avec votre Revue.

Je vous prie de croire, Cher Monsieur, à mes sentiments d'admirateur et de profonde sympathie.

SADE, FOURIER, LOYOLA

à Maurice Blanchot,
de son vieil ami
qui lui est profon-
dé'ment attaché

Roland Barthes

pour Maurice Blanchot,
en me souvenant avec
émotion de ce qu'il
m'a écrit au mo-
ment de cette élection
avec la fidèle amitié
de

Roland Barthes

Aou 1950

Cher monsieur

Je suis ravi d'avoir de
nouvelles de Robert Régnier
qui m'a montré, a Cannes, une
grande gentillesse. Je rentre
en Septembre. J'habiterai
la campagne. Milly
Seine et Oise

Si vous envoyez le livre
envoyez une dactylo. Je crois
que les manuscrits se s'égarent.
Je le trouverai à mon retour.
Votre
Jean Cocteau
x

à Roland Barthes
avec ma très vive
sympathie
R. Char

**RECHERCHE
DE LA BASE ET DU SOMMET**
SUIVI DE
PAUVRETÉ ET PRIVILÈGE

DANS LA PLUIE GIBOYEUSE

à Roland Barthes
cette espèce de deuxième
vie de Rancé...

En très fidèle souvenir
et amitié
Jean Cayrol

Georges Perec   6 15.6.70
53 rue de Seine
Paris 6ᵉ

Cher Roland Barthes,

la lecture de votre article sur
Massin dans un récent Observateur
me fait regretter, une fois de plus
(et je dois le dire, de plus en plus
amèrement) votre silence.

l'influence que vous avez
eue, par votre enseignement et vos
écrits, sur mon travail et sur
son évolution a été et demeure
telle qu'il me semble que mes
textes n'ont d'autre sens, d'autre
poids, d'autre existence que
ceux que peut leur donner votre
lecture —

Croyez, cher Roland Barthes,
à mes sentiments amicaux   G P

Mardi 19 février 1980.

Mon cher Roland

J'ai trouvé hier ton livre dans mon casier au journal, et je t'en remercie. Ta dédicace, flatteuse, m'a fait plaisir.

Je viens juste de le refermer, par cette matinée douce, ensoleillée, qui va très bien à ta voix. A une première lecture rapide, survolante, je l'ai trouvé bien ; c'est tout ce que je t'en dis pour l'instant, car j'ai envie de le relire, et d'écrire un article dessus, si on me laisse le faire.

C'est la deuxième partie, bien sûr, qui m'a le plus touché : tout ce qui touche à la mère. J'ai écrit il y a quelques mois un texte sur une séance de photos avec ma mère, et je te l'envoie, il devrait te parler. Je t'envoie aussi les textes qui étaient à l'exposition (véritable échange d'écriture, si tu l'acceptes, puisque je viens d'absorber la tienne) ...

J'espère que tu vas bien, et je t'embrasse :

hervé

P.S. (Ne remettons pas éternellement le projet de redîner une fois ensemble : je t'appellerai un matin. Et je te remercie aussi pour ta précédente réponse).

4

A Few Letters Regarding a Few Books

Regarding *Sur Racine*

Louis Althusser to Roland Barthes

The first encounter between Barthes and Althusser took place on October 5, 1962, over the course of an evening spent with Michel Foucault as well.[1] Althusser wrote to his friend Franca: "I think I am going to cultivate him [Barthes] because I undoubtedly have much to gain from his (theoretical) experience."[2] They saw each other again, always with Foucault, on November 11 that year and during the year of 1963. Althusser distanced himself from Barthes and from structuralism beginning in 1966 for reasons involving his position within the Communist Party.

*   *   *

[Paris,] May 7, 1963

Dear Barthes,

What a true pleasure it is to read that Racinian "psychology" and the famous "passions" to which, it seems, we owe this drama (to the greatest relief, no doubt, of those who would very much like to have such passions! or else have such "disreputable" ones!) *do not exist*. To read that language alone can offer a solution that the logic of the situation cannot possibly offer, and that from this language a universe is born. Not for a moment do you risk the dangers that, through modesty or through tact regarding your predecessors, you evoke; the words of Freud are perfectly at home here, in one of the worlds from which he borrows them.

I also liked very much your article at the end. . . . I don't think that you have ever presented this challenge to the Universities so well, to have the courage of their thoughts!

How convincing and illuminating your book is. I say this to you without reservation, not only because it's yours and one can read through the reasons of a friend, but because it's true.

Yours with all my heart, gratefully,
L. Althusser

Regarding *Critique et vérité*

Louis-René des Forêts to Roland Barthes

March 17, [1966]³

Dear Roland Barthes,

This simple note to thank you very heartily for your magnificent book that I read immediately in one sitting. Such reading today has a kind of hygienic virtue for each of us. And how, finally, to tell you this without indiscretion: there is courage in truth and we can rejoice that you oppose a frivolous, inconsequential polemic with the sole violence of the serious, which is your distinctive characteristic.

Thank you again and with best wishes,
Louis René des Forêts

Jacques Lacan to Roland Barthes

April 12, 1966

Thank you, dear Roland Barthes, for sending me your book. It was necessary to respond—and in that way.
    It seems to me that the situation is looking good.

Yours,
Lacan
I am working pretty well.

Jean-Marie Gustave Le Clézio to Roland Barthes

Place Île-de-Beauté, Nice, April 29, 1966

Dear Sir,

You are right, I'm completely on your side in the quarrel that sets you against traditional criticism. I read your response to Picard.⁴ I think that you are right not only because what you say is true, but also because that truth is expressed with nuance, fineness, and force—in a word, because it is intelligent. It's no longer possible today to ignore the depths of literature; it's no longer possible to remain in cozy comfort, easily satisfied, not when there is Rimbaud, Mallarmé, or Lautrémont. Your point of view is completely *current* and, for that reason, truly reasonable. But all that you must have already realized, given the quality of your friends and the mediocrity of your enemies. And the jealousy of the mediocre is sometimes very entertaining!

Thanks you again, yours with deep admiration,
JMG le Clézio

Regarding *S/Z*

Michel Foucault to Roland Barthes (BNF)

February 28, [1970][5]

Thank you, dear Roland, for sending me your *S/Z*. I've just read it in one sitting. It is magnificent, the first true analysis of text that I've ever read. I'm leaving soon for America—Buffalo, where I must, in two months, teach "French Literature." I'm taking *S/Z*, which I'll assign to the students as a basic text. And we'll get some practice.

Morocco? Will I see you when I return in May?

Yours, dear Roland, in friendship and admiration,
M. Foucault

Michel Leiris to Roland Barthes (BNF)

July 10, 1970

Dear Roland Barthes,

Don't be surprised by my slowness in writing to you to acknowledge receipt of your *S/Z*.

In a way, I'm learning to read there, and this—exciting—apprenticeship is clearly quite long!

So, thank you,
And with best wishes,
Michel Leiris

Roland Barthes to Alain Bosquet (BLJD)

Rabat, May 22, 1970

Dear Alain Bosquet,

I don't really know where to write to you, having no access to your address here; and nevertheless I want to tell you how touched I was by your text on *S/Z* in *Combat*.[6] It's a new way of taking a book seriously, of incorporating it without enslaving oneself to it, expressions of great joy, a way of recognizing a work without bringing an immediate judgment to bear on it; in short, a *dialogue* (an overworked word, but made new here), full of subtlety and soundness, that's able to find and say what unites us: love for the text.

All that is poorly said, but I assure you that, among the few articles devoted to *S/Z*, yours "resonates" especially—and I'm deeply grateful to you.

Very cordially yours,
Roland Barthes

Regarding *L'Empire des signes*

Roger Caillois to Roland Barthes (BNF)

May 18, 1970[7]

Dear Roland Barthes,

I found your letter when I returned from Morocco. Thanks for being so kind as to try to find me a car that fulfills my wishes. In fact, I've come up with a simpler solution, which I should have thought of immediately: bringing my own car. But I didn't know there were boats that specialized in that kind of transport. I'm no less grateful to you for the trouble you took. I only passed through Rabat, so I didn't try to come by to say hello.

I very much liked your Japan, which made me see more clearly into many impressions that had remained vague and that your analysis gave meaning by locating in a new, convincing coherence. I think that you received *L'Écriture des pierres*.[8] And I would be happy if that book gave you a small portion of the pleasure I found in your book (your books).

Very attentively yours with all sorts of good wishes for the happy progress of your work,
R. Caillois

Jean-Pierre Faye to Roland Barthes (BNF)

[1970]

Dear Roland, thank you for the wonderful empire (of signs)—and also for your wish to see "the clouds *pass*."
(Even clouds that build from "old women's gossip.")[9]

With best wishes,
J.-P. Faye

Regarding *Sade, Fourier, Loyola*

Louis Althusser to Roland Barthes

December 4, 1971[10]

Dear Roland Barthes, thank you for your book, your attention, and your friendly note, which touched me deeply. Alas I won't be among the number celebrating with you on December 8 at Seuil, and I'm sorry. Nevertheless let me tell you from a distance—a very close distance—in what high esteem I hold your effort and your writings, your lucidity and your courage. Yours with very best wishes, L. Althusser

Alain Jouffroy to Roland Barthes

December 6, 1971

Dear Roland Barthes,

I was very happy to receive your book on Sade-Fourier-Loyola, the most beautiful, the most effective of your books, perhaps. I had many encounters there, and you may catch a glimpse of yourself by reading the PS of the poems attached. I also found you intact and enigmatic in the penetrating, unexpected answers you gave to Thibaudeau's first questions for the ORTF interview reprinted in *Tel Quel*.[11] Warmly yours,

Alain Jouffroy

André Pieyre de Mandiargues to Roland Barthes

36, rue de Sévigné, Paris IIIᵉ, May 1, 1972

Your *Sade, Fourier, Loyola* delighted me, dear Roland Barthes. It is, for my tastes, the most "ravishing" of your books. I truly thank you for it and send you my most cordial regards.

André Pieyre de Mandiargues
(In Venice, saw SADE on equipment for electrical power distribution equivalent to the EDF; thus the lofty name is often read in big letters on lightning cables, transformer boxes that contain mortal power . . .).[12]

Regarding *Nouveaux Essais critiques*

Louis Althusser to Roland Barthes

October 4, 1972[13]

Thank you, dear R. Barthes, for your book, where it's good to re-read *Degré zéro* and (for me) to discover many of your luminous articles (Loti!).[14]

Yours in faithful friendship,
Louis Althusser

Regarding *Plaisir du texte*

Hélène Cixous to Roland Barthes (BNF)

Montreal, March 2, 1973[15]

Thank you, Roland, for the pleasure of finding many unexpected sources here, from a kind of primitive exasperation, a vast and mobile blank, a language that struggles. Rarely seen such a contrast between the moments of repression and of such strong censures lifted. Quick and slow.

With love,
Hélène Cixous

André Green to Roland Barthes (BNF)

Roussillon, February 23, 1973

Dear Barthes,

Thank you for sending me *Le Plaisir du texte*—I think I too can say, "That's it!" I say this even more because sometimes it has happened that I can't say it at all. I'll tell you this in person when we see each other. This latest work seems to me, in any case, to mark a break. A break that projects a return from the repression that your linguistic period—I understand the need for it!—helped to delay.

Nevertheless, if you'll permit me this criticism, I believe that we haven't grappled with the suffering of the text. Pleasure, no doubt, but as triumph over what grief? Well, the important thing is that life goes on.

Until soon, yours truly,
André Green

Regarding *Alors, la Chine?*

Roland Barthes to Christian Bourgois

February 14, 1976[16]

I'm very happy with all these reactions—surprised even that your correspondents took the trouble to *talk* about the text and so freely, given that their remarks—for once—were not addressed to me, but to you.[17] So thank you for all that.

Yours faithfully,
RB

Roland Barthes to Marcelin Pleynet (BLJD)

Paris, February 25, 1979

Dear friend,

I read your travel journal immediately and all in one sitting.[18] Truly, I was delighted by the simplicity, accuracy, and precise kindness. You can imagine how sensitive I was to the absence of all dogmatism, arrogance, and hysteria. You can also imagine how at each instant, as in the margin, my personal memories linked up with what you were reporting, but you remembered for me as well, recalling things that I had no doubt repressed. And then, it's quietly novelistic, to the extent that you were able to convey to each of us a "mood." And the poems are very beautiful.

Thanks for your thoughtfulness in letting us read your text first. I'm yours, dear Marcelin, in faithful friendship.

Roland Barthes

Regarding *Fragments d'un discours amoureux*

André Pieyre de Mandiargues to Roland Barthes

April 12, 1977[19]

Delighted, in the purest sense of the word, by your *Discourse amoureux*, dear Roland Barthes, I thank you for this beautiful gift, which I hope to have the opportunity to talk with you about someday, and I remain yours in friendship.

André Pieyre de Mandiargues

Michel Tournier to Roland Barthes (BNF)

Choisel, August 26, 1977

Dear Roland Barthes,

I'm very struck by a passage in the interview with you in *Playboy*. It concerns that particular category of pickup artists, those who "look for pickups to find someone to be in love with." You add that this category is quite common in homosexual circles. I expressed something similar in my novel *Les Météores*.[20] There, I have the homosexual Alexandre say, "I am all of a piece, I'm a whole man! Love = sex + heart. The others—most of them—when they go out hunting leave their hearts at home. Tied to their wife's or mummy's apron strings. It's safer. When love is sick or old it breaks down into two component parts. Sometimes—it is the usual fate of heterosexuals—desire is extinguished. Only affection is left. Affection based on habit and knowledge of the other. Sometimes the reverse is true: the faculty of affection becomes atrophied. Only desire is left, fiercer and more demanding the more it becomes barren. That is the usual fate of homosexuals.

"I am not threatened with those two kinds of degeneration. Physical desire and the need for affection are fused in me in a single ingot. That is the very definition of health and strength. Eros athlete. Yes, a formidable strength, a dangerous health, an energy liable to explode and strike back. Because the absence of a quarry, which to others only means desire unsatisfied, rouses me to despair, and the presence of a quarry, which to others brings only satisfaction of desire, in my case calls forth a display of all the panoply of passion. With me, everything always comes down to emotions." End of quote (pp. 91–92).

In short, this is a particular kind of pickup that could be called "total" as in "total war." That pickup artist is an anti–Don Juan type. It's likely that he's more often homosexual than heterosexual, but why?

Yours sincerely,
Michel Tournier

Regarding *La Chambre claire*

Marthe Robert to Roland Barthes

February 22, 1980[21]

A very, very beautiful book, my dear Roland, and for me at this moment a moving friend. Because I lost my mother last November and I'm also searching for the image of her that would contain all the others, that would be the only essential one. Because of that, I wasn't able to read your book as I would have under other circumstances, but I did read it all the same. I know it by the mixture of sadness and strange sweetness in which it continues to immerse me.

Thank you for sending it to me. But, my dear Roland, why don't you come here? We would be so happy to see you, you really must sacrifice an evening to us.

With love,
Marthe

Other Letters

Roland Barthes to Christian Prigent

Urt, August 25, [1973]

Thank you very much for thinking to send me these texts of yours.[22] As you can imagine, they affected me; I read them with interest and they resonated totally. I would like very much to discuss them with you but am, for the moment, still too tired.

Perhaps we can see each other?

In the meantime, thanks again,
R. Barthes

*   *   *

June 28, 1974

I've received your texts (for which I thank you) just as I'm leaving and I cannot bring them along.[23] But what I skimmed, from that "perspective of writing" from which phenomenology should be done, captivates me; it seems excellent. I would like to talk with you someday *on texts*; we'll try to do that in the fall when school starts—and we can talk about this mailing then. For now, thank you.

Yours,
Roland Barthes

*   *   *

Paris, April 2, 1977

I'm very concerned at the moment with my mother's health, and I can only offer these few lines to tell you that your letter touched me—and that I feel much sympathy with your problems. I would truly be happy to talk to you about them, as soon as things improve here and I'm available. Be in touch with me as we agreed when the third term starts.

Best wishes,
R. Barthes

*   *   *

Dear Prigent,

Thank you for this very unsettling text.[24] It's your "Prigent par lui-même"—and amusingly corrosive—and very beautiful. Thank you for including me among your first dedicatees.

Yours,
Roland Barthes

Roland Barthes to Jude Stéfan

May 17, 1975

I very much liked your utterly friendly text and I thank you for it.[25] You taught me, among other things, that even our differences turn out to be false because what I like in Satie is precisely . . . *La Mort de Socrate*, and so forth.

Thanks again for so much elegance and sympathy.

Yours,
R. B.

Jude Stéfan to Roland Barthes

May 30, [1975]

Dear Sir,

Thank you for your note, which reassures me, because writing this text was rather an honor, but the result could be misunderstood by a bad reader, who could see in it only the humorous reduplication, for example, or supercilious friends who may not feel how much it was prompted by fervor and gratitude.[26] But that fervor is concealed by the writing. I had to write it quite—thus, too—quickly and left out some remarks (for example, on the first name R., whose resonances it would have been instructive to hear). In any case, this lexicon operates like a charm.

Please accept my gratitude and admiration.

Jude Stéfan

Roland Barthes to François Châtelet (IMEC)

Paris, January 11, [1976]

Dear François Châtelet,

It was good of you to write to me; I'm answering in haste, as always: I'm very much involved in the Benveniste problem (you know how much I like and admire him), with Foucault and Julia Kristeva.[27] There is actually nothing to be done 1) because—in fact—his financial situation is not bad, 2) because his sister, a timid and stubborn person, evades any initiative. The only way to improve his lot—and it's terrible, I went to see him—is to get him out of the suburban hospital where he is (very miserable) and into a more humane nursing home. But it's not a question of money; in fact it's his sister who is standing in the way. So, for the moment, we have given up. The obvious conclusion is that *at all costs* anything resembling a charity event (which he doesn't need) must be avoided. If the radio wants to do an *intellectual* tribute to Benveniste—independent of his financial situation and without alluding to it—by all means, yes, of course; but that's a whole other project.

Can you explain that to Gonzoles—who strikes me as enterprising?

Yours faithfully,
Roland Barthes
I haven't yet read your book—always months behind—but I'm happy it's out and being discussed.[28]

Roland Barthes to Bernard Faucon

Paris, May 12, 1977

Your photos are marvelous; for me it's *ontologically* (if you'll allow me this pedantic word) the photo itself, to the point that speaks of the being: that fascination.[29] Thank you.

Would you like to try calling me again? My mother is doing better—but availability is still very much a problem for me. We'll see.

Yours,
Roland Barthes
326 95 85

Roland Barthes to Pierre Klossowski (BLJD)

Paris, Thursday February 16, 1978

Thank you, dear friends, for this marvelous film, enigmatic and obvious from beginning to end.[30] Denise was very beautiful and Pierre absolutely saturnine—the perfect manipulator. Thanks for this pleasure, this reflection. Your friend,

R. B.

Roland Barthes to Philippe Rebeyrol

Paris, March 25, 1979[31]

My very dear Philippe,

I'm a little unhappy about not coming, about failing to show up one more time, and I've been tormented by it for days. It's so difficult to be sure of oneself! I would like to come see you, because now, very mysteriously, since the death of Maman, I have a great resistance to travel "in and of itself." But this is what is happening: throughout these last months I've suffered from the endless intervention of "things to do" (courses, texts, theses, etc.) coming constantly *to quash* my personal work and separate me from it. There's something about this work that's essential to me, emotionally. I have to (for a commission by *Cahiers du cinéma*, which is beginning a book series) and want to do a text (a short book) on the Photo, but this text, on every level, as I've planned it, is profoundly tied to images of Maman. Hence my latent grief for months at not being able to do it. Now, free of the Course and all the rest, I can get started on it—and I have started immediately (although I'm not yet writing). I don't have the heart to quash this project one more time, even for a brief trip, or to postpone it once more, even for a few days. I want and I need to continue, without a break; in short, a kind of deep, stubborn unavailability keeps me from leaving (except, of course, for Urt, where I can work as I do here). Of course, I was hoping to put a few days' hiatus between the preparation of the text (the current stage) and the beginning of writing; but that's very difficult to plan in advance. If by chance I finish this preparation soon, then, given about a day, I could plan to leave, and I'd telephone you immediately. But it's more complicated because it's Easter vacation and flights will be booked up. I'm sorry, Philippe, to hem and haw so—a little neurotic, I know. But I live in the fantastical idea of a kind of *necessity* of work that Proust expressed well when he cited for personal reasons these words from the Gospel, "Work as long as you have light."

I know you'll understand. Maybe I can call you soon; that depends on the meanderings of my work; but of course don't trouble yourself in the least about this "suspended" plan.

With all my love, Philippe,
Roland

The Postage Stamp

This "mythology" on the postage stamp, dating from June 1964, is the text of a short film made that same year by Jean-Marc Leuwen, *Microcosmos*. The text is spoken by Pierre Santini, the musical accompaniment is Beethoven's *Diabelli Variations*.

*   *   *

What is a stamp? For the State, it may only be a convenient way of paying for postal service. But for us, when we stick that little bit of paper onto the envelope we are about to mail, it is no longer a fee that we're paying, it is an image that we're looking at. And what has more prestige than an image? A stroke of genius: we're enchanted by an image without considering that we're paying a tax.

If that image distracts, instructs, and makes us dream, it may be due to its small size; because what is small must be full and can be varied. In the past, for centuries, our civilization was nourished by the art of the miniature. That art was both very free imaginatively and very precisely designed; it treated two great subjects: everyday life and spiritual adventure. Our postage stamp is today's miniature; precise and inexhaustible, it too reminds us of how we live and how we think. An album of postage stamps is a bit like the book of hours for modern times.

In the stamp, we find represented all daily human employment, as it occurs throughout the world. Stamps tell us what work humans do, what their occupations and businesses are; they tell us what humans build: palaces, bridges, dams, monuments. Finally, they make an inventory of everything humans want to know: countries, faces, sites, strange animals, and unfamiliar flowers. The stamp is an illustrated dictionary of all the subtle objects that humans or nature construct and perfect.

The stamp shows us all the creators of our art, our thinking, our technology, and our sciences: the creators of images, music, and words, from Clouet to Mozart, from Carpeaux to Apollinaire; the creators of thought, like Descartes and Bergson; the creators of history, like kings and revolutionaries; the creators of the unknown, like sports heroes and scientific inventors.

Thus a kind of spiritual Olympus is assembled here; and since the stamp is a fluid image, given to all combinations, among these Olympians from all times and all countries, an immense conversation goes on. On the same envelope, Beethoven can converse with Maryse Bastié, Bugeaud with Michelangelo, Gargantua with the Queen Mother.

The stamp has its moral code. Wherever it goes, its responsibility is to give expression to a certain idea of the Good. This idea is that man must act, must overcome the obstacles of nature, the resistance of matter. In this code of usefulness and solidarity, there is no place for worry. Revolutionaries are only admitted if time has rendered them inoffensive, and accursed poets only if they have been converted. The stamp represents only what has been consecrated by society. The stamp is well behaved, well behaved as an image.

And nevertheless the stamp is a conqueror; it endlessly annexes unexpected new subjects like colombophilia, haute couture, pelota, or the Smiling Angel of Reims. On the stamp one finds all the objects that could go into an encyclopedia. Thus the stamp involves a confident possession of the world, all the objects of which are caught and acclimated by the image. And the reassuring order of the products over which man rules is restored. Unflaggingly, the stamp makes everything signify.

The first stamps were austere, and occupied primarily with allegory: Ceres, Peace and Commerce, the Sower. Since then, this little paper rectangle has gradually absorbed the representation of the entire world, of all it contains in the way of famous beings, sites, monuments, flowers, animals, memories, and achievements. Meant to travel the world, the stamp has itself become a world; succeeding the universe of stained-glass windows, illumination, and heraldry, a new microcosm is born.

On Seven Sentences in *Bouvard et Pécuchet*

We know Barthes's taste, even his fascination for the work of Flaubert and for *Bouvard et Pécuchet* (1881) in particular.[32] The chapter "L'Artisanat du style" in *Le Degré zéro de l'écriture* testifies to this ongoing passion as early as 1953. Characterized as a "marginal work," that is to say, atypical and unclassifiable in a writer's opus, Flaubert's last novel occupies a major place in the seminar that Barthes gave at the École Pratique des Hautes Études in 1971, which, for the most part, revolved around the bêtise and the copy. A few years later, in the spring of 1975, but this time within the framework of a seminar at the Université de Paris 7, Barthes once again devoted his research to the Flaubert novel, establishing a dialogue with his earlier work. In fact, he took long passages from his notes from 1971, as the manuscript clearly shows. But quite quickly he moved away from his first work and defined a new subject for study: the sentence. For him, of course, the subject was not new; as something between intellectual fascination, affective projection, and moral investment, Barthes, we know, "idolized the sentence" ("Deliberation," 1979). The article "Flaubert and the Sentence" (1967) already emphasized the importance of syntax in Flaubert's aesthetics and ethics. Here, Barthes selects and isolates seven sentences from *Bouvard et Pécuchet* for which he proposes analyses far removed from the usual means of explicating texts. For supplementary reading, see the lecture "Phrase—Modernité" given in the spring of 1975.[33]

Beginning of Research

It's a matter of a simple *point of departure* for research, with an uncertain future, of an uncertain duration. (Maybe, if this doesn't work, we will stop to do something else—and in any case, we have only a few sessions together.) What *point of departure*?

1. In contact with the guardian-text, it's a matter of discovering *pleasures* (mine? for the moment, that's inevitable). Desire, that's what is displayed by another. Desire is not imposed, but displayed; it takes or it doesn't take. Professors of Utopia? We are the puppet masters of desires.

2. I must anticipate roughly what I'm doing with them; in what field of knowledge they may take place, what *digressions* (and thus, potentially, what writing) they may trigger.

1. So I'm rereading (once more, this spring 1975) *Bouvard et Pécuchet*. I'm searching: What is it I savor? What is it that gives me pleasure, *responsive to the text*? What makes *a bell go off* in me? The work? Too vague. The "construction"? Surely not. The passages? I believe this for a moment and I begin to try to make for myself a personal anthology of *Bouvard et Pécuchet* (which would

lead me to a series of textual explications, but no matter). I keep at least one passage that pleases me: the peacock episode.[34] But, in searching for others, I get bogged down; impossible to *mark them out*, to *cut them out*. The attempt fails.

Nevertheless, in searching for my passages, I manage to locate my pleasure (my emotion? my excitement?), which I more clearly understand to be intermittent (sensual delight is based on *intermittence*). The discursive form of this intermittence is the *sentence*. I'm fascinated by certain sentences. So that's where I must go; what makes *a bell go off* in me is the sentence.

2. Object of pleasure, the sentence (Flaubert's sentence in *Bouvard et Pécuchet*): What does it have to do with knowledge? Can I hope to *work* on these sentences that delight me?

A vague "dispatching" of knowledge takes shape. What do I potentially have at my disposal?

(a) What general knowledge of the sentence? It is not assembled and remains very fluid. Here and there, piecemeal, there are some propositions:

—In Saussurian linguistics? Very little, because the sentence falls into the domain of speech (and thus the combinative). We find a little in Martinet.[35]

—In Chomsky? Yes, we find a theory on the sentence. But the Chomskian sentence is statutorily infinite. It proliferates (until the death of the subject) through interlocking parts, according to rules. And I already know that the fascinating point of *my* sentence is the closing. We'll see, of course; but this is not the *stylistic* φ, the written φ.[36]

—Maybe we'll find more things looking into rhetoric: Aristotle, the Stoics, Dionysius of Halicarnassus, *peri hypsous*,[37] the medieval *dictatum*.[38]

—I sense that there would be many things to look for in the vast field of ethnology, in civilizations (especially through the angle of religion) where production is regulated by formulaic expressions, verses, "coined" phrases.

(b) There are two clearer approaches that we can mention right away—and we are going to do that:

1—On the *ideology* of the sentence, which greatly interests us, we find a decisive, new, accurate approach by Julia Kristeva, *La Révolution du langage poétique*. Part B: "Le Dispositif sémiotique du texte," chap. 2, "Syntaxe et composition" (with regard to *Un Coup de dés*), p. 265 and following.[39] This will be our theoretical reference text, the framework that will allow us to ask questions, *our* questions. That is the purpose the work of others serves, if it is intelligent.

2—On Flaubert's sentence? I go back to a first approach I made with the *value-sentence* that I will evoke again (not the sentence *in* Flaubert [this is not a grammatical or stylistic study], but the sentence *for* Flaubert).[40]

[. . .]

So, our research principle is to learn why a relationship of pleasure (and for the moment let us not refine the distinction between pleasure and sensual delight)[41] is established between certain sentences in *Bouvard et Pécuchet* and my reading—and in that way, perhaps, *as though in passing, in sideswiping*, we will start toward some knowledge on the sentence, as an object composed of ideology and sensual delight.

Choice of These Sentences?

(a) I will proceed according to a principle of individuation (according to an arbitrary point of departure): I will retain the ones that *interest me*—without yet knowing by virtue of what type of interest (we can also say of someone we desire: you interest me).

(b) How many? At first I considered a very large inventory (sometimes two or three per page), even if that meant noting and listing, without always commenting. That would be the *proper* method, because the *quantity* of the inventory can engender a new perception of the issue. But it's impossible because of the very limited number of sessions (three or four still).

I will choose about twenty "good" sentences—from throughout the work—potentially rich in commentary, that is, in possibilities for knowledge, according to a *chrestomathic* principle (the most "useful" sentences). But chrestomathy differs from anthology; anthology is a matter of a principle of pleasure. Realized as sensual pleasure, a text is always *anthologic* (made up of islands, marks, losses, isolates). It is a *centon* (*cento, onis*), a patchwork. We must retain the anthologic principle—and not the chrestomathic one.

Consequently, we will analyze a very small number of sentences—by necessity—but without being obliged to choose from throughout the work. We will take them in the order of reading, thus by remaining—by necessity—at the beginning. This is the point of departure, the prefiguration of an inventory that we cannot take very far but that will thus be postulated.

Method of Commentary?

Even though aimed at an object that is formal in principle (the sentence), we will not exclude the pleasures or interests of content.

Of course the point of departure will be linguistic (see our introduction on the normative syntactical structure), but with the linguistics maintaining a Saussurian imperative (the meaning is part of the language; semantics, part of the linguistics).

The distinction between form and content constitutes a false dichotomy. Content is itself a form (a code). One cannot *halt* a sentence at its form. One can limit its extension, not its intention.

What interests us is the sentence-*object*. That object is *voluminous*; it is made of *layers*, like an onion (we must retain the metaphor of the onion, which is different from the one of fruit; with the onion, no "pit," no secret hidden beneath the skin).

Consequences of the "Anthologic" Operation?

By isolating sentences, by treating each one as a separate object, we are subjecting these sentences to an operation of *disconnection*.

Under cover of a simple operating option, we approach a radical transmutation of consciousness. We are going to start *seeing* the sentence, to disconnect it from its *fabric* within which we don't see it. See Bataille, *Méthode de méditation*: "The system of known elements in which our activity is inscribed is only the product of it. An automobile, a man entering a village: I do not see either one, but the fabric woven through an activity of which I am part. There where I imagine *seeing* 'what is,' I *see* the subordinating *ties* to the activity that is there. I do not see; I am within a fabric of knowledge, reducing to itself, to its servitude, the freedom (the primary sovereignty and nonsubordination) of what is."[42]

To *see* the auto, we disconnect it from its everyday function within the space of the village—just as, to *see* the sentence, we disconnect it from its narratological or reasoning (discursive) function. To disconnect is to separate from a use, a function; it is to convert an instrument into an object (see Duchamps and the *ready-made*). We separate the sentence from its (supposed) function of communication that itself conceals a *thetic* function (it's a matter of setting out a truth). We pass from paranoia to perversion (disconnected, the sentence can become a fetish). Thus from the very beginning—and no matter what sentences are chosen—we must speak of a sensual pleasure of disconnection. The disconnected sentence thus takes on the power to fascinate, to *shatter* us (see the root in Sartre's *La Nau-sée*).[43] That is how we must understand the *sovereignty* of the sentence.

We must never forget in our commentaries and digressions that our point of departure is the shattering obviousness of an object of language that we have cut from its discursive artifice, its ideological artificiality.

1

"As the temperature had climbed to thirty-three degrees, Bourdon Boulevard was absolutely deserted" (p. 31).[44]

1. Form in the Traditional Sense

—We note a binary cut with two well-separated limbs since they are nearly as long as one another; we almost have a metrical organization.

—The cut is reinforced by the *é/è* phonetic opposition (degrees/desert).

—It is a matter of a "logical" cut (in the classical sense of the word, as in treatises on rhetoric): with a subordinate and main clause. Fontanier speaks of the *subordinate* clause (Fontanier, p. 51) if the *proposition* (subject and predicate) is related to the general sense of the main clause and does not apply specifically to the subject or the attribute (in this case, it is a matter of an *incidental* proposition).[45] Here we note a logical relationship par excellence: the causality (*as*). The cause and its effect create a logical *saturation*, a "complete and finished meaning," according to the canonical definition of the sentence (Fontanier, p. 52).

2. Disconnection

Flaubert's sentence is eminently disconnectable, yet without being gnomic, lapidary. Its status is subtle, in a subtle and solid in-between; it is neither maxim nor inextricably held in the weave of other sentences. It is *extricable*, extractable. It has something like the scent of maxim (but only the scent). This sentence is *the insignificant promoted to the order of pseudomaxim*.

From then on, the sentence is *copiable*. It calls for the *copy*. The monumental (lapidary gnomism) is turned, collapsed into its practical joke: the copy (see copies of Venus de Milo, the Eiffel Tower). The sentence plays at eternity: the sentence of tomorrow, of forever, infinitely copiable. Flaubert knew it; he copied this sentence for his niece: "To his niece Caroline: 'It is to obey you, my Loulou, that I have sent you the first sentence of *Bouvard et Pécuchet*. But, since you describe it or rather dignify it with the name of relic, and since false ones must never be worshiped, know that you do not possess the true (sentence). Here it is: "As the temperature had climbed to thirty-three degrees, Bourdon Boulevard was absolutely deserted."' (1874)"[46]

Disconnectable, copiable, the sentence is a *parody* of itself. Moreover, here, through connotation, it constitutes a parody of scientific discourse (33 degrees). This parody of the scientific serves here as emblem for the whole book (as parodic variations on the discourse of scientific popularization). It is already a bit like Bouvard and Pécuchet were saying this sentence. Ensuring an emblematic, diagrammatic, and *inaugural* function, it provides and establishes the *tone*. It recalls the function of the prelude, or the *proem*, when the rhapsodist tries out a passage before really beginning.

3. Ellipsis and Catalysis

Let us proceed in approaching the sentence object. Proust will be very helpful to us here. Let us read what he says about Balzac's sentence—which he clearly saw transgressing the nature of the sentence—and then we will compare a contrario our sentence from Flaubert: "Not conceiving of the sentence as *made of a special substance* from which must be eliminated and no longer be recognizable all that forms the subject of conversation, of knowledge, etc., he adds to each word the notion that he has of it, the thought that it inspires in him. If he speaks of an artist, immediately he says all he knows, through simple apposition."[47]

In other words, Balzac *catalyzes*: he saturates (even though the sentence—as we know through Chomsky—is not saturatable). His mode of catalysis is *apposition* (Proust practices comparison). "Idle chatter" returns to the register of speech (in contrast to the sentence, writing).

Flaubert practices the *ellipsis* ("special substance"). He does not appose. He makes causality dominate ("as," "considering them stupid," sentence no. 6), from which he makes the very armature of the sentence (conforming to the ideology of the ratio). For him, the sentence is like an object, a microsystem having its internal hierarchy (as opposed to Balzac, who accumulates multiple *incidents*). All logic must be contained in the sentence. The sentence is a logical *envelope* (its origin, its matrix is very much the *proposition*: a logical notion, not a grammatical one).

What Balzac would have catalyzed, Flaubert evacuates; Flaubert's one simple sentence would have provided a whole first paragraph (climatic considerations regarding Paris, sociology of the Paris summer, topography of the Bastille and Gare de l'Arsenal area).

It's useful to note the relationship to science, to scientific discourse. Balzac is closer to science than Flaubert is. The ellipsis is not scientific; to be elliptical is not a good thing. The ellipsis assumes that one has chosen another value system—art. In art, the *implicit* is (at least in classical art, it *was*) a value.

Or again: silence. Without ever being hermetic, the Flaubertian sentence lets *silences* be heard. Silence is the constitutive place of the sentence, as of music.

Let us note again a major research and conference topic: the *implicit*. See the book by Ducrot, *Dire et ne pas dire*.[48]

4. Anacoluthon of Two Truths

However, not everything is simple, orthodox, and conforming to a logical ratio in Flaubert's sentence. This sentence is very sly (hence its appeal). On the level of content (on the form of content, see Hjemslev),[49] we find a rupture in the construction, an *anacoluthon* between two types (two registers) of truth: (1) a physical, thermometric truth (33 degrees), (2) a phenomenological truth that corresponds to what the subject sees ("completely deserted"). We discover a prosaic truth, a descriptive tautology, almost a conversational remark. Once the two truths are stated, their link is sanctified by logic ("as" is the degree zero of all subordinations: *cum*). Here again we find "art"; the sentence is description supported by reason. It is the space of great Dutch painting (inert physical space combined with the trembling of the "lived").[50] But always with a slight parodic smile that opens the *dislocation of languages*.

Or again: the combination of description and cause constitutes a form of mixed thesis. One states the fact, one states the cause, one plays at the truth. But the dislocation (the parodic) comes from an accident of unevenness. There is the fall of the pure, noble cause *matched*, through the eternal abstraction of the sentence, to the flatness of the effect. No need to measure in degrees (33 and not 30 or 35) to understand that it is too hot for people to go out! We can imagine the gag: solemnly consulting a thermometer and discovering that Bourdon Boulevard is deserted!

The anacoluthon is a kind of linguistic hold that *fixes*, that solidifies a *state of things*. There we return to the *shattering* through the detour of irony. Bataille: "If necessary, there is certainly no better means of treating the rational than with the help of *that involuntary irony* of sentences, which marks a simple state of things" (*OC III*, p. 12, note).[51] This absolutely defines our sentence: it posits the state of things, gives it a rational turn, all of it caught in the irony of the sentence (the sentence as irony)—this irony being, if not involuntary (too psychological a word), at least uncertain, *indistinguishable*.

5. Truth/Bêtise

The sentence might be like a *tableau vivant* of truth. Let us recall the theory (from Kristeva) of the Mallarméan antisentence. Mallarmé[52] maintains a thetic moment, as possibility of truth and thus of denotation (there is a denoted referent: the deserted Bourdon Boulevard). Flaubert proposes a fixed, frozen (if we can say that in this case!) representation of the thetic, the denoted, the truth. The sentence is like a tableau; or again, the sentence (Flaubert's sentence) is an *object* (*ob-jectum*), a gift set before us, set on the table (*propositio*). Whereas that formal parody of truth through the thetic nature of the sentence is the bêtise itself. Our sentence is a (sly) production of bêtise. The bêtise is not the error, on the side of error. The bêtise needs the thetic; it is a truth copied, frozen: a *doxa*, the *doxa* (for Cicero, the *sententia* goes back the *doxa*, to that which is sententious, which is our sentence).

Thus we understand the *scent* of this sentence: the aesthetic production of an endoxal object of language.

2

"Suddenly a drunk staggered across the footpath; and, on the subject of workers, they began a political conversation. Their opinions were the same, although Bouvard was perhaps more liberal" (p. 32).

1. Form (in the Traditional Sense)

This is not a sentence in the typographical, official sense (between two periods), but in the macrosemantic sense as presentation of a full, closed meaning.

So this sentence is different from the first one: no cut, no meter. The form is not in the "structure" but only and completely in the *launch* of the sentence. With Flaubert, we must note the major place of adverbs (at the beginning or at the end). Here, the opening of the sentence is through an adverb, abrupt: *Suddenly*. Ensuring a diagrammatic function, the sentence finds its emphasis through the displacement of the adverb to the beginning (far from the verb), imposing a logical rupture of time and place.[53]

Be careful, however: the displacement of the adverb, which often marks the "special substance" of the sentence (Proust), especially in Flaubert, can be obeying nonanalogic, nonimitative motives. The adverb can be displaced in order to, in some way, *get rid of it*, clearing the sentence for the coming of the noun or verb phrase. Thus it is a matter of a true presentation (art production, *preparation*).

2. Metonymy

The "logical" armature is a metonymic chain: drunk workers politics. Thus this is not true logic (the noble logic of causality). From the perspective of the ratio and the sentence, metonymy, like normative structure, is a cheap logic, a parody of logic. The bond of location is taken for a bond of implication: post hoc, propter hoc.[54] Metonymy corresponds to a narrative logic. The metonymic chain gets started with an external *release mechanism* (see animals and children).[55]

From then on, we can understand the value of this specifically Flaubertian operator: "and." "And" is a metonymic operator; pure contiguity is given the alibi of a grammatical—thus pseudological—link (the sentence as a place where grammar and logic are supposed to coincide, according to a classical conception). A tenuous but existing link, a sort of place, degree zero of metonymic movement, "and" has it both ways. It has the appearance of a logical *enumerator* (which adds equal units: the *worker* is thus supposed to be equal to the *drunk*, logically) and the function of a *joiner* of spaces, heterogeneous objects (a specifically metonymic function). It is the *articulation*, the movement of the body (of the child, the animal) that turns its head suddenly in response to an incongruous signal. A drunk? A worker.

3. The Voices

To write—to produce a writing, a text—is to produce a statement in several voices (many fictions of origin for the stated) and to confuse those voices more or less, pass from one to the other without warning, make them more or less indistinguishable. Flaubert is a classic writer; the voices are multiple, subtle, but *just about* distinguishable:

(a) *A drunk staggered across* . . . : This is the voice of the witness, the typical narrator. Let's not forget (see Jakobson)[56] that certain languages have a special mood for *reporting* what one sees, what one saw, that for which one bears witness: the testimonial.

(b) *And, on the subject of workers* . . . : We note an ellipsis (and a metonymy): "drunks" refers to "workers." We perceive Flaubert's voice as he possesses, through his status as writer and his own "vocation," a critical knowledge on the discourse of others. Flaubert knows the routines, the channels of conversation, the prejudices (drunks/workers), and he reproduces them as a realist artist of language. This is the voice of mythology, of parody, of irony, the voice of the specialist in endoxal discursivity, of the archivist of stereotypes, received ideas, fashionable ideas (in Balzac, we might have found here a whole moral and social *apposition* on the proletariat and wine).

(c) *A political conversation*: the stated imposes the abstraction of a *genre*: the political conversation. Thus, we hear the voice of an abstracter, a poser of genres and names, a namer, an onomothete,[57] a nominalist voice on the way toward a possible stereotype: the "political conversation" (with the quotation marks). Nomination, at this level, implies a *distance*.

(d) *Their opinions were the same*: it's a matter of the narrator's voice, the reporter's voice. But at the beginning, it was a matter of the narrator-witness. Here, it's a matter of a narrator-historian who begins to *interpret*, to generalize, compare, manipulate the *meanings*.

(e) *Although Bouvard was perhaps more liberal*: we find the same voice again of the historian, but of a particular variety and type, that of the scrupulous historian. This historian cancels out the narrator-demiurge; he doesn't know everything and he acknowledges that. He thereby substantiates the external existence of a referent. This realist artifice allows the probable to be reinforced, creates a "reality effect."[58] Let us note that the effect of the real does not necessarily depend upon the precision of detail or the certainty of evidence, but precisely on its modesty, on its scruples. One seems more accurate in saying, "I may be biased," and more honest in saying, "I could be wrong." "Perhaps" is, according to the cultivated doxa, the word that best substantiates the real. Through that voice, one enters the complex space of narrative imagination.

All these quick, fragile voices form a kind of *moire*.[59] Let us draw from this analysis the feeling that in good narrative methodology, the study of *points of view* (as a prestructural phase of the structural analysis of the story) must subtilize in the extreme the fabric of voices. The Flaubertian sentence is a very complex, but nevertheless analyzable stereophony.

4. The Doxa

In this sentence, we find three clear *doxa*: (a) the drunk-worker link, (b) the worker-political link, (c) the political conversation itself, forever rich in stereotypes. (In politics, opinions are never revolutionary; revolution itself is an object of doxa.) The sentence thus connotes—in fact—an appropriation of the doxa (by Bouvard and Pécuchet). The doxa as object of theft; it cannot be destroyed, only stolen. Bouvard and Pécuchet inhabit it, by force. They are the squatters of the doxa (their vice, their originality, by which they are going to become paradoxical, is that they change doxa a hundred times).

3

It's useful to reclarify the link between sentence and pleasure. It's not a matter of an *introspective* task, of gradually knowing *why* it gives me pleasure. Rather it's a matter of using pleasure as *release mechanism* for all ideas, all leads, without yet knowing if they are good.

"Bouvard had the advantage in other ways. His hair watch-chain and his manner of whipping up the mustard sauce revealed the graybeard, full of experience, and he ate, the corners of his napkin under his armpits, giving utterance to things that made Pécuchet laugh" (p. 34).

1. Form

Once again we encounter the Flaubertian "and." Thibaudet characterizes it as "the *and* of movement."[60] But that's a bit brief. In fact, the "and" marks an anacoluthon in the rhetorical thread.

Canonically, "and" links equal, homogeneous units, phrases of the same grammatical nature (a trick for Latin versions). No doubt here, "and" links two properties. It is grammatical, but *on the level of discourse*, there is rupture, heterogeneity. "And" links a metalinguistic generality (revealing the graybeard) and a contingent, fragmented notation. It is, literally, *unsound*. Unless there is distortion between form and content: "and" in fact linking two examples of the "graybeard."

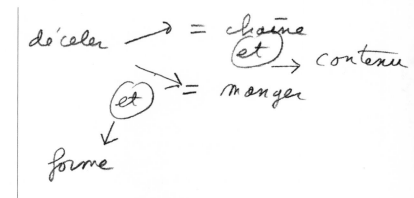

In any case, it's *trouble*. "And" creates a troubling shift in the rhetorical organization (the type is converted into species). We will note the troubling accolade:

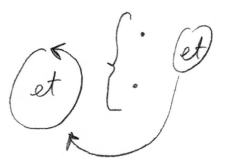

2. The Scene Is Kitsch (Hair Watch-chain, Mustard Sauce, Napkin Under Armpit)

But it corresponds more exactly to a lower variety of kitsch: vulgar kitsch.

Kitsch (Munich, 1860) comes from the southern German *Kitschen*: to throw together, to make new furniture from old. Kitsch refers to the negation of the authentic (to pass off something else in place of what was specifically asked for) according to a connotative, not denotative, phenomenon.

Ordinarily one encounters the connotations of objects, of settings. Here we have objects as well as behaviors (whipping the mustard sauce, placing his napkin). Let us note here, in the aesthetic analyses, the primacy given to the object, since there is an aesthetic, not even of gestures, but of behaviors, that is to say, functional gestures. What can be the artificiality, the inauthenticity of a gesture, its past *reference*? We may recall that the *schema* is the attitude of the body in action (athlete, orator, *statue*).[61] The idea of a *schematology* is very important for Bouvard and Pécuchet.

Kitsch is achieved in an *assemblage* of objects: a collection, a display, the exhibit of a whole. It is connected to the notion of *display* (exaggerated show, "making a fuss"). That is very much the case; Bouvard is on full *display*. *Display* corresponds to the complexity of objects present at a certain moment in a whole. This is the Flaubertian sense of *enumeration*; there is always a sense of kitsch. It is impossible to really understand Flaubert without referring to kitsch (see the stereotype and the bêtise).

With regard to kitsch, let us note the kitsch of the whole and the functionality of the parts (lamp, bed, pedestal table, etc.). Here, gestures are functional: making a sauce, eating, wearing a watch. The whole is *struck*, through disengagement and immobility, with kitsch. And the whole is the sentence. The Flaubertian sentence is constituted through *display*; it is the support of kitsch.

Each behavior (each praxemy), however functional, is *excessive*, *emphatic*. It includes an excess of function (see Sartre and the analysis of the café waiter).[62] The fact of whipping sauce like a graybeard corresponds to an excessive ease of experience, to the fact of protecting oneself excessively with tasks, with utterances. This accumulation of excess is kitsch as the drunkenness of consumption.

In general, Bouvard and Pécuchet are kitsch. Or rather, in Chavignoles (their garden, their galleries) they make kitsch. They have the pleasure of producing it (after which they unmake it for another kitsch like the garden). This highlights the proximity of kitsch to tinkering, like making an instrument with pieces meant for some other use, making drama with functions that were not meant for drama.

3. Bouvard Is Parading (on Display)

A *roquentin* (graybeard) is an old soldier in retirement, a part-timer in castles and citadels, and the word also refers to a singer of vaudeville songs, as well as a ridiculous old man who pretends to be young (*roc, roquette, forteresse*). Amorous display to seduce women, the amorous laugh of Pécuchet who is himself caught up in kitsch.

4

"Bouvard smoked his pipe, loved cheese, regularly took his demitasse; Pécuchet took snuff, at dessert ate only preserves, and soaked a sugar lump in his coffee. One was confident, flighty, generous; the other unassuming, thoughtful, thrifty" (p. 38).

1. Closure

This is a very rhetorical sentence with a list of contingent traits (an analysis) and a psychological synthesis. Thus the succession of analysis and synthesis, with an antithesis in each part, forms a canonical sentence.

What's interesting for us is the antithesis (and not the analysis and synthesis that correspond to the parts of the content). Why? The antithesis is a strong operator of closure. Because it is the mirror image: impossible to add anything. When the second term is given, it's finished (symmetry establishes completion). Thus closure is what defines the sentence (stylistically). Let us recall another definition of the sentence, that of Chomsky (J. Rychner, *Mort Artu*, cited by Kristeva, p. 288),[63] as statement unit limited by a conclusive pause. Let us also recall that for Flaubert, the bêtise was conclusion (in Latin, "closed" is *conclusus*). Flaubert's sentence continually mimics the bêtise. He evades the conclusion of content (syllogistically), but shifts it, fixes it, parodies it in the form: the sentence *concludes itself*. That form creates the laughable for nothing.

2. All the Same, Let Us Return to the Analysis/Synthesis Split

The analytical part focuses on "tastes." In themselves, tastes signify nothing: *I like/I don't like*. What's so interesting about that? It doesn't interest anyone, but it always *concerns* the other. It presents a body opposite my own, *a body that is not my own*. By individuating the body, tastes initiate the process of intersubjectivity. The other is other for me; I am other for him. Each *I* is an other; each other is an *I*. That's what every *taste* tells us, in its very gratuitousness.

The duller and more anarchic tastes are, the more disturbing. Hence the great effort immediately to give them meaning, to return them to a meaningful order, in an *interpretation* (meaning is soothing, reassuring: it undoes the body of the other by dialecticizing it into a reading space).

That's the role of the final synthesis. It gives tastes a *psychological* meaning. It transcends them through a well-known, very socialized order, the order of everyday psychology (through adjectives): characterology. We discover the reifying, pacifying function of psychology, of predication.

3. Through Psychological (Final) Synthesis, Contingency Is Outstripped by Meaning

Here again antithesis intervenes; it serves to produce paradigm, to produce meaning. Everything is literally paradigmaticized, term by term:

Smoking a pipe	Taking snuff (women take snuff)
Cheese: savory	Preserves: sweet
Demitasse	"Canard"
= coffee—black	= the idea of coffee, its taste, not its power
Confident	Unassuming
Flighty	Thoughtful
Generous	Thrifty
Bouvard	Pécuchet
Man	Woman

It goes without saying that the paradigm has a double meaning:

(a) It's a matter of differentiating Bouvard and Pécuchet (the ongoing enterprise is to differentiate without dissociating them), of making them recognizable without separating them. This recognition of pure identity is in some way gratuitous, nonfunctional, justified by the simple pleasure of intellection (of distinction), because they are not at all opposed on the level of action (see Plick and Plock).[64] Their character distinctions have no diegetic effect.

So it's a *plausible* constraint; for them to be *readable*, there must be a fiction of *meaning*—even if it serves no purpose—since the overall meaning is *Bouvard and Pécuchet*.

(b) The paradigm allows for the implicit opposition of Bouvard-man/Pécuchet-woman, mythologically (pipe/snuff, savory/sweet, arousal/fear of arousal). The masculine/feminine opposition has no genital, sexual import (or depth). Its function is to establish *the couple*. The couple is distinguished from the pair (twinship) of strictly identical organisms. The couple implies a split cell, the confinement of differences (literally, term by term). The sentence is basically *the envelope* that makes the couple, a sack of oppositions.

So the "meaning" of the sentence is the *couple*.

5

"On one occasion they attended a lecture on Arabic at the Collège de France, and the professor was astonished to see these two strangers attempting to take notes" (p. 39).

Here is a sentence that never ceases to fascinate me—ever since I first read it long ago—and, because it fascinates me, I don't really know how to dismantle it; isn't fascination *just short of* explanation? An abutment? The abutment of the Mirror.

Nevertheless I do see what it is that, analytically, I am "circling" (this is an action, a research method, that clearly recalls the action of the child at the originary scene, itself "fascinating").[65]

1. The Anacoluthon

An anacoluthon again—and a sizeable one. Who else knows so precisely that *to write* (to write *in the classical sense*, because clearly it's a whole other question with "modern" writers) is *to establish an order and subvert it*? And that is precisely what the anacoluthon does; it establishes and subverts a logic of construction, of sentence, of discourse.

This anacoluthon is reversal, sudden inversion of points of view, without warning, not only within the sentence, but the sentence *itself*, according to the even line of its delivery.

To really understand the power of this reversal, to imagine the shot, *it would take two cameras*. With one, we enter the room with Bouvard and Pécuchet from the rear (view of the room, desks, dais in the distance, etc.); the camera is through the eyes of Bouvard and Pécuchet (no doubt tracking). Now, *without warning*, camera two is substituted for this one, opposite it, from the eyes of the professor (no tracking for this one). The professor raises his head and sees a scene (speaking generally, this is a process to study: Flaubert is very cinematic). In short, the sentence implies *two technicians*.

Nevertheless the two levels glide over each other without the solution of continuity (the anacoluthon is glued, joined, as though clandestine). The operator of this glide is the "and" (another appearance of that famous "and"). "And," as slack link, conveys the heterogeneities on the same level and gives them a single skin, like a lock, like a vestibule in a railway car, a well-oiled rotating plate. Now the surreptitious joining of two heterogeneities produces the *monstrous*. Maybe the monstrous is always that: members of different classes (or even just members) joined without warning, as though this were *natural* (think of Hieronymus Bosch's creatures, of Bataille's pineal eye, etc.)[66] The Monstrous is a Flaubertian category to investigate, the episode of the Melons, for example.[67] One can say that, as with disordered botany, the second *buds* suddenly from the first, as opposed to Michelet's analyses by which it's the alliance of homogeneous bloodlines, *themselves*, that produces the monster. Kings are caught in the closed circuit of heredity. A sanguine stasis characterizes the Anjou kings; the Plantagenet kings present abnormal size (William the Conqueror did not fit in his tomb); they are voracious, hateful, satanic.

Another effect—or content—of the anacoluthon: two subjects approach ("they attended") and suddenly, without warning, they are transformed into *objects* ("these two strangers"), or, worse, into vague, anonymous objects (silhouette). It's a truly magical effect (conversion of one class into another: lead into gold, etc.), but an evil kind of magic: the *familiar touched with a wand* (verbally) that transforms him into *stranger*. It's the very process of the nightmare when the beloved is transformed into a distant, unknown being; it's the painful theme of *fading*.[68] That strangeness, that vertiginous remove, that *fall* (hemorrhage) from nature, constitutes the very domain of *enchantment* (fascination).

2. The Allocutory

I would like to connect this (gentle) rupture, this *fading* with a general feature that often strikes me in *Bouvard et Pécuchet*. We might say that in *Bouvard et Pécuchet*, *there is no allocutory framework*. No one addresses anyone; we never know where the message comes from. For example, Bouvard and Pécuchet perfectly mirror each other (that's the meaning of their partnership); they don't address each other with words. They form an amorous block (amorous Discourse is not allocutory, being a closed image). But—this is all Flaubert's work—that block is not projective; the book is not addressed to us—and that's the trouble with it. Here is what Sartre says (*L'Idiot de la famille*, p. 629–40) on the *Dictionnaire des idées reçues*: "Strange work: over a thousand articles and who feels addressed? No one, except Gustave himself."[69] I will express a reservation on this last idea because, for me, it doesn't account for the fascination. What is specifically fascinating is the absolute loss of the allocutory, as the anacoluthon produces something like a perversion of the statement. We have a *fading* not of the message (that's very clear, very readable), but of the allocutaries, the addressees; we could say that we are (monstrously) faced with a *language* (and not a *speech*) block.

This loss of allocution (but not of signification, because the fiction of denotation, of referent always survives in Flaubert) is tied to another loss that marks *Bouvard et Pécuchet* throughout: the loss of the gift. Bouvard and Pécuchet never give anything. Everything is exchanged, but all exchanges go wrong; there is no *expenditure*. The world—of nature and of language—is *dull*. Even excrement (see the episode with the dung that's worth gold) is salvaged, but that fails as well. Expenditure is negated by Exchange, but Exchange fails. The world is doubly closed; it is abolished in a kind of *tableau vivant* without addressee (*tableau vivant* or *tableau mort*, as we say *nature morte*, still life). What makes the book's tableau vivant terrible is that the "subjects" of the story (Bouvard and Pécuchet) are continually within; they are never cast out (that's why they are never bored). But Flaubert is always tidying up, *through the sentence*, so that nothing ever remains outside of the tableau vivant: the enormous paradox of an *elliptical art with nothing leftover nonetheless*. That is the very *effect* of our sentence.

6

"The monotony of the desk became odious to them. Continually the eraser and the sandarac,* same inkwell, the same pens, and the same companions! Considering them stupid, they talked to them less and less" (p. 40).

There is nothing to say (I have nothing to say) on the *form* of this sentence. Except: (1) to recall the dominant relationship of causality, naturalized by the present participle ("Considering them stupid"); (2) to note there should be a subtle analysis of the *rhythm* of the enumeration and the place of the two "ands." Thus I will formulate two remarks on content:

1. Cleavage

The sentence marks a split between Bouvard and Pécuchet, on the one hand, and their occupation, other people, everyday life, that is to say, the world (the worldly) on the other. The world invites or incites separation in two forms: work and language (the "stupidity" of others as language event). This cleavage, which fills the world with distance, boredom, and a vague nausea, is generally characteristic of the Lover; he feels the world as an absolute void. That feeling comes over Bouvard and Pécuchet as soon as, having discovered each other, they form a *couple*. This term typically involves passion.

---

*A resin used for blotting paper to keep ink from soaking in.

Whereas for them, passion illuminates the alienation of work. It serves as initiator, mediator of truth; it is pedagogical.

2. Copy

Again, the copy. It is not copying that disgusts them; it is the protocols of the copy (which otherwise could give one pleasure). Objects are no longer fetishes, mediums for bodily acts (the mania of "stationers"); they become flat objects once again, without resonance, without symbolism (neither metonymy nor metaphor). The copy is then returned to what general opinion considers it to be: a fastidious bêtise.

For Bouvard and Pécuchet, freedom (through an inheritance) will involve taking financial responsibility for the management of the copy ("applying" books to reality). And from then on, it becomes exciting. From slaves, they become *amateurs* (while awaiting the finale: the *nothing* of the copy freely assumed).

*　　*　　*

I would like to end this analysis of the sentence with a very short digression: the place of *Bouvard et Pécuchet* in the vast panorama of the copy, of copied languages (I mean in Flaubert's work). That would come back—methodologically—to presenting fictional characters as *creatures of language*, agents of language. These characters could be divided (classified) according to their relationship to the copy of language. In Flaubert, we would have:

(a) the consistency, the persistence of a single language, a single copy, the confinement of the idiolect with its model: this is linguistic monomania (Homais, Madame Bovary);

(b) the varied, hysterical, circular copy of *languages*; this is a matter of changing languages as one changes a shirt (clothes), of making languages revolve, of listing languages (a library of languages) as in *Bouvard et Pécuchet* and, but only shifting the field a bit, in *La Tentation de saint Antoine*;

(c) the nonlanguage, the just-short-of language, aphasia, the affective as that for which one does not take responsibility, *noted* through phraseology: Charles Bovary (Charles dies from the death of Emma); Berthe, proletarianized, disappears from language;[70]

(d) the ideal language, outside of social nature, the ideality of language, the beyond-copy as in *Saint Julien l'Hospitalier*.

These four categories correspond to the bêtise, hysteria, stupidity, art.

7

"To learn where to settle, they reviewed all the provinces. The north was fertile, but too cold; the south delightful for its climate, but unpleasant due to the mosquitoes; and the central part, frankly, possessed nothing of interest. Brittany would have suited them, were it not for the sanctimoniousness of its inhabitants. As for the eastern regions, because of the Germanic patois, they were out of the question" (p. 43).

1. The name flushes an image (as we say, "to flush game"). That was Proust's whole theory (place names: Guermantes, Balbec, Parme, Coutances).[71] The name is the foundation; the name expresses nothing, it does not translate, it is not subsequent. In the case of *Bouvard et Pécuchet*, the name doesn't flush an image, but a *stereotype*: the geographical touristic dictionary of received ideas.

Note that all tourist advertising, the endoxal geography of mass travel, functions according to this same mechanism, but positive—not deceptive.

2. The stereotype does not *express* a distaste ("I don't like that"); it establishes it. To form and to support are the same operation here; I let myself be formed by what supports me. Now as we know, the stereotype is a sentence, a phrasal strike: "the central part, frankly, possessed nothing of interest." This is a sentence, closed: period, that's all, neither, nor, it's done. I am formed by the sentence of others (like Sartre's *Genet*).[72] Thus it is enough to *undo* the sentence to undo the stereotype and reverse the value. That is the case with Michelet regarding the Center of France (in the *Tableau de la France*):[73] France functions historically because the Center has nothing of interest.

3. The sentence as a whole is doubly disappointing:

(a) within each proposition, it's fine, *but* there is a little something that makes *the whole* (moment of choice) not work. The object is *de-ceived*—through a point of hemorrhage: it *turns* (like mayonnaise turns);

(b) *enumeration* is obviously a powerful operator of deception. By becoming general and systematic, it escapes contingency, the aleatory, and returns to structure. Perhaps there is a hysteria of disappointment (as there are hysterias of boredom, sleepiness, failure). Psychologically, it is a matter of Distaste, the Difficult, the (infantile) *chaouchoun*.[74]

Now, interestingly, the disappointing enumeration of *Bouvard et Pécuchet* reproduces homologically and symbolically the disappointing enumeration of sexual practices, presented in a popular song, the Gallic "guardroom" song, which I'm going to quote in its entirety regardless, because it's so symbolically exemplary: "The Complex of Jean Gilles" ("Jean Gilles My Son-in-Law"). I'm omitting nothing except the repetitions:

—Father-in-law, my father-in-law,
I've come to complain to you.
—What's your complaint
Jean Gilles, my son-in-law?
My daughter is all yours.
—Yes, but what should we do
When we're by ourselves?
—Don't you screw her?
My daughter is all yours.
—Yes, but if I screw her
She'll stick me with kids.
—Don't you feel her up,
Jean Gilles, my son-in-law?
My daughter is all yours.
—Yes, but if I feel her up
Her breasts will sag.
—Don't you fuck her,
Jean Gilles, my son-in-law?
—Yes, but if I fuck her
We'll be fucked over.
—Don't you bugger her,
Jean Gilles, my son-in-law?
—Yes, but if I bugger her
I'll lose my taste for it.
—Don't you ball her,
Jean Gilles, my son-in-law?
My daughter is all yours.
—Yes, but if I ball her
She'll be a pain in the ass.
You're the pain in the ass,
Jean Gilles, my son-in-law.
Shit! Shut up and fuck off!

In one heterological leap, let's return to analytical discourse: the obvious relationship between the enumerative form and disappointment should be investigated. The list (no matter what its contents) may always be deceptive, basically, and Flaubert would be the author who has best realized the essential nature of enumeration (*La Tentation de saint Antoine*, *Salammbô*). What's interesting is that enumeration assumes an inventiveness (of inventory) and sometimes takes the appearance of triumph (Aeschylus, the catalogue in *Perseus*; children listing, between gasps, everything they've done, everything they want). We are at the heart of the imaginary with a frantic increase of the self (as in Kleinian manic triumphalism),[75] followed by a merciless deflation of that self. That manic-depressive structure corresponds to infantile depression: this is obviously the case with *Bouvard et Pécuchet*. And in our song, it's clear that Jean Gilles and his father-in-law form a single subject, master of enumeration (sexual triumph) and its disappointment.

*   *   *

To close . . .

"Yes," says Flaubert, "the bêtise consists of wanting to conclude." So I will not conclude—although not without risking the bêtise, nevertheless. Because even if I don't conclude, I must put the analysis of these seven sentences into the perspective of what continues to interest me in *Bouvard et Pécuchet*: *the engine of languages that never stops running*. Or again: the freewheel of languages. Or again: the levels, the gradual stepladder of the statement ("the bathmology").[76]

1. We must first establish what is it in the sentence, as Flaubert complies with it (and he exaggerates this obedience to the code), that produces a stop to language, a *stasis* of statement, the *static illusion*:

(a) We will first note the illusion of *complete meaning*, of the sentence as a space saturated with a complete meaning (classic definition, Classical rhetoric, in combination with the logic of Port-Royal, the center for predication).[77] Complete meaning? That's an illusion that proceeds from two devices:

—The prevalence of the relationship of causality, presented as often as possible (one moves from cause to effect: everything seems to be said).

—The control, that is, in fact, the restriction of catalysis. Yielding to catalysis would be to open the sentence, the meaning, to infinity, would be to lack the "special substance" of the sentence (according to Proust with regard to Balzac). The *measured, studied* ellipsis, the ellipsis that doesn't present itself as such, produces a disregard for everything that could extend beyond the meaning. It produces the illusion of a sentence that might be made *to measure* to the very body of thought (Flaubert is very good at that, he is a luxury tailor).

b) Next we will note all the operators of closure, all the devices that say, "attention, full stop, period, nothing more after!" (which, given the linearity of language, of the sentence, stands for "nothing more below"), all the internal symmetries of the sentence, the antithesis. In sentence 4, we saw the sentence functioning as an envelope, a sealed membrane that encloses, and therefore constitutes, the couple, an ideologically complete meaning, if ever there was one.

The stasis of statement (that is to say, in fact, the *stated*) is so strong in Flaubert that the Flaubertian sentence seems to achieve the very essence of the classical (predicative) sentence. *Thetic*, it *poses* the truth. That is why I could say this: the Flaubertian sentence is the tableau vivant of Truth, Reality, the Referent, and Denotation. It is *the simple state of things* that Bataille discusses.[78] Flaubert's sentence always has the air of being *without rest*, like Nature (only not including the *et caetera*, according to Valery).[79]

2. That all makes the Flaubertian sentence *a pure block of language*, a finished block, within which language is stopped, does not escape, does not drift, is not delivered to anyone (see the allocutory deficiency). Nevertheless, this block has surreptitious fissure points, which Flaubert desired, according to a clandestine, surreptitious disintegration from within the structure.

(a) We must recall that when a particular form, an idiolectal structure, repeats itself, renews itself (as is the case with Flaubert's sentence), it seems to copy itself, to recopy itself, it becomes a paradigm of itself. Every author is in a parodic relationship with himself. Moreover, and paradoxically, that is why writing *takes language for* the world. Bataille: "It is clear that the world is purely parodic, that is to say, that each thing seen is the parody of another, or the same thing in a deceptive form" (*Anus solaire*).[80] Flaubert's sentence is this deceptive parody: parody of itself, but also, since "content" and "form" can never be separated, parody of truth, of denotation. Perhaps Flaubert's pride and achievement was to found an art of *deceptive parody* thanks to a "perfect" (finished) form that, through its perfection, makes the referent escape in a sort of hemorrhage. Because, inversely, to feel one's way, so to speak, would allow the understanding that there is a truth. Only the lie, the void, the ungraspable, the unstoppable are *tidy*: we must get used to that paradox.

(b) Another point of disintegration: What I have called the *anacoluthons* (the places of anacoluthons) as ruptures in construction, not in grammar, but in discursivity, in the underlying schema of the statement. As examples, I will cite the anacoluthon of the two truths, the scientific and the mundane (no. 1), the Collège de France (no. 5), and I will come back to the paradoxical role of the Flaubertian "and," which is often an anacoluthon marker. We constantly see this double movement in Flaubert: cracking, breaking, and making the rupture slip. Is it a matter of a "Hypocrisy" of subversion? I think that's something to study; there is a hypothesis there, a lead.

(c) We will note once again a surreptitious disintegration: The enumeration—a typical feature of Flaubert—which is not unrelated to the anacoluthon. The enumerative "and" has the appearance of a logical enumerator, of an accumulator that joins homogenous units, which, in fact, are nothing of the kind. What is accumulated, *spun out*, is heterogeneous, heteroclite. What underlies the Flaubertian list is an aesthetic of the *preposterous* (see the child or bird who suddenly turns its head). This is clearly seen in Proust's pastiche. On the other hand, we have seen (sentence 3) that enumeration is the very essence of kitsch: the *display*, the preposterous parade. Finally (sentence 7), enumeration is a powerful operator of *disappointment*: it denies any possible conclusion, *exhausts itself* in failure, defers pleasure even further (Jean Gilles's complex).

What is the principle of these processes of phrasal disintegration and how are they related to the general question of infinite engines of language? I will summarize in this way: Flaubertian production both establishes (the sentence in all its classic splendor) and perverts its order. *It establishes it all the better to subvert it* as in *Little Red Riding Hood*: "Grandmother, what big teeth you have!—All the better to eat you, my child." With all the submission of a zealous slave, Flaubert accepts the order of classical language (and, coincidentally, through the sentence, the order of logic and grammar), but *on the sly*, through certain *pretenses*, he perverts that order. And therefore he repeats once more, on the level of the sentence, what *Bouvard et Pécuchet*, as macrostructure, never stops saying, that there is no bottom or end to language, to languages, that languages circle round and round until finally the truth of language is revealed, that is, the fatal exemption of Truth: the Copy.

3. Thus we come back to the copy—and through the same dimension of theme, we arrive at History, great and monumental History: How are Bouvard and Pécuchet inscribed there?

(a) All European literature, for centuries, was based upon *mimesis* (the referential function defines realism, in the broad sense). Here (maybe earlier, here and there), another *mimesis* is established: *the mimesis of languages*. Now, immediately, this *mimesis* is defined (described) as *bottomless*. It's all copy, the original endlessly recedes and, in this recession, engenders other copies. For example:

—all sciences are covered; like so much discourse, they all collapse in failure, only the copy remains;

—Bouvard and Pécuchet successively cover all the "roles" of psychoanalysis: obsessional, hysterical, perverse;

—each language is a level of bêtise for the higher level. But that level itself is topped with a new one that renders it stupid, and this continues with no end in sight:

—Chavignolles (France) is stupid;

—Bouvard and Pécuchet top Chavignolles, bêtise A: they are intelligent and subversive, morally and politically;

—Flaubert tops A and B: he makes the bêtise appear before us;

—we can top A, B, C (Sartre and Flaubert), etc.

On this decoding, we can refer to the second argument of the Neo-Skeptics (Sextus Empiricus):[81] infinite regression. But regarding languages, it is better to say *perpetual* than *infinite*. Language has the structure of a perpetual calendar (see *Argo*, the ship).[82]

(b) One could conceive—and of course refine—a typology of subjects according to if they stop language or not, provide it with a gear wheel, a catch, or let it go freewheeling:

—those that don't stop language: the chatterbox, the lunatic, the baby (babble), the text-writer, Bouvard and Pécuchet;

—the one who stops it: essentially, the (dogmatic) militant, political, theological, sexual, the ideological subject.

(c) So, it bears repeating: Flaubert's *object* is language, languages. The *subject* is man grappling with language, languages, like an onion, being nothing other than layers, skins of language. How is this located in History?

It is said that Leibniz was the last man who was able to hold all (scientific) knowledge in his head. After him, this assembling could only be done by many, hence, the idea of the encyclopedia. Likewise, in France, Balzac was the last fiction writer able to contain by himself all social knowledge; after him, a "social" novel could only be written by many.

The Encyclopedia of knowledge? It triumphed with Diderot. After him, it returned (or remained) as farce: *Bouvard et Pécuchet* is an encyclopedia-farce ("a kind of encyclopedia as farce").[83] Today *Bouvard et Pécuchet* would be two typists who would buy a small farm, read the Alpha or Bordas Encyclopedia, raise chickens (this would be a failure), do hand weavings (which wouldn't sell), go through phases of Marxism, structuralism, psychoanalysis, biology, etc.[84]

Thus the Encyclopedia of knowledge, in the Flaubert-moment, corresponds to the farce stage. But with Flaubert, the Encyclopedia of knowledge is replaced by another encyclopedia: the *Encyclopedia of languages*. This one cannot be serious: its *tone*, its *ethos* is uncertain, because language, languages are neither within nor outside of truth. And that is very much Flaubert's *ethos*. Uncertain, no one has yet been able to fix him: Flaubert as *neat* and *uncertain* enunciator.

Flaubert is stuffed with languages, but none definitively, "truly," prevails. One object has the same hypersemantic, underdogmatic function: not the Encyclopedia, relegated to the rank of farce, but the *Dictionary*, and better yet the *Dictionary of phrases* (articles by Littré). In the *Dictionary of Received Ideas*, the important, generative word is not "received ideas" (the bêtise); it is the word "dictionary."

5

Exchanges

1. Roland Barthes to René Char

There is no reason to think that René Char (1907–88) and Roland Barthes ever met, nor that there was a silent dialogue between them like the one Michel Foucault persistently constructed with the poet's work, from *Histoire de la folie à l'âge classique* (Gallimard, 1961) until *Souci de soi* (Gallimard, 1984). Nevertheless, Char's was the first living poet's name to appear in Barthes's first book, *Le Degré zéro de l'écriture*. In that book, which, in some way, returns poetry to a mythological form of "literature," Char himself, along with Francis Ponge and Henri Michaux of course, escapes the collapse of poetic writing into artificiality, "this diffuse tone," "this precious *aura*," which are "usually" called "poetic feeling." With Char, it's "the Word" that is "the dwelling place" and that "gratifies and fulfills like the sudden revelation of a truth." Barthes then adds, "To say that this truth is of a poetic order is merely to say that the Word in poetry can never be untrue because it is whole."[1] Barthes would subsequently refer to Char's work, either through his own readings or through those of his friends like Maurice Blanchot or Roger Laporte.

*   *   *

March 5, 1955

Dear Sir,

I was very touched that you thought to dedicate your latest and very beautiful book to me.[2] Perhaps, if I feel capable of it, I will try to talk about it. . . .[3] That would be the best, least rhetorical way to convey to you my friendship and my deep admiration.

Roland Barthes

*   *   *

November 18, 1968

Let me express my gratitude for your kindness in thinking to send me your text—and for the words that you thought to send with it.[4] And let me convey with my gratitude my deep and faithful friendship.

Roland Barthes

2. Roland Barthes to Georges Perros

Barthes never cites the name of Georges Perros (1923–78) in any of his books; however, the letters from Barthes to Georges Perros, like Perros's references in his texts to Barthes's work, testify to great closeness. They met in 1954 and, with Michel Butor and Pierre Klossowski, formed a small group of friends who shared the same taste for piano, the theater, and writing.[5] Perros's exile in Brittany in the early 1960s no doubt contributed to this "correspondence" that geographic separation encouraged. Geographic, but also "mythological" separation, as Perros's Brittany was very different from Barthes's Basque country. Beyond theater and piano (which Barthes and Perros practiced four-handed at the Klossowskis' home in Paris), there was writing, and primarily fragmentary writing. It was the "fragment" that prompted Barthes to ask Perros to participate in the Blanchot venture, the "Revue internationale," in 1962. Barthes wrote this to him: "You, the triumphant hero of the successful fragment, are the man for the job; the note from Blanchot, attached, will give you a sense of this column: to be presented there through a few fragments, flashes of that *indirect* light that literature ought to shed on the world."[6] Beyond Perros's public comments on Barthes, the letters from Perros to Michel Butor suggest a mutual admiration and no doubt the same friendly reservations: "I received Barthes's little book [*Critique et vérité*]. Very interesting as always. But, beneath all that, what extraordinary nostalgia for the work. Shh! That said, there is more "creation" in three lines of Barthes than in a hundred pages of our young creators today. Again, shh!"[7] The letters from Georges Perros to Roland Barthes have not been found.

*   *   *

[Paris,] Tuesday, [June 1, 1954]

Dear friend,

I'm afraid you don't have my new address: it's 11, rue Servandoni, Paris VIᵉ, Danton 95–85.[8]

I wonder if you have moved, and I don't really know how to get in touch with you. If this note reaches you, please be kind enough to call me so we can arrange to meet.

Very best,
R. Barthes

*   *   *

[Paris,] February 7, 1955

Dear friend, I haven't forgotten you and I was glad to get your note, however sad you may be right now, so very far from Paris.[9] For me, the year is sinking into the displeasure of increasing dispersion, the whole thing complicated by "systemic" trouble over the theater. We are in full Brechtian crisis, fascinated by the power of this man's theory and, as we haven't yet assimilated the issue very well, we only have a totally negative take on all the theater we see anymore (bad theater, moreover, even empirically); furthermore this creates tensions and ruptures in the review.[10]

Otherwise, I'm forever trying to get clear of the papers I promised, to be able to begin some "disinterested" writing finally; but I never manage it, and that's a bit of a grind. Now I'm going to have to get busy on my application to the CNRS, because it's only in some serious sociology that I see the means to find my way anymore.[11] I am, in fact, sick and tired of the theater, and I don't know how to extract myself *victoriously*, that is to say, making something out of this nothing.

You see that not much has changed since your departure. Won't you come to Paris for a bit? I would love to see you.

At least send me your news and trust in my faithful friendship.

R. Barthes
11, rue Servandoni, Paris VIᵉ

*   *   *

Friday, [February 18, 1955]

Dear friend,

Try to come to Paris, so we can see you a bit; let me know as soon as you arrive, but keep in mind that I'll be in England from March 6 to 12.[12] It would be a shame to miss you.

Until soon, I hope. Is there anything you need here that we can do for you?

Warm regards,
Barthes

*　　*　　*

Friday, [May 18, 1956]

Thanks, my old man, for your note. I'm still so sorry to have missed your call. Don't give up, try me again; I would like to come have lunch or dinner with you one day next week.

I'm still doing very badly! And that leads me miserably into laziness. I have only one idea in mind: to produce my collection of mythologies. But even that is very hard and I'm working completely in the dark, with the feeling that I have no justification for what I'm doing. I have the impression of persisting in publishing them *against* all. Probably that's what it means *to write*.

Awaiting your call, and sending my best,
RB

*　　*　　*

Sunday, [mid-September 1956]

I was happy to get your news; don't forget to keep me updated. I just spent a month in Hendaye, total solitude and absolute work; you see that we are even beyond the superlative! But truly, whatever daily panic there was over the point of my work, I retain a happy memory of that month that contrasts so sharply with the bogged down, indecisive intellectuality of the last year. I did nothing but write my theoretical text on the mythologies.[13] It's finished, except for a few edits. Sadly, I myself haven't gotten away from it, or rather, I haven't gotten myself out of it, as I had hoped; but, from an intellectual perspective, I don't think that it's insignificant for me. I believe I've taken a step forward in daring to confront the notion of *formalism*, beyond the Marxist taboos.

Since returning to Paris, I haven't done anything much. And I'm leaving again in a few days for Zurich with Nadeau to meet the Russian literati there.[14] Then I may go to Italy for a bit. I'll return to Paris about October 15.

Won't we see you in Paris at all this winter? If I get three days and a car, I'll try to come for a bit to share your sardines and see the country that I know nothing about.[15]

Yours truly, my dear Georges,
Roland

*　　*　　*

December 9, 1956

My dear friend,

Won't we see you for a little? Come for a bit to restore the sanity of all these Paris intellectuals with your wisdom; they've gone completely mad. As for me, I'm resisting it as best I can with a great influx of sociology (it's very quietist), and minor desertions. Seriously, when are you coming? I would really love to see you.

Roland

*　　*　　*

Saturday, [January 26, 1957]

I would really love to see you, my old man. To end procrastinations, I'll propose to you Thursday, January 31, at 6:30 PM at l'Arche.[16] We can get a quiet drink.

If that suits you, no need to respond, and see you Thursday. If not, give me a call, Danton 95–85.

Till very soon,
Your friend,
R. Barthes

*　　*　　*

La Spezia,[17] [Italy, August 26, 1957]

My old man, tied up here for the last month with a friend, Olivier, who broke two vertebrae.[18] A very hard month in all respects. But health is improving. We're returning to Hendaye. Drop me a line there to let me know if you'll be in Paris early September.

Faithfully yours,
Roland
Etchetoa
Hendaye-Plage BP

*   *   *

Sunday, [September 22, 1957]

Dear Georges,

I do nothing but look at the sea, but I really ought to do more and I am *dry*.[19] It's crazy that I have to be damp to be so unhappy about being dry.

I'm returning to Paris soon and will get in touch immediately. We can *really* work on something for the piano.

Roland

*   *   *

Wednesday, [October 23, 1957]

Dear Georges,

Hardly back, and off again! With this bronchitis, I'm leaving for Milan—because of something to do with publishing, or for nothing! I don't know.

I'll be back Thursday, the 31st. Be in touch?

Your friend,
Roland

*   *   *

[Hendaye,] Friday, [January 1958?]

Dear Georges, I have the impression that I left you with many worries. Where are you? At home? TNP? Brittany? I would really love for you to come here. But when? Maybe my next trip? I'm going back soon, even though my work is only beginning to take off. If I could still believe in the obscure work of laziness! But, with my kind of writing, that hardly holds. The weather continues to be wonderful. Till soon. Faithfully. RB

*   *   *

Hendaye, Sunday, [April 27, 1958]

I'm returning next week after a good month of work that has hardly
made a dent in my agenda nevertheless. Be in touch? I'll no doubt
be leaving Paris again about May 15 to return here to finish my
classwork. I leave for America June 17.

Yours,
RB

*   *   *

Battell North, Middlebury College, July 6, [1958][20]

You know the type? I'm having my little metaphysical crisis here.
But New York, what a wonderful city! In a few hours, I was at home
there; 12 million people all to oneself and freedom. Thinking of you.

RB

*   *   *

[New York, August 19, 1958][21]

I think of you often. Terribly rough stay inland. I hope that, despite
myself, I have registered the—astonishing—surface of things regardless. I'm returning soon. I need to catch my breath.

Faithfully,
R. B.

*   *   *

Hendaye, Friday, [autumn 1958?]

Yes, my dear Georges, it's true, I'm guilty, as they say. Nevertheless I
did ask Voisin for your address as soon as I got back from America.[22]
You see that I had good intentions. . . . I came back from there in
excellent shape; loads of personal problems seemed to get straight-
ened out—not all by themselves, because I had bad moments over
there, but that itself worked like some kind of excellent purgative.
I'm still doing well, but obviously bad conditions mounted again
in Paris, and the machinery is a little blocked again. Still overall
it's going well. I came here alone, though the family arrives this
evening—to have a go at this Racine—infamous, like all the things
I don't do—for the Club Français du Livre.[23] I am now very far into
it; but it's endless and basically I would rather be doing something
else, coming back to more mythological, lighter takes on things.

This Racine is really an exorcism of self, with all the bad faith it takes to beat up on a fellow who, in one sense, just resembles me too much (I mean the core, not the art). I'm thinking of returning to Paris about November 10, but I have all of November with him. After that, it would be good to do a little sociology since they persist in giving me grants.[24] The trouble is I don't know when we'll see each other. I suppose you're in Brittany for the winter. I might be able to swing by there in December when I come back here for Christmas. Why not? The sea here—even today when the weather's bad—outdoes any spectacle. Maybe yours is dreamier.

I think of you with all my faithful affection.

Roland

*   *   *

[Paris, January 28, 1959][25]

Be in touch? Racine is finished.[26]

Roland

*   *   *

Hendaye, Thursday, [April 1959?]

My dear Georges,

I haven't worked as well as I would have hoped or thought. It's idiotic, one never thinks that the work has its internal stops. It's crazy that there is still inspiration in all that. And finally, in short, always at the heart of my difficulties, always believing in exerting the intellect and only ever managing to take orders from the subjective.[27] I really worry over all that; I keep writing only through will, stubbornness, and it's not good. For some time, I've been afraid to fool around. I'm searching for something new and I can't find it. I'm afraid of losing the old—which is always a kind of security: the approval of my friends, etc.—and finding myself all alone and completely foolish at the end of this beautiful path. Finally: *etc*. Don't abandon me.

I return—we return—late Sunday probably. Try to be in touch during the week. I had my piano brought from Paris and I was finally able to get my fill of playing it. But in the end I think I only like Romantic music (though not Chopin), it's funny.

Your friend,
Roland

*   *   *

[Dubrovnik,] Saturday, May 2, [1959]

I'm plagued with a sprain that happened the second day and the trip
has lost a bit of its spice; I have to take care of myself. But on the
human side, as they say, there's boundless sympathy: a lively people
and yet no drama! I believe that's a profound quality.

Faithfully yours,
Roland

*   *   *

Hendaye, Saturday, [July 4, 1959?][28]

Finally the weather is fine. I'm working hard but I'm going in circles; it's like a problem that I can't find the solution to. First time in
my life that I've done a summary—and it's killing me.

Till soon,
Roland

*   *   *

Thursday, [September 1959?]

My dear Georges,

At last, to have—I won't say your news (I got a vague and essential
version of that through friends)—at least your address.[29] I wanted
to write to you, to tell you, if only in a note, that I'm here, and to
ask if there's anything I can do, whatever it is! Would you like a bit
of money—we can work things out later. I maintain that friends are
there for that, to make a flow of goods, a circulation of means, possible. And what else? You say nothing about returning. Could we,
the rest of us, arrange for that in one way or another?

Things are going well for me, uneventful. I did a lot of work this
summer on clothing, doing frenzied structuralism. All that is disturbing, and despite my rage for work, I fundamentally doubt my
efforts, I can't calm down, and I'm not even sure of being able to
write up these kinds of methodological imaginings. It's uninspired
madness, Fourier without the genius. I'm without a position;
they've—vaguely—promised me things.[30] I can hold out for three
months, if I can settle into this suspended sentence. January 1, I'll
decide; if nothing's come through, I'll say good-bye to the university,

to science, and I'll go back to teaching high school and work on the essay evenings and Sundays.[31] Basically, it's that sort of *simplicity* that tempts me. I've seen very little of people, and that's why, despite everything, I'm not doing badly.

Be in touch, tell me if you want anything at all.

Yours,
Roland

*   *   *

Sunday, [November 29, 1959]

My dear Georges,

With so many difficult things, I know that Gérard Ph.'s death must have added to your sorrows.[32] I'm sorry that you are so far away; it all makes more sense when you can talk about it; otherwise, isn't it absolutely absurd?

We continue to be in rather a fix here; my brother has not recovered. Everything is uncertain, the diagnosis, the prognosis; we're demoralized. He has never been sick and doesn't bear it very well, with that terrible fragility of the physically strong. This problem has practically become my whole life, nothing gives me pleasure, and I hardly leave the house. Like everything else the weather is dismal.

Give me your news. I can't wait for you to come back.

Yours,
Roland

*   *   *

Sunday, [December 13, 1959]

My dear Georges,

Your note made me happy. We're always talking about you with Pierre K[lossowski], but in fact we only say one thing: how much we want to see you return. I must go play a little piano at their place this week—which makes you envious, I know—I'll try to offer a bit of Schubert, I'd like to. Nothing much is new; we've been troubled by my brother's mysterious disease, two episodes of it. No one knows what he had, *so*, they say, it can come back. And we are worriers; we don't do well with this sort of thing.

I'm still making no progress in my clothing—and I'm at a standstill because I can't imagine more destructive work. Sometimes, rarely,

I tell myself that it's great, but most of the time I see the impasse where I am *cornered*, and I panic. And maybe this will only ever be a subject that I can talk—but not write—about; that will all become clear in a few months. Moreover, it's making me withdraw intellectually; I'm reading even less than before, I never go to the theater, neither Sartre nor Genet.[33] Except the lamentable *Crapaud-Buffle*, what a pretense of goodwill. [34]

We await you.

Roland

*   *   *

Hendaye, December 28, 1959

My dear Georges,

Here I am again in Hendaye for a few days. It's deserted and wet, but it's much more beautiful than summer. I'm recuperating a bit, what a lousy term. It ended in spades; my brother relapsed for the fourth time (it seems to be over for now), and I had to leave suddenly for Switzerland to help my advisor and friend Georges Friedmann, who was trying, unsuccessfully, to get over a severe depression.[35] It's the first time I've been responsible for a problem of that kind. I was worried sick about it; what a fright! As Mother Courage says, *such is the world, need it be so?*

Saw Klossowski and Butor; we talk about you, want you to come back. Can't we do anything to hasten it, arrange for it? I'm returning to Paris at the very beginning of January and I'm thinking of staying there right through until Easter. It's crazy that after all these disruptions and derangements I want—stupidly—order, regularity, reason, friends without problems and conflicts, in short, soundness—all those horrible words. I'm still working on clothing and nothing else; but I think what I'm doing is *infantile*.

I think of you very much.

Roland

*   *   *

February 7, 1960

My dear Georges,

You must be cursing me for my silence. But in short, I'm a little out of practice writing letters, my pen goes much more slowly than my mind, and all that I have to tell you, all that I need to tell you (because friendship is so self-centered) will be very quick: in short, a conversational rhythm includes silences. I have only two bits of practical news for you: I'm now established in this new position as "head of work" at the École des Hautes Études.[36] There is no work and I am head of nothing. I continue my idle life, worried about never working enough, tortured by what I believe to be dissipation, etc.

The only service asked of me is to contribute a little to the history review *Les Annales*.[37] A few reviews, occasional breaks from this interminable linguistics of clothing, strange masterpiece that I doubt I will ever complete. I see Pierre and Denise, superbly indifferent to any piano later than Mozart.[38] Michel, I saw before he left; I've begun *Degrés* and that makes me happy (but I think it's because I'm teaching).[39]

One more note, and you must forgive this entirely practical assault of mine. Picon, the editor of *Arts et Lettres*, has money to help writers and asked me to help him make use of it.[40] Will you allow me to direct him toward you? The money is anonymous, very much so, not even photos as for America; in short, ideal patronage. (I can't take advantage of it because I get a stipend from the State.)

Your friend,
Roland

*   *   *

[Hendaye,] Saturday, [April 9, 1960]

My dear Georges,

I'm in Hendaye, as planned, and in a now classic situation for me, here, in this dense crowd of swimmers and strollers, and here I am shut up inside my work as in a kind of schizophrenia. My rage for work moreover essentially stems from my desire to be finished with this futile book that I talk about all the time and that never seems to get done. All the same, I'm organizing my index cards one last time before drafting it, which will begin about August 10, because I have to take a break in eight days to go to Besançon to give three summer classes; and still it's down to the wire; if I don't finish this *Système de la mode* before I return to Paris in October, I'll be out of time.[41] A thousand other tasks await me next year, and the need to come up with a subject more *human* that this mad abstraction about the most "futile" of subjects. If all goes well, I should say, if all goes miraculously, so that I'm almost out from under by the end of summer, I'll try to come see you before starting a new year. I'm considering it, rest assured; but, like all weaklings, I only work by plunging in; without that madness, how to find the courage to write?

You see, always these same struggles: timing, torments of work, in short, all difficulties that undoubtedly undercut, quite simply, a dream of power, of inspired ease, etc. Nevertheless, this Clothing is important for me, it's a way of exorcising, of eliminating that internal abstraction that is something like my utopia. But what an outrageous prospect!

I beg you not to be discouraged by my silences. You know that nothing is interrupted by them. Start sending me letters again, you always make me very happy.

Faithfully yours,
Roland

*   *   *

Hendaye, Monday, [April 1960]

My dear Georges,

Well, I read the *Papiers collés* in one sitting, more quickly than any book I've read for a long time.[42] It's extraordinary what can be *captured* with only the imagination. But, finally, what you write is always intermediary between dream and thought, and that's what makes you inimitable—so profoundly different from Valéry, whom you admire but to whom you owe so little. What you have here is very distinctive; it is, if you will, *thought disappointed*, the object, through the literary function's sort of sly emphasis, of a *de-ception*, in Latin to render the *release* of literature's hold over reality. You know too well how convinced I am that herein lies the very ontology of writing, so you can have no doubt with regard to the writing that I am profoundly by your side. It's true that, if I were to take some of your *facts* at their word, I would debate them, at the gut level. But it's for that very reason that you are—wonderfully and incurably—a writer; with you, it's the *movement* that's true, not the element. Hence the famous mediation that makes good literature. And then naturally, beyond that *function*, is also that inimitable something, like a good spice, that is you, and that makes your book essentially *friendly*, simultaneously beyond you and greater than you, increasing your friendships.[43] You know all that. What remains to be seen is what you're going to do now: begin again? That's not possible, it's never possible.

So, one leap further, the next mediation, the last: that of an *order*?

It seems to me, sooner or later, that's where you must head; and maybe your new life, the end of your solitude, will help you in this.[44]

Thank you, my dear Georges, for this moment spent with you, a moment *more true* than reality, as in photogenic. Until soon, with other news.

Your friend,
Roland

*   *   *

Sunday, [June 12, 1960]

My dear Georges,

I'm very late in answering you, but you understand that my incapacity to write letters is one of those deep tendencies that require indulgence! You know that those tendencies are significant but not intentional. There I go again with my language. I'm on the point of coming to the end, if I can say that, with signifiers of Fashion; a few hours of organizing and nothing more will keep me from finally drafting this essay that I always announce in a fixed way like the march of the choir at the Opera. I'm leaving in a few days for Italy for a conference on the Image, then afterward Hendaye and Fashion (I hope to come see you returning from Hendaye, in the fall). I've seen a little theater (that hasn't happened to me in a long time), a few mediocre standards (among them, sadly, *Le Balcon*[45] and, shining above the mist like a distant star, the incomparable Brechtian *Mère*).[46] Once again I was sick from this beauty; well, affected, moved, freed, rendered powerful, intelligent, in harmony with the world—and then depressed that this work is all *alone*; what to do with a single piece of evidence?

Write me a note. I keep track of you through Pierre and Denise, but your own writing would make me happy.

Faithfully yours,
Roland

*   *   *

Thursday, [November 10, 1960]

My dear Georges, a small sign of friendship—no big news otherwise. I'm unhinged by renovations that are making a mess of my room, which I was able to enlarge. But at the moment I have no place to go, and I'm reduced to *reading* (because I can do it on my bed)! Well, I found Pierre's book *dazzling*, for reconciling you with *art*.[47] For the rest, the sociology wave, day to day—and Fashion too often at a standstill—interminable. With all that I take on, I would need an explosive cenaesthesia, and I'm so slow, so lazy! You see that I've resolved nothing, I carry on; and as for politics, well, I think that on the contrary I'm rationalizing more and more—that is to say, paradoxically, that I'm going straighter, a little.[48]

Yours, dear Georges, faithfully,
Roland

*   *   *

[Thursday,] November 19, 1961

My dear Georges,

Your note made me very happy, as you well know; but even when we don't write to each other, it seems I always know your essential news through Pierre, and I even saw photos from last summer, of Tania and the little one, as if I had been there.[49] But of course it's not the same thing, all the same; and I must really come pay you a short visit in your Brittany. But what can you do, it's another year of stress; for three or four years, I've been trying to escape my annual difficulties with work once and for all. I would like to try someday to be full faculty at this École des Hautes Études, where I only teach irregularly.[50] If I manage that, I believe that I would be free (if one can believe such a thing), free at least to return to more relaxed writing, to literature, in short, to the slightly informal life of a writer. To that end I must provide certain evidence to the University. I'm trying to transform my Fashion into a thesis and settle that issue this year; that's to tell you that I still can't give it to you to read. I estimate that I have two more months of work on the manuscript, for which I've written and typed up three hundred pages. I promise to send you a copy, as soon as it's final. In short, another tunnel-year, but I believe, yes, I really believe that it's the last one—at least for this tunnel! And consequently, you get the picture: I can't do anything but that, I can't read, except a little linguistics for myself, I hardly write, and basically see no one. Evenings, of course, I go out a bit, but it's mostly to rove the streets. But you, no Paris? Even spoiled and exhausting, a little visit here would let us see each other and play a few scales together. Try.

Your friend,
Roland

*   *   *

Urt, Tuesday, [spring 1962]

My dear Georges,

I know that I'm beating my own records in silence. I always plead
work; but it's true. I was supposed to submit a part of the manuscript before vacation, in such a rush that this past month I really
believe I didn't have a single engagement or write a single letter.[51] I
worked all day long and went out a bit in the evening, late, like
cats do. And that will be true, I think, for May as well, when many
things must be decided for me. But, if one can say this, the heart
keeps watch, you know. I hope that you have had spring there. I
arrived here four days ago, and there were three glorious days, but
today it's gray and I'm returning in haste to resume my manuscript
and my little worries at Hautes Études. Perhaps this is the last
month before something decisive, either that I get that post as Director of Studies which would give me stability and freedom, or
that I renounce completely this endless flirting with the University.

Be in touch, my dear Georges, and I beg you, never hold my silences against me.

With all my affection,
Roland

*   *   *

Urt, Sunday, [June 17, 1962]

My dear Georges,

I'm in our Southwest for three days, having come here to take a rest
from professional tumult; I was named director of studies at the
School of the same name.[52] All the feelings for the Collège de France
or the Academie. But also, this is important for me: I am free here,
independent, two hours of a little teaching per week, months of vacation, no more bosses, no more annual reapplying for a position—
and maybe, beyond all these objective reasons, the obscure satisfaction of returning to this University for which I basically have a
weakness; a plaything that I wanted as an adolescent and that I undoubtedly still desired, since I have struggled to obtain it in middle
age, by "retiring" from literature for three or four years. There, I've
acquired a taste for big plans; so I'm telling myself: one more year
of pseudouniversity tasks (Fashion and the little thesis),[53] after

which, provided with an occupation of two hours of work per week, I will get to the real writing. And there it is. That changes nothing about my work at the moment. Fashion is moving forward (when have I said that to you?), but I believe it will take me the summer; afterward: the little thesis, and the first year's seminar to prepare. I can do that on *signs*.[54]

I'm returning to Paris next week, but I think only for a few days. I'm tired, ready for my Italian vacation. After that, in the summer, I don't know: no doubt Urt and work. Are you coming to Paris someday? Give me a bit of your news, tell me what you're reading, what you're writing.

Yours,
Roland

*   *   *

Sunday, [early October 1962]

My dear Georges,

You know, it's always in my plans to write to you, but in one sense, since I am no longer an adolescent, I no longer know how to write letters, and that's why I regret it so much that you are far away. It seems to me that I have nothing to tell you beyond the realm of conversation and the hand is too slow and too heavy (you can see that, moreover, in my handwriting!). But, as for me, selfishly, I really like receiving your letters. We returned late from the Southwest this year, that golden-green grape seed color of this Basque Béarn, that was described so well by Francis Jammes when he was the famous poet of the region.[55] I didn't work so much during the summer, I lazed about, and now, coming back, I've spent all this October on an infinite number of thankless, inessential tasks. The essential one would be Fashion, but it remains only half typed up and there's still much left to do. So there you have it. I begin my seminar for Hautes Études in November; but this year I'll be obliged to improvise week by week.

When will we see you? I missed you again in September.

Your friend,
Roland

*   *   *

December 28, 1962

My dear Georges,

You've heard about the plan for an Italian-German-French publication developed here by a group that I'm part of (in extremis), centered on Blanchot and Mascolo.[56] I'd like to give you a long explanation of what all this means, but time is short and we need to take the plunge. Now, we need you, and I have everyone's support to contact you and beg you to join us: the new essential thing being—in our eyes—an ongoing column (*le Cours des Choses*) composed of *fragments* coming from each of us. You, the triumphant hero of the successful fragment, are the man for the job; the note from Blanchot, attached, will give you a sense of this column: to be presented there through a few fragments, flashes of that *indirect* light that literature ought to shed on the world—the world of others and our own.[57] If you can send us those fragments by January 10, that would be ideal (we have an international meeting in the middle of the month).[58]

We're counting on you, dear Georges; and as the *need* one has of others is basically the most tenacious of our affections, I am not ashamed to add to this appeal my warm and faithful wishes for you and yours, from your old friend.

Roland

*   *   *

Monday, [January 14, 1963]

Thank you from the bottom of my heart for these beautiful fragments that you were so kind to send us; everyone thanks you for them. I'll keep you posted on what the review (which doesn't yet exist) will do with them.[59] Just as they are, they constitute an invaluable contribution to build upon: thank you.

I had the pleasure of reading you as if it was a good letter to me; you should send these notes regularly to your friends! They give the impression of living with you.

Thinking of you faithfully, my dear Georges.

Roland

*   *   *

Friday, [April 19, 1964]

But no, my dear Georges, I love you as from the very first day, I think of you always with the most faithful affection, how could you doubt it? You'd have no doubt if you knew (but you do know, since I've told you) how much trouble I have writing letters; *existential* trouble, but it's nothing more than one of those little neuroses or even schizophrenias that go gallivanting between the pen and the head—and the heart—of those who write. I'm a good fellow for conversation (at least I hope) but, sadly, not for letters. That's why, with you so far away, I miss you even more. As for the book, I plead not guilty.[60] This time, Seuil stuck me with my twenty-five author copies and let me mail them myself; thus a considerable delay precisely for my friends. Your book has been here on my piano, all wrapped up to send, since before vacation, but since I returned from Urt only yesterday, that explains the delay. Yes, I would like very much to hear the good news of your son from you soon—and that you'll be coming to Paris soon as well, and that this time I won't miss you.

Yours truly with all my faithful affection.

Roland

*   *   *

Urt, July 2, [1964]

My dear Georges,

I learned through Michel that you have suffered the loss of your father.[61] I'm here, my dear Georges, and I'm thinking of you. Write to me, it seems to me that I'm the one who needs your words.

Your friend,
Roland

*   *   *

Urt, August 16, 1964

My dear Georges,

A small sign of friendship, since *signs* seem all I'm capable of! I made a little jaunt from Morocco to Italy, and now here, for rest, that is to say, work (relentless). I'm working on Rhetoric, I'm reading Quintilian. My heart is heavy, my overly sensitive "soul" is troubled, but Quintilian sets many things right. No doubt I'll be here for a few more weeks. And then, Paris, which is not to be envied.

Thinking of you faithfully.

Yours,
Roland

Baltimore, October 6, [1967][62]

My dear Georges,

It gave me great pleasure to see your writing, but I'm furious just the same! Why attack me so? You know quite well that my silence between letters means nothing; I've explained to you how difficult it is for me to write "intransitively," how I refuse to consider the letter an obligatory sign of faithfulness. For me, if I could see you again, I would find you as before, with the same affection and confidence, that's certain. And Fashion, that's another misunderstanding; regretfully, I let that semiological tome come out, with the firm intention of not boring friends with it, except in special cases[63] (Pierre, for example, being interested in the "suit").[64] It's not a book that can represent a "gift," a "souvenir," a "sign." Certainly, since you would like it, I'm going to have Seuil send you a copy. There you have it. But I would really like you to come to Paris sometime when I'm there (I return in February, after this American ordeal, which has just begun) and when we can see each other in the usual way.

Your faithful friend,
Roland

*   *   *

Rabat, May 1, 1970

My dear Georges,

Far from being "bêtises," the things you've written me give me *pleasure*.[65] That pleasure which sounds *right*, and thus *makes good*, justifies a work—justification that, in the barbaric slosh, only comes from friends anymore; because the press, the public . . .

    I'm having Japan sent to you (I don't get complimentary copies from Skira, hence the confusion); I think it ought to please you, because it's a rare genre: a *happy* critique!

Yours faithfully,
Roland
11, rue Pierre-Sémard
Rabat

*   *   *

Paris, April 28, 1973

My dear Georges,

I was very happy to receive the *Papiers collés II*; already, before one reads you, you offer the pleasure of the journey, of gleaning (and I also immediately fell on the lines that you devoted to me, and they made me happy).[66] In short, you are not boring—and I end up being fascinated by this quality—so difficult to define. I'll take advantage of this note to tell you that I was sorry to miss you on your last visit. When are you coming back? Write to me a little in advance.

Thank you,
Your friend,
Roland

*   *   *

March 8, 1975

Thank you, Georges, your letter is magnificent.[67] True criticism is in letters, more and more. Please, when you're coming to Paris, let me know a bit in advance, and we'll get together. I would like that.

Yours,
R. B.

*   *   *

March 28, 1976

My very dear Georges,

Lambrichs let me know about your disease and your operation.[68] It touched me deeply—all the more so because I had just reconnected with you through those "fracta" of memories that I loved so much, that I would have loved to have thought of and been able to write.[69]

Heal quickly and well, and trust in my steadfast and faithful affection.

Roland

3. With Jean Starobinski

Many factors connected Roland Barthes and Jean Starobinski. The writers they worked on Michelet, Racine, La Rochefoucauld. . . . But most importantly, a shared rigor, a shared ethics in their conception of critical writing. Starobinski's support of Barthes during the episode of the quarrel with Picard is proof of that.[70] Although the letter that Starobinski wrote at that time shows, despite his "constant support," there were not so much differences as particular problems that could not be resolved, for which the *Neutral* might have been the stumbling block. Starobinski's invitation to Barthes to teach a seminar at the University of Geneva in early 1971 strengthened the warm ties between the two "writer-critics" who both contributed to Skira's "Les Sentiers de la création" collection by publishing two very beautiful books the same year, *L'Empire des signes* and *Portrait de l'artiste en saltimbanque* (1970).

Jean Starobinski to Roland Barthes

Geneva, July 18, 1954

Dear Sir,

Thank you for getting your *Michelet* to me. I found your book upon my return from America, where I spent the winter.

The "method" that you applied seems to me singularly fruitful. That is very much the way analysis should proceed, I'm convinced. Whatever Kemp or Coiplet say, do not renounce thematic research![71] But I don't think you need my encouragement to feel that you haven't betrayed your author or failed in the essayist's difficult task. Give us more counterpoints like this one.

I will be in Geneva all summer; be in touch if you are passing through. For my part, I would be very happy to meet you (at Seuil?) during my brief stay in Paris, late September, on the way to America.

Yours cordially,
Jean Starobinski

Roland Barthes to Jean Starobinski (BNS)

[Paris,] April 30, 1961

Will you forgive me for my long delay in thanking you for your book, and for the words that you so kindly sent with it? Do you know how I searched for your text before writing my little *Racine*?[72] I should have written you to get the exact reference; I was torn between the fear of contradicting you and the fear of repeating you. Thus I have only just read yours and the perfection, the *rightness* of what you write allays all my fears; I couldn't *agree* with you more.[73] It's a very beautiful book, with which one forms a secret understanding, so thank you for all that. I hope very much to meet you one day, and if you come to Paris, it would make me very happy if you would get in touch with me.

Let me convey to you my feelings of admiration and deep regard,
R. Barthes
11, rue Servandoni, Paris VIe
Dan. 95–85

Jean Starobinski to Roland Barthes

Geneva, June 3, 1961

Dear Roland Barthes,

Your letter gave me great pleasure. I value everything you write too highly not to be pleased by the warm reception you give my book.

Passing through Geneva, Bernard Pingaud told me about a La Rochefoucauld that you're doing. Has this book been published? I myself have a study in the works on the same subject, and your essay would be extremely valuable to me. (A part of my essay—the preamble—appeared in *Médecine de France*, no. 107, 1959, but is subject to revision.)[74]

Will you be in Paris at the end of the month of September or beginning of October? If no obstacles arise, I am hoping to spend two weeks in France at that time.

Yours cordially,
Jean Starobinski

* * *

Geneva, May 16, 1966

Dear Roland Barthes,

I read *Critique et vérité* with a feeling of constant support: because you restore to criticism its full capacity for experience and risk. The truth upon which your adversaries pride themselves is a brief truth; the "convincing critic" wants to stop everything with his decree. There is nothing more to say, he believes, after he has spoken; he imposes silence upon the works and all future criticism.

Thus we would remain surrounded by studies characterized as "definitive" that forbid resuming discussion on the subject of an author. Gag criticism!

The only point that leaves me a little hesitant is what you say about the "void of the subject." Hesitant and fascinated. This writer is very much a subject who "weaves an infinitely transformed speech." Or is it previous speech that is transformed, that is transported? Then the subject would be speech right through, always *beyond* him in speech; but exteriority loses its sense of exteriority if there is no interiority. Thus there would remain, as Blanchot suggests, a certain *neutral*, neither objective nor subjective. . . . But no doubt we will take all that up again in Cerisy.[75]

Warm regards,
Jean Starobinski

Roland Barthes to Jean Starobinski (BNS)

Rabat, March 4, 1970

Dear friend,

I'm very touched by your letter, your confidence, your invitation—and won over by the preciseness of your request.[76] A broader invitation, as gratifying as it would be, would actually pose problems; but the idea of regular contact for two months with your university is very attractive to me. I've just decided to resume my seminar in Paris next year—and so not sign on for another year in Rabat (too many difficulties, despite many attractions). This is to tell you that it would be very possible for me to come to Geneva in January and February—but also (since you need to agree in principle) that I couldn't drop my Paris seminar and so I would have to be able to spend two days per week in Geneva (Monday and Tuesday would work very well)—two days, moreover, that I would devote entirely to all that is asked of me. Thus, in principle, yes, I accept, and with great pleasure.

I'm thinking of a quick trip to Geneva about the 20–25. But we could meet at the event for the Japan book at Skira (and I would be happy to do that in any case) and discuss the details of our project.[77] Arlette Perrenoud will give you the information for this trip. In any case, I'll be in Paris March 19.

Thanks again,
Warmest regards to you,
R. Barthes

[Paris,] March 21, 1971

Dear friend,

I don't want to let silence fall between us; it wouldn't do justice to the faithful thoughts I carry with me after those few weeks of contact that were a joy for me. I won't tell you again, or rather I will tell you again how *sincerely* happy that experience made me; I came away from it not the least bit tired. So thank you for all that you did for me; and would you express my gratitude as well to Jean Rousset.[78] And please let him know, with regard to a conversation we had in his office, that there is a treatise on propriety (in the opposite sense, as you can imagine) in de Sade (*Philosophie dans le Boudoir*).[79]

I am going to Morocco for Easter, but I'm hoping to come through Geneva after Easter—and so to see you there again.

Please remember me to Mme Starobinski, and kind regards to the little pianist who plays "Le Coucou."[80]

Kind regards, faithfully yours,

R. Barthes

Sadly, I think I'm going to give up the Skira series.[81] After *serious* reflection, I don't dare take on this work that will keep me from writing. I'll write to Skira one of these days.

4. With Georges Perec

"My true master is Roland Barthes," said Georges Perec (1936–82), one year after Barthes's death.[82] These words must be understood not simply as those of a disciple, although Perec was a "student" of this master, but as those of a writer. If *Les Choses* (Julliard, 1965) can be read as the novelistic transposition of *Mythologies*, the disproportion between the two works must be fully registered, the particular genius of Perec, and of course the writing processes so specific to *Oulipo*. Roland Barthes's support of Georges Perec's work is conveyed by the decisive backing he gave to *La Vie, mode d'emploi* (Hachette, 1978) when it won the Prix Médicis. Nevertheless, Barthes never quotes Perec and never writes about him. The moving letter from Perec in 1970 conveys his dismay faced with the "master's" silence. Barthes's promises ("I will do a text on you soon," he writes to him in 1965), which are unkept, do not quite tell the story: a real admiration for the work, but a lack of support for his aesthetic; a closeness all the more impossible as it hinges on a subtle difference: Perec's formalism and Barthes's formalism are not the same thing.

Roland Barthes to Georges Perec (BA)

Monday, [1962?]

Dear Georges Perec,

I thank you for having sent me your articles.[83] I've read them carefully, with interest, with the constant thought that they very much concerned me. Certain things seemed right to me, others less so: right, the demanding but unreal idea that you seem to make for yourself of literature, of its being, that is to say, its ends and means. I don't know if one can effectively discuss this (that is, in a way to modify them both), because the options, that is, the freedoms, seem to me different in your case and in mine. That said, I'd be only too pleased to talk with you about it. At the present moment, I have *too much* to do; but if you would be kind enough to call me a month from now, we could arrange a meeting.

Best wishes,
R. Barthes

*   *   *

Tuesday, [1962?]

Dear Perec,

A quick note, because your manuscript would have to be discussed in person.[84] I mean, I would have to hear what you say about it. My immediate reaction is divided: *If one accepts your project*, how not to appreciate the extremely sure way in which it is carried out? As before, with what I've read of yours, I have the feeling of admiration for the solidity of the writing, its intelligence, its obedience to the project, something like its perfection. But, for reasons that may be ones of personal censure, I cannot really support the choice of enterprise; I cannot really bear *imitated* writings (intentionally so, of course), even if the model is subtly blurred. This is not a criticism, but the explanation for a certain discomfort; but maybe you intended that. When we see each other, you can explain all that to me and tell me what perspectives you see in this text.

Yours,
R. Barthes

* * *

Dear Georges Perec,

A very quick note—now that I've finally read you quietly. I find your text *very good*.[85] And I was even surprised (not in relationship to you but in relationship to what one ordinarily reads) by the success, the simple, elegant maturity, the clear and nevertheless discreet (in the literary sense) sense of your work. I believe I see all you can expect once again, a realism not of detail but, in the best Brechtian tradition, of situation; a novel, or a story on poverty, inextricably mixed with *the image* of wealth. It's very beautiful, very rare today; yours is the one of "petite alienation," and all in all it's quite heart-rending—all the more so as the question, simultaneously emotional and social and human, arises from the successful treatment of those famous objects, to which you restore a mythic flavor. I don't know what you want to alter or add, but in any case, finish quickly and publish it. I think your book will be incontestable and that through this "simple" text, you will resolve many things that aren't working in the narrative today.

We will talk about it again—better than I am now.

Until soon,
Yours,
R. Barthes

* * *

Tuesday, [autumn 1965]

My dear Perec, how happy I am![86] Miracle of good news, news coming just now from the world of Letters. No, it isn't luck; it's the power of good in you that has triumphed. You will help us to emerge from obscurantism. Work well.

Yours,
R. Barthes
I will do a text on you soon.

* * *

May 9, [1967]

My dear Perec,

As soon as I read the extract from your text in *Les Temps modernes*, I wanted to send you a note simply to tell you the kind of peaceful and certain shock I experienced again in the presence of your writing: the certitude of a kind of writing being—who is *very rarely* given to us.[87] I haven't yet had time to get the whole book, because I can't do one more task. But I would like to tell you that I'm always thinking of writing a text on everything you've written. I still need a few months, but you should know that "I'm on the lookout" and the lamp of your texts is always there, by my side.

I hope we'll get together—one day.

Yours,
Roland Barthes
Duvignaud tells me that you've taken an interest in my Fashion.[88] Thank you.

* * *

January 28, 1968

Dear friend,

I was in the United States from October until just a few days ago, and it's only now that I found your invitation to Getzler's exhibition.[89] Excuse me for missing it; it wasn't intentional.

I too would be happy to see you again. Get in touch one of these days, if you have more will and energy than I do to shake off this depressing dispersion.

Yours,
R. Barthes

* * *

March 26, 1968

My dear Perec,

Excuse me for being so late in thanking you for your text on my Fashion; it made me happy that you're interested in this work, enough to write a few lines on the subject.[90] Frankly, I don't really see how a system could exist without a code, or what reason there is for basically comparing the system to terror, except to fall back into the old romantic myth of "spontaneity," anti-intellectualism, etc., which, I hope, is not your aim. We should discuss all this—and especially your much more interesting projects.

Until soon then,
Warm regards,
R. Barthes

Georges Perec to Roland Barthes (BNF)

June 15, 1970

Dear Roland Barthes,

Reading your article on Massin in a recent *Observateur* makes me regret, once more (and I must say, more and more bitterly), your silence.[91]

The influence you have had, through your teaching and your writings, on my work and its evolution has been and remains such that it seems to me that my texts have no other meaning, no other weight, no other existence than those your reading can give to them.

Please accept, dear Roland Barthes, my warm regards.

Georges Perec

Roland Barthes to Georges Perec (BA)

11, rue Pierre-Sémard, Rabat, July 4, [1970]

My dear Perec,

Your note touched but also saddened me. You know very well that I write almost no pieces of criticism, both because I have *absolutely* no time (I mean now that only writing books interests me and I can't endure anything that stands in my way) and because of what it costs me to get involved in judgmental discourse. When by chance I release something in a weekly, it's always under pressure from some contingency that weighs on me. This is to tell you that there is no *silence* with regard to your work; for me to talk about it (and I'd like nothing better), it's not a question of it interesting me (because that has been true since your first manuscript) but of it fitting *naturally* into the work I'm doing. So you must be patient until our respective works merge—or until some contingency brings them together.

At that time, I will try as best I can to repay your confidence and your friendship, and I will do so with joy.

Yours,
R. Barthes

*   *   *

December 17, 1972

My dear Perec,

I think I'll find pleasure in reading you, I sense that.[92] Your ideas point the way, like the "Great Rhetoricians," and we need an *end of the Middle Ages*. So, thank you in advance.

Until soon?

Faithfully,
R. Barthes

*   *   *

June 25, 1973

My dear Perec,

I was very touched that you wanted me to read your *Boutique obscure*.[93] I was happy to receive the proofs and the book. I will have to take the book with me on vacation, because I'm exhausted at the moment, but I will read you quietly and am already very attracted by what I see in this fragmentary writing. So thank you, and until soon.

Yours,
R. Barthes

5. Claude Simon to Roland Barthes

The ties between Roland Barthes and Claude Simon (1913–2005) were very discreet; only a few letters provide evidence, as well as Barthes's dedications to Simon. They were both orphans whose fathers died during World War I, part of the same generation, and, above all, deeply connected by a very close literary engagement. Roland Barthes never wrote on Claude Simon; he quotes him here and there, noting readings and an ongoing affinity. *L'Orion aveugle*, which appeared the same year as *L'Empire des signes*, and with the same publisher, Skira, links them. But what these letters show us is Barthes's admiration for a little-known text by Simon, his play *La Séparation*, adapted by the author from his novel *L'Herbe* (Minuit, 1958).

*　*　*

Perpignan, May 10, 1963

Dear Roland Barthes,

Infinite thanks for sending us your book.[94] At this moment I'm overwhelmed by practical tasks that make the mind go numb (setting up a new house, moving) and I'll wait to regain calm to read you. However I've not been able to keep myself from stealing a few quick glances here and there.

After all that you said to me about *La Séparation*,[95] I'm a little embarrassed (I seem to be offering you the same, and yet . . .) to tell you in turn the extent to which I am once more (I read—and reread—your remarkable preface to Morrissette's book on Robbe-Grillet)[96] stupefied by the rigor and penetration of your thinking (struck in finding in your afterword that very carefully formulated distinction between *quavering* meaning and *closed* meaning).

Being only an autodidact and intuitively feeling my way, I confess to you that I'm a bit intimidated by the interest that you show in me, as I've been intimidated by the regard with which Maurice Merleau-Ponty has honored me. I know that, as he would tell me, all that goes to the individual who is not completely me and who only appears by dint of work—and alas, disappears when I leave my desk. But that would be the other whom you recognize.

We would be happy to see you in Paris. We have found a little pied-à-terre there. But that means another move and settling in!

Réa joins me in sending you our best wishes.[97]

Claude Simon

*　*　*

Salses, March 9, 1964

Dear Roland Barthes,

Thank you from the bottom of my heart for your book and your dedication, which touched me deeply.[98]

Selfishly it makes me happy that you have collected in one volume all your essays from these last years. I was familiar with most of them, but each time I've wanted to refer to them, I've had to find them in old issues of reviews. And then, there are others I didn't know, like the one on *La Sorcière* (a book I like very much) and those on criticism in *Modern Language Notes* and *Times Literary Supplement*.

I've already told you this: I think your analyses are of major importance. For me, you have formulated (and in what a fashion!) lots of things that I have felt, but vaguely. No one has ever before spoken of the problems of writing as you do, and I think there are many among us who admire and owe you thanks for that.

After all sorts of difficulties, I think that soon we are going to be able to move into a little pied-à-terre that I found in Paris, and that will allow us to come more often. As soon as we are almost settled (that is to say—barring unforeseen circumstances—toward the end of May), we will ask you over some evening.

Réa joins me in saying how much we're looking forward to this time together and in sending you our best wishes.

Claude Simon

* * *

Salses, April 9, 1966

Dear Roland Barthes,

Thank you for being so kind as to send me your latest book, and thank you for saying these things.[99]

So happy that you are there.

In sincerest friendship,
Claude Simon

6. With Julia Kristeva

That Barthes titled his article on *Séméiotikè* "L'Étrangère" speaks volumes about the appeal, even the fascination, that Kristeva held for Barthes.[100] For Barthes, only "l'étrangère" is in a position to bring the "bonne nouvelle" about what alone matters, in his eyes: language, the sign. . . . It is very clearly in those terms that he presents her. She is the one who shifts and changes the place of things; she is the one who continually warns, "we are always going too slowly," "we are wasting time, 'to believe,' that is to say, to repeat ourselves and to please ourselves." In naming her "the foreigner," in assigning to her an origin associated with the East ("the one to whom we owe new knowledge, coming from the East and the Far East"), in writing of her that she "sideswipes, scars our young semiotic science with a foreign mark (which is much more difficult than foreign)," Barthes also says something about himself, his own quest, and in this sense clarifies the fact that, from his first intellectual act, in 1947, it is also from a foreigner, Viggo Brøndal (1887–1942), that he borrowed a major and, for him, essential concept, "the degree zero of writing," thus shifting the very old French rhetorical tradition over to an elsewhere alone from which "the new" can come. Throughout his work, Roland Barthes never stops referring to the theoretic shifts advanced by Julia Kristeva, always mixing deep affection with intellectual recognition.

Roland Barthes to Julia Kristeva

Urt, September 12, 1967

Dear friend,

Thank you for your *very important* text; I feel disturbed, transformed, transported by it, as with each of your texts. As you can imagine, I never saw or desired all that in writing *La Mode*, a work entirely immersed in the old semiology; but it's also true that the doubt you transform into victory was already present in the analysis of multiple systems. That doesn't change the fact that only your sympathy toward me was able to transform what could have been severe criticism into a *complement*, a *supplement* as Derrida would say, more important and much more advanced than your guardian-text. Thus I'm grateful to you on many levels for this text: thank you for having taken the trouble, for wearing yourself out writing, especially in your present state of fatigue. Your texts need to be published soon in one volume; we are in urgent need of this instrument for work, for revolution. I am naturally very eager to have your study published soon in *Critique*.[101] It seems to me the only problem may be the length, but that's minor. To save time, I think the wisest thing would be for me to send your text to Derrida, who is part of the *Critique* committee and who will be thrilled in any case. Piel would send it to him anyway. So I will mail it off to him with this post.

I would now like to tell you that I'm worried about your health. I'm sure that you don't get enough rest; you must take a two-month rest in a *rest home*. I myself was in a sanatorium (which is not the same thing) and I assure you that only there can one rest, because there is no effective rest without the *methodical*, *pragmatic* awareness one has of it there. I must soliloquize a bit here to defend the law of health.

I return to Paris in two days and I leave again for Baltimore on October 2.[102] I hope to be able to see you in that interval, if it isn't too tiring for you. If you have the opportunity, try to call me.

Please, take care of yourself. And again, a big thank you.

Your friend,
R. Barthes

Julia Kristeva to Roland Barthes (BNF)

Friday, [1977]

I'm making an effort to tear myself from my cares (now augmented with a new "love object" referred to proudly—God knows why—as "maternal")[103] and from my only reading—the only reading in which I truly rediscover myself—of *Fragments*, to tell you how happy I am to read your text. Perhaps because it's the only thing, right now, that wrests me from exile, this grief of the imaginary, and grounds me in what is very much your own—neither a surge of passionate delirium, nor the terra incognita of neutral contact, but a dream of after-sleep, a morning dream, already light, where I find my way in strangeness but also in delight.

It's been more than ten years (already!) that I've been reading you, and finally always this way, at each departure, and afterward— a gift of happiness in lightning flashes.

Love to you with all my heart.
Julia

7. With Pierre Guyotat

The ties between Roland Barthes and Pierre Guyotat are inseparable from the event of the publication of *Éden, Éden, Éden* by Gallimard in 1970, and the literary, aesthetic, and intellectual impact that its appearance produced. Beyond the question of this book's censure (it could not be publicly displayed in bookstores despite the triple preface meant to protect it, by Roland Barthes, Michel Leiris, and Philippe Sollers), in Barthes's eyes, the real event is what he specifies in his letter from September 13, 1969, even more clearly than in his public text, that is, the possibility of a literary revolution free of the "alibis" that had previously accompanied earlier ruptures, and notably alibis of the "fault" that transgressions always assume: "nothing remains but desire and language," he writes in his letter as in his preface.[104]

Roland Barthes to Pierre Guyotat (BNF)

September 13, 1969

Dear Guyotat,

Thank you for wanting to have your manuscript sent to me.[105] I was *delighted* by it. That word will surprise you but it expresses the contentment and relief that I feel in experiencing a *free* text: free of any subject, any object, or any symbol, produced as a vital substance, still unknown, already dreamed, new and nevertheless immediately accessible, with all the flavor and infinitude of language, beautiful in its unique matter, in its unique sentence, and beautiful in the repetition of that sentence. It seems to me that your text constitutes a kind of thrust, a historic shock: you inherit a whole previous action, from de Sade to Genet, from Mallarmé to Artaud, you shift it, you purge it of its age's alibis. There is no longer either Account or Fault (no doubt it's the same thing); nothing remains but desire and language, not one canceling the other, but placed in a reciprocal, indissoluble metonymy, in such a way that your text condemns all the attempts at censure that would be (will be) brought against it, censuring *at the same time* sex and language, being immediately excessive, that is to say, revealing the essence of censure. This is to tell you how much, and with what strength and certitude, I support the publication of your manuscript; all critical work will be advanced by it. It is also to tell that I will defend it as best I can and I'm sure I will not be the only one. Your text has such power of inscription, it is so unclassifiable and indubitable that it will act both as appeal and as landmark, a very rare combination—*not to be missed*!

Please keep me updated as to the fate of this text, its adventures, and let me express my feelings of warm admiration.

Roland Barthes

* * *

November 23, 1969

Here is my short text.[106] I hope that it's acceptable (I'm afraid that in switching from "you" to "he," from letter to text, from Guyotat as addressee to author/referent, I made the admiration I have for your text less apparent). Keep me posted about its publication. I'm very happy to have met you, yours

R. Barthes
11, rue Pierre-Sémard
Rabat

Pierre Guyotat to Roland Barthes (BNF)

December 18, 1971

Dear friend,

I did receive your book: *Sade, Fourier, Loyola*; I thank you. I in turn admire this magnificent work that you have been producing for twenty years and that summarizes, as exactly, as *naturally* as possible, all the historical phases (in History and in the history of a single man) of the production of literature. There is no one but you so attuned to writing, to writing alone; also you bring up to date—in a movement of words that now marks a complete line of the "literary" production of this time—the most "intimate" processes of the work, and "greater still," the larger thrust long called "inspiration."

Let me express here once again my admiration and my very faithful friendship.

Pierre Guyotat

Roland Barthes to Pierre Guyotat (BNF)

May 13, 1973

Dear friend,

Excuse me for leaving immediately after the play last night without finding you to thank you.[107] My friend André Téchiné was frozen stiff and I was worried about him. I deeply share François Wahl's opinion: you've gone *very far*, as far as possible, with absolute rightness: a wonderful text, indisputable (and *clear*) principle, *memorable* (haunting) show, astounding performance by the actors. My only reservation involves two important points of dramatic art: when two actors speak at the same time, the text isn't audible and from then on every-thing collapses—because the phonatory clarity of the signifier is *vital*, much more so even than with a so-called "realistic" text. For example, Kuki's solo toward the end is *wonderful*, almost tender.[108] Everything relies, as you know, on *understanding/hearing* (not on hearing/under-standing); the text must be *heard* and that isn't the case, at least not for long. The second point is that the actors, regardless of their perfor-mance, don't speak the text as they must; *they don't seem to believe what they're saying*. They are "theatrically" passionate; they act as if they naturally possess a meaning we lack. They undermine the ex-posed unconscious through the expressiveness of passion, but the un-conscious, as you know, is neither soul nor passion. I imagined a somewhat Asian or Gregorian "diction" (*actio* as Ancient Rhetoric said). That isn't their fault, of course; there would have to be a whole tradition behind them, an ancestral matrix—and we're back to the alienation of our civilization. That said, thank you to them, to Kuki for his entrance, his exit, and his solo, and thanks to you as well.

Your friend,
R. Barthes

8. With Jacques Derrida

There is nothing better than Jacques Derrida's (1930–2004) hom-age to Barthes—"Les Morts de Roland Barthes"—for capturing their relationship, a relationship without fanfare or indiscretion, in the image of what united them: writing.[109] Writing as a practice, but also a word present at the heart of their respective first books, *Le Degré zéro de l'écriture* and *L'Écriture et la Difference*, which Der-rida would not have been able to privilege as its own category with-out Barthes's earlier works, even beyond any reference to the thing itself.[110] In his homage, Jacques Derrida doesn't limit himself to Ro-land Barthes's "deaths," memory, the mother, and the person of Barthes himself; he also talks about the importance of concepts, for example, those of *studium* and *punctum* that he finds in *La Cham-bre clair*. The first mention of Jacques Derrida's name in Barthes's diaries appeared March 2, 1964, the date of a dinner with Philippe Sollers and Gérard Genette. Afterward, it seems that Paule Thévenin played a large role in their meetings. In any case, Barthes was much impressed by Derrida's early works, where their shared thinking made for deep connections.

Jacques Derrida to Roland Barthes

March 26, 1966

Dear friend,

Warm thanks for having sent me—and above all having written—*Critique et vérité*. This text that I've just read with joy—and a kind of jubilation—goes far beyond the polemical "circumstances." You haven't only retorted, you have provided a rigorous justification to all those "well-born" minds who were on your side. You have woven or reconstituted the theoretic network of their complicity. In that way as well, this essay is historic.

Thanks again. In warm friendship,
Jacques Derrida

Roland Barthes to Jacques Derrida (IMEC)

Johns Hopkins University

Baltimore, Maryland, November 20, 1967

Dear friend,

I am very late in answering your letter, and that already tells you "in a roundabout way" that I'm as disorganized here as in Paris. The fault is not with Johns Hopkins (to reassure you completely about the utmost freedom—the total freedom one has here) but with me, letting myself be dragged into lectures here and there, getting to see a bit of the country all the same; thus I spend my time reworking courses as lectures, articles as courses, etc.

I hear that you've agreed to come here next year (Girard told me).[111] Students are already looking forward to meeting you. I'll tell you about "my" America (but you already know it); in my eyes, there is just one single merit here that justifies the trip: the peace to work. I say that with longing because I haven't achieved it; but being surrounded by those you love, not being alone, you will manage it much better than I have.

There it is. I don't want to get started on the written account of my American "madness." I would risk being unjust (because in short I am *against*, basically), and in person that will be less serious!

I return in January, I don't know exactly when, looking forward to seeing you all again.

With warmest wishes to you,
R. Barthes
A thousand times yes regarding the Japanese fellow, whom I answered; I know him, he's splendid.

And thanks, an *immense* thanks for *La Grammatologie*.[112] Here, it's like a book from Galileo in the land of the Inquisition, or more simply, a civilized book amid barbarism!

Jacques Derrida to Roland Barthes (BNF)

March 22, 1970

Dear friend,

I very simply want to express my gratitude and admiration for *S/Z*. And with regard to no other text do I now find myself as absolutely in agreement, engaged. Everything in the arrangement of the page, in the production, should constitute what would be called, in the old code, a model, or a method, or an exemplary reference. In any case, to design, to multiply, to "free" a new space for reading and writing: I'm sure that *S/Z* does this and will do so for a long time to come.

Until soon, I hope,
Faithfully, your friend,
Jacques Derrida

*   *   *

Nice, March 30, 1972

Dear friend,

I just received *Les Lettres françaises*.[113] May I very simply offer you an immense *thank you*? And gratitude, which truly I've felt for a very long time (today more than ever, as you know), for your supreme and generous open-mindedness? Even before I begin to write, it is and always has been there, assisting me like an irreplaceable critical resource, but also as one of those most complicit looks, whose severity limits nothing, but on the contrary, allows, encourages writing, play. That tie, which thus proceeds from that solitude of which you speak, is in the work, and yes, so familiar, secret, discrete that—for my part—it has never become the object of discourse. That isn't right, and I blame myself, as I blame myself for Blanchot, the only one, no doubt, with whom I share a similar relationship of closeness, gratitude, and complicity, and to whom I can now say this, despite endless discourse, in a new and confident way.

I am very often tempted, as today, to speak to you about yourself at length. But what could I tell you that you don't already know? And I never dare retain you.

Be certain in any case of my faithful and deep friendship.

Jacques Derrida

9. With Maurice Pinguet

Maurice Pinguet (1929–91) played a fundamental role in the interest Japan prompted in the French intellectual world. He spent a large part of his life in Japan, teaching at the University of Tokyo or directing the Institut Franco-Japonais (1963–68), and he wrote a major book that is now a classic, *La Mort volontaire au Japon* (Gallimard, 1984). A close friend of Michel Foucault, whom he also brought to Japan, he was Roland Barthes's initiator and guide in his discovery of the "empire of signs," so that the book by the same title was naturally dedicated to him. Pinguet wrote two texts on Barthes, both of them shortly after his death, "Le Texte Japon,"[114] and "Aspects de Roland Barthes,"[115] rediscovered by Michaël Ferrier. Thanks to Ferrier, we know that Barthes and Pinguet met in 1957, and Pinguet captures Barthes very well in this brief note recalling him in Tokyo: "He would leave to take long walks alone, aimlessly. He would wander about the city like 'the man of the throngs' of whom Baudelaire spoke."

Roland Barthes to Maurice Pinguet (IMEC)

Paris. Thursday, June 9, [1966]

My dear Maurice,

My first break, after a sad and busy week, to reconnect with you.[116] I arrived in Paris yesterday, coming from Pesaro and Turin, without physical mishap, but morally I'm a bit depleted; ah well, that was expected.[117] I am in mourning for Japan, that feeling of distant separation from what one loves, so close basically to pure existentiality, to the point that certain languages, like Romanian or Portuguese, merge into a single word (*fado*), the idea of nostalgic separation and that of fate (*fatum*).[118] My flight went without incident, although long and enervating, and I was plunged immediately, thanks to Air France, into an unbearable French bath. I've been very sad throughout this return. Even in Italy, everything seemed to me difficult to bear except the country itself, which was radiant with sunshine and roses; the people were kind, of course (much more so than the French), but so physically coarse. Briefly, in a word, the Japanese enchantment continues; and of course, I keep myself going only by thinking of returning to your country. What made me put up with Pesaro was that I earned a few *liras* there, which immediately became the start of my Japanese stash.[119] I already have almost a third of a round-trip ticket, but God knows how long it'll take me to come up with the rest! Moreover, all that is excellent ethically: desiring one thing passionately puts others things one doesn't desire back in place. I'm in the process of reconsidering all my policies regarding articles and lectures in view of the money they could add to my stash, and that's basically very healthy. Japan is going to make me thrifty. The objects that I brought back are helping me very much; some have made those around me very happy; others are gradually finding their places in my room. I have before me the samurai portrait of the fine actor Kazuo Funaki[120] (think of my enlargement, a little shop in Yurakucho),[121] and I am returning, slowly, to the idea of a text on the Japanese face[122]—that is to say, step by step, on Japan. If I manage to do that, it will be dedicated to you. I've also thought many times of little Yuichi; some of his expressions are unforgettable.[123] I think about and see again many of the things that I did, that I saw over there; the important thing now is to "dialecticize," as they used to say fifteen years ago, that investment as a way of retaining it without neuroticizing it. I think that the work will help there; it's basically the only thing I find bearable here. I saw François again, which was deeply comforting, because he never contradicts the Japan in me, as you know.[124] Before settling down to work (I have a pile of things to catch up on), I'm going to write a certain number of letters for Japan, as we talked about; I don't want to lose the intellectual contacts you suggested. I'm also thinking of having as peaceful a summer as possible, even canceling some travel plans, among them Warsaw. In any case, Maurice, keep me posted about your return, so that I don't miss you on your way through Paris; I will really need to talk to you. I have still not seen anyone; I don't know what either Robert or Michel are doing.[125] Dear Maurice, you must give my great and faithful love to all of Tokyo, to André,[126] Hashimoto-san, Nikko-san,[127] and on my behalf, to all the Yuichis of Japan, all the Mikatas, and all the students.[128]

Your friend,
Roland
In fact, I am very sad.

*　　*　　*

Paris, June 20, 1966

My dear Maurice,

Your report gratified and touched me; it had an *overall* effect on Cultural Relations, where my standing right now is very high, thanks to you. And your second letter, received this morning, moved me and did me very much good. In the two weeks since my return I've been quite depressed. Japan, as we have said, constitutes a terrible mirror for Western civilization; going for walks along Saint-Germain-des-Prés these hot evenings is truly to confront collective hysteria: no thoughtfulness on faces, nothing but a will to *appear* insane. Seeing these boys *in disguise*, I never stop thinking of the race of young Japanese. First contacts upon returning have been difficult; mixed up with that (Japan having nothing to do with it, the West either) is the onslaught of responsibilities of all kinds, articles, procedures, paperwork, intellectual problems, all overdue work that I can't really manage to catch up on. Too many things to do gives me a sort of *ennui*, because then I can't make out very well the meaning of my work; it's an old problem, heightened in the last few years. Here again, Japan only helped to crystallize this need for *another* dimension in daily work, the necessity of balancing intellectual hypertrophy with a true art of living. Moreover, I have reflected many times on this notion of the *art of living*, and if I lived a bit in Japan, I would try to draw something from it. What has, if not diverted, at least occupied me for the last two weeks is that I have kept my resolve to resume contact with Japan; I do a little Japanese each day in the conversation book (while awaiting something more serious). I'm not under any illusions, but at least linguistically that's teaching me something—and it's fascinating. I'm also doing a bit of calligraphy everyday following the Vaccari that I bought.[129] It's very relaxing (but also diabolical). I'm taking notes for that text on Japan that you were kind to remind me about and that I haven't forgotten, but I don't want to go too quickly, because writing is tricky, and doing it to create an effect is, at least for me, very difficult, whereas, by intellectualizing, *I look like* I'm destroying what I love (that's what happened with my *Michelet*). I'm also busy with the Yama-mouchi grant, in a bad way, a bit of a crank, but what do you want of the Japanese! Finally and most importantly, I'm thinking about my next trip; paradoxically, things are falling into place almost too well, or too quickly. I'm going to the USA for a few days in October.[130] And, in all probability, I'm going to earn enough there for my Japanese travel and stay; the kitty filled in one fell swoop. What's more, it wouldn't be unreasonable—financially—to add this Japanese trip onto the American trip, because going around the world is no more expensive than Paris-Tokyo and back, and Paris-New York and back is already paid for.[131] The real problem is the date; in September-October, Robert will be there, and I don't dare cut into his trip too much with my presence, even incognito.[132] And in November my seminar starts again. All that is swimming around in my head, but reasonably so; in any case, there's no hurry, and I would love to talk with you. I would like to talk to you about the way I'm envisioning my next stay (whenever it happens) (a little like an experience of "immersion"). I would like to explore with you the possibilities—even vague ones—for a teaching position of two or three years in Japan (a temporary break that I've already thought of with regard to Morocco). Also, dear Maurice, I'm asking you to let me know as soon as you arrive in France. I will be in Urt early July, but you know that I can return to Paris easily and often from there, and I want very much to see you (I have in fact given up talking about Japan with my friends). Can you try calling me in Paris (Danton 95–85) and if I'm not there, writing to me in Urt, giving me some way to meet you? I hope this note reaches you before your departure; in which case give all my love to Hashimoto-san (whose "characters" really touched me) and André. For you, my dear Maurice, my strong and faithful affection.

Roland
Urt
Basses-Pyrénées
Tel. 47

Maurice Pinguet to Roland Barthes (BNF)

April 17, 1970

My dear Roland,

Your Japan was waiting for me here![133] I am returning from a trip to Spain—with no other bonus than the charm of things *to see* and the climate—and your Japan was waiting for me. You can imagine the whiff of nostalgia.

I leafed through it without reading it yet in detail because I like approaching it gradually and I would like my best attention to be available. But I already sense through this rapid glance the extremely exciting ideas and emotions that this book is going to offer me.

And what joy to have been, for you, its first addressee! How to thank you for so fond a thought? You know in any case, dear Roland, that this affection is totally reciprocal. You may trust in my friendship as I do in yours.

Thank you,
Maurice Pinguet

*   *   *

Tokyo, November 26, 1979

My dear Roland,

I often think of you, very often, but I hardly write to you, forgive me, I'm in a difficult phase of dejection, depression that often makes the smallest effort to get out of myself impossible even to write a few lines. This isn't out of negligence, as you well understand; it's disarray. The irony is that this return to Japan, which I awaited with so much joy, which was my constant dream for more than ten years, is turning into such a cruel existential crisis! Sometimes I tell myself it's simply a nervous, neurological disease whose onset just happens to coincide with this return. Sometimes I tell myself, like Bretécher of Thérèse d'Avila, "all this, it's psychosomatic"—a less disturbing but more humiliating hypothesis because, no matter what I do, I don't see a thing in my symptoms.[134] Dear Roland, I've already talked too much of ills that only interest me [. . .][135] and I've said enough to gain your indulgence for my silence. You have no doubt remained under the impression left by our last Rue de Sèvres meeting, that story of love, my hypomanic energy. Now it's the other side of the coin. But you, what has become of you? In Paris, even if I didn't telephone you often, the possibility of doing so, of seeing you, always existed, always verifiable. And your plan to come to Japan—to the Philippines? If you need me to do something, tell me, I would be happy to help you carry out a plan that may perhaps give me the joy of seeing you again in a few months. In principle, it was the spring you had in mind? I'm going to spend a week in the Philippines with André from December 21 to 28. If that still interests you, I'll give you recent information. Dear Roland, do you know that a critic for the *Japan Times* (which is the big English-language newspaper in Japan), Donald Richie, recently listing the five best works written on Japan since he's been writing about it, included *L'Empire des signes* in his ultraselective choice? Where do things stand with the plan for a new edition in France? Ah, dear Roland, I still have much to tell you—these aerograms are too short—but I'll write to you again—please note my new address.[136] Yours affectionately. Maurice

10. Roland Barthes to Renaud Camus

This is what Renaud Camus writes about first meeting Roland Barthes: "Regarding the date when I first met Roland, it was Saturday, March 2, 1974. I was at the Café de Flore with a few friends, we were getting ready to go see Warhol's *Nude Restaurant* at the Palais de Chaillot movie theater, and I (very audaciously) proposed to him that he join us—he accepted without hesitation." In Barthes's diary it reads: "March 2, [1974]. Flore with Renaud and William. Movie theater Andy Warhol." Their friendship was expressed by critical support on the part of Roland Barthes, notably on the occasion of the publication of Renaud Camus's first book, *Passage*, published by Flammarion in 1975,[137] and again by the preface that Barthes wrote for *Tricks*, published by Mazarine in 1979.[138] Their relationship is largely associated as well with contemporary art. It was through—among others—Renaud Camus, who kept company with Andy Warhol and a certain number of American artists, that Roland Barthes discovered the work of Cy Twombly. Moreover, it was with Camus that Barthes must have gone to Venice in spring 1980 for the major retrospective on Pop Art, for which he wrote one of his last texts, "Cette vieille chose, l'art. . . ."[139]

*　　*　　*

Urt, Wednesday, March 27, 1974

My very dear Renaud,

Here I am thinking about you and wanting to stop working to write to you. Since my arrival, despite all reason (a thousand things to do for the fall term), I'm working only "for myself," a complicit and accurate expression, all told, except if we could write for those we love, but, as we said the other night, we can certainly "offer" a text (dedicate it to) but never, sadly, "make" it for another. It would even be easier to make it *with* another. So, I'm organizing ancient index cards, getting a bit bored (it's evening and there's a fir tree, too dark green, out my window), and thinking that what I would like, as a reward for this work, would have to be seeing you again this evening and having dinner with you (with champagne, I'd like that). So it will be Tuesday, then? I'll arrive during the day (by train); I propose that we meet this *Tuesday, April 2 at 8 PM at the Café Apollinaire* (it's grim but we won't stay there). Only reply or call if there's a problem. It has been very beautiful and I would love it if you were here, writing your book not far from me.

With love,
R.

        *   *   *

Milano, Monday, June 2, 1974[140]

Dear and desired Renaud,

Thank you for your note; knowing you a little, I think that you paid me the greatest compliment I received on the China article—and one always needs that to continue.[141] The Conference drags needlessly on, it's warm and sunny, but Italy is losing its art of living.[142] We'll have to come back here (together) soon if we still want to take advantage of it.

I'll be returning Wednesday evening, no doubt. Try to telephone me very soon (if you can, please: morning, even Friday, this time).

Lovingly,
R.

        *   *   *

1) I'm on Fragment no. 285; there are 165 left to do, plus the supplements, plus the appendixes, plus the correcting, plus the typing, etc., plus the *act* of releasing all that to put it into circulation.[144]

2) I have decided, since the summer break is here, to exonerate my life from its unhappy loves.[145]

3) I would love to know a) what you are doing with your summer, b) where you are in your manuscript, c) if I'm going to be reading it soon.

Lovingly,
R.

*   *   *

Saturday, [February 15, 1975]

Renaud, your letter is adorably intelligent; to my mind, you pointed out what was necessary (I won't let it happen often). And your book—just glanced at it—is moving.[146] In short, two beautiful things coming from you and that made me happy.

We will see each other soon, surely.

With love,
RB

*   *   *

Urt, July 22, 1975

My very dear Renaud,

Your letter is very delightful as always—apart from the bad news. I would happily join you in Greece; I can well imagine the pleasures of it. But you see, it isn't likely. My summer is already practically arranged, and since it's an arrangement that has a few affective roots, shifting things is inconceivable. And then, you tell me nothing at all about how one gets to this godforsaken place—not even, among other things, if Lesbos is Greek or Turkish—or even how long you're staying. Try to send me word from there. In principle (because affectivity includes an aleatory dimension), I'll be at Juan with the Cordiers (Rapa Nui, Saramartel Parc) from August 2 or 3 until the end of the month.[147]

What you say about my writings is, as always, very flattering; but your talent, your elegance (let me say, isn't elegance a condition of truth, contrary to what so many brutal imbeciles think) is *to be recognized*. As for little Visage (that's his name), well, he's wrong about

RB.[148] I will say that, from the perspective of the "theory of the text"—which no doubt obsesses him—it's an important book—although still completely clandestine!

I send much love with many wishes for sunshine, rest, romantic diversions. Give my love to W.[149]

R. B.
With regard to Lesbos, stereotype oblige, this from Sappho:
"That one seems to me to be equal to the gods, the man who, seated,
    facing you, very close, listens to your sweet voice.
And that enchanting laugh that, I swear to you, made my heart
    pound in my chest; for when I look at you, even a moment, I can
    no longer utter a word;
But my tongue shatters, and, beneath my skin, a thin fire is racing;
    my eyes are sightless, my ears buzz,
Sweat streams from my body, shivers run through me; I turn greener
    than the grass, and it's almost as though I feel myself dying."[150]
—Are you familiar with this?

*   *   *

Urt, August 18, 1977

No, I'm not in Venice, alas[151]—but in Urt, inexorably, where I received your card. It's true—and I think of it with regret and remorse—that we no longer see each other; but my life has changed since my mother's illness. Not only am I unavailable—but I feel cut off from the availability of others. Don't forget me.

Your friend,
RB

11. Roland Barthes to Antoine Compagnon

The first mention of Antoine Compagnon's name in Barthes's diaries appears in May 1975. He participated in the first year of the seminar on amorous discourse (1974–75) and gave a talk titled "Music and Repetition." During the second year, he proposed an exchange with Contardo Calligaris on the discourse of psychoanalysis. Antoine Compagnon was then a fellow at the Thiers Foundation, where he prepared his thesis on the citation, with Julia Kristeva as his advisor. Roland Barthes put him in charge of organizing and directing the Cerisy Colloquium that took place in

June 1977, "Prétexte: Roland Barthes." Subsequently, and after Barthes's death, Compagnon wrote many texts on him, notably in his book, *Les Antimodernes: De Joseph de Maistre à Roland Barthes* (Gallimard, 2005). As professor at the Collège de France, Antoine Compagnon has, on many occasions, devoted majors sessions of his courses to his friend who preceded him there. From among the letters Barthes wrote to him, we have chosen a small, unified group involving the genesis of *Fragments d'un discours amoureux*.

*　　*　　*

Urt, June 23, 1976

My dear Antoine,

I just finished talking with you on the telephone. It's 3 o'clock, and there is that sweet calm of the afternoon here; no household noises, no kids on the road, the sun behind the shutters, my workspace awaiting me. Everything would be perfect, truly, if, . . . for example, I knew it was possible to spend the evening with you. I have almost finished my hundred figures.[152] According to some of them, I encounter you; either I might formulate things you've said to me (taught me), or here and there I might write a figure's index thinking of you and, in short, of what is original (how to say this?) in our relationship. If this book is ever printed, you'll recognize yourself in it, as in a rebus drawing, hidden and obvious in the tree. That is all very literary, but has literature ever served any purpose other than *telling all* without telling all? It alone can present the "slip" (the leftover, the badly said, the on-the-tip-of-the-tongue, *kataleipsis* and not *katalepsis*).[153]

Until soon, with love,
R.
Practical matter (that is to say, as always, a purely obsessional remark): save me a little time next week—from Tuesday to Saturday, no doubt.

*　　*　　*

Urt, Friday, June 25, 1976

My dear Antoine,

Your letter this morning gave me very great pleasure (in the ancient style, I would say, was very sweet to me) and I worked better because of it. I finished my "Figures," and since yesterday I've begun the "Codes."[154] I've buried my head in the sand a bit regarding this part of the book, and I'm now distressed to see many problems, difficulties, choices, that is to say, irresolutions; I'm very close to knowing what I would like to do, but as always, I'm afraid of it. And once again, I come back to you, because my problem, I think, is close to your work.[155] My problem is how to "comment on," to refer, to anchor, to reinforce what I just wrote by putting forward as proof discourses other than "mine" (which is, to shake up this "mine"). I would really like you to tell me everything you have compiled, from history and in your head, on this subject, especially since what I need is a certain mirroring of practices, and that's much of what you've focused on, isn't it? My problem being to "existentialize" the reference, I thought a lot about those first pages of yours that you showed me (on the découpage-collage).[156] I like them all the more for giving me courage (but, sadly, I never manage to say *I* without egotism, which was completely absent from your text and achieved a success that filled me with enthusiasm, you'll recall). I would really love to see the rest of what you've done. If it's not too much trouble, think about showing it to me: *I need to see it.*

We'll continue this chat about work in person. I can't wait to see you again, to talk travel with you. Let's telephone each other Tuesday morning (in Paris); yes, I'm in a great hurry to see you and send you my love. R.

*   *   *

Urt, Saturday, June 26, 1976

A quick note to tell you that I made a little start on *Lettura*.[157] I won't get much further on it until my return, so it's invaluable that you have written a great many pages. My laziness and my confidence would tempt me to let you do the whole thing, but I would like the pleasure of cosigning something with you. So don't worry about having written too much; on the contrary that will be of great use to us. We must anticipate things to cut (and be able to do so) even insofar as we will have to adjust our two texts (disproportionate as they are).

Until Tuesday (by telephone)—in haste—and impatiently. R.

*   *   *

Urt, Monday afternoon, July 5, 1976

I'm writing to you in the midst of a terrible thunderstorm. Here, it's "nature," again, and, as everyone knows, it's typical of nature to be disproportionate. Thunder booms from every side, already a torrent of water on the little road in front of the house, whirlwind in the plane trees—which I wouldn't mind if they weren't shaking the telephone lines dangerously (the town forgot to prune)—which makes me worry about another outage. By the time you arrive, I would like to have finished the revision of my hundred figures (but I doubt I'll manage that) and prepared new fragments for our *Lettura*. I would also like to arrange the books in the house a little so that you can have a few reading pleasures during your stay. That's the plan for this week. I'm looking forward to seeing you and send you love. R.

*   *   *

Urt, Friday, July 16, 1976

I've just finished the first revision of the hundred Figures, and you have been too linked to the (sometimes tiresome?) confession of this *labor* for me not to signal the end of it by writing you this short note: the desire to talk to you, to see you, to extend by this gesture the three *exquisite* days (see the etymology) that I spent with you (right after you left, there was a huge thunderstorm and the weather turned cloudy).

I miss you (*pothos*)[158] and send you love. R.

I began this very afternoon on *Lettura*; I'm a bit encouraged, since I'll be sending it to you.

*   *   *

Urt, July 18, 1976

My dear Antoine,

So I have "mounted" our fragments together, and here is the result.[159] Anticipating that the Einaudi scribes would remove our subtitles, I did away with them—arranging only the "parts." But I'll make sure they always leave a sizable gap between our old fragments (I've indicated our old titles in the margin, but that's just for you, in case you would like to make corrections to the montage; we can remove them afterward). I didn't change a thing in your text—which seems to me so much better than mine. I truly love what you write: something *inimitable* and nevertheless untheatrical; a simplicity and a power, a simple power that is, in the end, a kind of delicacy—atopic, not hysteric! that's the squaring of the circle, in writing. And you really make me jealous—so, no changes, except one or two transitions that I inserted between your fragments and my own. It seems to me that the whole thing has class, but I don't really know what will happen, because I've decided not to accept the rejection of the first article, even if it means terminating the whole contract.[160] That's what I'm going to write to Romano (at Einuadi's); I'll keep you posted.

It was quite a help to me, the whole day that I worked on this montage, to think that I was doing it a bit for you, with you. Alas, it doesn't have a written inscription, but perhaps there are *continued gestures*, and it makes me happy, at the end of one of your fragments, to *continue*—as in polyphony—and that polyphony I would be very happy to resume with you on another occasion, free of the irritating constraints of this commission.

I am now going to take up my "cross" again, a less sweet because more solitary one—more solipsistic one, the Figures. Now comes the moment of truth; I must decide: *what this is worth*.

Your friend R.
I think you'll have to send the text back to me (careful: I haven't made a duplicate) here in Urt. I'll arrange to have a photocopy made.

Naturally, you can correct, reorder, all you like, including my own text.

*   *   *

Urt, Tuesday, July 20, 1976

When you write to me (I received your note this morning), I'm always very pleased. It makes the day warmer for me. I love to feel your work progressing alongside mine (I could reverse the terms of the sentence), with the same problems. You tell me about your fear of rereading; I've begun mine (the second, which begins to be a true reading, because I stop less for corrections, already mostly made, the "first rinse" all finished).[161] I have a less bad impression; but I'm not rejoicing too much yet because I haven't reached the middle of the Figures, which left me with a very bad memory. The lesson that I'm drawing from this is that after the "first rinse," you have to read a second time, without getting discouraged, very slowly and very attentively, sentence by sentence, in a very critical fashion *at the detailed level*. To keep a slightly fresh perspective, I only do this work in the morning; in the afternoon I began to organize my file cards for the introduction (and what's more, new problems in sight there).

I'm really thrilled about that evening, Sunday, August 1, when we'll see each other. Isn't that right?

Good mid-day, dear Antoine, with love, until very soon, R.

*   *   *

Collège de France, Paris, July 28, 1976

Maybe to try out new stationery—surely to send you greetings and say until Sunday.[162]

R.
I'll arrive in Paris Friday evening. I'll leave Tuesday morning.

*   *   *

Bayreuth, August 5, 1976[163]

I miss you very much; I think I know what you wouldn't have liked here: the city, heavy and comfortable, that kind of German stone that, for me at least, still has the stench of Nazism—and what you would have liked: in the end, the festival itself: its folklore, so close, actually, to the bullfight (infirmary in the wings, cushions brought along for the too-hard seats, brio, the excitement of the ceremony, its danger as well) and its spectacle: a kind of essence of spectacle, through the accumulation of feats, of options, of fascinations—first and second (I was very close to the stage, you understand). As for me, I'll say it again, I bitterly regret not being here with you; I've told you why, the long chain of events.[164] But I can't get used to this contretemps, because, except for the city, this was made for you—for us.

I'm working a bit, on that initial "argument" we discussed our last evening.[165] I imagine you're making better progress in your writing than I am in mine. I truly can't wait to see you again. I'll get in touch as soon as I return to Paris—Wednesday or Thursday—if you're still in Paris—which I hope for my own sake.

Your friend R.

*   *   *

My dear Antoine,

As if by magic, my fear in leaving you came true to some extent: once again I'm behind in finishing my manuscript because the day after I arrived, getting ready to go down to work (finally, without interruption), I was stricken with a violent backache (at the level of the kidneys*). It isn't rheumatic, rather its mechanical (says the doctor); the result is that I'm almost completely immobilized, in bed, obviously. All the same, I can do a little work there, although I'm very badly set up for writing and my mind is really not alert, dazed by the aspirin and the reinforced austerity of the stay: Urt + bed + bad weather! Well, this manuscript, if it's ever finished, will be proof at least of stubbornness; but there's still much to do and I'm getting impatient.

I hope that, in contrast, yours has unfolded calmly and sweetly right to the anticipated end and that you're free, with only the concern of having to rewrite it. Leave, break off the year with a true emblem of vacation; there must be signs in a year. If you see the painting, don't forget to pick out some image (or some detail) that could serve as the "mark" for this book on Love.

I'm already very anxious to see you again. I hope that you can telephone me from Paris—and that when we do see each other again (early September), we will celebrate—with expensive champagne in an elegant place—our two manuscripts completed, my back healed, and our reunion.

With love. R.

*   *   *

Having you on the phone always gives me a kind of peace and balance; that comes from the "Zen" side of the relationship, I think, but as it is the nature of Zen to stop (suspend) reflexiveness, verbalization, self-commentary, well, I'll stop. I'm working at my table now, constantly trying to find a good position (because my back is still very painful, there's hardly any improvement) and good inspiration. There too, the manuscript is running out of steam; endless

---

Rheingold obsession! [Barthes spells *reins* (kidneys) with an "h" (rheins). Hence this is a pun, alluding to the prologue of Wagner's *Ring* (see the preceding letter).— Ed.]

new difficulties, new stumbling blocks arise. Nevertheless I'm moving forward, still without knowing when I'll be finished. You already know that, beyond the manuscript, nothing is happening. The weather is mild, a bit hazy, already autumnal; every time I perceive this euphoria of light and atmosphere, I wish that you were here. I eagerly await your return phone call, as you know.

Enjoy Italy,
Your friend R.

*   *   *

Urt, Wednesday, September 1, 1976

I received two letters from you that made me happy—because I missed you, and I was disappointed—maybe even a bit worried—that you didn't telephone me from Paris, as you said you would. Everything was alright, wasn't it? I'm awaiting your return call or letter. As far as I'm concerned, you only have to say the word and I can return to Paris toward the middle or end of next week (about the 10th). Because the madness of the manuscript (finished) was immediately succeeded by the madness of typing it up. It became clear to me that unless I almost completely finish the typing before returning to Paris, the editing will be delayed much too long. So I'm in the process of typing it, without a break: at a mad pace, almost Stakhanovist. But the book is hysterical enough an object that it doesn't exist if it doesn't appear. In this frenzied work, in which each hour counts, with the rain, outside (it's raining), I feel a certain solitude and it would be sweet to see you. I feel a bit alone with this strange manuscript on my hands, the very material of which isolates me from the world. I await your news—news of your trip. I really can't wait to see you again.

With love. R.

*   *   *

Urt, Thursday, September 9, 1976

My dear Antoine,

I'm sending this note—although I will certainly call you today or tomorrow and see you again Saturday or Sunday—because I really want to write to you, because I received your card from Venice (the image would only go on *Discours amoureux* through great metaphorical contortions, but it will go very well on "Tenir un discours"—as a launch),[166] and because yesterday evening I finished typing my entire book. That was a bit crazy, since, all told, I typed the whole thing in just over two weeks. I am really very tired—and very depleted—and perhaps all the same, despite the Zen rule! it would do me good to talk to you about it. We will see how that transpires—I'm going to call you and we can then arrange for our next meeting. I am anxious to see you again, with love. R.

12. With Hervé Guibert

In a certain way, the meeting between Hervé Guibert (1955–91) and Roland Barthes is the stuff of literary legend. Barthes was the first great influence on Guibert, but the tie that binds them together was more complex and more ambiguous than that of disciple and master. The legendary part essentially involves the posthumous publication by Hervé Guibert of the now famous "Fragment pour H."[167] that Roland Barthes sent to him following an encounter cut short by Guibert. It is a kind of supplement to *Fragments d'un discours amoureux*, but it seals both the impossibility and the inevitability of the *non-voulour-saisir* (non-will-to-possess), the last figure in the book that makes the nonpossession of the other's body ("not to possess the other") a form of inscription of the Neutral at the heart of amorous discourse. The letters from Barthes to Guibert, like those Guibert sent to Barthes, without ever contradicting the legend—the exchange of a text for a body, and the rejection of that exchange—nevertheless color it with affects, delicacy, friendship, admiration, and a kind of reciprocity we can glimpse from this rediscovered epistolary writing.

Roland Barthes to Hervé Guibert

January 25, 1977

I thank you for your book.[168] I read it all in one sitting, carried along by the writing, which is true writing. I would love to talk with you about the relationship (in your case) of writing to fantasy; it's difficult by letter, and at the moment I'm a bit sick. Maybe you'd like to call me again for us to arrange a meeting—for when I'm no longer ill.

Thanks again,
R. B.
326 95 85

Hervé Guibert to Roland Barthes

Paris, February 1, 1977

So here is the text that I wrote for you, beginning with your question on the relationship between writing and fantasy. First of all, it's an attempt. I consider it a starting point to prompt a conversation, a response, an exchange of letters, or a discussion.

I wrote it quickly and there are things you can take or leave. Most of all there are things to develop.

Until Saturday then,
Looking forward to meeting you,
Hervé Guibert

Roland Barthes to Hervé Guibert

Paris, Friday, [March] 4, 1977[169]

Hervé, your text is very good. Something that belongs only to you: very modern, very obscure feelings, with very clear writing, a clarity that reinforces them. Talent, talent, talent . . . to be published, that's for sure (do you want to send it to a review?).

Until soon,
(Pardon me for being so unavailable, you know the reason, don't underestimate it.)[170]
R. B.

*　　*　　*

June 4, 1977

My dear little Hervé,

I so desire to please you, to respond to your impatience, that I tried today, between two tasks, to begin a short text that I want to do on you. But you see, I'm too tired, too pressured, and I didn't get very far. I like what you write too sincerely to do something quickly. I must ask you to accept that I will not be able to do this text until I've finished with all my other commitments, that is, practically speaking, not before the month of July. I think that you could clear it with Régine Deforges that your text (with mine) won't appear until the fall.[171] I promise to write something on you—and of course, without a contract (this was only a fantasy, a mental caress!). And what would help me, to write this text, is to have access to the one that you redid and that clearly you must get published. I'm quite sad about disappointing your impatience, because your impatience is part of what I like in you, what links us, what marked our meeting. But all the same, it's only your impatience I'm disappointing, not your request, because I will write this text, without fail. It will be brief, I can't write any other way, but at least it won't be hasty.— You can telephone me without misgivings, I like hearing your news.

Work well, write,
With love,
R. B.

*   *   *

[Urt,] August 9, 1977

Forgive me, Hervé, for having let your letters go unanswered, letters that please me so much nevertheless, as well as the package with your manuscript that I have not yet been able to look at. I haven't written one letter since I've been here; first because of my mother's health, which, upon our arrival, presented problems (doing better now), and then continuing to be a bit depressed, unable to connect with the world, even the world of dear friends. You must never read into my silence; I think of you with much tenderness—and always a lively, real admiration for all your writing (I'm thinking of your letters). I still can't work on my text for you; I can hardly write, and only read a little. Don't be impatient, and above all, don't misinterpret.

With love, my Hervé,
R. B.

*   *   *

October 17, 1977

My dear Hervé,

Forgive me for not getting in touch with you. My mother's health is once again (since summer) very bad and I'm going through a very difficult period, entirely caught up by this concern, this occupation, incapable of attending to anything else and arranging a meeting. I wouldn't want you to think by that, foolishly, that I've turned away from you; but it's as though my life is *suspended*.

With love,
Roland

*   *   *

Paris, December 7, 1977

Hervé, you are adorable because . . . innocent. Because I found our evening atrocious.[172] I resented you for planting yourself five meters from me in my room and walking out on me after five minutes! You questioned me about my friends, with a certain envy, it seemed to me; well, I would characterize them this way: none of them would ever have done that. But, as I think that, like everyone else, you must not be very at ease with yourself, I can't hold it against you. I simply believe, in fact, that the ties between us must be strengthened no further; one of them remains very strong: the unfailing admiration I have for the *charm* of your writing.

With love—tenderly—from a distance,
R. B.

*   *   *

Paris, December 14, [1977]

My dear Hervé,

Your letter is full of delicacy (so, no doubt, you wrote it!) and I thank you for it. There is nothing more between us, except a little history, eliminated (catharsis!) by this exchange. We will see each other, if you really want to, after the vacation, in January.

With love,
R.

*   *   *

Paris, January 12, 1978

Hervé, I'll mention your wish to André T. when I see him.[173] But the question seems complicated, to say the least. I already know of two fellows who put in for the part, passionately and stubbornly.

    —I'm going to Morocco for a few days to do a seminar. Will we get together, as planned, when I return in February?

Your friend,
R. B.

*   *   *

Paris, March 14, 1978

But no, Hervé, it was absolutely nothing. It's *only* because you were with someone and I tend to be unsociable when introduced to a stranger *under the gaze of one I know*, with whom I can basically only make small talk since the third party is there: in short, truly Nathalie Sarraute! (But why wouldn't I be a character in a novel?)

With love (kisses on the cheek) and will see you when you wish.

R. B.

*   *   *

January 21, 1980

My dear Hervé,

Your note is very sweet and I thank you for it, but also there's a little bitterness, and that must not be. Often I'm so overwhelmed, so panic-stricken over tasks that I have to sacrifice the simplest acts of friendship; as for your opening, I thought that it didn't matter since I had seen and liked your photos.[174] If there are additional texts, why not send them to me? That would make me happy. Maybe we could see each other one day in February as well? Do you want to call me some morning?

With faithful affection, my dear Hervé, love,
Roland Barthes
633 92 92

Hervé Guibert to Roland Barthes

Tuesday, February 19, 1980

My dear Roland,

I found your book yesterday in my box at the newspaper, and I thank you for it.[175] Your flattering dedication made me happy. I just closed it again, on this mild, sunny morning, which goes very well with your voice. At a first, quick, skimming read, I found it good; that's all I will say for the moment, because I want to reread it, and write an article on it, if they will let me.[176]

It's the second part, of course, that touched me most: everything regarding your mother. A few months ago I wrote a text on a photo session with my mother, and I'll send it to you, it should speak to you.[177] I'll also send you the texts that were at the exhibit (a true exchange of writing, if you agree to it, since I have just absorbed yours). . . .

I hope you're doing well, with love,
Hervé
P. S. Let's not forever keep putting off the plan to have dinner together again; I'll call you some morning. And thank you, too, for your earlier response.
P. S. 2. I couldn't find the text on my aunts, and it's also because I really don't want to overload you, the envelope would have been too heavy. . . .

"Vita Nova"

How far back does the "Vita Nova" project go, that is, the plan to move to entirely fictional, novelistic, creative writing? It goes back to the very beginning, one could answer, since, for example, by the time of *Le Degré zéro de l'écriture,* the work was starting to take shape as a utopian idea, as a future work that had to be seized in the moment, an undertaking that involved one's entire life, one's entire existence organized around the "preparation of the novel," as Barthes's last course at the Collège de France indicated as well, in which he proposed a kind of "simulation" of the work in the process of being made.

Its genesis, like any genesis, is hard to reconstruct in detail. We can offer a few stages and a few signs. In 1979, the project crystallized around this title, as is evident by the eight outlines that Barthes drafted between late August and mid-December, evident at well by the countless "file cards" or "pages" that he filled at the time. But as early as 1969, we can see the first concrete gestures toward writing that moves away from even the freest forms of the essay and is organized around the word *Incidents.* On a file card from the time (November 1969) offering no other details, that term is associated with Raymond Queneau, no doubt the Queneau of *Le Chiendent* (Gallimard, 1933) where the word appeared in a cover letter, but Queneau uses the word elsewhere as well. This is the term Barthes later chose in 1978–79 as a title for the collection of fragments he wrote on Morocco during his stay there in 1970–71, only one chapter in the vast collection that "Vita Nova" was meant to be. Initially, nevertheless, "Incidents" designated all the microfictions of reality, notations, and events that are offered as events in the structure of the novel. Moreover, it was in this same period that Barthes used the term in *L'Empire des signes*.[178] Here it names the mode of fiction of haiku that he would later construct in *La Préparation du roman* as the model of the event suited to the work he planned to write.

The term *incident* is undoubtedly essential but not sufficient to encompass the project that from then on, in 1969–70 and the years following, would be associated with other names and other titles, like "Our France," which points the work toward the mythologies, "Restaurant Phrases," or more generic terms like *novel* (in 1974 for example) or *fiction* (in 1975). Sometimes at the top of a page we find terms like "Dream," or "Novel: Incident," "Novel: Text," or what might appear to be chapter titles: "Futile Evenings" (on this topic see "Soirées de Paris," which Barthes was writing at the same time as the "Vita Nova" outlines, between late August and mid-September 1979),[179] or "Anamnesis," for which he offered a foretaste in *Roland Barthes par Roland Barthes*, a book that as a whole and like *L'Empire des signes* may appear to be one of the prodromes for "Vita Nova." Other titles were published in the mid- and late 1970s: "Notre littérature,"[180] "Scènes," "Le Roman impossible," "Mémoire," "Stromates," "La splendeur de passé."

Throughout this file we find "production notes," instructions Barthes wrote to himself for the future composition of the work that he was in the process of putting together. For example, in October 1977, even though he was also "keeping" his "Journal de deuil"[181] tied to the death of his mother, he wrote on one page, "Maybe insert here and ventilate the Journal of grief." Or again, we see appearing a plan for a more classical, narrative novel titled "The Conspirators," which at times recalls André Gide's *Les Faux-monnayeurs*, and which Barthes ties to current events; thus, in a file titled "Supports for the conspirators," dated August 18, 1979, he includes the project for the "Mesrine theft," a reference to the famous gangster shot by the police that same year, on November 2, 1979. The project is occasionally altered with a competing title, the "Dispensers of Justice novel" (September 26, 1979). In October, we find many hypothetical titles: "Confession of a writer," "Dictionary of my life," "History of my perversions." We also find present or future titles in the plans for "Vita Nova," like "Futile evenings," previously cited, "Maetri e Autori," and "Patricians and Plebeians."

"Vita Nova" never took form definitively enough for Barthes to imagine the transition from notes to overall writing, but in fact some of his chapters had already been written at the time of his death. These are, in short: "Incidents, au Maroc naguère . . . ," "Soirées de

Paris," "Journal de deuil," to which we may add the last two courses at the Collège de France on the preparation of the novel, which were offered as one uninterrupted course, a kind of endless speech for which the key word is that rare term that Barthes exhumed from the decadent Latin of Sidoine Apollinaire, *scripturire*, which names in a dead language the "desire to write," the endless craving to write more. *Le Chambre claire*, the last part of a kind of trilogy that begins with *Roland Barthes par Roland Barthes*, followed by *Fragments d'un discours amoureux*, constituting three treatises on the Self, love, and death, is not the "Vita Nova." It is like one of its sources, one of its insights, or one of its prefaces. The epilogue lies elsewhere.

We are presenting here eight outlines of "Vita Nova" previously reproduced at the end of *Oeuvres complètes*.

Transcription and Translation of "Vita Nova"

Translated by Kate Briggs

"Vita Nova" comprises eight sheets of paper in 21 x 29.7 format. The first seven pages were written on typewriter paper, the eighth on squared paper. The pages were filed in a red cardboard folder marked VITA NOVA in capital letters. The first draft was written in ink; additions were made in black or red pencil.

Abbreviations Used

< > word crossed out
<illeg.> word rendered illegible
{ } interlinear addition
Italics indicate additions made in black pencil, **bold** indicates those made in red pencil.
The square brackets [ ] are Barthes's.

<u>Vita Nova</u>

Meditation. Taking stock
Morality with no hope of application.

<u>Prologue</u> – Bereavement[182]

I. The World as a contradictory object of spectacle and
indifference [*as Discourse*]
 —Archetypal objects: —[Evil?]
                              —The Militant
                              —Bad Faith

I. (a) *"pleasures" are impervious to . . .*
                              —Music

II.   —The decision of April 15, 78[183]
             —Literature as a substitute for love

             —

                              —Writing

III. Imagining a V.N.
                              —Regimes

IV. Literature as disappointment (it was an Initiation)
                              —Done already: the Essay
                              —The Fragment
                              —The Diary
                              —The Novel
                              [—Humor?]
                              —Nostalgia

                              {*compact*}
V. <The> Idleness [The Neutral? The Heap / Tao]
             {*philosophical <u>Doing Nothing</u>*}

<u>Epilogue</u>: The Encounter

Vita Nova

Make
more dialectical
Plan too edifying   Meditation. Taking stock
       too disappointing   Morality with no hope of application

<u>Prologue</u>   —Bereavement
             —The vital problem of <u>Action</u> (with respect to what
                                             ensues:
                                             what to do? how to
                                             act?)

I.   Amorous acedy
           —What came after RH[184]
           —Half-hearted pursuits

II.   "Pleasures" are impervious to force
           —Music | Cruising
           —Giving up painting
           —Derisory things: Knitting, *Komboloï*[185] |

III.   The World as a contradictory object of spectacle and
       indifference. Analysis and Typology of <u>Discourses</u>
       "Evil"? The Militant. Bad faith.

IV.   The decision of April 15, 1978. Literature as a substitute,
       <illeg.>[186] of love.

V.   Imagining a V.N.
       Regimes.

VI.   Literature: is only an initiation? Disappointments,
       incapacities?
               — Done already: the Essay.
               — The Fragment. The Diary. The Novel.
               — Humor.
               — Nostalgia

VII.   Pure Idleness: "philosophical doing nothing." (The
       Neutral. Tao / the Heap).
             —Friends (Fantasy of devoting myself entirely to them)
             —*The Return to former positions. Carrying on.* No
             V.N.

<u>Epilogue</u>: The Encounter

<u>Prologue</u>　　　— Bereavement
　　　　　　　　— <To Live, A[187]>

—To live, to act, to invest, to desire　　　Fields, Circles, crossings
→ Quest
The "Return————Loss of the true guide, the Mother
to Childhood"　—Maestri e Autori*　　　　　　　　Cruising
(without Mother)　　　　　　　　　　　　　　　　Futile
　　　　　　　　　　　　　　　　　　　　　　　Evenings

Masters of—The Writer (*Never was a philosopher*
Discourse　　　　　　　　*my guide*)
　　　　　　—The Gigolo – as Other—Ordinary People
　　　　　　　　the Baker
　　　　—The Friend
　　　　—*the unknown young man*

—Figures – Woman – as Irritation
　Anti-
　Discourse　　<Proust?>
　　　　　　　? – the Militant – as Other-Priest

?　　—The decision of April 15, 1978 Maestro Tolstoy takes the
　　　place of Proust?
　　　Lit.

?
　　? — VN

　　? — *The absence of a master*　｜　*The Moroccan Child*
　　　　　　　　　　　　　　　　　from the Zenrin
　　　　　　　　　　　　　　　　　Poem[188]
　　　　　　　　　　　　　　　　　Pure Idleness

? <u>Epilogue</u>　　　　　　　　　　　　The Encounter

　Index of people and places (e.g., *the Flore*)

　　　　　　　　　　　　　　　　　Inferno II 139–42[189]

<u>Prologue</u> – Bereavement
>—The Loss of the Guide (the Mother)

—To live, to act, to desire, to fantasize

—Quest: what force, what form, what <u>discourse</u> in order to write?

— Anti-Discourse:
- — Woman as Irritation
- — The "Scholar"
- — The Militant (Priests of Power)

— Mediators: "Maestro et Autore"

- — The Gigolo
- — The unknown Young Man
- — The Friend

- — The Writer → *Vita Nova*

- — The (Moroccan) child: the Guide-less
                          Idleness

-Prologue

↓ *Mam.*[190] *as guide*

___ Futile Evenings
+ Politics (Le Monde at the Flore?)[191]

"This is how I spent my evenings"

? ┬ –Quests[192]

Journeys, Circles   Dialectic: —Evil and Good Mingled
    Guides   —Positive and Insufficient
    _____   —Fantasies where every
                                   journey is a success.
                                   Talent to the very end

        —The gigolo
        —The unknown young man
        —The Friend
        —The writer

        —*Mam. still the guide*

↓ Decision of April 15, 1978

        —VN
        —"I'm withdrawing from the world to begin a great
           work that will be an expression of . . . Love"

I didn't know   ⎧
whether I was   ⎪
withdrawing   ⎪
do to this or   ⎨   ≠
its   ⎪
opposite   ⎪   the (Moroccan) child   the Guide-less
                   ⎩   Idleness

-*Idea of Poikilos,*[193] *of the Romantic Novel, of the absolute Novel.*
See notes for the 79–80 <u>Lecture</u> <u>Course</u> # p. 11

<u>Forms:</u>

> —*Narrative, account of an (intellectual) quest*
> cf *Photography*
> —*Account of my evenings (endless, futile diachrony)*
>
> —*The Frgmts of a "great work" (cf Pascal's* <u>Pensées</u>*)*
> # *observations, aphorisms*
> *Frgmts: like the remains*[194] *of an Apology for*
> *something*
> —*Fake dialogues (would be good for Politics, which*
> *is interminable contestatory hair-splitting)*

[Reading Pascal] Desire to:

— <Frag> Proceed as if I were writing my major work (Summa) <the illeg.> but an Apology for what? That is the question! Not for "me" at any rate!)—of which only ruins or contours, or erratic portions would remain (like the foot in Porbus's painting):[195] Fragments of varying lengths, <possibly illeg.> (neither aphorisms, nor essays)

—The Frgmts: would bear out the theory of *Poilikos*, of the Romantic Novel, of the Absolute Novel: densely written, elliptical even, always very "intelligent" (a tight watch to be kept on this) → Slow, unremitting labor—not only of the Form but also (new for me) of the Thinking.

—Give up playing the Foolish game, the scare quotes, the refusal to assume a position in relation to the enunciation (excuse of the Novelistic, of the diversity of my ego). Without Self-indulgence. No Pretence.

—Which law? the absolute law of mam.
[The Neutral? at any rate: firm and brave]

—No more *I*. At any rate, no more than Pascal.
—That will be difficult: he could say: <the> man, men

—Organization? "Sheafs": indecipherable plan that's still ordered.

—The idea about the Circles, Mediators, e.g. <Illeg.>
won't be *inflated*: it will be what it can be:
a Fragment—a two-page Apologue, etc.

—"Pensées" in which, References to the Scriptures (quotations)

        [would be replaced by References to literature (quotations)
—All of this would mean giving up the childishness of the Vita Nova Narrative: those efforts of the frog who wished to make itself as big as . . .[196]

or   [-Bereavement]
at the end

  —Acedy

  —Life hypotheses   [Virgil]
      —Cruising. Bolge[197]   Gig.
      —Encounter. Celebration   The unknown ym
      —Struggle (G[198] Politics etc.)   Militant
      —Charity   The friend JL[199]
      —the Heap   The Moroccan child
      —*Music Painting Retreat*

  —[Mam. as guide]   *Journal of Mourning*[200]
  —*'The Circle of my possible'* * = Lit.
  —Decision of April 15, 78:[201] Literature

*See Heidegger quotation in the lecture § on Idleness.[202]

NOTES

Foreword

Epigraph: Maurice Blanchot, *L'Écriture du désastre* (Paris: Gallimard, 1980), 183.

1. The letters from Barthes to Frédéric Berthet are found collected in Frédéric Berthet, *Correspondances, 1973–2003* (Paris: La Table ronde, 2011).

2. Leyla Perrone-Moisés, *Com Roland Barthes* (São Paulo: WMF Martins Fontes, 2012).

3. Roland Barthes, *La Plus déchirante des fêtes*, followed by *À propos de Roland Barthes*, with original drawings by Josef Nadj (Paris: Archimbaud, 2001).

4. *L'Amitié de Roland Barthes* (Paris: Seuil, 2015).

Death of the Father

1. The chapter in this book, *Sur les bancs de Flandre* (Les éditions de France, 1927), was reprinted by Antoine Compagnon in his anthology *La Grande Guerre des écrivains: D'Apollinaire à Zweig* (Paris: Folio, 2014). See also (identified by Antoine Compagnon [*Romantic Review*, January-March 2014]) Louis Dours, "Les Marins bayonnais tombés à l'ennemi," *Bulletin de la Société des sciences, lettres et arts de Bayonne* 3–4 (1917): 14–20.

2. Baron Antoine Exelmans (1865–1944) was the descendant of an illustrious French military family, the grandson of the Marshal of France, Rémy Joseph Isidore Exelmans (1775–1862).

Chronology

1. See *Le Théâtre antique à la Sorbonne* (Paris: L'Arche, 1961).

2. *Oeuvres complètes*, vol. 1 (Paris: Seuil, 2002), 29–32 (henceforth OC).

3. According to his diary, Barthes returned to Leysin in 1972 to revisit these places while he was staying in Geneva.

4. Roland Barthes would publish all of his work with Seuil—with the exception of *La Tour Eiffel* (Delpire, 1964), *Élements de sémiologie* (Denoël-Gonthier, 1965), *L'Empire des signes* (Skira, 1970), and *Alors, la Chine?* (Christian Bourgois, 1975).

1. From Adolescence to the Romance of the Sanatorium

1. A reference to texts read during the awards ceremony for the 1931–32 school year. The Prince of Conti (1611–68), after having been Molière's supporter, turned against him, assuming a pious stance, notably in the *Traité de la comédie et des spectacles* (1666), in which he attacks his former protégé.

2. An allusion to the three "Fragments du Narcisse" by Paul Valéry, collected and published in *Charmes* in 1926.

3. This phrase appears in "Pour le latin," *La Vie littéraire* (Paris: Calmann-Lévy, 1925), 281 (first series published in 1888–92).

4. Jean Huerre and Sadia Oualid: classmates of Barthes.

5. The Section Française de l'Internationale Ouvrière, ancestor of the present-day Parti Socialiste, was then led by Paul Faure and Léon Blum, while Frédéric Brunet then led the Parti Socialiste Français (1919–35), which brought together the right wing of the socialist movement.

6. There were two Jaurès anthologies at the time: *Pages choisies* by Paul Desanges and Luc Mériga (Reider, 1922), and *Morceaux choisis* by Émile Vandervelde (Alcan, 1929).

7. *Histoire socialiste de la Révolution française* (Librairie de L'Humanité, 1922).

8. *L'Armée nouvelle* was published by Rouff, 1911.

9. Édouard Herriot (1872–1957), a member of the Parti Radical, was president of the Conseil in 1932.

10. A mistake by Barthes. There is no article by that title in *La Vie littéraire* by Anatole France, but there is a "famous" one published as "L'Esprit normalien" in the posthumous book by Jules Lemaître (1853–1914), former student of the Rue d'Ulm: *Les Contemporains: Études et portraits littéraires* (Paris: Boivin et Cie, 1914).

11. Barthes alludes here to *Un Amour de Swann.*

12. Barthes is referring to the Spanish dancer Teresa Boronat (1904–2011), whose stage name was La Teresina.

13. Both by Nicolas Berdiaff, the first appeared in 1931 from Éditions Je Sers, and the second the following year from Éditions Demain. Barthes alludes to *De la dignité du christianisme* in 1975 in connection with Bertolt Brecht: "Brecht et le discours: Contribution à l'étude de la discursivité" (*OC*, vol. 4, 789).

14. A text by Barthes inspired by the figure of Diodorus of Sicily.

15. Barthes began writing a novel in 1934, whose hero, Aurélien Page, offspring of a provincial bourgeois family, gradually comes to understand that family's tyrannical structure.

16. The house in Bayonne, Allées Paulmy, now gone, is mentioned in the beginning of *Roland Barthes par Roland Barthes*, where Barthes provides a photograph of it (*OC*, vol. 4, 586–87).

17. Berthes Barthes, Barthes's grandmother, "good, a provincial: steeped in the bourgeoisie," whom Barthes talks about in *Roland Barthes par Roland Barthes* (*OC*, vol. 4, 590).

18. This text from Barthes's juvenilia has not been found.

19. This is "Divertissement in F Major," dedicated to Philippe Rebeyrol, dated January 17, 1934.

20. *The Birth of Tragedy* by Nietzsche appeared in a French translation in 1901 as *L'Origine de la tragédie dans la musique ou hellénisme et pessimisme*, published by Mercure de France.

21. A classmate of Barthes and Rebeyrol who belonged to a prominent family of Protestant ministers, the Monods.

22. An allusion to the work of Robert Shumann, *Davidsbündlertänze*, which features "the march of David's companions against the Philistines," that is, against bourgeois conformists in the Romantic reading.

23. Roland Barthes suffered his first attack of tuberculosis in May 1934, with a lesion in his left lung. He was first in Bayonne and then, prevented from taking the baccalaureate, he was sent to Bedous in the Pyrenees for a free cure in September 1934 until summer 1935. He lived there with his mother and brother Michel.

24. Gaston Doumergue (1863–1937) was president of the Conseil from February to November 1934, when he resigned.

25. Charles de Saint-Évremond (1614–1705). Barthes must have been reading the *Oeuvres mêlées*, published by Techener in 1865.

26. The Gospel According to Luke.

27. The League of Nations, precursor to the United Nations.

28. Thermopyles is one of the names for Saint-Étienne-de-Baïgorry.

29. Named after the owner of the building; Barthes mentions it (mistakenly transcribed as "Carricq") in "Biographie," in *Le Lexique de l'auteur* (Paris: Seuil, 2010), 256.

30. Clément Vautel (1876–1954), writer, journalist, author of popular novels, among them *La Petite-Fille de Madame Angot* (Albin Michel, 1934).

31. Barthes's mistake, August 13, 1935, was a Tuesday.

32. "Un je ne sais quel charme encore vers vous m'emporte" (*Polyeucte*, 2.2).

33. Jean Brissaud, classmate of Barthes and Rebeyrol, the son of Doctor Brissaud, who treated Barthes for his tuberculosis until 1946.

34. The name given to Sorbonne students who were members of the medieval theater group started by Gustave Cohen.

35. Line by Giosuè Carducci (1835–1906) in "Idillio maremmano," in which Carducci mocks romantic speculations.

36. Philippe Rebeyrol had gone to Lyon for the examination in history, postponed because of the war, and had just passed it.

37. Louis Séchan (1882–1968), Hellenic scholar, professor at the Sorbonne. It was before him and Paul Mazon that Barthes defended his graduate thesis, "Evocations et incantations dans la tragédie grecque," in October 1941.

38. The spelling adopted in the first French translations of *The Idiot* by Fyodor Dostoevsky for the character Myshkin.

39. Barthes has his first serious relapse of tuberculosis in October 1941 and was first treated in Paris by Doctor Brissaud, who then sent him to the sanatorium for French students in Saint-Hilaire-du-Touvet in early winter 1942.

40. Michel Delacroix, son of philosopher Henri Delacroix, was a classmate with whom Barthes took singing lessons given by Charles Panzéra. Michel Delacroix died October 28, 1942. Assy is located in Haute-Savoie.

41. Barthes was confined to bed rest in Paris from October 1941 until February 1942.

42. "Temporal" in the sense that mysticism gives to this word, that is, related to the worldly realm.

43. Jean Girodon was a student with Barthes at the Louis-le-Grand Lycée.

44. For example, "a girl with whom I could hardly achieve an erection and only discharged when thinking of another," in *Oeuvres intimes*, vol. 1 (Paris: Gallimard, 1981), 709.

45. In early February 1945, Barthes left Saint-Hilaire-du-Trouvet with a group of patients for the sanatorium in Leysin, Switzerland, a major center for treating tuberculosis and home of the Clinique Alexandre.

46. A reference to Pascal's phrase "I will also have thoughts in the back of my head," in *Pensées* (Paris: Gallimard, 1977), 404, fragment 659.

47. Barthes's graduate thesis on Greek tragedy, with Paul Mazon at the Sorbonne, which he defended in October 1941.

48. Linked to the Swiss banking system, the "clearing" permitted exchanges between banks without requiring money orders or any other means of sending funds.

49. Barthes spoke of him in a long interview titled "Réponses" (*OC*, vol. 3, 1025). On May 3, 1936, this group's first performance of *Perseus* took place, with Barthes in the role of Darius. See *Roland Barthes par Roland Barthes* (*OC*, vol. 4, 613); and "Lettre au sujet du Groupe de théâtre antique" (*OC*, vol. 2, 25–26).

50. Jacqueline Mazon (1918–2008) was the niece of the great Hellenist Paul Mazon, the professor of Barthes and Jacques Veil.

51. There is no Wednesday March 24, 1944, but in any case it was indeed in March 1944 that Barthes made a visit to Paris, after which, upon returning to Saint-Hilaire, he had to remain immobile for a long time because of a new pulmonary attack.

52. Removal of one or a group of ribs in the case of a failed pneumothorax.

53. A tomography is an exploratory procedure using radiology that allows one to observe a cross section of an organ or tissue at a given depth.

54. Illegible.

55. *Existences* was the magazine for the Saint-Hilaire-du-Touvet sanatorium. Barthes had already had several pieces published in it, beginning in 1942. He published "En Grèce" in the July 1944 issue (*OC*, vol. 1, 68–74).

56. In the inclined position, the patient lies flat with feet higher than the head in order to relax the lungs.

57. René Cohen was a doctor at the Saint-Hilaire-du-Touvet sanatorium.

58. Canetti's book, *Le Bacille de Koch dans la lésion tuberculeuse du poumon*, appeared in January 1946 in the monograph series from the Institut Pasteur.

59. Gilbert de Rham, a great Swiss surgeon born in 1899, was the author of a *Traité sur la Thoracoplastie* (Imprimeries réunies, 1944).

60. Robert David (see the letters addressed to Robert David).

61. Illegible.

62. Again, referring to Robert David.

63. October 10.

64. One line is missing.

65. One line is missing.

66. We do not know what the CED is, probably a European center or committee for health or education that approached Georges Canetti.

67. The end of the letter is missing.

68. A word is missing.

69. The word here in French, *fricarelle*, means erotic practices between women and, by extension, lesbian love itself.

70. One line is missing.

71. One line is missing.

72. Daniel Douady (1904–82) was the first doctor and first director of the Saint-Hilaire-du-Touvet sanatorium, beginning in 1933. Barthes had already done a postcure in his establishment in Paris between January and July 1943.

73. One line is missing.

74. A section of the chapter "Sa Majesté la femme" from *Michelet par lui-même* (1954) is titled "Lesbianisme de Michelet" (*OC*, vol. 1, 393–94).

75. The end of the letter is missing.

76. Speleostomy was a method of healing tuberculosis invented by Doctor Bernou at the Châteaubriant sanatorium (Loire-Atlantique) that, in response to the failures linked to pneumothorax and thoracoplasty, consisted of healing up pulmonary cavities with silver nitrate.

77. Barthes is alluding to the editorial by Sartre in the first issue of *Temps modernes*, which appeared in October 1945, reprinted in *Situations II* (Gallimard, 1948). See the letter from December 20, 1945, to Robert David. *Temps présent*, a weekly publication founded by Stanislas Fumet in 1937, reappeared in 1944 after having been banned during the Occupation. It was supported by the Dominicans who were connected to the Éditions du Cerf.

78. Barthes is alluding to his article, "Le Style de *L'Étranger*" (by Camus), which appeared in the journal *Existences* in July 1944 (*OC*, vol. 1, 75–79).

79. *Sursis*, the second volume in the *Chemins de la liberté* (Gallimard, 1945), has a printing date of August 31, 1945.

80. *Mouvement républicain populaire*, Christian-Democrat party founded in 1944.

81. Olivier Messiaen (1908–92) had just given the first performance of *Trois petites liturgies de la présence divine* (1943–44) in December 1945 and was considered a Christian composer.

82. Barthes will make much use of this idea henceforth, especially in period of *Mythologies*. See, for example, "The Vaccine of the Avant-Garde," *Les Lettres nouvelles*, March 1955 (OC, vol. 1, 563–65).

83. André Siegfried (1875–1959), historian and sociologist; Pierre Emmanuel (1916–84), writer and poet.

84. A nickname for one of the patients at the Saint-Hilaire-du-Touvet sanatorium.

85. As we have seen, Doctor Brissaud has followed Barthes's disease since Paris.

86. For example, like the convoy from Saint-Hilaire-du-Touvet of which Barthes was part.

87. OC, vol. 2, 254.

88. Barthes's mistake; there is no Thursday, December 8, 1944. It must have been Friday.

89. A piece of the letter is missing.

90. Illegible because the letter is damaged here.

91. André Mosser, medical student and patient at the sanatorium.

92. One line is missing.

93. The pianist Vlado Perlemuter (1904–2002) fled France in 1943 because of anti-Semitic persecution and took refuge in Switzerland, where he contracted tuberculosis, from which he recovered in 1946 after the war (see the following letter).

94. The end of the letter is missing.

95. Barthes is alluding to the "right extrapleural pneumothorax" that he had just undergone at the Clinique Miremont in Leysin, which took place Wednesday, October 10. In a letter from Thursday, October 18, Barthes describes the aftermath of the operation: "Wednesday 10 absolutely not suffering from the operation, complete calm—Thursday, Friday: the worst of the suffering: breathlessness, erratic pulse, asphyxiaton; I thought I was done for (will tell you about that, too). Saturday: draining, relief, fatigue, discomfort, misery [. . .]."

96. Duet with Perlemuter took place in the second half of September (see the preceding letter).

97. A part of the letter is missing.

98. On Barthes's return from the Clinique Miremont to the sanatorium in Leysin.

99. Doctor Klein was the head doctor at the sanatorium.

100. Cut.

101. Sartre's editorial appeared in the first issue of *Temps modernes*, published in October 1945 (see the letter to Georges Canetti from December 20, 1945). In a letter to Robert David from December 17, of which we have only a fragment, Barthes took up the question of the opposition between the analytical mind and the synthetic mind: "Try to find the first issue of the review, *Les Temps modernes*. There you will read a very fine manifesto by J.-P. Sartre; you will see how the analytical mind, the bourgeois mind, the mind of 89 [. . .], and how the modern world seems to call for a more 'totalitarian' concept of man. It is very clear that 89, whose death echoes across the continent, will have its last stronghold in the legal mind, in the legal structures, cherished offspring of the Revolution and high priests of the analytical, bourgeois mindset. Thus, within the citadel of the Law, there must be revolutionary minds, applying revolutionary methods to the very subjects of the Law. You will be

one of them, I am sure of it. One can be a revolutionary and very gentle. I really hope that, more and more, the new Revolution will be a question of work rather than of blood."

102. *Le Sursis* (once again, see the letter to George Canetti mentioned earlier).

103. The end of the letter is missing.

104. Tuberculosis cures required patients to be exposed to fresh air and sun.

105. In January Barthes wrote "two pages" on Albert Camus at the request of a certain Russo, an Italian intellectual who edited a journal in Milan, about whom we have not been able to uncover any information.

106. In a letter to Robert David from January 18, 1946, of which we have only a fragment, Barthes lays out this dialectic in detail: "Love, you see, is a kind of inverse reason, and therein lies its terrible, and terribly beautiful, nature. Love has all the characteristics of reason. It is the most logical action possible, accepting no compromise and basing its progression on a logical line of thought. In reason, logic has the power of royalty; in love, it has the power of tyranny. I cannot *do otherwise* than accept the panic (before a word, or silence), not through intellectual fidelity to a principle, but through the absolute pressure of an inner dialectic that for me merges with love itself."

107. This is the title of a famous book by Maurice Barrès ("devoted to love and pain") published by Juven in 1903.

108. A word is missing.

109. The Milhits were one of the Swiss families that Barthes often visited, in addition to the Chessex and Sigg families. He also visited their daughter Heidy in Berne. Their house in Lausanne is where, we assume, Barthes wrote this letter to Robert David.

110. A word is missing.

111. Grasset, 1929.

2. The First Barthes

1. Barthes arrived in Alexandria in November 1949 and taught at the university.

2. Charles Singevin (1905–88), whom Barthes met in Bucharest, was a philosopher and author of *Essai sur l'un* (Seuil, 1969) and many articles. He spent a major part of his career in French institutions abroad.

3. Algirdas Julien Greimas (1917–92), linguist and semiotician. In 1948, he had just defended his doctoral thesis on the vocabulary of fashion, under the direction of Charles Bruneau. He was then an assistant professor at the Alexandria University.

4. That is what Barthes eventually did, by starting on a thesis in lexicology in autumn 1952 under the direction of Charles Bruneau, thanks to which he became a student researcher at CNRS and received a grant.

5. After his return from Egypt, Barthes worked at the Department of Cultural Relations for the Ministry of Foreign Affairs.

6. In 1947, Barthes had contemplated a training course in social services and public education.

7. In 1956, Philippe Rebeyrol was a cultural consultant in Cairo. This is undoubtedly an allusion to the failed Anglo-French invasion in November 1956 following Nasser's nationalization of the Suez Canal—which Barthes calls "sinister buffoonery" here.

8. Following the uprising of the Hungarian people against the Communist dictatorship in October 1956, Soviet troops invaded Hungary and surrounded Budapest on November 4. The repression left twenty-five hundred Hungarians dead. A large portion of the anti-Stalinist left supported the uprising. The found-

ing of the journal *Arguments* by Edgar Morin, Roland Barthes, Jean Duvign-aud, and Colette Audry in December 1956 marked the left's renewed opposition to Stalinism.

9. The uprising in Poland in June 1956, harshly repressed, produced a sort of "thaw" with Gomulka's speech in Warsaw in October in which he strongly criticized Stalinism.

10. See their exchanges later in the chapter.

11. *La NRF* reappeared under the name of *Nouvelle Nouvelle Revue française* in 1953, and readopted its current title in 1959.

12. After publishing "Le Degré zéro de l'écriture" and "Faut-il tuer la grammaire?" in August and September 1947, *Combat* published five articles by Barthes that would constitute the core of the book to be published by Seuil, but not until 1953. The first of them was titled "Triomphe et rupture de l'écriture bourgeoise" and appeared November 9, 1950. Thus Queneau wrote to Barthes the very day the article was published. At the end of the introductory paragraph Maurice Nadeau wrote, "He [Roland Barthes] has made no secret of having to oversimplify and exaggerate his views, and he expects they will raise questions." Queneau is cited in a list that includes "Flaubert, Mallarmé, Rimbaud, les Goncourt, les Surréalistes, Queneau, Sartre, Blanchot or Camus."

13. It is still a question of the manuscript for *Le Degré zéro de l'écriture*.

14. This is one of the first "mythologies" to appear, published in *Esprit* in October 1952, and it will come first in the collection.

15. Evidently a reference to "L'Encyclopédie de la Pléiade" project that Queneau was in the process of assembling, the first volume of which appeared in 1956. Barthes did, in fact, participate in it. His article "Le Théatre grec" appeared in the 1965 volume, *Histoire des spectacles* (*OC*, vol. 2, 724–44).

16. Apparently there was a misunderstanding; Barthes does not follow up on this proposal.

17. There is no trace of such a study in the Barthes archives.

18. Roland Barthes was a student researcher in lexicology at the CNRS, beginning in late 1952.

19. Barthes lost his CNRS grant for his thesis in lexicology at the end of 1954 and applied for a new grant in sociology, which he obtained in 1955. In the meantime he worked at Éditions de l'Arche, thanks to Robert Voisin (see the "Author of the Theater" section, p. XXX).

20. A promise Barthes did not keep.

21. Barthes participated in the major conference on "the structuralist debate," organized by René Girard at Johns Hopkins University in Baltimore, Maryland, in October 1966.

22. In reality, Barthes's article in *Combat* dates from August 1947. Astonishingly, Béguin anticipates by a month a new series of articles by Barthes in *Combat* that will become part of *Le Degré zéro de l'écriture*, the first of which appeared November 9, 1950.

23. Barthes's text titled "Michelet, l'Histoire et la mort" did, in fact, appear in the April 1951 issue.

24. Jean-Marie Domenach (1922–98) was an intellectual close to Emmanuel Mounier, and was the noted author of *Retour du tragique* (Seuil, 1967). He became friends with Michel de Certeau and Michel Foucault.

25. No text by Barthes on Cayrol appeared in the December or January issue of *Esprit*. This must refer to a long article, almost essay length, titled "Jean Cayrol et ses romans" that appeared in the March 1952 issue of *Esprit*.

26. The title Barthes chose was "Le Monde où l'on catche," published in *Esprit* in October.

27. On Cayrol, see our note, p. XXX.

28. In the Dolomites, north of Venice, where Genet stayed to treat his rheumatoid arthritis, contracted during his time in prison. He probably stayed with his Russian patron, Gala Barbisan, who owned a chalet there. See Catherine Robbe-Grillet, *Jeune mariée: Journal, 1957–1962* (Paris: Fayard, 2004), 122.

29. The abbreviation is crossed out in the letter.

30. This "mythology" appeared in the February 1955 issue of *Les Lettres nouvelles* under the title "Pour une histoire de l'enfance, enfants-vedettes, enfants-copies, jouets."

31. Of course Genet means Marguerite Duras, who lived with Dionys Mascolo on Rue Saint-Benoit.

32. Jean Guéhenno (1890–1978) published *L'Évangile éternel: Étude sur Michelet* with Grasset in 1927.

33. André Frénaud (1907–93) was a French poet, in particular the author of *Il n'y a pas de paradis* (1962).

34. Frénaud's letter probably addressed *Mythologies* and the "final text" in particular, that is, "Le Mythe, aujourd'hui."

35. Jean Lacroix (1900–86), French philosopher, was the teacher and friend of Louis Althusser. Barthes probably met him at Saint-Hilaire-du-Touvet, where he came to give a lecture on friendship in 1943.

36. Robert Coiplet, journalist at *Le Monde* and former representative for the Vichy censorship board at *Le Temps*, published a very critical review of *Mythologies* in *Le Monde* on March 9, 1957. Jean Lacroix's article appeared on May 5 that same year.

37. See photos, page XXX.

38. There was, in fact, quite a violent exchange between Jean Paulhan and Roland Barthes; Paulhan, using the pseudonym of Jean Guérin, attacked Barthes in *La Nouvelle NRF* in June 1955, and Barthes responded to him in *Les Lettres nouvelles* in July–August. See *OC*, vol. 1, 569.

39. Robert Pinget published *Le Renard and la Boussole* with Gallimard in 1953.

40. Upon the death of his maternal grandmother, Noémie Révelin, in July 1953, Barthes moved into her apartment on the Place du Panthéon until spring 1954.

41. © Catherine and Jean Camus. Having learned of Barthes's very critical text on *Le Peste* before its publication, Albert Camus responded to it through an open letter to Barthes that appeared in the January issue of the *Bulletin du club du meilleur livre* following a review by Barthes titled "*La Peste*, annales d'une épidémie ou roman de la solitude?" Barthes published a response to that open letter in the April issue of the same journal. See *OC*, vol. 1, 540–47 and 573–74.

42. Robert Carlier (1910–2002) was the founder of Éditions du Club du Meilleur Livre, which issued the journal with the same name.

43. *Les Lettres nouvelles*, edited by Maurice Nadeau.

44. Marcel Péju was the office manager for *Les Temps Modernes*.

45. Marcel Arland accepted Barthes's invitation but had to cancel his visit at the last minute for personal reasons.

46. The book must be *Planétarium*, published by Gallimard in May 1959.

47. See "Le Grain de la voix" (1972) and "La Musique, la voix, la langue" (1978) in *OC*, vols. 4 and 5, 150–53 and 524–27.

48. On the review, see Marco Consolini, *Théâtre populaire, 1953–1964: Histoire d'une revue engagée* (Paris: Éditions de l'IMEC, 1999).

49. See the letter to Jean Cayrol from July 1953, p. XXX. The article in question is "Pouvoirs de la tragédie antique" (*Théâtre populaire* 2 [July–August 1953]).

50. Guy Dumur (1921–91), writer and drama critic, member of the editorial committee for *Théâtre populaire*.

51. Morvan Lebesque (1911–70), journalist and essayist, member of the editorial committee for *Théâtre populaire*.

52. Jules Roy had just published *La Bataille dans la rizière* with Gallimard. In fact, a play by Arthur Adamov, *Le Professeur Taranne*, appeared in the July-August 1953 issue of *Théâtre populaire* (see the following letter).

53. The play by Jules Roy that Barthes alludes to is titled *Les Cyclones* and does, in fact, address the army's attempts at ultramodern airplanes. It was published by Gallimard in 1954.

54. Here Barthes is criticizing Roy's presumed stoicism, through Vauvenargue's (1715–47) moralism.

55. Barthes is on vacation in Groningen in the Netherlands, where he writes this letter and the two that follow.

56. *Le Professeur Taranne*.

57. Jean Duvignaud (1921–2007), one of the review's founders.

58. "Pouvoirs de la tragédie antique."

59. The Groupe de Théâtre Antique de la Sorbonne, which Barthes founded after the war.

60. In the VIᵉ arrondissement in Paris.

61. August Baumeister (1830–1922).

62. Margarete Bieber (1879–1978).

63. Michel de Ghelderode published "Les Entretiens d'Ostende" in the March–April 1954 issue.

64. Name illegible.

65. Jean Duvignaud published "Trois petits mythes du théâtre bourgeois."

66. Jean Laude published "À l'origine du drame."

67. The March–April 1954 issue of *Théâtre populaire* published a French translation of the play by Heinrich von Kleist.

68. Roland Barthes published a simple note on *Ruy Blas* directed by Jean Vilar (*OC*, vol. 1, 486–88), but the same issue ran a text by Vilar, "Ruy Blas: Notes pour les comédiens."

69. In early April Barthes had to go to Avignon to give a lecture for the branch of the Amis du Théâtre Populaire that had just been created. See "Avignon, l'hiver," *France Observateur*, April 15, 1954 (*OC*, vol. 1, 472–75).

70. Jean Paris, the author of a *Hamlet* published by Seuil the year before, which Barthes reviewed (*OC*, vol. 1, 472–75).

71. The editorial in the March–April 1954 issue was, in fact, written by Jean Paris on the subject of an exchange between the Comédie-Française and the Moscow Ballet.

72. Jean Rouvet, senior official at the Ministry of Culture, was then the administrator of Jean Vilar's TNP.

73. This concerns the "Amis du Théâtre Populaire." On the conflicts—especially the ideological ones—between the Amis du Théâtre Populaire and the TNP as represented by Jean Rouvet, see Émile Copfermann, *Le Théâtre populaire, pourquoi?* (Paris: Maspero, 1965), 64–72.

74. The subject proposed by Barthes appeared in the editorial in the next issue.

75. Michel Zéraffa (1918–85), writer and essayist, researcher at CNRS, also literary critic for *France Observateur* and *Lettres nouvelles*.

76. Barthes attended the Nîmes drama festival. See his columns on *Julius Caesar* and *Coriolanus*, directed by Raymond Hermantier, in *Théâtre populaire*, July–August 1955.

77. This must be Jean-Paul Richard and his wife; Richard was born in Marseille and owned a house there.

78. Barthes is probably alluding to a text related to the Hungarian anti-Soviet revolution of 1956.

79. Etchetoa is the name of the villa in Hendaye where Barthes was then staying.

80. The first play by George Schehadé, *Histoire de Vasco*, was performed by Jean-Louis Barrault's company on Monday, October 15, 1956.

81. Barthes was in Zurich for a cultural-political meeting organized by Ignazio Silone and Maurice Nadeau, following the cultural "thaw" linked to relations with Khrushchev. Georges Bataille, Albert Béguin, Jean Duvignaud, and a certain number of intellectuals and apparatchiks from Russian and central Europe were present. Maurice Nadeau mentions the event in his fine portrait of Ignazio Silone in *Grâces leur soient rendues* (Paris: Albin Michel, 2011), 179–80.

82. There were many tensions at the review that pitted the formalists against the political activists, the Brechtians against the Vilarians, the theoreticians against the practitioners. Jean Duvignaud did not support the Brechtian turn of *Théâtre populaire*, especially after the publication of the fifth issue in January–February 1955, devoted to Brecht, with a very radical editorial by Barthes ("La Révolution brechtienne," in *Essais critiques*; *OC*, vol. 2, 314–16). Jean Duvignaud no longer wrote for *Théâtre populaire* after March 1956, although he and Barthes remained connected through another undertaking, the founding of the review *Arguments*, with Edgar Morin, that same year.

83. See the review that Barthes published in *Théâtre populaire* in May 1958 on the production of *Ubu roi* by Jean Vilar at the TNP (*OC*, vol. 1, 929–32).

84. Barthes is speaking here of his work on fashion for the CNRS.

85. Barthes is probably referring to the prefaces to Racine's plays published in 1960 by the Club Français du Livre (volumes 11 and 12 of *Théâtre classique français*), which became the first part of *Sur Racine* (1963). In the March 1958 issue of *Théâtre populaire*, Barthes published a study titled "Dire Racine," which became the second part of the book.

86. In the September–October 1955 issue on the production of *Ubu* by Gabriel Monnet.

87. A reference to payments Voisin made to Barthes every two years for his work for *Théâtre populaire* (see the letter to Jean Cayrol from July 1953, p. XXX).

88. Roger Pic (1920–2001) was a photographer whose photographs of Brecht's production of *Mère Courage* were the subject of Barthes's commentary in the 1959 third quarter issue of *Théâtre populaire* (*OC*, vol. 1, 997–1013), and especially of the preface to *Mère Courage* published by Éditions de l'Arche in 1960, with photos by Pic (*OC*, vol. 1, 1064–82).

89. The sale of the villa, Etchetoa, located in Hendaye, inherited by Barthes's mother from her family, and not actually sold until 1961.

90. John Willett (1916–2002), English translator of and commentator on Brecht's work. He published *The Theatre of Bertolt Brecht* with Methuen in 1959.

91. Jacques Robichez published *Le Symbolisme au théâtre* with Éditions de l'Arche in 1957.

92. In his preface to Bertoldt Brecht's *Mother Courage*, with photos by Robert Pic, Barthes quotes Walter Benjamin: "Rupture is one of the fundamental methods of formal elaboration" (*OC*, vol. 1, 1075), translated by Anna Bostock as "interruption is one of the fundamental methods of all form-giving" in "What Is Epic Theater?," which appears in Walter Benjamin, *Understanding Brecht*, trans. Anna Bostock (London: Verso, 1998), 19.

93. Based on the novel by Maxime Gorki, Brecht's *The Mother* was produced by Brecht at the Théâtre des Nations (*OC*, vol. 1, 400–2).

94. *Système de la mode*, which was not published until 1967.

95. In 1960, Barthes published several texts on fashion, preliminary to *Système de la mode*.

96. In 1960 and 1961, Barthes published only one article in *Théâtre populaire*, on Genet's *Le Balcon* (issue 38, second quarter 1960).

97. It was T. S. Eliot (1888–1965), an American and then naturalized British poet, in his famous text on Dante: "A state of mind in which one sees certain beliefs, as the order of the deadly sins, in which treachery and pride are greater than lust, and despair the greatest, as possible, so that we suspend our judgment altogether." Eliot, "Dante," in *Selected Prose* (London: Faber and Faber, 1975), 221–22.

98. Allusion to *Victory*, the novel by Joseph Conrad, published in 1915.

99. "Aujourd'hui ou Les Coréens" appeared in *France Observateur* on November 1, 1956, a review of Vinaver's play, which opened October 25, 1956, at the Théâtre de la Comédie in Lyon, produced by Roger Planchon (*OC*, vol. 1, 666–67).

100. That is, for the performance on October 27.

101. Jean-Marie Serreau did a production of *Le Coréens* at the Théâtre d'Aujourd'hui (Alliance Française) in January 1957, parallel to Planchon's. Barthes mentions this production in "Note sur *Aujourd'hui*" (*OC*, vol. 1, 646–49).

102. Written by Vinaver between 1957 and 1958, this play was produced for the first time only in 1980, by Gilles Chavassieux at the Théâtre des Ateliers in Lyon. It was first published in March 1958 in *Théâtre populaire*.

103. The play in question is *Iphigénie Hôtel*, written at the same time as *Les Huissiers* and first produced in 1977 by Antoine Vitez at the Centre Georges-Pompidou.

104. An allusion to Vinaver's play *Iphigénie Hôtel* (see the preceding letter).

105. Stories by Ueda Akinari, written in 1776 and considered to be among the most important works of eighteenth-century Japanese fiction.

106. This is a reference to Barthes's review of Michel Foucault's *Folie et déraison: Histoire de la folie à l'âge classique* (Plon, 1961) that appeared in the November 1961 issue of *Critique* and was reprinted in *Essais critiques* (*OC*, vol. 2, 422–27).

107. Georges Plekhanov (1856–1918), Russian Marxist theoretician, *Notes sur l'histoire de la littérature française de Lanson*, and G. Lanson, *L'Histoire de la littérature française* (Hachette, 1898), 394–97.

108. Ernst Robert Curtius (1886–1956), eminent German Romanist, author of *Balzac* (French translation published by Éditions des Syrtes, 1923).

109. A reference to Georges Duhamel.

110. *OC*, vol. 5, 233.

111. A reference to Karl Marx: "Religion is the sigh of the oppressed creature, the heart of a heartless world, and the soul of soulless conditions. It is the opium of the people." Marx, *A Contribution to the Critique of Hegel's Philosophy of Right*, trans. Joseph O'Malley (1844; Oxford: Oxford University Press, 1970), 3.

112. An Edith Piaf song.

113. A popular singer (1889–1978), still very famous at that time.

114. "Le Grand voyage du pauvre nègre," sung by Édith Piaf (1936).

115. Report by Roland Barthes from July 1949; Archive of the Ministry of Foreign Affairs, Nantes, Bucharest (Institut Français, no. 126PO/1/23).

116. The name of Ivan Mitchourine was associated with that of Trofim Denissovitch Lyssenko when Lyssenkoism was developed in 1948, which was intended to suppress genetics, deny the existence of genes and chromosomes, and promote a proletarian overhaul of biology and agriculture.

117. Romanian People's Republic.

118. Alexandru Rosetti (1895–1990), linguist and rector at the university from 1946 to 1949.

3. The Great Ties

1. In a letter to Robert David from January 1946, Barthes wrote this about his encounter with Fornié: "I am learning a lot here from a fellow, Fornier [*sic*], a militant returned from the camps, tough and sensitive intelligence, a frightening world for me who remains silent, gasping for breath, but he's teaching me much because he claims to sense in me a certain intellectual integrity (so he says), and thus, though very reserved, he's very open with me." Later in "Réponses," Barthes pays homage to this friend in naming him as one of those who introduced him to Marxism (*OC*, vol. 3, 1026).

2. The book is *Littérature présente* (Corrêa, 1952), a collection of articles that appeared in *Combat* and *Le Mercure de France*.

3. Alain Robbe-Grillet published "Le Chemin du retour" in the August 1954 issue of *Les Lettres nouvelles*. This short story was reprinted in *Instantanés* (Minuit, 1962).

4. The psychiatrist Cyrille Koupernik (1917–2008) published an article entitled "Le Pavlovisme sent la poussière" in *France Observateur* 226 (September 9, 1954) on " Le Grand Robert," a famous hypnotist on whom Barthes had written a text.

5. In fact, Barthes published "Le Grand Robert" in *Les Lettres nouvelles* in October 1954. The "second article" that Barthes substituted for the one on Le Grand Robert for *France Observateur* was a fierce criticism of *Le Figaro*'s drama critic, Jean-Jacques Gautier, titled "Comment s'en passer," which appeared in the October 3, 1954 issue (*OC*, vol. 1, 517–19).

6. The mythology on the Tour de France, which appeared in *Les Lettres nouvelles* in September 1955 under the title "Le Tour de France comme épopée," and was reprinted in *Mythologies* (*OC*, vol. 2, 756–64).

7. Barthes was then giving classes at the Sorbonne's Centre de Civilisation Française.

8. No doubt the one on "Le Guide Bleu" that appeared in *Les Lettres nouvelles* in October 1955.

9. The board of *Lettres nouvelles* that Nadeau directed.

10. Le Prix de Mai had just been started by Alain Robbe-Grillet with Georges Bataille, Maurice Nadeau, Louis-René des Forêts, Nathalie Sarraute, and Roland Barthes as judges. On *Théâtre populaire*, see the correspondence with Robert Voisin, who edited it. *Arguments* was a review founded in 1956 by Edgar Morin, Roland Barthes, Jean Duvignaud, and Colette Audry.

11. For foreign students at the Centre de Civilisation Française.

12. Nadeau's review, *Les Lettres nouvelles*, and the imprint bearing the same name had just been dropped by their publisher, Éditions Julliard. They would be picked up by Éditions Denoël.

13. "Situation du linguiste," regarding *Problèmes de linguistique générale* (Gallimard, 1966) by Émile Benveniste (1902–76), appeared in the May 15, 1966, issue of *La Quinzaine littéraire*.

14. *La Quinzaine littéraire* published an interview with the philosopher and journalist Jean-François Revel (1924–2006) in the March 1, 1966, issue on the occasion of his candidacy in the general elections, and a text by Lucette Finas on Barthes's *Critique et vérité* appeared in the April 15, 1966, issue.

15. Barthes's hostility toward Jean-François Revel stemmed from the fact that a harsh satire by Raymond Picard lampooning Barthes was published in Revel's "Libertés" series from Pauvert in autumn 1965.

16. An article titled "Plaisir au langage" on the book by Severo Sarduy (1937–93) *Écrit en dansant* appeared in *La Quinzaine littéraire* on May 15, 1967.

17. François Erval (1914–99), coeditor of *La Quinzaine* at that time, with Maurice Nadeau.

18. The book appeared in the "Tel Quel" series from Éditions du Seuil in 1969.

19. This was an important year for Michelet events: the reissue of *Histoire de France* by Pierre Gaxotte, the beginning of production for *Oeuvres complètes* (Flammarion), edited by Paul Vialleneix, who published simultaneously his *Voie royale: Essai sur l'idée de peuple dans l'oeuvre de Michelet* with the same publishing house, and so on.

20. Maurice Nadeau published a review of *Le Plaisir du texte* titled "Le Petit Kamasutra de Roland Barthes" in the March 16, 1973, issue of *La Quinzaine*.

21. An allusion to a very important article that Maurice Nadeau published on *Le Degré zéro de l'écriture* twenty years earlier in the July 1953 issue of *Les Lettres nouvelles*.

22. Nadeau proposed that Barthes write a review of *Roland Barthes par Roland Barthes* for *La Quinzaine littérarire*. Barthes's article, titled "Barthes puissance trois," appeared in Nadeau's journal on March 1, 1975.

23. Because of financial difficulties that *La Quinzaine* encountered, Maurice Nadeau organized a sale to support the review; many writers and artists participated by donating manuscripts or, like Barthes, "paintings"—drawings, watercolors, gouaches.

24. A reference to the "inaugural lesson" at the Collège de France that Barthes would give on January 7, 1977.

25. Pierre Nora, editor of the human sciences division of Gallimard.

26. It was Seuil that finally published the inaugural lecture in 1989, under the title of *Leçon*.

27. The theme of the debate organized at the Centre Georges-Pompidou in April 1977 was "The Intellectual and Power," with Leonardo Sciascia participating.

28. See the first exchange between Barthes and Cayrol in January 1951, p. XXX.

29. A linguist that Roland Barthes knew through Algirdas Julien Greimas; then teaching at the University of Groningen, Guiraud had lent his house to Barthes for the summer.

30. See the letter to Robert Voisin from July 19, 1953, p. XXX.

31. The pages in question are "Pouvoir de la tragédie antique," which appeared in *Théâtre populaire*, Robert Voisin's review, in July–August 1953.

32. *Michelet par lui-même* by Barthes would appear in 1954.

33. Jean Cayrol did not leave Éditions de Seuil at all; he went on to edit the *Écrire* review there from 1956 to 1966, as well as the collection with that same name. Barthes must be alluding to a vacation Cayrol is taking.

34. Cayrol lived with his mother in Saint-Chéron, a small village in Essonne, about forty kilometers from Paris.

35. The uncertainty of the date of this letter makes it difficult to identify Cayrol's novel. It is probably either *Le Démémagement* (Seuil, 1956) or *La Gaffe* (Seuil, 1957).

36. An allusion to a famous passage from *Volupté* (1834) by Sainte-Beuve (1804–69) in the novel's second chapter: "The movement of the trail, the morning freshness of air and sky, the momentum of conversation rising and falling every moment, the self-confidence that is awakened so lightheartedly in such circumstances, a trace of rivalry that, after all, is inevitable in a group of young

men and women intoxicated, emboldened me." Sainte-Beuve, *Volupté* (Paris: Garnier-Flammarion, 1969), 40–41.

37. Barthes published in *Esprit* three articles on Jean Cayrol's earlier novels, the last of which was on *L'Espace d'une nuit* (Seuil, 1954) in the July 1954 issue (*OC*, vol. 1, 506–8).

38. Barthes is referring to *Je vivrai l'amour des autres* (Seuil, 1947).

39. Karl Barth (1886–1968), the great Swiss Protestant theologian whose Christology Barthes defines perfectly here.

40. Jean Baruzi published *Aphorismes de Jean de la Croix* (Féret et fils, 1924).

41. A page is missing.

42. On Olivier de Meslon, see T. Samoyault, *Roland Barthes* (Paris: Seuil, 2015), 407.

43. The "preface," which will in fact be a postscript, is dated September 1956 by Barthes in his book, and in the manuscript August 20, 1956 (see the letter to Georges Perros from September 1956, p. XXX).

44. *Coup de grâce*, written with Claude Durand and produced in 1964, which Barthes saw on January 13 with François Braunschweig, with whom he left for Italy on January 14.

45. This note was written on a card with the Collège de France letterhead.

46. This book may be *Les Enfants pillards* (Seuil, 1978) or *Histoire de ciel* (Seuil, 1979).

47. The book in question in *Gommes*, Robbe-Grillet's first novel, which had just been published by Éditions de Minuit.

48. Robert Coiplet was a journalist for *Le Monde*. Barthes would have direct dealings with him when *Mythologies* appeared (see the letter to Jean Lacroix from May 11, 1957, p. XXX).

49. Bernard Dort, for example, would explain that *Les Gommes* is "halfway between Simenon and Joyce" (*Les Temps modernes*, January 1954).

50. The review *Écrire* was founded three years later in 1956 by Jean Cayrol and its last issues would appear in 1966.

51. Robbe-Grillet then lived in Brest, Brittany, in Kerangoff to be precise, one of the city's suburbs, where his family home was located.

52. Robbe-Grillet was writing many short stories then, some of which would appear in *La Nouvelle NRF* in 1954 and the years that followed, and then would be reprinted in *Instantanés* (Minuit, 1962).

53. Barthes discusses *Les Gommes* for the first time in "Pré-romans," *France Observateur*, June 24, 1954 (*OC*, vol. 1, 500–2); the text solicited by Piel was published in the July–August 1954 issue of *Critique* under the title "Littérature objective," and reprinted in *Essais critique* (*OC*, vol. 2, 293–303).

54. *Le Degré zéro de l'écriture*, published in 1953; since Robbe-Grillet never published anything on Barthes's book, this must refer to one of the letters in their correspondence.

55. In the September-October 1955 issue of *Critique*, Barthes published "Littérature littérale" on Robbe-Grillet's *Voyeur*; this text was reprinted in *Essais critiques* (*OC*, vol. 2, 325–31).

56. A strip-tease club frequented, for example, by Raymond Queneau in the same era: Queneau, *Journaux, 1914–1965* (Paris: Gallimard, 1996), 903. Barthes discusses the Moulin Rouge strip-tease competition and Robbe-Grillet's *Voyeur* (Minuit, 1955) in the "mythology" titled "Strip-tease" (*Les Lettres nouvelles*, December 1955; reprinted in *Mythologies*; *OC*, vol. 1, 785–88).

57. This mythology was very severe with regard to the round table practices of Robbe-Grillet and was not reprinted in *Mythologies* (*OC*, vol. 1, 960–62).

58. See the letter to Michel Butor from June 6, 1960, p. XXX, in which Roland Barthes announces to his correspondent that he supported Yves Velan's

novel for the Médicis prize, prompting anger from Alain Robbe-Grillet. Through Bernard Dort's indiscretion, Robbe-Grillet knew that Barthes had reservations about *L'Année dernière à Marienbad*, a film released in 1961 (Catherine Robbe-Grillet, *Jeune mariée: Journal, 1957–1962* [Fayard, 2004], 416). See also the letter from September 17, 1961, to Jean Piel, p. XXX, in which Barthes says he is abandoning the idea of discussing this work in *Critique*; the question will arise obliquely nevertheless in Bruce Morrissette's preface to *Romans de Robbe-Grillet* (Minuit, 1963). (*OC*, vol. 2, 458–59).

59. *Projet pour une révolution à New York* appeared in November 1970 from Éditions de Minuit.

60. Michel Butor and Georges Perros, *Correspondance, 1955–1978* (Nantes: Joseph K., 1996). In this correspondence, Barthes is often the subject (see the letters from Roland Barthes to Georges Perros, p. XXX). The correspondence between Michel Butor and Pierre Klossowski is forthcoming.

61. Barthes's text on *Mobile* is "Littérature et discontinu" (1962), reprinted in *Essais critiques* (*OC*, vol. 2, 430–41).

62. The content of this letter involves the Hungarian uprising in October 1956 against the Communist regime, which led to extremely important critical reflection by the Marxist intelligentsia in opposition to the Soviet system, in which the question of the nature of the Soviet Union is indeed posed—degenerate worker state or state capitalism, for example.

63. An allusion to Switzerland, where Michel Butor then lived and taught at the École Internationale in Geneva.

64. Georges Friedmann (1902–77) then taught at the École Pratique des Hautes Études. It was with him and Edgar Morin that Barthes would establish the Centre d'Études des Communications de Masse in 1960.

65. Poulot was the real name of Georges Perros.

66. The postcard on the back of which Barthes wrote shows Rembrandt's *Saul and David* (Mauritshuis, The Hague, 1657).

67. Butor was then traveling in Greece with his wife. See Butor and Perros, *Correspondance*, 22.

68. Barthes had just published "Dire Racine" in the March 1958 issue of *Théâtre populaire* and was working on the prefaces he had to write for the complete collection of Racine's plays in 1960; see Barthes, *Sur Racine* (Paris: Seuil, 1963).

69. Roland Barthes had to go to the United States that summer to teach there (see the following letter). Claude Bourcier's visit was part of the preparation for the stay. Michel Butor did indeed visit Middlebury College in 1960.

70. Middlebury College is located in Vermont. Butor taught there as well (see the letter from Michel Butor from February 16, 1960, p. XXX). Barthes's only reference to this experience appears in a remark during the Cerisy Colloquium: Antoine Compagnon, *Prétexte: Roland Barthes* (Paris: UGE, 1978), 413. One can also refer to the account by Richard Howard, friend and American translator of Barthes, in Steven Ungar and Betty R. McGraw, eds., *Signs in Culture: Roland Barthes Today* (Iowa City: University of Iowa Press, 1989) 32. However, Howard makes a mistake in dating Barthes's first visit as 1957.

71. Roland Barthes will use the critical pretext of a Bernard Buffet exhibition to sing the praises of New York in "New York, Buffet et la hauteur," *Arts*, February 1959 (*OC*, vol. 1, 937–39).

72. Barthes went to stay with Vinaver many times in his chalet in Haute-Savoie (see the letter to Vinaver from the preceding year, p. XXX).

73. Perhaps a reference to Richard Howard.

74. *Degrés* was published by Gallimard in 1960. Butor cites this letter from Barthes in a letter to Perros. Butor and Perros, *Correspondance*, 42.

75. In a talk at Royaumont in 1959 Butor explained his progression from philosophy (his first area of study) to the novel: Butor, *Répertoire* (Paris: Minuit, 1960), 271–74.

76. "Histoire ou Littérature?" *Annales*, May-June 1960; reprinted in *Sur Racine*.

77. Michel Butor was then teaching at Bryn Mawr College in the greater Philadelphia area.

78. Marie-Jo Butor (1932–2010), Michel Butor's wife.

79. Cécile Butor is one of Michel Butor's four daughters; she appears in *Boomerang* (Gallimard, 1978), a book about the trip to the United States.

80. See the letter that Georges Perros sent to Michel Butor a few days earlier. Butor and Perros, *Correspondance*, 41–42.

81. *Papiers collés* appeared from Gallimard in March 1960.

82. Denise Klossowski, née Morin, was the model for Roberte, Pierre Klossowski's heroine. The couple lived on Rue de Canivet near Rue Servandone, and then at Cour de Rohan, and Barthes often played piano with Pierre Klossowski's wife.

83. The birth of Agnès Butor.

84. Claude Bourcier and Vincent Guilloton were in charge of the French Summer School at Middlebury College where Butor was going to teach.

85. Again, the book in question is Georges Perros's *Papiers collés*, published in March 1960.

86. Tania Perros is the wife of Georges Perros, whose life, practically and financially, was quite difficult then. Butor and Perros, *Correspondance*, 47–48. Tania would have a miscarriage (56).

87. Illegible.

88. In reality, the genesis of *Système de la mode* will be less smooth; Barthes did not actually finish writing it until April 1964, and it was not published until 1967.

89. Marthe Robert published *Kafka* with Gallimard in 1960, on which Barthes wrote an article in *France Observateur* in 1960, "La réponse de Kafka," reprinted in *Essais critiques* (OC, vol. 2, 395–99).

90. Yves Velan won the Prix de Mai in 1960 for *Je* (Seuil, 1959). Roland Barthes devoted an article in *Critique* to this novel, "Ouvriers et pasteurs," reprinted in *Essais critiques* (OC, vol. 2, 389–94).

91. Georges Perros and Pierre Klossowski.

92. Klossowski published *Roberte, ce soir* in 1953 and *La Révocation de l'édit de Nantes* in 1959 with Éditions de Minuit, then *Le Souffleur, or le Théâtre de société* in 1960 with Pauvert.

93. See Barthes's letters to Perros, p. XXX.

94. Barthes was in North America from January 15 to February 5, 1961, when he went to Montreal to work on a film on sports with Hubert Aquin, *Le Sport et les hommes*, released in 1959. The text of the film was published by Presses Universitaires de Montréal in 2004.

95. Robert Kanters (1910–85), a writer and critic born in Belgium who was very hostile to modernity and the new novel, wrote a very negative review of *Mobile*: "L'Amérique en butorama," *Le Figaro littéraire*, March 2, 1962.

96. Barthes published an important article on *Mobile* in *Critique* in 1962, reprinted in *Essais critiques* (OC, vol. 2, 430–41).

97. Francisque Sarcey (1827–99), a fundamentally reactionary French critic and journalist.

98. Butor was in the United States.

99. The "Revue internationale" is the focus of Barthes's correspondence with Blanchot; Butor participated in it, as is evident from Dionys Mascolo's letter

from December 5, 1962. See "Le dossier de la 'Revue internationale,'" *Lignes*, September 1990, 264–65.

100. The subject of Barthes's seminar that year was "An inventory of contemporary systems of signification: systems of objects (clothing, food, lodging)."

101. Quotation inspired by Sébastien-Roch Nicolas de Chamfort, who wrote: "Nearly all men are slaves for the reason the Spartans gave for the Persians' servitude: for lack of knowing how to pronounce the syllable 'no.'" Chamfort, *Maximes et pensées*, 1795.

102. Butor and his family had just settled in West Berlin thanks to a grant from the Ford Foundation.

103. See the exchange on this subject between Butor and Perros with regard to Barthes the writer. Butor and Perros, *Correspondance*, 159–60.

104. *Essais critiques* had just appeared.

105. René Marill Albérès (1921–82) published a monograph that year on Butor with Éditions Universitaires.

106. Georges Perros.

107. Illegible.

108. Butor wrote the preface for Montaigne's *Essais* in three volumes for the UGE "10/18" collection, published in 1964.

109. Élisabeth was the daughter of his wife Tania. See Butor and Perros, *Correspondance*, 173.

110. The subject of Barthes's seminar that year was "Research on Rhetoric."

111. That is, the "point to judge" that Quintilian classifies according to conjecture, definition, and quality. "L'Ancienne rhétorique, aide-mémoire," in *OC*, vol. 3, 527–601.

112. Paris: Gallimard, 1964.

113. This is the dispute set off by the appearance of a violent tract by Raymond Picard, *Nouvelle critique ou nouvelle imposture* (Pauvert, 1965), against Barthes's *Sur Racine*, published in 1963. It was resolved with the publication of *Critique et vérité* in 1966.

114. Butor came to the March 10 session of the seminar.

115. *Critique et vérité*.

116. It is more a matter of Butor playing with graphics than actual cross-outs.

117. Barthes is writing on the back of a postcard showing Shugakuin, Kyoto's very famous imperial palace.

118. Mathilde.

119. Maurice Pinguet (see his letters, p. XXX).

120. Barthes left for a year to teach at the University of Rabat.

121. In early 1970, Butor published *La Rose des vents: 32 Rhumbs pour Charles Fourier* with Gallimard. Barthes would have read a manuscript of Butor's text.

122. Barthes had just published "Vivre avec Fourier" in Critique in October 1970 (reprinted in *Sade, Fourier, Loyola* in 1971).

123. Butor moved to Saint-Laurent-du-Var because he was then teaching at the University of Nice.

124. The statute of the École Pratique des Hautes Études allows the director of studies to advise theses without having a doctorate himself, which was the case with Barthes.

125. See the correspondence with Jean Starobinski, who invited Barthes to teach in Geneva, p. XXX.

126. For *Sade, Fourier, Loyola*.

127. Barthes was a member of the jury from 1973 on.

128. Michel Butel won the Médici prize for *L'Autre Amour*, and Hector Bianciotti won the foreign prize for *Le Traité des saisions*.

129. The letters from Roland Barthes to Jean Piel are in the Jean Piel collection held at the IMEC. Here we are using the transcription made by Sylvie Patron as an appendix to her thesis on the *Critique* review, defended in 1996 at the University of Paris 7, from which is extracted her work *Critique, 1946–1996: Une Encyclopédie de l'esprit moderne* (Éditions de l'IMEC, 1999) and which includes many pages on Roland Barthes (for example, 115–24).

130. In his article "La Fonction sociale du critique."

131. Roland Barthes published an article on the novel by Queneau, *Zazie dans le métro* (Gallimard, 1959) titled "Zazie et la littérature" in the August–September issue of *Critique*, reprinted in *Essais critiques* (*OC*, vol. 2, 382–88).

132. Barthes wrote only one article on Morin, which appeared in the July 1965 issue of Combat (*OC*, vol. 2, 718–19).

133. It is a question of *Histoire de la folie* published by Plon in 1961 under the title of *Folie et déraison: Histoire de la folie à l'âge classique*.

134. Henri Michaux published *Connaissance par les gouffres* with Gallimard in 1961. Yvon Bélaval did indeed address Michaux's book in an article in the November 1962 issue of *Critique* titled "Introduction à la poésie expérimentale."

135. René Girard published *Mensonge romantique et vérité romanesque* with Grasset in 1961. Barthes did not review it but he alluded to it in "Les deux sociologies du roman" in *France Observateur* in December 1963 (*OC*, vol. 2, 249–50). It was Michel Deguy who reviewed Girard's book in the January 1962 issue.

136. *L'Observatoire de Cannes* by Jean Ricardou appeared from Minuit in 1961 and *Nuits sans nuit et quelques jours sans jour* by Michel Leiris from Gallimard the same year. *L'Ordre des choses* by Jacques Brosse (1922–2008), with a preface by Gaston Bachelard, was published by Plon in 1958.

137. Barthes makes a mistake regarding the title; it was an extract from *L'Année dernière à Marienbad* that appeared in Tel Quel 5 (Spring 1961).

138. Barthes's review appeared in the November 1961 issue under the title "Savoir et folie" and was reprinted in *Essais critiques* under the title "De Part et d'autre" (*OC*, vol. 2, 422–29).

139. Girard's thinking, which is a Christian philosophy of mediation, directly opposes modern "nihilism," which he sees as an avatar of the "Romantic lie," as is evidenced by this paragraph from the ninth chapter of Girard's book, "L'Apocalypse dostoïevskienne," in which Barthes is directly targeted: "Ten years will not pass before we recognize in 'l'écriture blanche' and its 'degré zéro' the increasingly abstract, increasingly ephemeral and stunted avatars of the noble Romantic birds." Girard, *Mensonge romantique et vérité romanesque* (1961; Paris: Hachette Littérature, 2011), 297–98. Nevertheless Girard supported Barthes against Picard in the "quarrel" and invited him to the colloquium in Baltimore that he organized in 1966 (see the letter from August 27, p. XXX).

140. "Critique de la poésie" appeared in *Critique* in March 1966.

141. Pierre Verstraeten (1933–2013) never published anything in *Critique* during this period.

142. Following the publication of the violent tract by Raymond Picard previously cited.

143. Probably *Fleurs bleues*, published by Gallimard in 1965.

144. Critique did not take a position in the debate between Barthes and Picard. On this subject, see Sylvie Patron, *Critique, 1946–1996*, 218ff.

145. We have not been able to identify this name.

146. Tzvetan Todorov published his *Théorie de la littérature, textes des formalistes russes* with Seuil in 1965.

147. There is no article by René Lourau (1933–2000), but Roger Kempf published an article on the body in the October 1966 issue ("Sur le corps de Julie Beaujon").

148. This must be the article by Jean Batany on linguistics that appeared in the May 1967 issue.

149. Michel Deguy published "Théâtre et réalisme" in October 1966.

150. Jean-Pierre Attal published "Maurice Scève, la Délie" in July–August 1966.

151. Marc Le Bot published no articles in 1966.

152. We have found no trace of this Mr. Blemen.

153. Barthes went to the large colloquium on criticism at Johns Hopkins University in Baltimore, held October 18–21, 1966, under the direction of René Girard, with Richard Macksay, Charles Morazé, Georges Poulot, Eugenio Donato, Lucien Goldmann, Tzvetan Todorov, Jean Hyppolite, Jacques Lacan, Guy Rosolato, Neville Dyson-Hudson, Jacques Derrida, Jean-Pierre Vernant, and Nicolas Ruwet.

154. Alain Badiou published an article on Louis Althusser titled "Le (Re) commencement du matérialisme dialectique" in the May 1967 issue of *Critique*.

155. Jacques Derrida had the same response: "like Barthes, I find it irritating at least because of its tone, the airs the author gives himself, the 'notes' he distributes as on the day of general inspection or the last judgment," but he agrees to its publication (letter from Derrida to Piel from February 26, 1967, cited by Patron, *Critique, 1946–1996*, 88).

156. Alain Badiou notes in this article Michel Foucault's "powerlessness to produce, on the structural basis—however universal—that he designs, the distinctive operators of science and nonscience" and "the pretheoretic lightness of his judgments on Marx." See Foucault, *Les Mots et les Choses* (Paris: Gallimard, 1966), 273–74.

157. René Girard published "Symétrie et dissymétrie dans le myth d'Oedipe" in the February 1968 issue, number 249.

158. "La parole selon Constant" was published in *Critique* in August–September 1968.

159. Claude Hodin published an article entitled "L'Écrivain au travail" in the October 1970 issue of *Critique*, regarding especially *Le Journal d'un inconnu* by Jean Cocteau (Grasset, 1953). The article on *La Voie lactée* by Luis Buñuel (1969) was not published.

160. See our note 1 for the letter of April 5, 1970, p. XXX.

161. Barthes asked to meet with Lévi-Strauss regarding his thesis and did so on January 16.

162. This is a matter of the first version, or the rough draft of *Système de la mode*, which was not published until 1967. Here Barthes is hoping that Lévi-Strauss will agree to advise his thesis, which did not happen.

163. The two books must be *Totémisme aujourd'hui* and *La Pensée sauvage*, which were published respectively by PUF and by Plon in 1962.

164. "Pour une sociologie du vêtement," *Annales*, March–April 1960.

165. In *Le Monde* on December 18, 1965, there was a page devoted to the matter of "nouvelle critique" and the dispute with Raymond Picard that was very critical of Barthes, as we have seen. The newspaper published an inset in which appeared a text by Lévi-Strauss, brought to *Le Monde*'s attention by "a reader," that was published in the Italian review *Paragone* in April 1965 and that enlists Lévi-Strauss in the controversy on the side of Picard. The extract begins with this sentence, "The fundamental vice of literary criticism with

structuralist pretensions stems from the fact that it too often comes down to a game of mirrors, in which it becomes impossible to distinguish the object from its symbolic resonance in the consciousness of the subject." In its December 25, 1965, issue, *Le Monde* published Lévi-Strauss's clarification that Barthes mentions: "In a recent 'literary page,' *Le Monde* devises for a few sentences of mine a fate that troubles me, involving a text I wrote in June 1964, thus predating (if I am not mistaken) the controversy on which someone seems to have me taking a position. My response to an Italian review was only trying to explain that, contrary to what researchers seem to admit, structuralist criticism and historically dictated criticism, far from mutually excluding each other, mutually involve each other. A good structuralist study always assumes that one has passionately inquired into history and, in the case of a literary subject, linguistics: the best feature of both domains is submitting the hypotheses of the researcher to external controls. Thus the sentences you quoted were only aimed at allegedly structural criticism that appears unconcerned with this double truth."

166. Jacqueline Piatier (1921–2001) edited the literary supplement of *Le Monde*.

167. *Mythologiques*, vol. 2, *Du miel aux cendres* (Plon, 1967).

168. BNF.

169. A reference to the famous letter from Claude Lévi-Strauss to Roland Barthes regarding *S/Z*. Later, after Barthes's death, Lévi-Strauss told Didier Éribon in an interview that he had written the letter as a joke, ironically, to have a little wild fun with the book: Claude Lévi-Strauss and Didier Éribon, *De près et de loin* (Paris: Points-Seuil, 1990), 106. We are not reproducing this letter since Lévi-Strauss published it himself (Claude Lévi-Strauss, Paris: Gallimard, 1979). Reading this second letter, one may get the feeling that Lévi-Strauss is mocking himself just as much, as his parodic discourse here so closely resembles that of some of his *Mythologiques*.

170. To celebrate the publication of *Anthropologie structurale deux* (Plon, 1973).

171. *La Voix des masques* was published in 1975 by Skira, in the same "Les Sentiers de la création" collection as Barthes's *L'Empire des signes*.

172. "Plus loin que le degré zéro," *Nouvelle Nouvelle Revue française*, September 1953, reprinted in *Le Livre à venir* (Gallimard, 1959) under the title "La Recherche du point zéro"; and "La Grande tromperie," *Nouvelle Nouvelle Revue française*, June 1957, reprinted in *La Condition critique: Articles, 1945–1998* (Gallimard, 2010).

173. "It allowed me to see a man like Blanchot, a man whose thinking was extremely sharp, extremely elevated, the highest in literature, solitude, negativity, become engaged in an activity that had all the imperfections of activism." *OC*, vol. 5, 778–81. More generally on this project, see the cited dossier published in the September 1990 issue of *Lignes*.

174. Maurice Blanchot published *L'Attente oubli* that year with Gallimard.

175. Barthes was writing on the letterhead of the *Arguments* review, which was founded in 1956, as we have seen, by Edgar Morin, Roland Barthes, Jean Duvignaud, and Colette Audry, in reaction to the reemerging Stalinism, notably with the invasion of Hungary by Soviet troops, which would shut down, coincidentally, at the end of 1962.

176. The "Revue internationale" discussed in the introduction to this chapter.

177. The French editorial staff then included Robert Antelme, Michel Butor, Louis-René des Forêts, Marguerite Duras, Michel Leiris, Dionys Mascolo, and Maurice Nadeau. In Italy, it was mainly Italo Calvino, Pier Paolo Pasolini, Elio Vittorini, Alberto Moravia, and Francesco Leonetti. In Germany it was Hans

Magnus Enzensberger, Ingeborg Bachmann, Günter Grass, Uwe Johnson, Martin Walser. . . . Barthes would introduce Georges Perros into the enterprise (see his letter to Perros from December 28, 1962, p. XXX).

178. Gallimard would drop the venture very quickly, and Julliard would become the official publisher for France for this review that would never actually exist.

179. *OC,* vol. 2, 559–61.

180. This must be *Sur Racine.*

181. The Zurich meeting was difficult, revealing very strong political differences between the various groups (see the letter from Maurice Blanchot to Uwe Johnson from February 1, 1963, in "Le Dossier de la 'Revue international.'"); among myriad disagreements, let us cite, for example, the charge directed at the French for being abstract and ignoring the concrete (268–75).

182. We date this letter from May-June 1963 because that was when Mascolo left for Italy for a week to try to save the "Revue internationale" by making it a French-Italian venture. Ibid., 289–92.

183. Hans Magnus Enzensberger's position was to publish "three separate reviews with international leanings" (letter from Mascolo to Leonetti from May 22, 1963; ibid., 289). Beginning in 1961, Enzensberger and the Germans in general were tied up with the crisis linked to the construction of the Berlin Wall in August 1961. See his letter to Mascolo from September 19, 1961, calling into question "the German participation in the plan" (232) and ending in profound pessimism regarding history and a certain rupture in positions but also hostility toward the mandarin aestheticism of the French (letter from Enzensberger to Mascolo from February 25, 1963; ibid., 278–80).

184. Francesco Leonetti was one of the most persistent of the "Revue internationale" initiators; for example, in spring 1964 he published in the Italian review *Il Menabò,* under the title "Gulliver," a group of texts that constituted a kind of preliminary issue, even though the review seemed to be abandoned.

185. It must be *Critique et vérité.*

186. We are reproducing here the carbon copy of the letter retained by Barthes, which explains why there is no opening or formal closing, which Barthes would have added by hand to the typed original he sent to Blanchot, which has not been found.

187. As early as 1959, in response to an investigation into General de Gaulle's regime in the *14 Juillet* review, in which Blanchot participated, Barthes refuted all characterizations of de Gaulle as a "fascist" (*OC,* vol. 1, 984–86).

188. Barthes is alluding here to his refusal to sign the Manifeste des 121, a "Declaration on the right to rebellion in the war of Algeria," written largely by Maurice Blanchot and Dionys Mascolo, signed by André Breton, Jean-Paul Sartre, Michel Leiris, etc., and published September 6, 1960. Barthes preferred to sign the text by Claude Lefort, Edgar Morin, Maurice Merleau-Ponty, Georges Canguilhem, etc., published October 6, 1960, in *Combat* and less indulgent toward the nationalism of the National Algerian Liberation Front.

189. See his summaries in the school's annual (*OC,* vol. 2, 747–49 and 875).

190. See, for example, Barthes's letter to Butor from August 16, 1964, p. XXX.

191. At the end of the section "The First Barthes," p. XXX.

192. *OC,* vol. 3, 527–601.

4. A Few Letters Regarding a Few Books

1. Barthes, *Sur Racine* (Paris: Seuil, 1963).
2. *Lettres à Franca* (Paris: Stock-IMEC, 1998), 229.
3. Barthes, *Critique et vérité* (Paris: Seuil, 1966).

4. See our note 3 in chapter 3 in the letter to Michel Butor from November 21, 1965, p. XXX.

5. Barthes, *S/Z* (Paris: Seuil, 1970).

6. Alain Bosquet published a review of *S/Z* in *Combat* on May 14, 1970, titled "Roland Barthes ou la critique devient un rêve."

7. Barthes, *L'Empire des signes* (Geneva: Skira, 1970).

8. *L'Écriture des pierres* appeared the same year as *L'Émpire des signes*, also from Skira.

9. An allusion to the big quarrel between Jean-Pierre Faye and Philippe Sollers that same year, following an interview with Faye in *La Gazetter de Lausanne*, in which he violently called Sollers into question. See the letter from Roland Barthes to Philippe Sollers from October 25, 1970 (*OC*, vol. 5, 1044).

10. Barthes, *Sade, Fourier, Loyola* (Paris: Seuil, 1971).

11. An interview published in the fall 1971 issue (*OC*, vol. 3, 1025–42).

12. SADE stands for Societa Adriatica di Elettricita.

13. Barthes, *Nouveaux Essais critiques* (Paris: Seuil, 1972).

14. Éditions de Seuil had just reissued *Le Degré zéro de l'écriture* followed by *Nouveaux Essais critiques* in which appears the text on *Aziyadé* by Pierre Loti.

15. Barthes, *Plaisir du texte* (Paris: Seuil, 1973).

16. Barthes, *Alors, la Chine?* (Paris: Christian Bourgois, 1975).

17. Christian Bourgois did indeed receive numerous letters to thank him for publishing *Alors, la Chine?*—from, for example, Didier Anzieu, Jacques Rancière, Daniel Wilhem, François Di Dio, and Jacques Aumont.

18. The manuscript of *Voyage en Chine*, which would be published by POL in 1980, and later republished by Éditions Marciana, 2012.

19. Barthes, *Fragments d'un discours amoureux* (Paris: Seuil, 1977).

20. Paris: Gallimard, 1975.

21. Barthes, *La Chambre claire* (Paris: Gallimard-Seuil, 1980).

22. Poetic texts by Prigent.

23. Prigent sent pages from the thesis he was writing on Francis Ponge, under Barthes's direction.

24. Christian Prigent sent Barthes his book *Du Côté de l'imaginaire* (Terra incognita, 1977).

25. See the following letter.

26. Jude Stéfan's text on *Roland Barthes par Roland Barthes* was reprinted in *Xénies* (Paris: Gallimard, 1992). Later in a brief tribute, Jude Stéfan wrote, "Barthes has spoken of an 'erotic of the proper noun' and poets often think about the value of names. In his, there are many things: the initial 'B.' A literary 'B' especially for that generation of the 1950s that was reading Breton, Borges, Blanchot, Bataille. The word 'ART,' concealed in the name. There is also the 'H.' Essential, central, although slightly hidden, toward the end of the name. The 'H' with its horizontal bar that can link two human beings, he wrote. In his case, two beings of the same sex. The 'H' of "finding the H" of Rimbaud's poem, which he must search for and find in his homosexuality. And then: the 'H' that is both his English and Greek. The English, elegant, musician Barthes; the learned Greek Barthes, professor of classical literature Barthes. And finally, there is the 'ES.' A feminine ending that is not pronounced. The sign of a plural noun, which he was." *Globe Hebdo*, November 3–9, 1993.

27. Émile Benveniste suffered an attack in December 1969 that left him aphasic; he died on October 3, 1976.

28. François Châtelet had just published a novel, *Les Années de démolition*, with Éditions Hallier.

29. In October 1978, the following year, Barthes published a text on Bernard Faucon's photographs in Zoom (*OC*, vol. 5, 471–74).

30. In his "columns" for the *Nouvel Observateur*, Barthes will praise the film by Pierre Klossowski and Pierre Zucca, *Roberte, ce soir*, which he refers to here (*OC*, vol. 5, 650).

31. On Philippe Rebeyrol, see p. XX.

32. Fragments from a seminar given at the Université Paris 7 in 1975. Transcribed, presented, and annotated by Claude Coste with the help of Éric Marty.

33. This text was reproduced in June 2010 in the *Genesis* review, presented by Éric Marty and transcribed by Arlette Attali.

34. In chapter 10.

35. In 1967, the article "Flaubert et la phrase" appeared as a tribute to the linguist André Martinet in the *Word* review (April, August, December 1968), before being included in *Nouveaux Essais* critiques in 1972. The Barthes archives related to Flaubert include a collection of course notes, the first version of the article from 1967.

36. The greek letter *Phi* seems to designate the sentence here.

37. Greek name for *On the Sublime* by Pseudo-Longinus.

38. *Dictatum* or *Ars Dictaminis*: a collection of Latin composition techniques adapted from ancient rhetoric between 1070 and 1250 to respond to the needs of medieval society.

39. *La Révolution du langage poétique: L'avant-garde à la fin du XIXᵉ siècle: Lautréamont et Mallarmé* (Paris: Seuil, 1974). After summarizing the main points in the "Syntax and Composition" chapter, Barthes traces Julia Kristeva's argument step by step. Kristeva shows that the sentence is constructed like an ideological object that Mallarmé deconstructs by calling into question the predication, linearity, and normativity, and thus renewing, with the "holophrase," this mode of expression in which the original drive arrives at the "most solid refuge of symbolic normativity: syntax."

40. See our note 2 on p. XXX.

41. On this opposition, see Barthes, *Le Plaisir du texte* (Paris: Seuil, 1973).

42. *La Somme athéologique I*, in *Oeuvres complètes* (Paris: Gallimard, 1979), 5:204–5.

43. Antoine Roquentin, the main character in Sartre's *La Nausée* (Gallimard, 1938), is fascinated by the sight of a chestnut tree root and thus becomes aware of contingency.

44. Gustave Flaubert, *Bouvard et Pécuchet*, ed. Jacques Suffel (Paris: Flammarion, 1966).

45. The in-text citations to Fontanier are to Pierre Fontanier, *Les Figures du discours* (Paris: Flammarion, 1977), 51.

46. Gustave Flaubert, *Extraits de la correspondance*, or *Préface à la vie d'écrivain*, ed. Geneviève Bollème (Paris: Seuil, 1963), 262.

47. Marcel Proust, *Contre Sainte-Beuve*, ed. Bernard de Fallois (Paris: Gallimard, 1954), 247.

48. *Dire et ne pas dire: Principes de sémantique linguistique* (Paris: Hermann, 1972).

49. Barthes discovered Louis Hjelmslev's work—his *Essais linguistiques* were published in 1959—at the time when he was writing the mythologies, in the 1950s; see also Roland Barthes, *Élements de sémiologie* (Paris: Denoël-Gonthier, 1965). While Saussure conceived of the sign as the unity of signifying and signified, Hjelmslev distinguished the form of content (thought) and the form of expression (phonic chain).

50. In "Le monde objet" (1953), Barthes describes "the nature of classical Dutch painting, which has washed away religion only to replace it with man and his empire of things. Where once the Virgin presided over ranks of angels, man stands now, his feet upon the thousand objects of everyday life, triumphantly surrounded by his functions" (*OC*, vol. 2, 283).

51. This sentence from Georges Bataille does not appear in either of the two notes on page 12 of the third volume of the *Oeuvres complètes* (Paris: Gallimard, 1971). Nevertheless, the "sentence" comes up in the first note and this is what Bataille writes: "I speak as well, but in speaking I do not forget that speech not only will escape me, but that it does escape me" ("Preface to Madame Edwarda").

52. This is certainly Barthes's slip; he must mean Flaubert here, not Mallarmé.

53. Barthes's notes remain inexplicit: "Diagrammatic function: emphasis through displacement of the adverb to the beginning (far from the verb), logical rupture of time and place."

54. In fact, post hoc, ergo propter hoc: after that, therefore because of that. The motivating force behind narrative activity is the confusion of consecutiveness and consequence, "what comes after being read in the narrative as caused by ("Introduction à l'analyse structurale des récits," 1966; *OC*, vol. 2, 840–41).

55. Barthes explains this allusion a few lines further on.

56. "It seems that historical discourse involves two regular types of shifters. The first type we might call shifters of listening. This category has been observed, on the level of language, by Jakobson, under the name testimonial and under the formula C^eC^{a1}/C^{a2}: besides the event reported (C^e), the discourse mentions both the act of the informant (C^{a1}) and the speech of the "writer" who refers to it (C^{a2}). This shifter therefore designates all mention of sources, of testimony, all reference to a listening of the historian, collecting an elsewhere of his discourse and speaking it." Roland Barthes, "Le discours de l'histoire," 1967; *OC*, vol. 2, 1251.

57. Barthes creates the neologism "onomothete," no doubt evoking the "nomothete," which he uses metaphorically (in Athens, a nomothete was a member of the legislative committee that revised laws).

58. In "L'effet de réel" (1968), Barthes analyzes how certain concrete notations in Flaubert's *Un coeur simple* (1877)—"a pile of boxes," which is meant to avoid signification in order to directly denote the real—end up signifying realism.

59. *Moire* is a very reflective silk fabric. The metaphor recurs in Barthes to designate the way meaning in a literary texts shimmers and disperses.

60. "The *and* that Flaubert works magnificently is the *and* of movement that accompanies or signifies over the course of a description or narration the shift to a higher tension, to a more important or dramatic moment, a progression: 'Meanwhile clouds had gathered; the tempestuous sky roused the electricity that was in the people, and they kept whirling about of their own accord with the great swaying movements of a swelling sea; and one felt that there was an incalculable force in the depths of this excited throng, and as it were, the energy of an element.' (Éducation, 453)." Albert Thibaudet, "Le Style de Flaubert," in *Gustave Flaubert* (Paris, Gallimard, 1982), 265–66.

61. From 1974 to 1976, that is, parallel to the seminar on *Bouvard et Pécuchet*, Barthes devoted his seminar at the École Pratique des Hautes Études to *Discours amoureux*, published by Seuil in 2007, from which he would draw *Fragments d'un discours amoureux* (1977). In the postscript of this last work, titled "How This Book Is Constructed," Barthes defines the "figure" of amorous discourse like this: "These fragments of discourse can be called figures. The word is to be understood, not in its rhetorical sense, but rather in its gymnastic or choreographic acceptation; in short, in the Greek meaning: schema is not 'schema,' but in a much livelier way, the body's gesture caught in action and not contemplated in repose: the body of athletes, orators, statues: what in the straining body can be immobilized. So it is with the lover at grips with his figures: he struggles in a kind of lunatic sport, he spends himself, like an athlete; he 'phrases,'

like an orator; he is caught, stuffed into a role, like a statue. The figure is the lover at work" (*OC*, vol. 5, 29).

62. In a famous passage in *L'Être et le Néant*, Sartre describes the attitude of a café waiter who overplays his role and whom he presents as an example of "bad faith." Sartre, *L'Être et le Néant* (Paris: Gallimard, 1943), pt. 1, chap. 5, section 2, "Les Conduites de mauvaise foi."

63. Kristeva, *La Révolution du langage poétique: L'Avant-garde à la fin du XIXᵉ siècle: Lautréamont et Mallarmé* (Paris: Seuil, 1974).

64. *Les Malices de Plick et Plock*, a black-and-white comic strip by Christophe that appeared in *Le Petit Français illustré* from 1893 to 1904, recounts the adventures of two gnomes who pull many pranks and have many misadventures before learning their lesson.

65. Barthes regularly returns to Freud's "wolf man": the patient's castration fantasy goes back to witnessing the "originary scene," that is, coitus between his two parents. See, in particular, Barthes, *Le Discours amoureux: Séminaire à l'École pratique des hautes études, 1974–1976*, followed by *Fragments d'un discours amoureux: Inédits*, ed. Claude Coste (Paris: Seuil, 2007), 603.

66. Georges Bataille, *L'Oeil pineal*, in *Oeuvres complètes*, vol. 2 (Paris: Gallimard, 1970).

67. Pécuchet creates monstrous vegetables by inadvertently mixing up seedlings (*Bouvard et Pécuchet*, chap. 2).

68. "Fading": Barthes uses this English term and Lacanian concept very freely, with regard to the voice in particular. Fading is one of the figures in *Fragments d'un discours amoureux*: "Painful ordeal in which the loved being appears to withdraw from all contact, without such enigmatic indifference even being directed against the amorous subject or pronounced to the advantage of anyone else, world or rival" (*OC*, vol. 5, 145).

69. The whole of this book by Sartre addresses the bêtise. Barthes condenses the quotation. Sartre writes, "and who feels addressed? No one. Or rather, yes, one man. The strangest thing is that he is the audience and does not seem to realize it. It is the author himself. Sartre, *L'Idiot de la famille: Gustave Flaubert de 1821 à 1857*, Bibliothèque de philosophie 1 (Paris: Gallimard, 1971), 635.

70. Berthe, the daughter of Charles and Emma Bovary, who remains orphaned at the end of the novel.

71. On this question, see "Proust et les noms" (1967), reprinted in *Nouveaux Essais critiques* in 1972.

72. In *Saint Genet: Comédien et martyr* (Paris: Gallimard, 1952), Sartre analyzes how Genet forms for himself an identity in conformity with the images that others form of him.

73. *Tableau de la France: Géographie physique, politique et morale* appeared in 1875. In "Chimie de la France" (1953), Barthes offered the following commentary: "*Le Tableau de la France* itself, which is usually given as the precursor for geographies, is in fact the account of a chemistry experiment; the list of the provinces in it is less description than a methodical inventory of materials, necessary substances for the entirely chemical elaboration of the general nature of France. It is a bit like the list given at the beginning of a good recipe, if you will: take a little Champagne, a little Picardy, a little Normandy, Anjou, and Beauce, make them revolve around a central nucleus, the Île-de-France, absorb them in this negative pole and you will have the superlative nation of Europe: France. That is what Michelet does; once the elements are listed, described, weighed, and judged, he proposes the principle for blending them: thanks to that very specific polarity surrounding the negative center of France with a belt of marches, that is, positive (and thus incomplete) Frances, France is only a chemically infinite nation, it exists only in that void maintained by the very arrangement of its parts" (*OC*, vol. 1, 311).

74. Barthes explains this term in "Comment vivre ensemble," his first course at the Collège de France; Barthes, *Comment vivre ensemble: Simulations romanesques de quelques espaces quotidiens: Notes de cours et séminaires au Collège de France, 1976–77* (Paris: Gallimard, 2002), 109. In the southwestern France, in the Gascon patois, the word "chaouchoun" refers to a spoiled, temperamental child.

75. In his seminar on amorous discourse, Barthes refers regularly to the work of the psychoanalyst Mélanie Klein: "Triumphalism (recognized and described by Mélanie Klein with regard to certain moments in infantile depression, which, as we know, is closely related to amorous Discourse): the Self artificially reinforces and invests in itself. Whatever happens, I always remain Myself (see Médée by Corneille)" (*OC*, vol. 5, 240). On "triumph," see Mélanie Klein, *Essais de psychanalyse* (Paris: Payot, 1968), 349.

76. The neologism "bathomology" recurs in Barthes's work, and designates the plurality and gradual steps of the effects of meaning (*bathmos* means "degree" in Greek).

77. The "logic of Port-Royal" commonly refers to *La Logique, ou l'Art de penser* by Antoine Arnauld and Pierre Nicole (tied to the Port-Royal abbey and Jansenism), published in 1662. These analyses that make language the expression of thought would serve as reference point until the mid-nineteenth century.

78. See our note 51, p. XXX.

79. "Et cetera. Et cetera. / Mallarmé did not like that word-gesture. He banned it. As for me, I tasted it and was surprised. The mind has no more specific response. It itself is what this interlocution makes happen. / No Etc. in nature. Total enumeration. The part for the whole does not exist in nature—The mind cannot bear repetition. It seems made for the singular. Once for all. As soon as it perceives law, monotony, it deserts." *Cahiers*, vol. 1 (Paris: Gallimard, 1973), 983.

80. This is the first sentence in *Anus solaire* (1927), in *Oeuvres complètes*, vol. 1 (Paris: Gallimard, 1970), 81.

81. "The later skeptics hand down five modes leading to suspension, namely these: the first based on discrepancy, the second on regress ad finitum, the third on relativity, the fourth on hypothesis, the fifth on circular reasoning. . . . The mode based upon regress ad finitum is that whereby we assert the thing adduced as proof of the matter proposed needs a further proof and this again another, and so on ad finitum so that the consequence is suspension as we possess no starting-point for our argument." Sextus Empiricus, *Outlines of Pyrrhonism*, trans. R. G. Bury (Cambridge: Harvard University Press, 1933) 1.15.99.

82. The vessel *Argo*, on which Jason and his companions embarked to seek the Golden Fleece. Roland Barthes often repeats this reference. See in particular "Le vaisseau Argo" (1975): "Frequent image: that of the Argo (luminous and white) of which the Argonauts gradually replaced each piece, so that they ended up with an entirely new ship, without having to change its name or its form" (*OC*, vol. 4, 626). The ship and the perpetual calendar are structures that are endlessly renewed without ceasing to be themselves.

83. "It is the story of these two fellows who copy a kind of critical encyclopedia as farce." Gustave Flaubert, letter to Edma Roger des Genettes, August 18, 1872, in *Correspondance* (Paris: Gallimard, 1998), 4:559.

84. Bordas and Alpha edited encyclopedias meant for the general public. In the early 1970s, the Alpha encyclopedia published weekly installments to be bound into volumes.

5. Exchanges

1. *OC*, vol. 1, 196–202.

2. *Recherche de la base et du sommet*, followed by *Pauvreté et privilège*, appeared that year with Gallimard in the "Espoir" series edited by Albert Camus.

3. Barthes alludes to Char's collection and his title with regard to New York (*OC*, vol. 1, 938).

4. The dedication Char wrote in *Dans la pluie giboyeuse* (Gallimard, 1968) is reproduced in the images, p. xxviii.

5. See the note regarding Michel Butor, p. XXX.

6. Letter from December 28, 1962, see p. XXX.

7. Michel Butor and Georges Perros, *Correspondance, 1955–1978* (Nantes: Joseph K., 1996), 220.

8. Barthes left the apartment at Place du Panthéon for the one on Rue Servandoni, where he lived until his death.

9. Georges Perros left Rue Obeuf in the Meudon Bellevue district to go live in Saint-Malo. He would return to Meudon between 1956 and 1959, before his permanent exile to Douarnenez in Brittany.

10. See the letter to Robert Voisin from March 1954, p. XXX.

11. On February 26, Barthes submitted his project titled "Research on the Social Signs and Symbols in Human Relations (in the Contemporary French Domain)" and, thanks in part to enthusiastic letters of support from Fernand Braudel and Lucien Febvre, Barthes obtained a position as research assistant that lasted until 1960.

12. Barthes went to London for a series of BBC broadcasts.

13. The postscript to *Mythologies*, titled "Le Mythe, aujourd'hui."

14. See our note 3 in the letter to Robert Voisin from September 28, 1956, p. XXX. Georges Perros was in Douarnenez at the time.

15. Georges Perros was in Douarnenez at the time.

16. Éditions de l'Arche, where Barthes was literary advisor in 1954–55.

17. Postcard showing a panoramic view of La Spezia.

18. Olivier de Meslon, mentioned in a letter to Jean Cayrol from April 1956 (see p. XXX).

19. The letter was sent from Saint-Jean-de-Luz.

20. See the card to Michel Butor from the same time and our note 5 on Middlebury College, p. XXX.

21. The postcard shows Long Island.

22. Robert Voisin. Georges Perros was then staying in Brittany in Touldriz, in the region of Douarnenez. See Butor and Perros, *Correspondance*, 22–23.

23. One of the prefaces for the volume of Racine's plays for the French Book Club. *Sur Racine* itself did not appear until 1963.

24. Barthes was a research assistant at the CNRS from 1955 on, but each year he had to reapply for funding.

25. The postcard shows a Vermeer painting titled *The Little Street* (Rijksmuseum, Amsterdam, 1658).

26. See the preceding letter.

27. Barthes was then immersed in his structural research on fashion.

28. The postcard shows a still life by Heyman Dullaert (1636–84).

29. As we have seen, Georges Perros left Meudon, where he had lived since 1956, for Brittany. Financial reasons, as this letter indicates, explain this departure. He lived on Rue Émile-Zola in Douarnenez until summer 1960, and then, still in the same city, on Rue Anatole-France in the Richepin project.

30. Barthes was no longer able to renew his position as research assistant at the CNRS.

31. Barthes's situation was resolved in January 1960 by his acceptance into the École Pratique des Hautes Études (see the letter from February 7, 1960, p. XXX).

32. Gérard Philipe, with whom Georges Perros was very close, died November 25, 1959.

33. On September 23, 1959, François Darbon produced *Les Séquestres d'Altona* at the Théâtre de la Renaissance; on October 28, Roger Blin staged *Les Nègres* at the Théâtre de Lutèce (world premier).

34. The play by Armand Gatti was performed by the Théâtre National Populaire at the Théâtre Récamier, produced by Jean Vilar, October 23, 1959.

35. Barthes had been working on a doctorate since 1955 with Georges Friedmann, at the sociology research laboratory of the École Pratique des Hautes Études, on writing style. Hence Friedmann was his thesis "advisor."

36. The status of "head of work" was more or less equivalent to that of research assistant. Barthes was part of the "economic and social sciences" laboratory.

37. Barthes would publish a few articles in *Les Annales*, for example, in the September-October 1960 issue, the review of *Histoire de la civilisation française* by Georges Duby and Robert Mandrou, published in 1958 by Armand Colin (*OC*, vol. 1, 1059–63).

38. The Klossowskis.

39. See the letter from Roland Barthes to Michel Butor from February 14, 1960, p. XXX.

40. Gaëtan Picon (1915–75), writer and art critic who worked under the direction of André Malraux, then minister of culture.

41. This is the first time the book's definitive title appears. It would not be published until 1967.

42. This book by Georges Perros was published by Gallimard in March 1960 (see also the letter to Michel Butor from April 11, 1960, p. XXX).

43. In a letter to Michel Butor, Georges Perros wrote to him regarding *Papiers collés*: "Barthes wrote me that it's a 'friendly' book. I don't ask for more." Butor and Perros, *Correspondance*, 49.

44. Tania, Perros's companion, was expecting a child; unfortunately she would have a miscarriage (ibid., 56).

45. Barthes wrote a very harsh review of the production by Peter Brook at the Théâtre du Gymnase in Théâtre popular in the second quarter of 1960 (*OC*, vol. 1, 1037–38).

46. *La Mère*, a novel by Maxime Gorki adapted for theater by Bertolt Brecht, was performed by the Berliner Ensemble at the Théâtre des Nations. Barthes wrote a review of it for Théâtre populaire in the third quarter of 1960, reprinted in *Essais critiques* (*OC*, vol. 2, 400–2).

47. It's a question of *Souffleur, ou le Théâtre de société*, published by Pauvert.

48. The summer of 1960 saw the appearance of the Manifeste des 121 that Barthes did not sign.

49. Tania is Georges Perros's wife, the "little one" is Frédéric, their first child.

50. That is to say, Barthes would like a tenured position, which he obtained in 1962 (see the letter from June 17, 1962, p. XXX).

51. A reference to the manuscript of his thesis on Fashion tied to his candidacy for a position as director of studies at the École Pratique des Hautes Études? Barthes published no books in 1962.

52. The status of director of studies corresponds to that of university professor. Barthes worked in the research laboratory on "Sociology of signs, symbols, and representations" at the École Pratique des Hautes Études.

53. At that time, the State thesis was routinely accompanied by a secondary thesis, called the "little thesis." This one involved editing a text by Charles Fourier.

54. Barthes's first seminar (1962–63) was titled "Inventory of Contemporary Systems of Signification: System of Objects (Clothing, Food, Lodging)." Among

the students taking that seminar were Jean Baudrillard, Luc Boltanski, Olivier Burgelin, Jacques-Alain Miller, Jean-Claude Milner, and Robert David (*OC*, vol. 2, 253–54).

55. Barthes writes "raison" for "raisin" here, but surely he meant grape seed.

56. On this subject, see the correspondence with Maurice Blanchot and the introductory note, p. XXX.

57. We have not found that note; it must be the one titled "Mémorandum sur le cours de choses," composed by Maurice Blanchot and presented in "Le Dossier de la 'Revue internationale,' " cited file, p. 185–86.

58. See the correspondence with Blanchot regarding the meeting in Zurich on January 19–20, 1963, p. XXX.

59. As we have seen, the "Revue internationale" would never appear.

60. *Essais critiques* had just appeared. In a letter to Michel Butor from April 1964, Georges Perros commented on Barthes book in this way: "It's always very exciting. With something existentially sad about it. It's really true that we've passed from medicine to surgery, and then to, I don't know, whatever psychoanalysis verges on but ruins most of the time." Butor and Perros, *Correspondance*, 166.

61. See the letter from Michel Butor to Roland Barthes from June 2, 1964, p. XXX.

62. Roland Barthes was then teaching at Johns Hopkins University in Baltimore, Maryland.

63. *Système de la mode* appeared in 1967, and Barthes did not send it to Perros, as he did his earlier books, no doubt forgetting the promise that appears in his letter from November 19, 1961 (see p. XXX).

64. In most illustrations, Klossowski's heroine, Roberte, wears suits.

65. We don't know the content of Perros's letter, but can imagine it concerns S/Z, which had just come out.

66. In the section "Lectures," Perros devotes several pages to Barthes under the title "Barthes étoile" where it is a question essentially of *L'Empire des signes*. Perros writes, "And there is the subject of a world à la Fourier, bathed in his amorous time, writing becoming possible again, desirable beginning from nothing, this nothing so precisely manifest, but inexplicable, in haiku, with its inflexibility, its rigorous idleness that enchanted him." *Papiers collés* 2 (1973; Paris: Gallimard, 1998), 293–94.

67. Perros's letter must concern *Roland Barthes par Roland Barthes*.

68. Georges Perros, a victim of cancer of the larnyx, underwent an operation in early March at the Leannec Hospital in Paris. The operation, which involved the vocal chords, restricted him to silence, and he would relate that experience in *L'Ardoise magique* (Givre, 1978), published posthumously and reprinted in *Papiers collés* 3 (Gallimard, 1978).

69. Barthes must have reread *Papiers collés* 2 (Gallimard, 1973).

70. On this affair, see our note 3 in the letter to Michel Butor from November 21, 1965, p. XXX.

71. Jean Starobinski is making an allusion to the critics Robert Kemp (1879–1959) and Robert Coiplet (on the latter, see our note 36 in chapter 2 in the letter from Roland Barthes to Jean Lacroix from May 11, 1957, p. XXX). Barthes often treated Robert Kemp harshly in his editorials for *Théâtre populaire* (see for example *OC*, vol. 1, 524 or 591).

72. Jean Starobinski published "Racine et la poétique du regard" in *La Nouvelle Revue française* in August 1957, reprinted in *L'Oeil vivant* (Gallimard, 1961). Barthes published *Sur Racine* in 1963, but the first part appeared originally as the preface to the volumes 11 and 12 of Racine's play with the Club Français de Livre.

73. An unfortunate slip by Barthes in the original French here; he writes *je ne suis plus que d'accord* (I no longer agree with you) rather than *je suis plus que d'accord* (I more than agree with you).

74. Jean Starobinski would also publish a preface in *Maximes* (UGE, 1964).

75. This must be a reference to the ten days in Cerisy on "The Present Directions of Criticism" (September 2–12, 1966) in which the great names of the "Nouvelle Critique" participated (Gérard Genette, Paul de Man, Jean Ricardou, Serge Doubrovsky), but neither Roland Barthes nor Jean Starobinski.

76. Starobinski invited Barthes to teach a seminar at the University of Geneva in January-February 1971.

77. *L'Empire des signes* had just been published by Skira.

78. Jean Rousset (1910–2002), eminent critic and professor at the University of Geneva, author especially of *Forme et signification* (Corti, 1962).

79. It is in the part titled "Français, encore un effort si vous voulez être républicains" that this treatise appears in de Sade's work published in 1795.

80. "Le Coucou" is a piece for harpsichord by François Couperin that Jean Starobinski's son Georges played, who was then about ten years old.

81. Albert Skira had proposed to Roland Barthes that he direct a series for his publishing house.

82. *Entretiens et conférences*, vol. 2 (Nantes: Joseph K, 2003), 328.

83. It is probably a matter of texts that Georges Perec wrote between 1959 and 1962, related to the plan for a review titled "La ligne générale" that never materialized, although the texts would appear in the form of articles in 1962–63 in the *Partisans* review founded by François Maspero in 1961. They were reprinted posthumously in *L. G.: Une aventure des années soixante* (Seuil, 1999).

84. Is this the manuscript of "Portulan," Perec's attempt to rewrite Joyce's *Ulysses* that he was working on in 1962?

85. The manuscript titled "La Grande aventure" was delivered to Roland Barthes on December 11, 1962, according to Georges Perec's biographer, David Bellow, and the response from Barthes seems to date from January 1963. This novel was rejected by Gallimard in June 1964, and then accepted conditionally by Maurice Nadeau in his "Les Lettres nouvelles" collection with Julliard. Reworked by Perec, it would become the manuscript for *Les Choses*, which appeared in 1965. David Bellos, *Georges Perec: Une vie dans les mots* (Paris: Seuil, 1994), 313–18.

86. Georges Perec had just won the Prix Renaudot for *Les Choses, un histoires des années soixante* (see preceding note).

87. "Un Homme qui dort" appeared in the March 1967 issue of *Temps modernes*; the novel was published the same year with Denoël in the collection edited by Maurice Nadeau.

88. *Le Système de la mode* was published in 1967.

89. An exhibition of paintings and drawings by Pierre Getzler, a great friend of Georges Perec, took place in Perec's apartment, 92 Rue de Bac, Paris VIIe, in December 1967.

90. Georges Perec never published this commentary on *Système de la mode*, which was quite critical apparently from Roland Barthes's remarks.

91. It was not in *Le Nouvel Observateur* but in *La Quinzaine littéraire* from June 1, 1970, that Barthes published a text on *Massin, La Lettre de l'Image*, with a preface by Raymond Queneau (Gallimard, 1970).

92. Roland Barthes was responding no doubt to receiving *Oulipo: Créations, re-créations*, published in 1972 in Gallimard's "Idées" collection.

93. *La Boutique obscures: 124 rêves* appeared that year with Denoël.

94. *Sur Racine.*

95. *La Séparation*, as mentioned earlier, is the play for theater that Claude Simon took from L'Herbe. It was presented at the Théatre de Lutèce in a production by Nicole Kessel in 1963.

96. The preface to Bruce Morissette, *Les Romans de Robbe-Grillet* (Minuit, 1963), reprinted in *Essais critiques* (*OC,* vol. 2, 458–59).

97. Réa is Claude Simon's wife.

98. It is a matter of *Essais critiques*, which had just been published.

99. It's a matter of *Critique et vérité*.

100. *Séméiotiké, recherches pour un sémanalyse* is Julia Kristeva's first book, published in 1969 by Éditions de Seuil in the "Tel Quel" collection. Barthes devoted an article to it in *La Quinzaine littéraire* of May 1, 1970 (*OC,* vol. 3, 477–80).

101. The article by Julia Kristeva titled "Le Sens et la mode" appeared in the December 1967 issue of the *Critique* review edited by Jean Piel.

102. For Johns Hopkins University; see the letter to Jacques Derrida from November 20, 1967, p. XXX.

103. Allusion to her son David, whom she had with Philippe Sollers, born in 1975.

104. "Ce qu'il advient au Signifiant" (*OC,* vol. 3, 609).

105. The manuscript in question is *Éden, Éden, Éden* (as mentioned earlier). Barthes wrote this letter after reading the manuscript and before any mention of the plan for a triple preface.

106. Barthes was in Morocco, teaching at the University of Rabat, when he wrote his preface to *Éden, Éden, Éden*, which he compares to the letter he wrote previously regarding the book.

107. Guyotat's play, *Bond en avant*, was produced that year at the Recontres Internationales de musique contemporaine de La Rochelle, and again at the Cartoucherie de Vincennes from April 25 to May 20, where Barthes saw it.

108. The actor François Kuki, who with Alain Olivier performed the play, which previously involved four actors.

109. "Les morts de Roland Barthes" appeared in *Poétique* in September 1981, was reprinted in the first volume of *Psyché* (Galilée, 1987), and then in *Chaque fois unique, la fin du monde* (Galilée, 2003).

110. *L'Écriture et la Différence* appeared with Éditions du Seuil in 1967, in the "Tel Quel" collection, the same year as *La Grammatologie* (Minuit) and *La Vois et le Phénomène* (PUF).

111. René Girard was the head of the Department of Romance Languages at Johns Hopkins University at the time.

112. *La Grammatologie* appeared that year from Éditions de Minuit.

113. In the March 29, 1972, issue of *Les Lettres françaises* appeared a letter from Roland Barthes to Jean Ristat regarding Jacques Derrida (*OC,* vol. 4, 125–26).

114. Published in the issue of *Critique* devoted to Roland Barthes in 1982.

115. First published in *L'Infini* in spring 2004 accompanied by an introductory note, it was reprinted in a posthumous volume, *Le Text Japon, introuvables et inédits* (Seuil, 2009).

116. Barthes is alluding to the first trip he has just taken to Japan, from May 2 to June 2, at the invitation of Maurice Pinguet.

117. In Pesaro, Barthes read a paper titled "Principi e scopi dell'analisi strutturale," which covers the essence of his "Introduction à l'analyse structurale des récits"; in Turin, he presented the Italian translation of his *Essais critiques*.

118. For Romanian, it seems that Barthes speaks of *dor*, which means "lack," "languor," "longing," and "desire" as well. It is a favorite word of Romanian Romantic poets.

119. The lira, of course, is the Italian monetary unit now replaced by the euro.

120. His photo appears at the beginning and end of *L'Empire des signes* ("of the half-smile").

121. Yurakucho is one of Tokyo's busy shopping districts.

122. One chapter in *L'Empire des signes* is titled "Le Visage écrit."

123. Yuichi is a masculine Japanese first name; we don't know precisely who this is.

124. A reference to François Braunschweig.

125. Robert Mauzi and Michel Foucault, respectively.

126. André was Maurice Pinguet's companion.

127. Mutual Japanese friends of Pinguet and Barthes.

128. *Mikata* in Japanese means "friends," "those near and dear," "those on our side."

129. No doubt the book by Oreste Vaccari, *Pictorial Chinese-Japanese Characters* (Trubner, 1950).

130. To Baltimore, Maryland, for the colloquium at Johns Hopkins University and other lectures.

131. Barthes would have to wait until spring 1967 for his second trip to Japan (from March 4 to April 5).

132. This may be Robert Mauzi.

133. A reference to *L'Empire des signes*, which had just been published by Skira Editions and was dedicated to Maurice Pinguet.

134. Claire Bretécher had just published "La Vie passionnée de Thérèse d'Avila" in *Le Nouvel Observateur*.

135. A crease in the paper, text illegible.

136. Maurice Pinguet's letter was written on a preprinted, limited format "aerogram."

137. See our note 146 for the letter from February 15, 1975, p. XXX.

138. *OC*, vol. 5, 684–87.

139. *OC*, vol. 5, 915–28.

140. The lettter is written on letterhead from the Jolly President Hotel of Milan. An error in the date: it must be Monday, June 3.

141. Upon returning from China, Roland Barthes published "Alors, la Chine?" in *Le Monde*, May 24, 1974.

142. Barthes was attending the first conference of the International Association of Semiotics, which was held in Milan from June 2–6, 1974.

143. Written on a postcard showing the Glasgow theater's performance of *Cinderella* (1880).

144. Roland Barthes was preparing *Roland Barthes par Roland Barthes*.

145. In *Roland Barthes par Roland Barthes*, it reads, "X. tells me one day he decided 'to exonerate his life from its unhappy loves,' and that this phrase seemed so splendid to him that it almost managed to compensate for the failures that had provoked it; he then determined (and determined me) to take more advantage of this reservoir of irony in all (aesthetic) language" (*OC*, vol. 4, 719). We now know through this letter that "X." is none other than Barthes himself.

146. *Roland Barthes par Roland Barthes* was published in February and Renaud Camus had just published his first book, *Passage*, with Flammarion. In *La Quinzaine littérarire* from May 1, 1975, Barthes would publish excerpts from a dialogue with Renaud Camus broadcast on France Culture March 19, 1974.

147. Daniel Cordier, whom Roland Barthes knew by way of contemporary art. Barthes would write an important text on one of the artists, Bernard Réquichot, who showed in the gallery that Cordier owned: "Réquichot et son

corps" (*OC*, vol. 4, 377–400). In *Roland Barthes par Roland Barthes*, we find a photo of Barthes working in this villa, Juan-les-Pins (*OC*, vol. 4, 618).

148. A reference to Bertrand Visage, who was just twenty-three years old, contributed to the *Gulliver* review created by André Bercoff, and sent Roland Barthes a letter in hopes of an interview when *Roland Barthes par Roland Barthes* appeared. Barthes answered in a letter from February 23 (private collection): "In a general way, your questions would truly make for an excellent critical work. Do it. That would be much better than if I rehashed one more time my explanations on the subject—and even for the journal, because it has now become novel for a journal to offer a critical article." In 1973, Barthes had done a very fine interview with Bertrand Visage on *Le Plaisir du texte*, titled "L'Adjectif est les 'dire' du désir" (Gulliver, March 1973; *OC*, vol. 3, 463–68).

149. A reference to William Burke, Renaud Camus's companion at that time.

150. Barthes is citing fragment 31 from the Greek poet Sappho (630–580 BCE), which usually goes by the title "À une femme aimée" in French, as in the translation by Théodore Reinach: Alcée, *Sappho* (Paris: Les Belles Lettres, 1937). For an English translation, see *If Not, Winter: Fragments of Sappho*, trans. Anne Carson (New York: Random House, 2002), 63. He doesn't cite the very beautiful last line, which is incomplete, it's true: "But one must risk everything, since."

151. Allusion to the postcard on which Barthes was writing, showing a painting by Canaletto titled *The Giants' Stairway of the Doge's Palace* (Collection of the Duke of Northumberland, Alnwick, 1755–56).

152. The "figures" of *Fragments d'un discours amoureux*. In the end, Roland Barthes would only keep twenty-five of these hundred figures for the book.

153. The opposition between katalepsis and kapaleipsis is at the heart of the first session of the second seminar on amorous discourse (January 8, 1976). Katalepsis, a term from stoicism, designates the comprehension, the grasping of an object, thus mastery and hold, whereas, with kataleipsis, discourse, instead of the object being grasped, something slips, something is left over. See Roland Barthes, *Fragments d'un discours amoureux* (Seuil, 1977), 327–32.

154. This question is addressed in the postscript to *Fragments d'un discours amoureux*, titled "Comment est fait ce livre," not retained in its long version by Barthes, and replaced by a short version of a few pages, bearing the same title. By "Codes," Barthes means the sources, the "terroirs" of his own text, from Werther, which is the guardian-text of *Fragments*, to the citations from which they are woven, to the references present in the margins of the book, to language, to theoretical sources. Ibid., 690–704.

155. Antoine Compagnon was then working on his thesis on the citation, which would give rise to his book, *La Seconde Main, ou le Travail de la citation*, published by Seuil in 1979.

156. These pages appear in the first part of *La Seconde Main*, in sequence 1, "La Citation qu'en elle-même," beginning from the section titled "Ciseaux et pot à colle."

157. A reference to the "Lecture" article that Compagnon and Barthes were to write for the *Enciclopedia Einaudi* (Einaudi, 1977–82), in fifteen volumes, edited by Ruggiero Romano and for which Roland Barthes asked friends and students to write with him or to write a certain number of articles; among those asked: Jean-Louis Bouttes, Roland Havas, Éric Marty, and Patrick Mauriès.

158. Pothos, the brother of Eros in Greek mythology, is associated with amorous desire.

159. It must be a matter of the fragments composing the "Lettura" article for the *Encicloedia Einaudi*.

160. The first article written by one of Roland Barthes's recruits had been rejected by Einaudi; the compromise they reached was that Barthes corrected this first text and cosigned all the others to avoid any further rejections.

161. The *essangeage* ("first rinse") is the preliminary step of soaking or scrubbing dirty laundry before actually washing it.

162. This note is written on letterhead from the Collège de France, the first available to Roland Barthes, newly appointed.

163. Barthes went to Bayreuth to attend performances of Richard Wagner's Ring produced by Patrice Chéreau and under the direction of Pierre Boulez on the occasion of the centenary of the work's creation.

164. Barthes went to Bayreuth in the company of Romaric Sulger-Buël.

165. With regard to *Fragments d'un discours amoureux*.

166. See the letter from August 16, p. XXX, in which Barthes asked Compagnon to pick out an image for the book on amorous discourse. In the fall, Compagnon sent him from London a reproduction of the painting from Verrocchio's workshop *Tobias and the Angel* (National Gallery, London, 1470–75), from which Barthes would take a detail to illustrate the cover of his *Fragments d'un discours amoureux*. "Tenir un discours" is the subject Barthes chose for his first seminar at the Collège de France.

167. Published by Hervé Guibert, March 19, 1986, in *L'Autre Journal* (*OC*, vol. 5, 1005–6).

168. *La Mort propagande*, published early 1977 with Éditions Régine Deforges.

169. The shift to the use of the familiar "tu" between the letter of February 1, 1977, and this one is explained by the meeting between Roland Barthes and Hervé Guibert that took place on Saturday, February 5; we can thus hypothesize this response was by Barthes on March 4.

170. A reference to Barthes's mother's illness.

171. In an interview with Didier Éribon in *Le Nouvel Observateur* from July 18–24, 1991, Hervé Guibert spoke of a text titled *La Mort propagande n° 0*, for which Roland Barthes was to have written a preface. Barthes's defection apparently quashed the project. In the rest of the letter, Barthes alludes to the "contract" linked to this book as a "fantasy." He thus repeats the term present in *S/Z* with regard to the epilogue of *Sarrasine*, a text in exchange for a night of love (*OC*, vol. 3, 192–93).

172. Regarding that evening, a few days later (December 10) Roland Barthes sent Hervé Guibert "Fragment pour H.," which offers another reading of the event (as mentioned earlier).

173. André Téchiné was going to film *Les Soeurs Brontë* during summer 1978; the role in question was that of Branwell, which would be played by Pascal Greggory.

174. Hervé Guibert had a photo exhibition at the Agathe Gaillard Gallery, Rue de Pont-Louis-Philippe, Paris IVe.

175. *La Chambre claire* had just been published. Hervé Guibert worked at *Le Monde*, where he did the photography column.

176. Hervé Guibert's article "Roland Barthes et le photographie, la sincérité du sujet," appeared in the February 28, 1980 issue of *Le Monde*.

177. Reprinted in *L'Image fantôme* (Minuit, 1981).

178. *OC*, vol. 3, 409–13.

179. *OC*, vol. 5, 977–93.

180. In "Soirée de Paris," following an evening with Philippe Sollers, Barthes notes: "He (Sollers) ignited the idea that I'd had to write a History of French Literature (through Desire)" (*OC*, vol. 5, 982).

181. Published posthumously by Éditions du Seuil in 2009.

182. Barthes is evidently referring to the death of his mother, which occurred on October 25, 1977.

183. We know nothing specific about this "decision"; nevertheless, it is clear that it is a matter of a mythical conversion—in the manner of Pascal—to a "new life" wherein existence would be entirely taken up by "literature."

184. R. H. are the initials of the character-pretext that led to the writing of *A Lover's Discourse: Fragments*.

185. This Greek term, which is difficult to make out, has been transcribed here as Κομπολόϊ {*Komboloï*} rather than Κοβολι, as Barthes writes mistakenly. Meaning "beads" in modern Greek. In this instance *Komboloï* refers to the traditional pastime with which Greek men occupy themselves while the women knit: a secular pastime that involves manipulating a kind of rosary that is passed from one hand to the other.

186. Éric Marty: the word would appear to be "expansion." {Diana Knight, however, suggests "expression," which would fit with the phrase in the fifth plan: "I'm withdrawing from the world to begin a great work that will be an expression of . . . Love."}

187. {A is the first letter of *agir*, or "to act."}

188. The Zenrin poem is a poem in the Zen tradition from *Zenrin Kushu* (fifteenth century). Barthes alludes to it in *Incidents* as a way of characterizing the pose and the attitude of the Moroccan child he mentions here: "A kid sitting on a low wall, alongside a road he isn't watching—sitting, as it were eternally, sitting in order to be sitting, *without procrastinating*. Sitting quietly, doing nothing. Spring comes, and the grass grows of its own accord." See Diana Knight, "Idle Thoughts: Barthes's *Vita Nova*" *Nottingham French Studies* (Spring 1997): 88–98.

189. This is clearly a reference to Dante. "'Now go, for one same will is in both: you are guide, you lord, and you master.' So I said to him; / and when he had set forth / I set out upon the deep, savage path." *The Divine Comedy of Dante Alighieri*, vol. 1: *Inferno*, ed. and trans. Robert M. Durling (Oxford: Oxford University Press, 1996), 47. {translation modified}

190. {*Mam.* is used here as an abbreviation for *Maman*, a familiar term for Mother}

191. {The Café de Flore, in Paris}

192. {Barthes's term here is *Recherches*, echoing the title of Proust's *A la Recherche du temps perdu* (*In Search of Lost Time*).}

193. This Greek term signifies motleyed, multicolored, changeable. It is notably used apropos of the Romantic novelists to designate the total novel that combines all literary forms. In his 1979–1980 lecture course at the Collège de France, which was cut short by his death but drafted in full, Barthes wrote: "Romantic Novel or Absolute Novel. Novalis (*Encyclopaedia*, Book 2, Section 6, fragments 1441 and 1448): *Art of the Novel*: Shouldn't the novel include all kinds of styles, variously linked to and animated by the common spirit? The art of the novel excludes all continuity. The novel should be an edifice that is built anew in each of its eras. Each little fragment should be something cut out— something circumscribed—a whole worth something in itself." A little further on Barthes adds: "I forgot to give the Greek word: *poikilos*, daubed, spotted, mottled—the root of *pikilia* in modern Greek: various *hors d'oeuvres*—we could also cite the Rhapsodic, the tacked together (Proust: the Work as made by a Dressmaker) → the Rhapsodic distances the Object, magnifies the Tendency, the act of *Writing*." See p. **144**.

194. {Barthes's term here is *reliefs*, signifying remains or remnants but also the raised or visible portions of something. Both meanings are used in the seventh plan. See p. **405**.}

195. Allusion to François Porbus the younger, a Flemish painter, born in Anvers in 1570 and died in Paris in 1622, who appears in Balzac's *The Unknown Masterpiece*, to which Barthes is referring here. Yet Barthes makes a peculiar mistake: the actual author of the chaotic canvas—a "kind of formless fog"—from which a single fragment—a bare foot—emerges is Frenhofer.

196. {Allusion to the fable by La Fontaine: "The Frog Who Wished to Make Herself as Big as the Bull." See *Selected Fables*, trans. Christopher Wood (Oxford: Oxford University Press, 1995), 13–14.}

197. {A term adapted from the Italian *bolgia*, used by Dante to refer to the gulfs or valleys of the eighth circle of the Inferno.}

198. {Barthes's plan reads: "Politique H etc.," with the "H" shorthand for *Homosexuelle*; here the "G" should be read as shorthand for "Gay," as in "Gay Politics etc."}

199. Barthes is alluding here to Jean-Louis Bouttes, one of his closest friends.

200. {Barthes's *Journal of Mourning*, which belongs to that "panorama" of writings that form a background to *The Preparation of the Novel* discussed in the editor's preface (see pp. **xvi–xviii**), has recently been published in French: *Journal de Deuil: 26 octobre 1977–15 septembre 1979*, edited by Nathalie Léger (Paris: Seuil, 2009).}

201. Barthes initially wrote "79" here, but then corrected it by writing "78" over the top.

202. In the 1979–1980 lecture course, Barthes quotes this passage from Heidegger in the section on "Idleness": "Heidegger (*Essays*, XXVII, 'Overcoming Metaphysics'): 'The unnoticeable law of the earth preserves the earth in the sufficiency of the emerging and perishing of all things in the allotted sphere of the possible which everything follows, and yet nothing knows. The birch [the tree, that is!] never oversteps its possibility. The colony of bees dwells in its possibility. It is first the will which arranges itself everywhere in technology that devours the earth in the exhaustion and consumption and change of what is artificial. Technology drives the earth beyond the developed sphere of its possibility into such things which are no longer a possibility and are thus the impossible' → that, I think, is a good description of the Conflict between *Writing* (will, exhaustion, wear, variations, whims, artifices, in short, the *Impossible*) and *Idleness* (Nature, development—"sensitivity"—within the sphere of the Possible)." See pp. **156–57**.

INDEX

Academy of the Romanian People's Republic, 119, 123
Actors, with understanding/hearing, 272–73
Adamov, Arthur, 91–92, 93, 317*n*52
Adverb, 219, 332*n*53
Akinari, Ueda, 101, 319*n*105
Albérès, R. M., 150, 325*n*105
Alexandria University, 314*n*1, 314*n*3
Allées Paulmy, 310*n*16
Allocution, loss of, 227–28
Alors, la Chine? (Barthes, R.), 202–3, 309*n*4, 330*n*17, 340*n*141
Alpha, 235, 334*n*84
Althusser, Louis, 316*n*35, 327*n*154; Foucault and, 196; *Nouveaux Essais critiques* and letter from, 201; *Sade, Fourier, Loyola* and letter from, 200; *Sur Racine* and letter from, 196–97
American Journal of Ophthalmology, 119
Âme romantique, L' (Béguin), 79
Amis du Théâtre Populaire, 317*n*69, 317*n*73
Amour de Swann, Un (Proust), 310*n*11
Anacoluthons: disintegration and, 233–34; as reversal, 226–27; of two truths, 217–18
Analysis, of content, 105
Analysis/synthesis split, 224–25
"Ancienne rhétorique: Aide-mémoire, L'" (Barthes, R.), 180, 325*n*111
André (Pinguet's companion), 278, 279, 340*n*126
Annales, Les (review), 144, 165, 248
Année dernière à Marienbad, L' (film), 158–59
Annie, 12
Antelme, Robert, 328*n*177
Anthology, 213, 214–15
Antimodernes: De Joseph de Maistre à Roland Barthes, Les (Compagnon), 285
anti-Semitism, 313*n*93
Antisentence, 218
Antonomasia, 109

Anzieu, Didier, 330*n*17
Apollinaire, Guillaume, 210
Apollinaire, Sidoine, 299
Apollo, 7, 139
Aquin, Hubert, 324*n*94
Archambaud, Michel, viii
Argo (ship), 334*n*82
Arguments (review), 315*n*8, 318*n*82, 320*n*10, 328*n*175
Aristotle, 151, 152, 180, 212
Arland, Marcel, 147, 316*n*45; letter from, 78; letters to, 76–77, 78–79, 87; *La NRF* and, 73, 77, 78, 79, 147
Armée nouvelle, L' (Jaurès), 5, 310*n*8
Arnauld, Antoine, 334*n*77
Art, 330*n*26; dramatic, 272–73; Flaubertian sentence and, 217; of living, 278; with novel as antiartistic genre, 6–7; Pop, 281; supernatural and, 103; "tonality" of, 6
Artaud, Antonin, 271
Artifact, letters as, viii
"Artisanat du style, L'" (Barthes, R.), 210–11. *See also Degré zéro de l'écriture, Le*
"Aspects de Roland Barthes" (Pinguet), 276
Attal, Jean-Pierre, 327*n*150
Attali, Arlette, 131, 331*n*33
Audiberti, Jacques, 83
Audry, Colette, 315*n*8, 320*n*10, 328*n*175
"Aujourd'hui ou Les Coréens" (Barthes, R.), 319*n*99
Aumont, Jacques, 330*n*17
Authors: with historical method and literature, 106; in parodic relationship, 233; Sartre and, 333*n*69. *See also* Writers
"Avenir de la rhétorique, L'" (Barthes, R.): dreams and, 187–88; enemies of rhetoric, 180–81; language and, 181–83; with poetry and prose, 185–86; with rhetoric defined, 180; silence and, 181; with writers and language, 184–85

BA. *See* Bibliothèque de l'Arsenal
Bach, Johann Sebastian, 56
Bachelard, Gaston, 83–84, 157
Bachmann, Ingeborg, 329n177
Bacille de Koch dans la lésion tuberculeuse du poumon, Le (Canetti, G.), 312n58
Badiou, Alain, 162, 327n154, 327n156
Balcon, The (Genet), 319n96
Balzac (Curtius), 319n108
Balzac, Honoré de, 109, 216, 235, 343n195
Barbisan, Gala, 316n28
Barrault, Jean-Louis, 95, 318n80
Barrès, Maurice, 314n107
Barth, Karl, 322n39
Barthes, Berthes (grandmother), 310n17
Barthes, Henriette (mother), 25, 55, 63, 68, 71, 133, 208; death of, 298, 342n182; health of, 294, 342n170; letter from Exelmans, A., xii–xiv; letter from Le Bihan, xii
Barthes, Louis (father): death of, xi–xvi; Exelmans, A., on, xii–xiv; Le Bihan on, xii
Barthes, Michel (brother), 310n23
Barthes, Roland, *195. See also specific topics; specific works*
Baruzi, Jean, 322n40
Bastié, Maryse, 210
Bataille, Georges, 214, 233, 318n81, 330n26, 332n51; *Critique* and, 156–57; on irony, 218; Le Prix de Mai and, 320n10
Bataille dans la rizière, La (Roy), 317n52
Batany, Jean, 161, 327n148
"Bathomology," 334n76
Baudelaire, Charles, 5, 23, 109, 276
Baudrillard, Jean, 337n54
Baumeister, August, 92, 317n61
BBC broadcasts, 335n12
Beethoven, Ludwig van, 5, 209, 210
Béguin, Albert: cultural-political meeting and, 318n81; letters from, 79–81; support from, 73, 315n22
Béjart, Madeleine, 110
Bélaval, Yvon, 157, 326n134
Bel éte, Le (Pavese), 101
Belles Lettres, 114

Bellow, David, 338n85
Benedictine monks, 13, 14, 15
Benjamin, Walter, 97, 318n92
Benveniste, Émile, 128, 207, 320n13, 330n27
Bercoff, André, 341n148
Berdiaff, Nicolas, 6, 310n13
Bereavement, "Vita Nova" and, 300, 301, 303, 304
Bernac, Pierre, 89
Bernet, Daniel, 92
Bernou (doctor), 51, 312n76
Berthet, Frédéric, viii, 309n1
Bêtise, 256; as conclusion, 224, 232; copy and, 211, 229, 235; Sartre and, 333n69; truth and, 218
Bettencourt boulevard ou une histoire de France (Vinaver), 99
Bianciotti, Hector, 156, 326n128
Bibliothèque de l'Arsenal (BA), 262, 265
Bibliothèque Littéraire Jacques-Doucet (BLJD), 76, 78, 84–85, 87–88, 199, 202, 208
Bibliothèque Nationale de France (BNF), 64, 88, 92, 102, 115, 141
Bibliothèque Nationale Suisse (BNS), 258, 260
Bieber, Margarete, 317n62
Biology, 111, 120, 236, 319n116
Birth of Tragedy, The (*L'Origine de la tragédie dans la musique ou hellénisme et pessimisme*) (Nietzsche), 310n20
Blanchot, Maurice, vii, 237, 254, 276, 315n12, 324n99; arguments, 172; description of, 328n173; letters from, 172–73, 174–75, 176–79; letters to, 171–72, 173–74, 175–76, 179–80, 329n186; Manifeste des 121 and, 329n188; "Revue internationale" and, 170
Blank page, 22, 82, 97
Blatt (doctor), 119
Blemen, 161, 327n152
Blin, Roger, 336n33
BLJD. *See* Bibliothèque Littéraire Jacques-Doucet
Blum, Léon, 4, 310n5
BNF. *See* Bibliothèque Nationale de France
BNS. *See* Bibliothèque Nationale Suisse
Boltanski, Luc, 337n54
Bonniot, 28–29

Bordas, 235, 334n84
Boronat, Teresa, 310n12
Bosquet, Alain, 199, 330n6
Bost, Pasteur, 10
Bostock, Anna, 318n92
Boulez, Pierre, 342n163
Bourcier, Claude, 143, 147, 323n69, 324n84
Bourgois, Christian, 202, 330n17
Boutique obscure, La: 124 rêves (Perec), 266
Bouttes, Jean-Louis, viii, 341n157, 344n199
Bouvard et Pécuchet (Flaubert): "anthologic" operation and, 214–15; commentary, method of, 214; influence of, 210–11; with languages, engine of, 232–36; research for, 211–13; sentences, choice of, 213
Bouvard et Pécuchet, sentence 1: anacoluthon of two truths, 217–18; disconnection, 215–16; ellipsis and catalysis, 216–17; form (in traditional sense), 215; truth/bêtise, 218
Bouvard et Pécuchet, sentence 2: the doxa, 221; form (in traditional sense), 218–19; metonymy, 219; the voices, 219–21
Bouvard et Pécuchet, sentence 3: form, 221–22; kitsch, 222–23, 234; parading (on display), 223, 234
Bouvard et Pécuchet, sentence 4: analysis/synthesis split, 224–25; closure, 224, 233; example, 224
Bouvard et Pécuchet, sentence 5: allocution, 227–28; anacoluthon, 226–27; example, 225–26
Bouvard et Pécuchet, sentence 6: cleavage, 228; copy, 229
Bouvard et Pécuchet, sentence 7: disappointment, 230–31; enumeration, 223, 230–32, 234; name and image with, 230; stereotype, 230
Braudel, Fernand, 335n11
Braunschweig, François, viii, 277, 322n44, 340n124
Brecht, Bertolt, 96–97, 310n13, 318n88, 318n90, 318nn92–93, 336n46
Brechtism: influence of, 239, 263; *Théâtre populaire* and, 90,

314n103; first attack of, 310n23; inclined position and, 33, 312n56; Institut Pasteur and, 312n58; Perlemuter with, 313n93; pneumothorax with, 68–69, 312n52, 312n76, 313n95; relapse, 311n39, 312n51; speleostomy and, 47, 51, 312n76; thoracoplasty and, 31, 38, 312n76; tomographies and, 31, 38, 41, 312n53. *See also* Leysin Sanatorium; Sanatorium des Étudiants de France
Twombly, Cy, 281

Ubu (Monnet), 95, 96
Ubu roi, 318n83, 318n86
Understanding/hearing, actors with, 272–73
United Nations, 311n27
United States, 179, 264, 323n69, 324n79, 324n98
Universal science, 120
Université de Paris 7, 211
University of Rabat, 199, 260, 325n120, 339n106

Vaccari, Oreste, 278, 340n129
Valéry, Paul, 106, 249; influence of, 2, 3, 5, 23, 309n2; origins, family, 3–4; Pascal and, 182; poetry and, 112; rhetoric and, 180–88; on writers and language, 184–85
Vandervelde, Émile, 310n6
Van Gogh, Vincent, 133
Van Humbeeck, 55, 56, 60
Van Roleghem (doctor), 36
Vautel, Clément, 11, 311n30
Vauvenargues (Marquis de), 91, 123, 317n54
Veil, Hélène, 27–28
Veil, Jacques, 25–27, 311n50

Velan, Yves, 140, 148, 322n58, 324n90
Vermeer, Johannes, 335n25
Vernant, Jean-Pierre, 327n153
Verrocchio, Andrea del, 342n166
Verstraeten, Pierre, 160, 326n141
Vialleneix, Paul, 321n19
Victory (Conrad), 319n98
Vie, mode d'emploi, La (Perec), 261
Vie en fleur, Le (France), 5
Vie littéraire, La (France), 5, 309n3, 310n10
Vilar, Jean, 93, 99, 317n68; criticism of, 94; TNP and, 90, 317n72, 318n83, 336n34
Vinaver, Michel (Grinberg), 98, 99, 143; friendship with, 323n72; letters from, 100, 101–2; letters to, 100–1; plays of, 319nn102–4; Théâtre d'Aujourd'hui and, 319n101; Théâtre de la Comédie and, 319n99; *Théâtre populaire* and, 319n102
Visage, Bertrand, 283–84, 341n148
"Vita Nova": viii; "incidents" and, 297–98; with other titles, 298; transcription of, 299–308
Vitez, Antoine, 319n103
Vittorini, Elio, 175, 328n177
"Vivre avec Fourier" (Barthes, R.), 325n122
Voices, the, 219–21
"Void of the subject," 260
Voie lactée, Le (film), 163
Voisin, Robert, 133, 315n19, 335n22; letters to, 90–99; Perros, G., and, 243; *Théâtre populaire* and, 90, 94–99, 318n87, 320n10, 321n31

Voltaire, 5, 105, 111
Volupté (Sainte-Beuve), 321n36
Voyeur (Robbe-Grillet), 322nn55–56

Wagner, Richard, 290, 342n163
Wahl, François, viii, 160, 272
Walser, Martin, 329n177
Warhol, Andy, 281
Wilhem, Danile, 330n17
Willett, John, 96, 318n90
Work, of writers, 107–9
Work-model, 141
Writers: language and role of, 184–85; in parodic relationship, 233; rhetoric and work of, 107–9; signing of work, 180
Writing: bond of, 273; defined, 240; desire to write or *scripturire*, 299; difficulty, 8, 16, 20, 133, 155, 159; documents for, 103; dreams and, 187–88; evolution with act of, viii, 186; fantasy and, 292–93; novelistic, 203, 261, 297; piano, theater and, 141, 238; poetry and, 237; solicitations from *La Nouvelle NRF*, 73, 76, 77, 78, 79, 147; solicitations from *Les Temps modernes*, 86–87. *See also* Sentence, Flaubertian

Yamamouchi grant, 279
Yuichi, 277, 278, 340n123

Zazie dans le métro (Queneau), 157
"Zazie et la littérature" (Barthes, R.), 157
Zen, 290, 292
Zenrin poem, 303, 343n188
Zéraffa, Michel, 94, 317n75
Zucca, Pierre, 331n30

European Perspectives

A Series in Social Thought and Cultural Criticism

Lawrence D. Kritzman, Editor

Gilles Deleuze	*Nietzsche and Philosophy*
David Carroll	*The States of "Theory"*
Gilles Deleuze	*The Logic of Sense*
Julia Kristeva	*Strangers to Ourselves*
Alain Finkielkraut	*Remembering in Vain: The Klaus Barbie Trial and Crimes Against Humanity*
Pierre Vidal-Naquet	*Assassins of Memory: Essays on the Denial of the Holocaust*
Julia Kristeva	*Nations Without Nationalism*
Theodor W. Adorno	*Notes to Literature*, vols. 1 and 2
Richard Wolin, ed.	*The Heidegger Controversy*
Hugo Ball	*Critique of the German Intelligentsia*
Pierre Bourdieu	*The Field of Cultural Production*
Karl Heinz Bohrer	*Suddenness: On the Moment of Aesthetic Appearance*
Gilles Deleuze	*Difference and Repetition*
Gilles Deleuze and Félix Guattari	*What Is Philosophy?*
Alain Finkielkraut	*The Defeat of the Mind*
Jacques LeGoff	*History and Memory*
Antonio Gramsci	*Prison Notebooks*, vols. 1, 2, and 3
Ross Mitchell Guberman	*Julia Kristeva Interviews*
Julia Kristeva	*Time and Sense: Proust and the Experience of Literature*
Elisabeth Badinter	*XY: On Masculine Identity*
Gilles Deleuze	*Negotiations, 1972–1990*
Julia Kristeva	*New Maladies of the Soul*
Norbert Elias	*The Germans*
Elisabeth Roudinesco	*Jacques Lacan: His Life and Work*
Paul Ricoeur	*Critique and Conviction: Conversations with François Azouvi and Marc de Launay*
Pierre Vidal-Naquet	*The Jews: History, Memory, and the Present*
Karl Löwith	*Martin Heidegger and European Nihilism*
Pierre Nora	*Realms of Memory: The Construction of the French Past*
	Vol. 1: *Conflicts and Divisions*
	Vol. 2: *Traditions*
	Vol. 3: *Symbols*
Alain Corbin	*Village Bells: Sound and Meaning in the Nineteenth-Century French Countryside*
Louis Althusser	*Writings on Psychoanalysis: Freud and Lacan*
Claudine Fabre-Vassas	*The Singular Beast: Jews, Christians, and the Pig*
Tahar Ben Jelloun	*French Hospitality: Racism and North African Immigrants*
Alain Finkielkraut	*In the Name of Humanity: Reflections on the Twentieth Century*
Emmanuel Levinas	*Entre Nous: Essays on Thinking-of-the-Other*
Zygmunt Bauman	*Globalization: The Human Consequences*
Emmanuel Levinas	*Alterity and Transcendence*
Alain Corbin	*The Life of an Unknown: The Rediscovered World of a Clog Maker in Nineteenth-Century France*
Carlo Ginzburg	*Wooden Eyes: Nine Reflections on Distance*
Sylviane Agacinski	*Parity of the Sexes*
Michel Pastoureau	*The Devil's Cloth: A History of Stripes and Striped Fabric*